Lord Berners

Composer Writer Painter

Lord Berners: Self-portrait

Lord Berners

Composer Writer Painter

Peter Dickinson

Peter Dickinson

24-10-08

THE BOYDELL PRESS

First published 2008
The Boydell Press, Woodbridge

The publication of this volume has been assisted
by a grant from the Berners Trust.

ISBN   978-1-84383-392-5

The Boydell Press is an imprint of Boydell & Brewer Ltd
PO Box 9, Woodbridge, Suffolk IP12 3DF, UK
and of Boydell & Brewer Inc.
668 Mt Hope Avenue, Rochester, NY 14620, USA
website: www.boydellandbrewer.com

A CIP record for this book is available
from the British Library

This publication is printed on acid-free paper

Designed and typeset in Adobe Hypatia Sans, Adobe Myriad and
Adobe Warnock by David Roberts, Pershore, Worcestershire

Printed in Great Britain by
CPI Antony Rowe, Chippenham, Wiltshire

Contents

List of illustrations

Frontispiece Berners: Self-portrait

Titles in quotes are those originally given to the paintings.

Preface and Acknowledgements

I KNOW I heard some songs by Lord Berners (1883–1950) in a concert at the Cambridge University Music Club in the 1950s, but I remember them very dimly. My real introduction to Berners was due to Philip Lane, who was an undergraduate at Birmingham University when I was a lecturer in the Music Department. He came to me, as his supervisor, with a final-year project on Berners. A few weeks later he told me that he had been to Faringdon House, where Berners' heir Robert Heber-Percy had let him look through a pile of manuscripts and other material. Lane asked me if I would go with him to help sort things out.

As everyone who has been to Faringdon admits, the experience is unique. Heber-Percy had kept the house up in a comparable style ever since Berners died in 1950, but he had always been reluctant to answer letters of enquiry about Berners. As he says in his interview here, he was frightened of saying the wrong thing. But the ice was broken, and the 1972 Purcell Room concert, regarded as an official revival, soon followed. Then there was an LP, my edition of the complete songs and piano music, and the events of the 1983 centenary. Heber-Percy generously supported all of these, as well as further recordings in the 1980s.

In preparing the concerts I gave regularly with my sister, Meriel Dickinson, our recordings and broadcasts, as well as my editions, I have a large number of people to thank following Heber-Percy and Lane, whose own manuscript about Berners I have consulted. Berners' publisher, J. & W. Chester (later Chester Music, now incorporated into Music Sales) was represented by Sheila MacCrindle.[1] She was always unfailingly enthusiastic about Berners, loved his sense of humour, and got part of *The Triumph of Neptune* into the last night of the Proms in 1975, and *A Wedding Bouquet* was included in 1990. She worked tirelessly to get a TV documentary made about Berners, but sadly never succeeded, and there were problems because there seems to be nothing of Berners on film.

When it comes to this book, it would not have been possible at all without the support of Arthur Johnson, the producer of the 1983 BBC Radio 3 documentary, whose energy and unfailing interest in the subject propelled the project to its conclusion. The programme received a Certificate of Commendation in the Sony Awards for Best Radio Documentary of the year, but, of course, the broadcast used only a fraction of the interview material. I lent the tapes to Mark Amory when he was writing his delightful biography *Lord Berners: the Last Eccentric* (1998), so he was able to quote from them. But this book presents the complete interviews as well as other material to create a portrait of Berners in all his dimensions, largely from people who knew him. I am grateful to Jacquie Kavanagh at the BBC, who has approved the publication of these interviews and more specifically to those who were interviewed or their heirs. William Crack's daughter Sylvia and her niece Teresa Shurmer, who both lent me material, including the two Crack portraits; Lord Christopher Thynne for the interview with his mother, the Hon. Daphne Fielding; Sofka Zinovieff for approving the use of my interviews with her grandfather, Robert Heber-Percy; Charlotte Mosley for the use of the interview with her mother-in-law, Lady Mosley; Anthony Russell-Roberts for Sir Frederick Ashton; Candida Lycett Green for her mother the Hon. Lady Betjeman; Dominic Harrod for the interview with his mother, Lady Harrod; Dr Hugh Cecil for the interview with his father, Lord David Cecil; Lady Pamela Knyvett Berners for sharing her childhood memories and allowing me to quote from her letters and reminiscences; Dr Anthony Parton for

1 Hugh Wood, 'Sheila MacCrindle', 'Business as usual', Obituary, *Guardian*, 24 July 1993.

sharing details about the Larionov cartoons of Berners; Chris Mawson for confirming that there was never a Shell Guide to Berkshire; Elizabeth Ennion at the Archive Centre, King's College, Cambridge, for copies of Berners' letters to Clive Bell; Lady Preston, Richard and Rita Walker for lending me books; Michael Thompson for letting me have a photograph of Stanley Hall and giving me information about Shropshire families.

The interview subjects were the people who knew Berners best; what they have to say is of unique documentary value. But there are also three interviews from a later generation, also made in 1983. Gavin Bryars undertook considerable research on Berners in the 1970s until he found that his work as a composer prevented him from finishing. He shared his findings with me, which I used for the BBC Radio 3 documentary and many concert performances, and later with Mark Amory. I am particularly grateful to Bryars for letting me draw on his interviews with some of the subjects here and also include some of his notes about his encounters made at that period – and for reading the typescript. Sir Richard Rodney Bennett is another composer who values Berners' work, and the Italian musicologist Professor Fiamma Nicolodi has made a special contribution as the granddaughter of Alfredo Casella, friend and colleague of Berners from the World War I period in Rome.

Following Heber-Percy's death in 1987 the Berners Trust was formed under the chairmanship of Lady Dorothy Heber-Percy. The trustees owed much to her as founder, and it was during this period that Berners' published writings came back into print thanks to the enthusiasm of Jonathan Rabinovitch at Turtlepoint Press and Helen Marx Books, New York. *The Girls of Radcliff Hall* came out in its first trade edition, edited by John Byrne, and all Berner's music reached CD, masterminded by Philip Lane.

A more recent development is the scholarly work of Mary Gifford, who gained a PhD from King's College, London, in 2007.[2] She has generously shared her knowledge of the Berners Archives and associated data, and fielded many enquiries: her own detailed study of Berners and his family will be of considerable interest when it appears. Bryony Jones' enthusiastic study *The Music of Lord Berners: the Versatile Peer* (2003) explores a variety of connections between Berners and other composers, although her access to sources was limited.

I should like to thank R. A. Preston and the staff of Shrewsbury Public Library for their help in researching Berners' family history, and also Margaret Grieve at the Library of the University of Keele – all in the early 1980s.

I must thank further Arnold Goldman for drawing my attention to an article by Julian Cowley; F. G. L. O. Van Kretschmar and Paul Thwaite for providing Dutch translations; David Threasher for *Gramophone* archives; Dr A. Rob-Smith for information about the Tynchewycke Society for which Berners wrote his Polka in 1941; Dr Richard Shephard for help with periodical articles; the late Professor Eugenie Lampert for Russian translation; Chris Banks for information about the Stravinsky purchases of the British Library; my wife Bridget for reading the typescript and other materials about Berners; Mark Amory and Bruce Phillips, who also read the typescript and made suggestions; my son Francis, who helped with the book's title and other issues. I have also been extremely fortunate to have had Dr David Roberts as copy-editor and fastidious designer.

Many people have helped with the photographs: the Dowager Duchess of Devonshire and the archives staff at Chatsworth; Clarissa, Countess of Avon; Lady Panufnik, who advised on the purchase of a camera and how to use it; Sofka Zinovieff; Jeremy Hulme at Faringdon along with Peter and Michael White; Diana and Michael Parkin; Sylvia Crack and Teresa Shurmer; Anne Reille Jackson and Marie-Christine Jackson; Kate and Christine Caldwell;

---

2 Mary Gifford, *Lord Berners: Aspects of a Biography* (PhD thesis, University of London, 2007).

Melanie Gardner at the Tullie House Museum & Art Gallery, Carlisle; Philip Lane and Peter Meason; Shane Pictor; Gavin Bryars and Mike Webb at Boydell & Brewer, where I have also valued the enthusiasm for the project shown by Peter Clifford and all his colleagues.

I have had assistance through Eduado Blasi in Rome in locating one of the Tivoli pictures and in finding Berners' house at 3 Via dei Foro Romano, now the Rome headquarters of the firm of Pirelli, internationally known for its high-quality tyres and cable systems – and its series of calendars illustrated with photographs of beautiful women. The first-floor drawing room of the three-story corner house, which was then called simply 3 Foro Romano, would have looked out directly onto the Forum, although the trees have grown up since and now obscure the view. If Mussolini was visible parading on his white horse, as Lady Dorothy Heber-Percy suggested (p. 73), it was probably on the other side of the Forum on the Via dei Fori Imperali. The gate into the Forum, mentioned by Robert Heber-Percy, is across the road and there is now no access from there.

Judith Harris and David Willey kindly identified the ruins in Plate 27, one of several examples of Berners painting Roman views close to where he lived.

I must apologise to anyone I have inadvertently failed to reach or to mention and who may have been of assistance in my long connection with the subject.

My editorial method involved transcribing all the interviews, then cutting repetitions in the answers, removing or correcting occasional factual errors, and condensing the questions asked to make a more readable narrative. The original cassettes of the full interviews, not kept by the BBC, have been placed with the Berners Archive at the British Library. *Lord Berners: Composer, Writer, Painter* is not the last word about Berners, but it represents all aspects of his work and provides information collected over many years about one of the most fascinating figures of his period.

Finally, I am most grateful to the Berners Trust for a generous grant towards publication costs which has made it possible to produce this volume to a standard that I hope would have satisfied even the exacting taste of his lordship himself.

Peter Dickinson
Aldeburgh 2008

CHAPTER 1

Introduction

Peter Dickinson

LORD BERNERS is one of the most idiosyncratic and
fascinating personalities in the history of British music.
He is remembered as the versatile peer whom Nancy Mitford used as the basis for the character of Lord Merlin in her
novel *The Pursuit of Love*.[1] Berners has also been celebrated
for his eccentricities, some of which have become legends,
but he did use a harmless vegetable dye to make the white
pigeons all sorts of colours at his country house in Faringdon.
He was also said to have had a piano built into in the back of
his Rolls-Royce, but in fact it was a small clavichord housed
under the front seat. Stravinsky's memoirs and letters show
how much the great composer valued his friendship with
Berners and also admired his music.

Gerald Hugh Tyrwhitt, who became the 14th Baron Berners in 1918, was born on 18 September 1883. This was the
year that saw the birth of Clement Attlee, the British Prime
Minister whose Labour government in 1945 would confirm
the end of the privileged world within which Berners lived.
It was also the year in which the Italian dictator Benito
Mussolini was born – Berners worked in Rome and kept a
house there for over thirty years. During the final years of
the nineteenth century the European powers were competing to secure territory for their colonial empires and quar-
relling amongst themselves as they moved towards the onset
of World War I, the first of the two defining conflicts of the
first half of the twentieth century. The United States was also
acquiring territory, adding states to the Union, and moving
towards the position where it would take over in commercial
and political terms from the British Empire on the international stage. American culture was becoming pervasive: the
world watched Hollywood films, embraced American popular songs and musicals, and danced to rhythms derived from
African American music.

As a diplomat at the British Embassy in Rome during
World War I, Berners was not required to enlist in the armed
forces. In Rome he flourished within an international artistic
milieu attuned to all the latest ideas. By comparison with his
friendships with luminaries such as Stravinsky and Diaghilev,
his earlier studies in France and Germany and travels elsewhere were only a preparation. After inheriting his title he
was able to dedicate himself to the arts – composing, writing and painting – right through the uncertain period of the

1 Nancy Mitford (1904–73):
The Pursuit of Love (1945) became
a best-seller and was turned into
a film.

inter-war years. His jokes often seem to reflect the frivolity of the 1920s, but levity was not the dominant mood as the dictators gained control in Italy, Spain and Germany, and a totalitarian regime was entrenched in Russia. The United Kingdom flirted with fascism when Oswald Mosley founded the British Union of Fascists in 1932; the following year Hitler became Chancellor of Germany. Berners may have met Hitler and, although no fascist himself, his circle of friends included some British admirers of the Nazi regime. As the period between the wars came to an end – the 'long weekend' as Robert Graves called it – the political and social confusions of the 1930s became more intense. Renewed conflict was inevitable at the end of what W. H. Auden described as 'a low dishonest decade'. Berners retreated to live in Oxford, came close to a breakdown in reaction to the war, and passed the time by writing three novels, two short stories and a play before returning to composition with a final ballet and two film scores in the years before he died on 19 April 1950.

Berners' centenary in 1983 brought his work to a wider public than at any time since his death. All the main newspapers and periodicals marked the occasion with articles.[2] Some new ground was covered, especially with the BBC Radio 3 broadcast of Berners' only opera, allowing it to be heard for the first time in the UK.[3] An exhibition of pictures, photographs and documents at the Royal Festival Hall boasted the words 'LORD BERNERS' in large letters on the outside of the building. He would have enjoyed the irony. Honouring a member of the hereditary peerage was a surrealist gesture to come from a left-wing Greater London Council.[4]

The centenary concert at the Wigmore Hall was practically sold out and had to be repeated, which showed an advance on the impact made by the Purcell Room concert with readings by Sir John Betjeman eleven years earlier.[5] As another centenary tribute, two of Berners' books were reprinted in a single paperback with a foreword by Sir Harold Acton, who knew Berners in Rome from World War I onwards.[6] The long memories and longevity of several of Berners' friends were a feature of the BBC Radio 3 documentary.[7]

In it I referred to Berners as 'a rare type of polymath' in view of his versatility as a composer, writer and painter. The interviews in the programme, now transcribed in full in this book, establish that Berners was no conventional amateur in any one of these pursuits. And as an eccentric he clearly became a professional.[8] I concluded: 'All these elements combine to create a fascinating picture of a man at the artistic and social centre of an era, but hampered by no professional

2 Parts of this introduction were included in a lecture at the Royal Society of Arts delivered on 30 November 1983: 'Lord Berners (1883–1950): Composer, Author, Painter and Eccentric', subsequently published in the *Royal Society of Arts Journal* 132, no. 5333 (April 1984), 313–24.

3 *Le Carrosse du Saint-Sacrement* was produced at the Théâtre des Champs-Élysées, Paris, on 24 April 1924. The BBC performance is now on CD – Marco Polo 8.225155 (2000). There was another production in Paris on 2 June 1948.

4 The exhibition was arranged by the Greater London Council in association with Chester Music and Gavin Bryars. Private view, 29 September 1983.

5 *An Evening of Lord Berners*, with Meriel Dickinson (mezzo), Peter Dickinson (piano), Timothy West (readings). Presented by the Park Lane Group at the Wigmore Hall, on 25 September 1983, and repeated as *A Sunday Afternoon with Lord Berners* at the Purcell Room, South Bank, on 16 October.
　　An Evening of Lord Berners, with Sir John Betjeman, Meriel Dickinson, Peter Dickinson, Susan Bradshaw, presented by the Park Lane Group at the Purcell Room, South Bank, on 8 December 1972. An edited version of this programme, introduced by Peter Dickinson, was broadcast on BBC Radio 3 on 12 December 1973, and repeated on 20 April 1975: producer Elaine Padmore.

6 *First Childhood* (1934) and *Far from the Madding War* (1941), with a Preface by Sir Harold Acton (Oxford: Oxford University Press, 1983). *First Childhood* is now reprinted, and *Far from the Madding War* is included in *Collected Tales and Fantasies* (both New York: Turtle Point Press and Helen Marx Books, 1999).

establishments. He could afford his independence – he exercised it with distinction.'

In doing so he leaves us with plenty to think about in terms of the use of leisure in our own very different society today. But to find out who Berners was we can start by looking at his earliest influences and compare what he wrote about himself with the facts.

Berners published two volumes of autobiography – *First Childhood* (1934) and *A Distant Prospect* (1945) – and he left unpublished reminiscences of the time he spent in France and Germany around 1900.[9] In the first two volumes he deliberately created confusions by changing the names of people and places, often only slightly, a tactic he also used in the privately printed *The Girls of Radcliff Hall*, where the girls are thinly disguised boys.[10] In *First Childhood* he was writing from the point of view of a young person, a perspective he retained. Hugh Walpole recognised this:

> Lord Berners in this book shows that he is a poet who has never grown up, not because he cannot, but because he does not want to. The only people who write well about their childhood are those who have never left it ... Lord Berners has no illusions about himself as a child, and the sort of colour that inspires his pages comes from the contrasts between himself in rebellion against his elders in a sort of pontifical grandeur, doomed to destruction.[11]

Philip Larkin, in more incisive tones:

> The two chief characteristics of childhood, and the two things that make it so seductive to a certain type of adult mind, are its freedom from reason and its freedom from responsibility. It is these that give it its peculiar heartless, savage strength.[12]

I asked Philip Larkin whether he came across Berners at Oxford when he was an undergraduate: 'I am afraid my contact with Lord Berners was of the slightest. It consisted of attending a meeting of the English Club which he addressed ... most likely in 1940–41. I remember he had one lens of his spectacles darker than the other, or it may have been that both of them were dark; this gave him a slightly sinister appearance ... he may have read extracts from *Far from the Madding War*, which was published around that time.'[13]

The adult world into which Berners was born qualified his earliest memories and shows something of what he was reacting against. His deviations from the facts in *First Childhood* reflect his own angle of vision, so much a feature of his musical parody, his cut-and-paste assemblages or additions

7 *Lord Berners*, 18 September 1983, devised and presented by Peter Dickinson, producer Arthur Johnson. Sony Radio Awards 1984: Certificate of Commendation in category of Best Documentary Features Programme. Repeated on 2 January 1985.

8 But he was not always eccentric: 'In my early adolescence I was always anxious to do the right thing. I knew that any manifestation of eccentricity was considered to be in bad taste, whether it consisted in wearing brown boots on Sunday or in disliking cricket or fox-hunting. School and family life had taught me the necessity of concealing any lurking tendency to be different from other people, the necessity of conforming.' *The Château de Résenlieu*, 58.

9 *The Château de Résenlieu* (New York: Turtle Point Press and Helen Marx Books, [2000]) and *Dresden* (2008). On the flyleaf of *A Distant Prospect* there are three volumes of autobiography listed with Volume 3 (in preparation). It looks as if Berners envisaged *Résenlieu* and *Dresden* forming this volume together.

10 See interview with Daphne Fielding, Chapter 6, p. 67.

11 Sir Hugh Walpole (1884–1941), popular novelist. *The Book Society News*, February 1934. For further extracts from reviews see the back pages of *The Camel* (1936).

12 'The Savage Seventh', *Required Writing: Miscellaneous Pieces, 1955–1982* (London: Faber & Faber, 1983), 111.

13 Letter to Peter Dickinson, 21 December 1983.

14 This aspect of Berners is barely mentioned by the interview subjects here. In 1939 he went public with 'Brighter Royal Academy Pictures' in *Lilliput: the Pocket Magazine for Everyone* 5/1 (July 1939), Second Birthday Number. Berners proposed a cut-and-paste treatment of famous portraits in the same way that 'young ladies of the Victorian era used to compose scrap screens by cutting up coloured prints and sticking them on a background'. His collection of grotesques includes Dame Laura Knight's portrait of an old woman entitled *Gipsy Splendour* given the head of Neville Chamberlain; Ernest Gillick's picture of a woman carrying a pitcher on her head called *The Gift* becomes Lord Halifax; Sir John Lavery's portrait of the Viscountess Wimborne has a new face with comedian George Robey; Phyllis Dodd's picture of a little girl on a rocking horse becomes George Bernard Shaw; Charles Spencelayh's painting of an old man becomes Lloyd George; and finally a surrealist assemblage by Meredith Frampton has its head replaced by one of Anthony Eden. Each one is scrupulously labelled 'with apologies'. One wonders what these distinguished figures thought of this frivolity as war approached. Gladys, Duchess of Marlborough, was amused by it: 'She revelled in his collection of photographs of royalty, politicians, society beauties, actresses and other celebrities, whose features he had changed with skilful brushwork, adding moustaches, beards and odd head-gear. He also set the subjects of these witty compositions in scenes that were incongruous, with unsuitable companions creating amazing comical conversation pieces'. Daphne Fielding, *The Face on the Sphinx: a Portrait of Gladys Deacon, Duchess of Marlborough* (London: Hamish Hamilton, 1978), 67–8. Berners used his cut-and-paste technique less mischievously when he was asked to design the outside covers for *Wiltshire: Shell Guides*, edited by Robert Byron, general editor John Betjeman (London, 1935). See plate 16.

to existing drawings or pictures.[14] It would also spoil the impact of his youthful rebellion if some of his relations were found to have been hard-working, responsible and distinguished – which they were.

Berners was born as Gerald Tyrwhitt (his family name) at Apley Park in Shropshire (not Arley, as in the book, although there is a village of that name). The Gothic mansion (see plate 13) belonged to Berners' maternal grandfather, William Orme Foster (1814–99), called Farmer in the book, and this is how it looked in 1891:

Apley Park occupies one of the finest sites in South Shropshire, overlooking the Severn near Bridgnorth. The park itself extends over four hundred acres, and possesses abundant wealth in timber; it has an undulating surface, and is surrounded by thickly wooded hills, among its other attractions being a fine herd of deer.

The Hall is an elegant structure of Grinshill freestone, in the castellated style of architecture, with octagonal turrets at the angles, and a massive porch of three arches at the entrance of the eastern front; the left side is surrounded by a lofty tower, and at the north end stands the chapel. The building is a fine specimen of architectural skill and excellent workmanship, and is one of the most costly and imposing structures in the county. The interior of the mansion is appropriately fitted and decorated in accordance with its external character.

The pleasure grounds are of great extent, and are beautifully planted with a profusion of choice flowers and ornamental shrubs. On the south side of the Hall are artistically arranged gardens, below which is a sloping lawn supported by a fine stone balustrade; from this a flight of steps leads to an open space of greensward, whose borders are planted with various shrubs and flowering plants. The eastern edge of the slope is thickly planted with ornamental tress and fragrant flowers. At the western end of the ground lies a pretty pool, with a fountain in its centre, surrounded by beds of flowers. Close by is a rockery of huge blocks of stone, hidden by clusters of ferns, moss and ivy, surrounded by additional trees and graceful shrubs. The gardens extend some distance to the west of the mansion in which direction are magnificent rhododendrons. The south portion of the hall is fronted with lawns bordered by flowers. The terrace [a range of hills], which extends two miles, commands extensive views; its hanging woods rise to a great height above the Severn, of whose lovely valley it has a splendid prospect.[15]

Berners' own description is less prosaic:

> Arley [Apley] was a huge neo-Gothic house of grey stone, built towards the end of the eighteenth century. It was a little like Strawberry Hill in appearance and, if not so airy and fantastic in its architecture, was quite as adequately turreted and castellated. Its atmosphere was highly romantic … It was surrounded by a very lovely park, undulating and well-timbered, a wide valley through which the river Severn flowed. The house itself stood on a height overlooking the river, and the gardens were laid out with slopes and stone balustrades descending to the water's edge. The most striking feature of the park was a range of heavily wooded hills following the line of the river to Southridge [Bridgnorth], the picturesque and rather foreign-looking local town. This range was known as the Terrace. It was an earthly paradise for children, and the precipitous sandstone cliffs that stood out here and there from among the trees provided an inexhaustible field for exploration and adventure.[16]

None of this survives today, since the house and grounds had a long period of neglect. However, recent information suggests that the executant architect for the elaborate 1811 structure was the landscape gardener John Webb, responsible for other Gothic houses such as Eaton Hall and Cholmondeley Castle in Cheshire.[17]

William Orme Foster was an ironmaster who inherited John Bradley & Company, Stourbridge, from an uncle. The firm owed its prosperity to the rapidly developing railways, and at one time employed over 5,000 men. Foster bought Apley Park in 1867 from the Whitmore family, who had owned it since 1551. He paid over £300,000, which included 'a large portion of the town of Bridgnorth'. Berners called the town Southridge in *First Childhood*, typically turning the real name backwards and upside down. That £300,000 would be over £21m today, based on the Composite Price Index,[18] so it was no wonder that Berners wrote:

> I was given to understand that it would be necessary for me to earn my living. I was surrounded by people who seemed to have nothing to do but amuse themselves, and I thought it grossly unfair. Why couldn't my grandfather, who was immensely rich, provide me with sufficient money to enable me to live in luxurious ease like my uncles and aunts? What was the point

15 Francis Leach, *The County Seats of Shropshire* (Shrewsbury, 1891).

16 *First Childhood*, 5–6 (pages of the first edition).

17 See *Country Life*, 25 May 1907; Gareth Williams, 'Apley Hall: the County's Greatest Restoration Project: Past Deciphered, Future Assured', *Shropshire Magazine*, October 2005. Also detailed illustrated site http://www.apley-park.org/apley_post_1987/sec_shrop_mag/shrop_mag.htm .

18 Jim O'Donoghue and Louise Goulding, 'Consumer Price Inflation since 1750', *Economic Trends* 604 (March 2004), 38–46.

in becoming a grown-up gentleman if one had to be bothered with a profession?[19]

The 'immensely rich' grandfather took his responsibilities seriously. Berners, perhaps as a result, 'never took anything very seriously', according to Sir Harold Acton.[20]

Foster was a Liberal MP for South Staffordshire from 1857 to 1868; High Sheriff for Wexford in 1876 and for Shropshire in 1883, the year of Berners' birth. He was a magistrate and Deputy Lieutenant of Shropshire and Staffordshire, and was widely respected for his influence and generosity. Foster's eldest son, William Henry, continued this family tradition of benefactions and good works, and was MP for Bridgnorth from 1870 to 1885. He wasn't merely the kind of Philistine politician Berners complained about. In 1907 he was cited as 'a good judge of pictures', and possessed examples by Reynolds, Turner, Constable and others.

William Orme Foster seems to have been the best type of Victorian industrial baron and county landowner, lord of many manors and prodigal of endowments. When he died in 1899 at the age of eighty-four the grief of the county was genuine and lavishly expressed. 'The family and household mourners proceeded slowly from the house to the lodge, and here the procession was doubled and trebled in length twice over by hundreds who had come to pay their last respects to one whom all had recognised as a great benefactor and a true English gentleman.'[21] Gerald and his young cousins did not attend the funeral. But Foster had been in decline for many years. Much earlier, at the height of his activity, he had a stroke after losing his seat to a Roman Catholic in 1868 – by forty-nine votes. He then became an invalid, and by the time Berners was a child he was mentally unstable. This is how it looked to the young Gerald:

> My grandfather used to sit all day long in a darkened room. From his lips there came forth a never-ending stream of groans and curses … that could be heard from all over the house. At meals he always occupied his place at the head of the table, even when there were visitors, and every Sunday he went to church. But these public appearances involved many anxious moments, and I remember him once in the Parish Church, bursting into so violent a storm of expletives in the middle of the sermon that the service had to be hastily concluded.[22]

The young Gerald, as later in his music, couldn't resist imitation and parody:

> In the privacy of the nursery, I would sometimes entertain my small cousins by giving them a realistic

19 *A Distant Prospect*, 14–15 (pages of the first edition).

20 See interview with Sir Harold Acton, Chapter 3, p. 49.

21 *Shrewsbury Chronicle*, 13 October 1899.

22 *First Childhood*, 17.

imitation of my grandfather's peculiarities, a performance which relied for its effectiveness chiefly on the
fact of its being in the worst possible taste and, if over-
heard, by nurses or parents, of its being immediately
and severely punished.[23]

The 1881 census figures show the scale of life at Apley Park.
There were twenty servants employed inside the house, apart
from gardeners and workers on the estate. The housekeeper
was given her real name in *First Childhood* – Charlotte
Matchet, aged fifty at the time. She taught Gerald to believe
in fairies and magic. As a result he tried to turn his cousin
Emily into a toad with magic wand, but it didn't work.[24]

The uncle and aunt living at Apley, both unmarried, must
have been Captain James Foster and Constance Evelyn Foster.
Captain Foster was a distinguished soldier and a prominent
sportsman, serving on national hunt committees. The aunt
was a cripple as a result of the same enthusiasm – a serious hunting accident. But she loved fine clothes and would
show them off to Gerald. She told him his grandfather was
ill because he was under a spell. Gerald, having read his Russian fairy stories, tried to deliver him from it by crowning
him with a wreath of snowdrops. That didn't work either.[25]

Berners liked to describe himself as 'a sport, in the biological sense, in an exclusively sporting environment'.

It has been said that the English take their pleasure
sadly. Not sadly, I used to think, but too persistently,
and the pleasures of field sports were considered not
so much as pleasure but the fulfilment of some sort
of sacred national duty. The long days of hunting and
shooting against which it would have been criminal
to protest were as irksome to me at home as were
the organised games at school ... The most arduous
labours of agriculture, I used to think, would be prefer-
able to the long-drawn-out amusements enforced on
me by my social position. But I was obliged to bow in
the house of Rimmon and pretend that I was enjoying
myself.[26]

But even in 1929 Berners published a short article on 'Fox-
hunting'. He starts:

A musician on Fox-hunting! ... One might say that the
process of musical composition is not unlike that of
hunting a fox. The theme, like its vulpine counterpart,
may prove a 'flyer' and provide good sport, or it may
turn out to be merely a 'cowardly short-running trai-
tor, no better than a hare'. Or again, one might point
to the fact that nothing can more vividly express the

23 *First Childhood*, 18.

24 *First Childhood*, 34–5.

25 *First Childhood*, 23–4.

26 *A Distant Prospect*, 96–7.
But letters to his mother show
that he was more active riding and
swimming that this suggests.

exhilaration of the chase than music ... Beauty, excitement, courage, love; does not the hunting-field supply all the things that men most share?[27]

However, Nancy Mitford gave these words to Lord Merlin: 'Hunt as much as you like, but never talk about it. It's the most boring subject in the world.'[28]

Just three miles across the river Severn from Apley Park is Stanley Hall, one of the houses of Berners' father's family, which was the seat of Sir Henry Thomas Tyrwhitt, 3rd Baronet (1824–94). (See plate 14.) Berners says little about him. He was a lieutenant in the Rifle Brigade; JP for Norfolk and Shropshire; and High Sheriff for Shropshire in 1877. He succeeded his father in 1839 and married Emma Harriet, Baroness Berners in her own right, in 1853.[29]

According to the *Dictionary of English and Folk-names of British Birds*: 'A lapwing is said to have brought assistance by its cries to the wounded founder of the old Lincolnshire family of Tyrwhitt, who assumed three lapwings as his device in memory of the deliverance.'[30] The three birds are found on the Berners arms.

The establishment at Stanley Hall – called Stackwell in *First Childhood* – was slightly less lavish than at Apley. There were fourteen servants and a Swiss governess. She was Bertha Fasnacht – Mademoiselle Bock in *First Childhood* – brought in to teach Gerald after he and his parents had moved to Althrey – not a disguised name – near Ruabon.[31]

Gerald's paternal grandmother, Baroness Berners – Lady Bourchier in *First Childhood* – was probably the source of his anti-clericalism. Emma Harriet was the daughter of a clergyman, Rector of Ashwellthorpe, the family's seat in Norfolk. She had been converted to the evangelical wing of the church by Lord Radstock. According to Berners:

> She went so far as to have herself described in *Who's Who* as 'distinctly low', an epithet which must have caused some surprise to those unaware of its sectarian significance.[32]

She used to make visits to the poor and sick taking with her soup and propaganda. Berners must have recognised her type when he set to music a poem by Robert Graves: 'The Lady Visitor in the Pauper Ward'.[33] She was always giving young Gerald copies of the Bible, which left him with a problem:

> Disposing of a Bible was no easy matter. It would, of course, be sacrilegious to burn it. If deliberately left behind or lost it would invariably be returned because she always took the precaution of writing one's name

27 Berners, 'Fox-Hunting', *The New Forget-me-not: A Calendar* (London: Constable, 1929).

28 *The Pursuit of Love* (London, 1945; Harmondsworth: Penguin, 1949), 62. The character of Lord Merlin is a sympathetic portrayal of Berners, with many details taken from life.

29 *Shrewsbury Chronicle*, 2 February 1894. See Family Tree, Appendix 9.

30 H. Kirke Swann, *Dictionary of English and Folk Names of British Birds* (London: Witherby & Co., 1913).

31 Berners has created some more confusions in *First Childhood*. Baroness Berners lived in Norfolk at Ashwellthorpe Hall, 'a crenellated Tudor-style house built in 1831 and 1845 by Lady Berners on the moated site of the ancient seat of her Knyvett ancestors, and incorporating part of their house'. John Kenworthy-Brown *et al.*, *Burke's & Savill's Guide to Country Houses*, vol. 3: *East Anglia* (London: Burke's Peerage, 1981).

32 *First Childhood*, 36. But she actually put 'Distinctly Protestant', Mark Amory, *Lord Berners: the Last Eccentric* (London: Chatto & Windus, 1998), 2.

33 The second of *Three English Songs* (1920).

and address on the title page. I remember once when
I dropped one of them in the moat being horrified to
find that it refused to sink and continued to bob up
and down on the surface like a lifebuoy. Even this con-
tingency, I felt, must have been foreseen by my grandmother and in consequence she had had it lined with
cork.[34]

The marriage of Sir Henry Tyrwhitt's third son, Hugh,
with William Orme Foster's third daughter, Julia Mary, was
a union between two influential Shropshire families. Berners guessed that the Foster riches were a great incentive to
his father, and perhaps the Fosters were attracted by the
titles across the river. The wedding took place at Stockton
Church near Apley on 10 August 1882. The *Salopian Journal*
reported: 'The bride, given away by her father, wore a dress
of cream-coloured satin, trimmed with Brussels lace and a
veil fastened with dog roses and diamonds.' At the wedding
breakfast for eighty guests the decorations for a country dis-
trict were numerous and exceedingly attractive. 'No such
grand wedding had taken place at Stockton for ninety years.'
Arches were constructed with mottoes of celebration. The
list of presents and donors, given in small type, was eight
inches long. The tenantry gave a gold and sapphire bangle,
with stones set in silver, regretting that 'the time has now
come when your residence among us will be a memory only,
we heartily rejoice in the happy prospect of the future upon
which you are now entering ...' There was a dinner for two
hundred workpeople on the estate.[35]

All these good omens were to little avail, since the marriage was not a success. Julia Mary (plate 2) did stay at Apley
for about six years after her wedding, since Captain Tyrwhitt
(plate 1) was often abroad in the navy. Gerald saw little of
his father and was strongly affected by his mother. She once
tried to thrash him, but his father could never be bothered.
She took him to Eton in 1897 and removed him early. She
went with him in the spring of 1900 to Résenlieu in France,
where he stayed to learn French.[36] She would have taken him
to Dresden the following year, but it coincided with more
important matters – the hunting season.[37] These were the
first of his Continental visits designed to prepare him for the
diplomatic service.

Berners' artistic talents derived from his mother. She
preferred Walter Scott to Lord Byron, but on her marriage
rushed out to buy a copy of *Don Juan*, which she'd been forbidden to read. She further kicked over the traces by walking
down Bond Street unaccompanied. All this was in 1882.

In *First Childhood* Berners writes: 'As for my immediate

34 *First Childhood*, 42.

35 *Salopian Journal*, 16 August 1882.

36 *The Château de Résenlieu*, 3.

37 *Dresden*, 1.

ancestry I am unable to trace any single one of my distinctive traits to my grandparents, and still less to either of my parents.'[38] It may have been attractive for him to think of himself as *sui generis*, when writing his autobiography in the early 1930s. He may have felt like that, but he was wrong. It doesn't detract from his remarkable versatility and the nature of his musical gifts – it even explains them – but he did inherit significant characteristics from both his father and his mother.

Berners claimed that his mother thought the most important thing in life was to ride well, as he knew to his cost, although he apparently succeeded. But she was also the transmitter of culture, however thinly spread. Music in the drawing room in Victorian times was dominated by the female sex. Women played the piano, the harp or sang: men might occasionally accompany them with a violin or flute, instruments thought unsuitable for ladies. In E. M. Forster's *A Room with a View*, Lucy Honeychurch upsets the vicar by playing the tempestuous first movement of Beethoven's last piano sonata, op. 111. He said:

> I do not consider her choice of a piece happy. Beethoven is so usually simple and direct in his appeal that it is sheer perversity to choose a thing like that, which, if anything, disturbs.[39]

Mrs Tyrwhitt would have understood. Music was all right as long as it didn't disturb, could be tolerated as long as it was amateur and not taken seriously. In this spirit Mrs Tyrwhitt used to play the piano to Gerald and show him her sketchbooks – another of her accomplishments. He used to sketch landscapes when he was at Eton. But:

> As soon as I began to show signs of developing talents of my own, fearing perhaps that she might be calling into being a Frankenstein's monster, she put away the sketchbooks and closed the piano.[40]

His mother relented later on, and she planned his time abroad as a preparation for a career in the Diplomatic Service.[41] On the one hand, it may have been her superficial approach to the arts which gave Gerald Berners the facility he later developed in music, writing and painting: what Lord David Cecil called 'the graceful, easy understated accomplishment of an admirable stylist – a gifted man in whatever he took up.'[42] But on the other hand Berners' background was the artistically strangulating Philistinism of the middle and upper classes that hampered other British composers of the period such as Elgar, especially when he married the daughter of Major-General Sir Henry Gee Roberts, and Delius, struggling against his German-immigrant businessman father,

38 *First Childhood*, 23.

39 E. M. Forster (1879–1970, *A Room with a View* (London, 1908; Harmondsworth: Penguin, 1955), 35–6.

40 *A Distant Prospect*, 18–19.

41 *A Distant Prospect*, 121. In *Percy Wallingford* the narrator describes how one prepared to enter the diplomatic service by spending time abroad, *Collected Tales and Fantasies*, 11. Wallingford, like Berners, went to the embassy in Constantinople and then to Rome, 28–9. Through his narrator, Berners describes the atmosphere in Rome in 1914: the story is dedicated to Clarissa Churchill, later the Countess of Avon. See Clarissa Eden, *A Memoir*, ed. Cate Haste (London: Weidenfeld & Nicolson, 2007).

42 See interview with Lord David Cecil, Chapter 14, p. 117.

the Bradford wool merchant. The question of amateurism is important enough to make it worth looking more carefully at the term in Victorian England.

An earlier English composer, Henry Hugo Pierson (1815–73), had to live in Germany to resolve this conflict in the mid nineteenth century. Like Berners, Pierson composed music that was advanced for its period. Nicholas Temperley has discussed his case:

> The word 'amateur' once an honourable term that distinguished a cultivated gentleman from his Philistine colleagues, was rapidly taking on the pejorative meaning of 'untrained dabbler'. It neatly embodied the feeling of many that the strangeness of Pierson's music was in some way related to his alien social status. And so, in a sense, it was. With his education and literary connections, he was more likely to be in sympathy with the more extreme forms of romanticism than a man brought up in a narrow apprenticeship to the craft of music. Pierson found himself, then, a misfit in the world of English music. To those of his own class, above all his father, a musician was not a gentleman; to those in the profession, a gentleman was not a musician. In Germany [where he settled from 1839] he found no difficulty in being both.[43]

The problem was not new. A century earlier, in 1749, Lord Chesterfield wrote to his son, who was making the Grand Tour in Italy: 'If you love music, hear it; go to operas, concerts and pay fiddlers to play it to you; but I insist upon your neither piping nor fiddling yourself. It puts a gentleman in a very frivolous and contemptible light ... Few things would mortify me more than to see you bearing a part in a concert, with a fiddle under your chin.'[44]

Berners, too, solved the problem by living abroad. He liked it so much better than the Foster family, who once did a Grand Tour: 'It rained in Venice, Uncle Luke caught sunstroke in Florence, my mother lost a bracelet at the opera in Milan, and my grandmother found a bug in her bed in Bologna. These mishaps were often referred to when anyone spoke too enthusiastically about foreign travel.'[45]

Berners became Honorary Attaché at Constantinople in 1909 and at Rome in 1911, keeping a house there until after World War II. Not much has emerged about Berners' first diplomatic post at Constantinople, but Alan Wykes is the source of one anecdote:

> The footman at the head of the steps leading down to the ballroom announced: 'The Honourable Gerald

43 Quoted by Stephen Banfield in 'The Artist and Society', *The Athlone History of Music in Britain: the Romantic Age, 1800–1914*, ed. Nicholas Temperley (London: Athlone Press, 1981), 19.

44 Quoted in Bernarr Rainbow, *Music in Educational Thought and Practice: a Survey from 800 BC*, 2nd edn (Woodbridge: Boydell Press, 2006), 123.

45 *First Childhood*, 48.

46 Alan Wykes, 'Lord Berners', *Music and Musicians*, September 1983, 10–11. I asked Alan Wykes where this story came from, and on 10 October 1983 he replied to say that he thought Robert Helpmann had told him in the 1950s, and probably had the story from Berners himself. Mary Gifford told me that the Cunliffe-Owens arrived in Constantinople in 1913, and in her memoirs, *Thro' the Gates of Memory: from the Bosphorus to Baghdad* (London: Hutchinson & Co., no date, [1924]), Betty Cunliffe-Owen makes no mention of the episode. Wykes' article contained another story which he said was told to him by Vaughan Williams at a concert of music by Gerald Finzi at the Festival Hall in the 1950s: Berners 'was arrested by a village constable for causing a breach of the peace when walking down a country lane wearing a World War I gas mask … a little girl had fled in terror from the strange apparition. "I am a sufferer from hay fever", he told the constable, "the mask filters the pollen". All the same he was fined £2, which he paid in gold sovereigns adding another twenty for the Police Widows and Orphans Fund. As a compensation to the child … he wrote her a short piece for the piano in which reiterated notes imitated her running feet … called *Chlorine Caprice*.'

47 Beverley Nichols, *The Sweet and Twenties* (London: Weidenfeld & Nicolson, 1958), 161.

48 'The Late Lord Berners: Rt. Hon Raymond Robert, Baron Berners of Stanley Hall died aged sixty-three after some months' illness on 5th inst. at 4 Down Street, Piccadilly. He owned vast estates in Shropshire and Norwich and also in Leicester and he was very popular amongst all his tenantry and a large circle of friends.' *Shrewsbury Chronicle*, 13 September 1918. Obituary: *The Times* 9 September 1918.

Tyrwhitt-Wilson … and friends'. The announcement was in no way sensational … This was the ballroom at the British Embassy in Constantinople … His excellency in full ambassadorial fig stood on a dais, his lady, plumed and glitteringly jewelled at his side … receptions were noted for their unrelieved pomp … So it was hardly surprising that no laughter, merely shocked silence, greeted the arrival of the Honourable Gerald Tyrwhitt-Wilson … and friends. The heir presumptive to the Barony of Berners was dressed in a skin-tight black leotard that enveloped him from throat to toe, and he was accompanied by two attendant bodies skilfully playing pan-pipes and dressed in the fancy costume of satyrs. The ballroom was suddenly full of stiff upper lips, raised eyebrows and pained efforts at pretending not to have noticed. The military attaché Colonel Cunliffe-Owen said softly to his lady: 'His Excellency will be furious about it. Tyrwhitt-Wilson's gone too far this time.' The subject of his fury said: 'He was blue in the face with indignation. And little is so pleasing in the sight of God as a blue ambassador. I shall take azure memories of him to Rome – to which eternal city His Excellency is having me banished to do my penance.'[46]

Berners' travels in France, Germany and Austria before that had made him more of a European than almost any British composer of the first half of the twentieth century. In the 1890s Delius became part of the artistic scene in Paris and lived in France for most of the rest of his life. Berners made similar connections in Rome. Had he remained Gerald Tyrwhitt and not inherited his title and wealth in 1918 – the barony goes back to 1415 – his English background might have seemed less attractive, although his connection with Faringdon House began in 1910 when his mother and her second husband, Colonel Ward Bennitt, went to live there.

Berners may have preferred fantasy to fact when he inherited his titles. He told Beverley Nichols that three uncles fell off a bridge at the same time after attending a funeral.[47] In fact, the eldest son of Sir Henry Tyrwhitt died before he did, so the next son, Raymond Robert, inherited the baronetcy in 1894 from his father and the barony from his mother in 1917 on her death.[48] When the second son died, in 1918, also without issue, Gerald's father (the third son) was already dead, so both titles came to Gerald. Not unexpectedly, although it could not have been predicted when he was growing up. (See family tree, Appendix 9.)

When Berners' uncle Raymond Robert died at the age of

sixty-three the Shropshire seat, Stanley Hall, and the estates in Norfolk and Leicester were sold at once on the instructions of the new 14th Baron Berners, who did not want the responsibilities of his forebears. Long-standing family connections thus came to an end.

Berners' father, Captain the Hon. Hugh Tyrwhitt CVO, CSI, Royal Navy (1856–1907) died on board the P. & O. steamship Caledonia *en route* to Egypt for the winter. He had served in the naval brigade landed for service in the Sudan with the Nile expedition for the relief of General Gordon, which arrived too late, and then remained in the Mediterranean. In 1905 he commissioned HMS *Renown* for the Indian tour of the Prince and Princess of Wales. Accompanying him as chaplain was his brother Leonard, who, in the tradition of younger sons went into the church, and later became a distinguished churchman. He was Canon of Windsor and chaplain to three monarchs: Queen Victoria, Edward VII and George V. Captain Tyrwhitt was appointed ADC to the King not long before his death, and his funeral at Holy Trinity, Brompton, was attended by the full naval establishment, with the Admiral of the Fleet and seven other admirals.[49]

Berners had seen little of his father, and during childhood realised his parents' incompatibility. As he put it: 'My mother and father were like two cogwheels that forever failed to engage.'[50] But Berners did owe some of his qualities to this enigmatic man:

> I used to admire and enjoy my father's occasional flashes of wit. But I feared and disliked the long periods of silence and moodiness that intervened, and even his wit, within the family circle, was only exercised, as a rule, at the expense of my mother or her friends. His wit was too cynical to be comfortable.[51]

Berners learned that technique himself and mastered it so that some of his father's gibes were prototypes for his own. When Captain Tyrwhitt was asked whether his mother, Lady Berners, was really a baroness in her own right he answered: 'Yes, but she's everything else in her own wrong.'[52] Of Berners himself Edith Sitwell tells:

> One of his acquaintances was in the impertinent habit of saying to him: 'I have been sticking up for you.' He repeated this once too often, and Lord Berners replied: 'Yes, and I have been sticking up for you. Someone said you aren't fit to live with pigs, and I said that you are!'[53]

Captain Tyrwhitt had other qualities that affected his son, although he had no time for art or literature:

49 Tyrwhitt was born in 1856 and entered the navy at thirteen and a half. He became a lieutenant in 1881, and three years later was flag officer to the C-in-C in the Mediterranean. In 1893 he was promoted to commander, and raised again in 1899. He was flag captain to Admiral of the Fleet Sir John Fisher, then acting C-in-C with his flag flying on the battleship HMS *Renown*. On returning home he was private secretary to the Earl of Selbourne, then at Whitehall for three years, retained by Lord Cawdor. He was again appointed to the *Renown*, but had to resign owing to ill health. *Shrewsbury Chronicle*, 8 November 1907. Obituary: *The Times*, 1 November 1907.

50 *First Childhood*, 52.

51 *First Childhood*, 53.

52 *First Childhood*, 38.

53 Dame Edith Sitwell (1887–1964), *Taken Care of: an Autobiography* (London: Hutchinson, 1965), 127.

I was always very impressed by my father's elegance. He took a good deal of trouble about his clothes. He was a small, well-built man. He wore a neat, pointed beard and he walked with an imposing swagger. He had that easy superiority of manner which enables people to command attention whether on a battleship or in a restaurant. Anyone meeting him for the first time might have mistaken him for minor royalty.[54]

Distance perhaps lent enchantment. When he came to see Berners at Eton and gave him the money to buy a vocal score of Wagner's *Das Rheingold* it was the first time they had been alone together away from home.[55]

The diversity of his mother's tastes fascinated him: 'She admired indiscriminately Keats and Longfellow, Jane Austen and Marie Corelli. Paintings by Leader and Luke Fildes gave her the same emotions as those by Raphael and Titian.'[56] His mother may not have appreciated the distinction between great art and the more popular product. Berners, of course, did, but that didn't stop him disconcerting people by juxtaposing priceless objects and joke pieces at Faringdon in his own collection. One of his mother's engravings depicted a young lady seated at the organ. It was entitled *The Lost Chord*, after Sullivan's sentimental masterpiece. Berners – glad to poke fun – felt 'it was just as well she had lost it!'[57]

Unlike her son, Mrs Tyrwhitt had no sense of humour, and was always surprised if what she said was found funny. In this, Berners sided with his father, who sometimes found more to laugh at than was convenient. One of young Gerald's tutors, called Mr Pratt in *First Childhood* became a butt for his father's ridicule:

> I gathered that my father didn't much care for Mr Pratt and certainly his behaviour, when Mr Pratt was present, and his comments after he left, seemed to suggest that he understood him better than my mother appeared to do. I remember one day Mr Pratt saying: 'I often think some of the best things in life are behind us'. My mother was inclined to agree with the sentiment and was a little puzzled when my father broke out into a malignant guffaw of laughter which hardly seemed justified by the innocent nature of the remark.'[58]

When the Swiss governess came to teach Gerald he found her stuffy, prudish and dull. She deserved to be the victim of a practical joke, one that anticipated surrealist incongruity:

> During the summer months, when the weather was warm, I used to do my lessons in a little summer-house in the garden. Close at hand, concealed in a shrubbery,

54 *First Childhood*, 54.

55 According to Mary Gifford, Berners' letters to his mother suggest that his father did not visit him at Eton.

56 *First Childhood*, 76. Benjamin Williams Leader (1831–1923) and Sir Samuel Luke Fildes (1844–1927) were both fashionable Victorian painters. Leader concentrated on landscapes: Fildes became known for socially committed pictures and was in demand for society portraits, including royalty.

57 *First Childhood*, 76.

58 *First Childhood*, 101–2. This story is in Chapter 9 of *First Childhood* but most of that chapter was published two years earlier in *Little Innocents: Childhood Reminiscences*, with preface by Alan Pryce-Jones (London: Cobden-Sanderson, 1932), 5–9.

there was a rustic closet which Mademoiselle Bock, every morning, used to visit with clockwork regularity. The fact that she was the only person in the household to make use of it suggested to my mind a diabolical plan of revenge. The gardener's son had a natural talent for carpentering and, with his assistance, I constructed a very ingenious booby-trap. By an intricate system of leverage we succeeded in arranging matters so that, when you sat down, a small board came up and hit you a terrific blow on the behind. Next morning I anxiously awaited the moment for Mademoiselle's customary retirement and, as soon as she had set out, I made my way swiftly through the bushes, crept up to the door and listened for the result. I was rewarded by hearing the sound of a dull whack followed by a startled cry. A few moments later Mademoiselle Bock emerged with a distraught countenance.[59]

Of course, the governess gave her notice and Gerald was in trouble. As he put it: 'smarting Swiss buttocks overcame native prudery'. However, Lady Pamela Knyvett Berners remembers that her mother Elizabeth Maude was also involved. She was a child of about the same age as Gerald, and would have been staying at Apley with her parents at the same time as Gerald and his mother. Elizabeth was in league with Gerald, and they watched the incident from an upstairs window, laughing until she was sick. The governess was apparently spiteful with the children and deserved it, but there was such a row that Elizabeth was sent home in disgrace.[60]

Then he was sent to school: to Cheam (1893–7). This was part of the Tyrwhitt family tradition since all nine sons of Sir Henry Tyrwhitt went there. In *First Childhood* Berners calls his prep school Elmley and tactfully says it no longer exists. This is because he attacks the way in which imagination was constricted and the arts discouraged. 'The manner in which music was taught there was one of the methods of discouragement.'[61]

Berners found the music master's taste appalling. His favourite piece was the salon classic *Les Cloches du monastère* – Berners doesn't mention who wrote it, but it was by the French organist and composer Louis Lefébure-Wély (1817–69).[62] His own idol at the time was Chopin, disparaged by the music master as morbid, and thus forbidden. But his continued devotion to Chopin emerged in his waltzes and his late Valse for the séance scene in the film *The Halfway House* fifty years later. Berners documented the headmaster's sadism, but he still found Cheam 'good in its way', and its

59 *First Childhood*, 113–14. This story appeared first as 'The Swiss Governess: an Autobiographical Fragment', *The New Keepsake: a Christmas, New Year and Birthday Present for Persons of both Sexes* (London: Cobden-Sanderson, 1931), 131–6.

60 Telephone conversation with Lady Pamela Knyvett Berners, 2 October 2007.

61 *First Childhood*, 199.

62 *Les Cloches du monastère: Nocturne*, op. 54, by Louis Lefébure-Wély (1817–69). The final repeat of the saccharine melody imitates the monastery bells. *First Childhood*, 200 (1934); 184 (1999).

antagonism towards the arts must have been typical at the time.

Lord David Cecil, commenting on Berners' humour, said: 'You couldn't call it kindly, but it wasn't ill-tempered. They were mischievous boyish pranks.'[63] When Cecil Beaton stayed with Berners in Rome he considered him 'a very odd character with very little heart' who couldn't resist 'joking about one's softest spot and prodding one's Achilles heel.'[64]

The story about the Swiss governess was first published in an anthology decorated by Rex Whistler three years before it was included in *First Childhood*.[65] Compared with Harold Nicolson's essay in the same volume, called 'Early Influences', Berners' fragment is neat and well timed. Nicolson and Berners were both at the Embassy in Constantinople, and to some extent were rivals. Berners used to make fun of Nicolson, who was at the political centre of events in both world wars, and didn't appreciate it. Berners may have noticed – and he would have liked this – that he describes his own awakening of consciousness in *First Childhood* at the age of three and a half, whereas Nicolson identifies his at the age of eleven![66]

Berners couldn't resist deflating people. Apparently he advertised two elephants for sale in the personal column of *The Times* and then told the press that he had sold one to Nicolson and the other to Lady Colefax. Both were furious.[67] Lady Pamela Knyvett Berners knew Berners best when she was a child herself, and could describe him from that point of view:

> Until I was thirteen years old – in 1935 – I spent a great deal of time with Gerald and my wicked grandfather ... I was just 'enfant terrible' or 'that child' and never treated as anything but an equal – except when Faringdon was full of the then 'beautiful people'. Then I just slid about, sat behind chairs listening, taking it all in. Sometimes I was allowed to take dinner with the guests – to be seen and not heard! Even better, hardly seen! His dog and I were very good at this. Berners' really monstrous pranks – for that is what they were – did not always go down with his own generation, but they gave me (and still do) endless hours of sheer joy!
>
> He was all things to all people – sometimes quiet and shy. Always so polite even if, when you thought about it deeply, he had just insulted somebody – but so perfectly! But he was rarely unkind. He loved people ... he was never the upper-crust snob, but stopped at workmen's tea places, talking like mad to one and all ...
>
> My children have grown up with him as an almost living legend – his mark was upon me, being so young.

63 See interview with Lord David Cecil, Chapter 14, p. 120.

64 Hugo Vickers, *Cecil Beaton: the Authorized Biography* (London: Weidenfeld & Nicolson, 1985), 183.

65 *The New Keepsake*, 131–6.

66 *The New Keepsake*, 2. Sir Harold Nicolson (1886–1968) was born in Teheran, where his father was a diplomat. After Oxford Nicolson followed in his father's footsteps, and he overlapped with Berners at the British Embassy in Constantinople. His marriage to Vita Sackville-West was unconventional. His literary books include biographies of Tennyson, Byron and Swinburne, and the set of portraits, *Some People* (1927) which Margaret Drabble in *The Oxford Companion to English Literature* (Oxford: Oxford University Press, 1985) considered 'perhaps his most memorable work'. Nicolson entered politics, briefly supporting Oswald Mosley's New Party in 1931, but became a Labour MP in 1935. He was Parliamentary Secretary to the Ministry of Information in Churchill's wartime government. His view of Berners emerged in his obituary for the *Spectator*, 28 April 1950, 568.

67 See interview with Lady Mosley, Chapter 10, p. 94.

68 Letter to Peter Dickinson from Lady Pamela Knyvett Berners, 30 September 1983. Later she remembered a journey with Berners by car from London to Oxford when they stopped for some early tea at a workmen's café. The driver was not the chauffeur William Crack, but a friend who was very shocked. Berners would make up rhymes whilst travelling. Telephone conversation 2 October 2007.

I thought as he thought and learned so much about life – more perhaps than this grubby little person should have done. But it never hurt me – I think it made life all the easier to face – because he always made it a challenge![68]

Berners wrote to her most months when she was at school and enclosed naughty little poems and drawings mocking people they knew. He told her that he couldn't stand his own family. They represented the adult roles he refused to take seriously, especially in marriage.

In 1934 Berners was asked what he considered the essentials for a happy marriage. Perhaps he thought of his parents when he replied: 'A long purse, infinite credulity and no sense of humour, a combative nature and a stipulation that the man should be a man and the woman a woman – or vice versa.' He mocked conventional marriage in the two short stories *Percy Wallingford* and *Mr Pidger*.[69] In the first, Percy Wallingford, the author's brilliant school contemporary, makes an inexplicable marriage and finally takes his own life.[70] In *Mr Pidger* (the name of a dog) a young couple quarrel so badly over the wife's dog that they are disinherited by his uncle, and the husband throws the dog out of the train window on their return journey.

Berners' unpublished play, *The Furies*, staged in Oxford in 1942, has a hero who marries a tart to escape the competing attentions of three smart ladies. The ballet *A Wedding Bouquet*, produced in 1937 to choreography by Sir Frederick Ashton with costumes and sets by Berners himself, is a satire on weddings by way of Stravinsky's *Les Noces*. The bridegroom is surrounded by his former mistresses. One of them, Josephine, gets very drunk. The sung text, by Gertrude Stein, struck people as preposterous, which is why Berners must have chosen it. He didn't respect her work, even though he wrote realistic parodies of it himself. Berners didn't even set Stein's texts as she wrote them, and never bothered with punctuation. He even told the publisher to 'get the engravers to put a few full stops in' – an esoteric joke probably unshared until his letter surfaced at the publishers some forty years later. The whole celebration ends unpromisingly with the words: 'Bitterness is entertained by all: they incline to oblige only one.'[71] These words, taken out of their context, cause what had been an ebullient waltz to fizzle out at the end. There were divorces and unhappy marriages amongst the people Berners knew.

E. E. Cummings assessed Gertrude Stein: 'She's a symbol – she's an excellent symbol, like a pillar of Portland cement! You can't budge her. Philistines bump into her and get bruised.'[72]

69 The two stories were first published together as a paperback by Basil Blackwell, Oxford, 1941, and not reissued until they were included in *Collected Tales and Fantasies* (1999). Compare *Mr Pidger* with the story in *First Childhood* of Berners as a child pushing his mother's dog out of the window, 70. Lady Pamela Knyvett Berners knew about this through her mother, who told her the dog fell harmlessly into bushes (interview at North Creake, 6 October 2007). *Mr Pidger* was reprinted in *Diversion* (London, 1946), an anthology edited by Hester W. Chapman and Princess Romanovsky-Pavlovsky and published for the benefit of the Yugoslav Relief Society, 57–90. In that volume the short story by Elizabeth Bowen, 'The Good Earl', is set in exactly the social context into which Berners was born. She reviewed *A Distant Prospect* in the *Tatler*: 'It is the manner – the style, the shape, the mood – of the memory that gives *A Distant Prospect* its human value and high aesthetic claim.' Amory, *Lord Berners*, 223.

70 At the end of *A Distant Prospect* Berners wrote: 'I have known too many men whose lives have been too triumphant in their schooldays. There is a danger in one's golden age coming too early', 125–6.

71 Gertrude Stein (1874–1946), American avant-garde writer and collector of paintings who spent most of her life in Paris. *A Wedding Bouquet* was produced at Sadler's Wells Theatre on 27 April 1937 (not 1936, as on the vocal score). See interview with Sir Frederick Ashton, Chapter 11, p. 99, and Berners' Stein parodies, Chapter 18, p. 152.

72 Charles Norman, *The Magic Maker: E. E. Cummings* (New York: Macmillan Co., 1958), 53.

Berners liked her because she was fashionably modern – in the way that his avant-garde musical style was around World War I – and she did disconcert people. She was supported by the Sitwells, who represented a type of avant-garde chic which arrived in England during World War I with the magazine *Wheels*, edited by Edith Sitwell, and was exemplified by her collaboration with William Walton, *Façade*.[73]

Berners had musical targets too. 'The recent Sibelius Festival (Thank God) has considerably diminished public enthusiasm for Sibelius.'[74] Pretentiousness, which he disliked in any form, was equated with excessive length:

> The symphonies of Schumann and Schubert, beautiful as they are, contain passages one feels might conveniently have been shorter, whilst in Bruckner and Mahler there are moments that even an audience of tortoises might find tedious.[75]

Matters with Walton – another British composer who couldn't stand living in England – became more complex. During the Second World War, in Oxford, Berners returned to writing novels, as usual based on real people somewhat disguised. As many as four books appeared in 1941, following *The Camel* published in 1936, dedicated to John and Penelope Betjeman and partly based on them. Berners talked about his plans to have a composer as hero in the novel that became *Count Omega*, and Walton grew nervous. On 9 October 1941 Walton's solicitor wrote to Berners:

> Will you kindly respect Mr Walton's wishes by not using his name or referring to him in any way in this novel?

On 24 October Walton's solicitor reported Berners as having replied, but made matters worse by saying that he had reserved Walton for a forthcoming novel.

Meanwhile Walton had read *Count Omega*, with its composer hero, with relief, and wrote to Berners to say that he had 'enjoyed it very much: the composer is too like Edmund Rubbra for my liking.'[76] Further: 'I had hoped my action would cheer you up and give you something to gossip about and I'm sorry it seems to have had the contrary effect.' Berners, perhaps initially taken aback by Walton's seriousness – a crime in his eyes at any time – then returned to the fray:

> I informed your solicitors that my letter to you about 'putting you into a book' was not intended to be taken seriously. Something must have happened to your sense of proportion as well as to your sense of humour. You surely don't imagine that your personality is sufficiently

73 Edith Sitwell's verses were declaimed in *Façade* (1923) to music by Sir William Walton (1902–83); Sir Osbert Sitwell (1892–1969), prolific writer whose story 'The Love-Bird' was partly based on Berners and whose text was used by Walton for *Belshazzar's Feast* (1926), which was dedicated to Berners which occasioned a gift of £50; and Sacheverell Sitwell (1897–1988), who wrote the scenario for *The Triumph of Neptune* (1926) and whose poem was set by Constant Lambert in *The Rio Grande* (1928). In the period between the two world wars the Sitwells represented the literary avant-garde, although they were accused of pretentious publicity. However, Arnold Haskell, *Balletomania: the Story of an Obsession* (London: Victor Gollancz, 1934), 225 n. 1: 'Thank God for the Sitwell family and Lord Berners! They are the great exception to everything I have written about the narrow views of English artists. Their role has already been a great one ...'

74 Berners Archive. However, this didn't stop Berners from attending the reception after a Sibelius concert – see *The Times* report 2 November 1938.

75 See 'The Time Element in Music', Chapter 18, p. 150.

76 Edmund Rubbra (1901–86), pupil of Holst and Vaughan Williams, wrote eleven symphonies. Correspondence from the Berners Archive.

interesting to appeal to me as a literary theme. If you insist on trying to thrust yourself into my novels in this fashion, I shall be obliged to apply for an injunction to restrain you from doing so.

He went further and wrote to Walton's solicitors:

I am shortly bringing out a book called *Ridiculous Composers I have known*. If your client, Mr William Walton, should consider it necessary to see a copy before publication, will you kindly tell him to apply to Messrs Constable?

Constant Lambert, composer, conductor and friend of both parties, wrote to Berners on 2 January 1942:

What a fool Willie made himself about it. It's about time somebody reminded him that after all he's only an illegitimate Sitwell.

In *Far from the Madding War* Lord Fitzcricket is Berners' self-portrait, and Francis Paltry is another composer with some resemblance to Walton.

Francis Paltrey and Lord Fitzcricket didn't get on very well. Their temperaments and their aesthetic views were poles apart. Lord Fitzcricket was a dilettante and had always been interested in the pleasurable aspects of art, and he thought that a work of art should never be tedious. Francis, on the other hand, held that art should be austere, he felt that he himself had a mission. Lord Fitzcricket said that Francis believed in catharsis through boredom.

When Paltrey was asked about his symphony he replied:

'Certain people might consider it long. It lasts about an hour and a half, and it's in one movement. If a man has something to say, he must take his time about it. I haven't been able to acquire the modern knack of developing a theme in a few minutes or not developing it at all.'

'I think you're wise', said Lord Fitzcricket. 'If you're setting up to be a national composer. The English have a tendency to judge art by size and weight'.[77]

It must have appeared to Berners that Walton, with *Belshazzar's Feast*, the concertos for violin and viola, the First Symphony and especially *Crown Imperial* behind him, was in danger of becoming a natural successor to Elgar. That was a disaster – from Berners' point of view – that couldn't be tolerated. The values of his Victorian childhood might triumph after all.

77 *Far from the Madding War*, 164 (1941); 422 (1999). In *The Camel* the vicar and his wife went to a lunch party where the guests include 'a female composer who had written a symphony of such incredible length and dullness that it had been immediately hailed by all the leading English musical critics as a masterpiece', 64 (1936); 79 (1999).

In his own work, from 1926 onwards Berners met the problem by turning to the collaborative medium of ballet, where the composer would not be assessed on his own, seriously. He'd never written a piece of absolute music, except perhaps the orchestral Fugue of 1924. He was more at home in a situation where several artistic elements could be combined, not with the tepid and unselective enjoyment of his mother, but with the sharp discrimination of a connoisseur fluent in four languages and cultures.

Berners countered Walton's type of single-minded intensity by deliberate diversification, spreading himself more thinly. In the 1930s he exhibited and sold about a hundred oil paintings, as well as starting to publish his books. It has been hard to assess Berners as a painter because very few examples are in galleries.[78] No wonder, with this diversity, that the *New Statesman* published a clerihew:

> Lord Berners
> Told a crowd of learners
> That if they wanted to compose
> They should paint or write prose.[79]

Walton, from a working-class background in Oldham, Lancashire, was fortunate to get the chance to become 'an illegitimate Sitwell' and develop his work exclusively as a composer in a congenial atmosphere. Berners couldn't do this because of the conditioning of his early life – in spite of meeting Stravinsky in 1911, who became a good friend and told Berners' publisher that he was 'not only a composer of unique talent but a typical and very representative character of his race.'[80]

Perhaps he was too representative of the Victorian conflict between the arts and society. But it was society, in a more glamorous sense, that became a distraction after Berners came into his inheritance. During World War I he became part of the futurist movement in Rome, writing some of the most advanced music by any British composer up to that time. Apart from unpublished juvenilia his first published works show that he began his composing career as an avant-gardist. He didn't follow up the discoveries that caused him to be regarded as a leading British modernist well into the 1920s. His tactic was to take on or take off fashionable styles, including national idioms in songs – *A Lieder Album*, *Three French Songs*, *Three English Songs* – and orchestral pieces such as the *Fantaisie espagnole* or *Chinoiserie*, the first of the *Three Pieces for Orchestra*. Then he supplied the needs of dancers in the five ballet scores more in the tradition of Delibes and Tchaikovsky than Stravinsky. Berners showed himself a master of the salon style in the song to his own

78 This book contains the largest selection seen since 1936.

79 One of the winners of a clerihew competition set by Raymond Mortimer in the *New Statesman* in 1939. Amory, *Lord Berners*, 104.

80 *Chesterian*, October 1917, 156.

poem, 'Red Roses and Red Noses', and capable of what ought to have become a smash-hit in the risqué music hall number 'Come on Algernon'.[81]

In all this talent for mimicry so plentifully illustrated, where is Berners himself? The enigma of Berners, disguised as Robert Mainwroth, is the starting point for a short story by Osbert Sitwell called 'The Love-Bird'. 'To those who did not care for him, Robert Mainwroth gave an impression of being a scoffer, one who was eccentric and outside life.' But his friends saw him as 'a pivot of very modern, if mocking activity. He was so intensely aware of all that was going on in the many different worlds around him, albeit so much of this action and effort appeared to him in itself to be ridiculous.'[82] Sitwell probes the reason for his being engaged in keeping life at arm's length, and suggests that perhaps 'he had so much felt the fear, love, excitement, terror and beauty of existence, had been so early singed by these things, that he would rather avoid life if he could ...' He goes on to ask if emotions that used to exist were now being hidden 'under the mask of fun and witty observance'. He characterises Mainwroth: 'He was, in fact, a dilettante, but one in the best sense: for he aspired to be nothing but what he was. He talked well and amusingly; painted and wrote fluently, even with talent of an order.' Whilst allowing many endearing qualities to Mainwroth, Sitwell observes: 'Creative talent might have cured him, but he had, and by so little, missed it ... However, whether he loved or did not love, whether he felt so deeply or did not feel at all, there was no doubt that he was a delightful companion and a very good friend.'

Osbert Sitwell was writing a story which happens to be an astute attempt at a character analysis of someone like Berners, although much younger. But, from that point of view, there are some flaws. First, he fails to recognise the real value of the music, which he barely mentions, and which everyone agrees, including Berners himself, was his most important single contribution; secondly, he underrates his late Victorian context, although he goes into surprising detail about the contents of the country houses that Mainwroth (Berners) sold when he inherited them; finally, he is wrong to be so nostalgically negative. Creative talent did save Berners from the unacceptable alternatives provided by his family background, although, as I have shown, not by a simple reaction against it. He was a child of his time, but more like Wilde and Firbank than Elgar or Kipling.

Much later, in the fourth volume of his autobiography, Osbert Sitwell returned to the subject of Berners. He remembered how they were together at the 1923 festival of the International Society for Contemporary Music at Salzburg,

81 This song, with lyric by T. E. B. Clarke, was used in the film *Champagne Charlie* (Ealing Studios 1944), where it was sung by Betty Warren. Meriel Dickinson sang it at the London concerts in 1972 and 1983, and she made the first recording.

82 Osbert Sitwell (1892–1969), 'The Love-Bird', in *Collected Stories* (London: Duckworth & Co., 1953), 64–82. The story first appeared in *The Argosy*, February 1934.

83 Amory, *Lord Berners*, 83.

84 Osbert Sitwell, *Laughter in the Next Room* (London: Macmillan, 1949), 180–1.

85 At the time of *Cupid and Psyche*, Sadlers' Wells Theatre, 27 April 1939, Berners wrote in *Illustrated*, 20 May 1939, a kind of ballet credo based on enjoyment:

> There can be no doubt that ballet is now more appreciated in England than in any other country: that England is now the spiritual home of ballet. Formerly the cult of a restricted public, it is now acquiring every day a wider and more varied following of enthusiasts. Literature treating of the ballet grows daily. Nearly every month brings a new book on the subject (often by people whose enthusiasm is their only merit) and soon libraries will be as cluttered with books on ballet as they formerly were with books on theology.
>
> The modern type of ballet which, to borrow pictorial terminology, might be described as 'genre' ballet, was invented by Diaghilev. Originally a real offshoot of the Imperial Russian Ballet, it broke away from the classical tradition and then assumed new and more exciting forms.
>
> Serious composers of every country, Stravinsky, Ravel, Richard Strauss, de Falla, wrote music for it. Painters such as Picasso, Derain, Utrillo designed costumes and scenery. This was all through the initiative of Diaghilev and his death seemed at first as if it would be the death-blow to ballet. But, after a chaotic interval, a new order became established. Sadler's Wells is now the principal home of ballet in England … no other ballet company in the world could boast of so gifted a trio as Ninette de Valois, Frederick Ashton and Constant Lambert … combined with a band of dancers displaying such individual technique, such fascinating and varied personalities.

although he had forgotten that Berners' *Valses bourgeoises* for piano duet were performed as well as Walton's First String Quartet. Berners acted as interpreter when Alban Berg took him and Walton to meet Arnold Schoenberg.[83]

> At Salzburg … we saw much of our friend Berners, with his keen understanding and appreciation of everything that is fine, and his particular gift of reconciling the irreconcilable, both in people and circumstances, so that you are conscious, when in his company, that anything may occur … Melancholy I believe by nature and with a number of talents of uncommon degree most evenly distributed among the arts, when not at work he is addicted to humour, as less gifted individuals are victims to drink or to drugs … rarest of attributes in a conversationalist, he listens as well as he talks. In the years between the wars he did more to civilise the wealthy than anyone in England. Through London's darkest drawing-rooms, as well as through the lightest, he moved, dedicated to their conversion, a sort of missionary of the arts bringing a touch of unwanted fun into many a dreary life – perhaps all the more funny for its being unwanted.[84]

Creative talent enhanced not only Berners' life, but also the lives of those who were fortunate enough to come into contact with him. This is where his multifarious activities governed by enjoyment are an example to us today in a society with increased and even enforced leisure and thus eminently worth exploring.[85]

He wrote his own epitaph:

> Here lies Lord Berners
> One of the learners.
> His great love of learning
> May earn him a burning
> But praise to the Lord!
> He seldom was bored.

One of the reasons for the great popularity of ballet at the present moment is perhaps that it is one of the most palpable manifestations of Art for Art's Sake. It represents what left-wing highbrows call 'escapist art' in its purest form. There is in ballet no insidious motive of edification and uplift. And although ballet companies may call themselves 'educational' their primary object is, or should be, to entertain rather than educate. It is to ballet that you may flee from the wrath to come and from the wrath that seems almost at hand. In these troublous times we may at least escape for an hour or two to Sadler's Wells and other places where there is ballet.

1 *(below)* Berners' father, Captain Hugh Tyrwhitt, RN, CSI, CVO

2 *(right)* Berners' mother, Julia Mary Tyrwhitt (*née* Foster, later Bennitt)

3 *(below right)* Berners about 1922

4 Aldous Huxley, Phyllis de Janzé and Berners outside Faringdon House, *c.* 1936

5 Frederick Ashton, Constant Lambert and Berners in the drawing room of Faringdon House, 1937

6 Berners wearing a monocle at the première of *Cupid and Psyche*, 1939

7 Berners, Ira Belline, Frederick Ashton and Francis Rose at the première of *Cupid and Psyche*, 1939

8 Berners and dancers at the première of *Cupid and Psyche*, 1939

9 Berners, Gay Margesson and Richard Cecil in Broad Street, Oxford, early 1940s

10 Berners, Lord and Lady David Cecil and William Walton, outside the Sheldonian Theatre, Oxford, 1942

11 *(above)* Robert Heber-Percy, 1930s

12 *(right)* Robert Heber-Percy, 1980s

13 Apley Park, Shropshire, Berners' birthplace and early home

14 Stanley Hall, Shropshire, the seat of Berners' uncle Raymond Robert Tyrwhitt-Wilson, 13th Baron Berners (photograph by courtesy of Michael Thompson, the present owner)

15 Faringdon House, Oxfordshire (formerly Berkshire), Berners' country house, built *c.* 1770 under the ownership of poet laureate Henry James Pye

16 Berners: photomontage for the covers of the *Shell Guide to Wiltshire*, 1935

CHAPTER 2

Critical responses

Peter Dickinson

T HERE ARE several periods when Berners was in the
news, initially as a composer, but later as a polymath and
eccentric. The first was when his early music was published
and gained prominent performances – the years during
World War I and into the 1920s, when Berners was seen as
part of modern music, even of the avant-garde. He brought
an international sophistication to British music to offset the
obsession with folk music, impressive enough in major figures such as Vaughan Williams, but often tedious and provincial in the minor exponents. Then Berners' contributions
to ballet in the inter-war years were his principal route to
a larger public, which was also kept informed of his eccentricities. From 1918 onwards there were articles from some of
the leading critics, reflecting the initial impact of his music.
During the 1920s and 30s Berners was in the public eye when
his travels and attendance at receptions, as well as his latest
works, were reported in the press. In the dark days of austerity after World War II there were obituary tributes in 1950,
but by his centenary in 1983 he attracted more public attention. The record does not stop there, since by the later 1990s
virtually all his music was on CD, all his published writings
were back in print, and there was a very readable biography
by Mark Amory.

Berners first became known as a composer when he was
an Honorary Attaché at the British Embassy in Rome from
1911 to 1920. He was Gerald Tyrwhitt until 1918, when he
inherited, and it was under that name that his music was
first published in England by the house of J. & W. Chester
in 1917. Their association began with Tyrwhitt's *Trois petites
marches funèbres* for piano, and he arrived with a fanfare and
an impressive recommendation:

A British composer hitherto completely unknown in
his own country is to be introduced by the publication
of these three little humorous marches ... The *Little
Funeral Marches* [for a statesman; a canary; and a rich
aunt] are humorous miniatures of a peculiarly British type, and they are clearly the work of a musician
with an amazing insight into the musical techniques
of our day. Daring as they are, these pieces never give
the impression of deliberate or strained modernism;
the hearer cannot help feeling their spontaneity and

the sureness of touch which makes their meaning so convincing.

We are happy to record the testimony of one of the greatest living composers, M. Igor Stravinsky, who has voiced his appreciation of this work in an interesting letter to us recently. In M. Stravinsky's opinion Mr Tyrwhitt is not only a composer of unique talent, but also a very typical and very representative character of his race.[1]

The composer's manuscript dates the triptych precisely 'Rome, May 13, 1916. Moon ¾ to full', and at the head of the last piece he wrote: 'enfin, nous allons pouvoir acheter un automobile', which did not reach the published score. There was also an undated Italian edition of the *Trois petites marches* by a firm in Florence. This could have been a private printing overtaken by events when Berners was taken on by Chester, who were given the copyright of this work for all countries on 30 June 1917. The first performance of the *Three Funeral Marches* was given by Berners' friend and colleague Alfredo Casella at the Accademia di Santa Cecilia in Rome on 30 March 1917.[2]

Then Casella encouraged Berners to use all three funeral marches in a group of five pieces scored for small orchestra, and he conducted this version as *L'uomo dai baffi* [The Man with the Moustache] for Fortunato Depero's marionette theatre.[3] In 1919 Casella wrote *The Evolution of Music: throughout the History of the Perfect Cadence* with the last eleven bars of the third march provided as an illustration.[4]

In 1919 Chester published Berners' *Fragments psychologiques*, planned under the name of Tyrwhitt, but the two-page announcement in the *Chesterian* starts: 'Gerald Tyrwhitt – now Lord Berners ...' and mentions the *Three Orchestral Pieces* to be premièred by the Hallé in Manchester on 8 March under Eugene Goossens.[5] When the *Chesterian* advertised these pieces it referred to a great impression made by 'the audacious, descriptive and ironic qualities of the music, no less than its profound originality'.[6] The piano duet version was given in Paris through the Societé Musicale Indépendante in a concert of British music sponsored by Lord Derby at the Salle Gaveau on 25 April 1919. The French composer, pianist and writer Florent Schmitt reviewed the concert, mentioning Berners as the composer of the 'notorious little funeral marches, played last year, the titles of which did not fail to scandalise some critics'. Schmitt said he felt the influence of Stravinsky in the *Chinoiserie* and went on, revealingly, 'but Lord Berners could not possibly deny his master'. In the *Valse sentimentale* he even found 'a kind of

1 *Chesterian*, October 1917, 156.

2 Alfredo Casella (1883–1947), leading Italian composer and pianist. For more details about the solo piano music see Berners, *The Collected Music for Solo Piano*, ed. Peter Dickinson (London: Chester Music, 1982; 2nd edn 2000).

3 See interviews with Harold Acton, who was there, Chapter 4, p. 48, and Fiamma Nicolodi, Chapter 18, p. 144. Philip Lane has scored the two pieces which Berners did not use as Intermezzo 1 & 2 to make a set with all three Funeral Marches, all three *Fragments psychologiques* and *Portsmouth Point*. Recorded on Marco Polo 8.223711 (1998). The British première of *L'uomo dai baffi* was given by Aquarius under Nicholas Cleobury at the Queen Elizabeth Hall, London, on 1 November 1983. That concert ended with Cleobury's arrangements of Berners' *Three Songs*, 'Red roses and red noses' and 'Come on Algernon', sung by Mary King.

4 Alfredo Casella, *L'evolution della musica: a traverso la storia della cadenza perfetta* (with parallel texts in French and English) (London: J. & W. Chester, 1924); new edition enlarged by Edmund Rubbra, as *The Evolution of Music through the History of the Perfect Cadence* (English only) (London: J. & W. Chester, 1964).

prim sensibility. A crocodile would weep over it.' The final
Kasatchok was 'extremely picturesque and alive, and reveals
a remarkable virtuosity of technique'.[7]

Looking back, there must have been some strong reactions
to the Funeral Marches, as Chester acknowledged in offering the *Fragments psychologiques*: 'The work just announced
will doubtless arouse violent controversy, and in order to
illustrate how this new music is viewed by prominent critics,
we cannot do better than quote the following ...' Then came
extracts from reviews of the Funeral Marches. Ernest Newman, writing in *The New Witness*, hailed 'the spirit of irrever-
ence' allowing us to laugh 'at ludicrous things'. He noted the
'expansion of harmony, and of the harmonic sense that makes
a thousand combinations acceptable to us which would have
driven our fathers mad'. Like *Alice in Wonderland* it was
'absurd but logical'.[8] The review that – very characteristically
– Berners liked best came from Julien Tiersot[9] in *Le Courier
musical*. He must have been the scandalised critic referred
to by the *Chesterian*. First of all Tiersot named the subjects
– the victims – of the *Trois petites marches funèbres* then he
went on:

> I will not stop to enquire whether the period through
> which we are passing is one that permits of the railing
> at death, and making it the subject of jokes which are,
> moreover, out of fashion. I only draw attention to the
> first title as a contrast to the other two. It is evident that
> to the composer's idea it is as gratifying to celebrate the
> funeral of a statesman as that of canaries or rich aunts
> – and all at a time when these men devote and exhaust
> themselves to serve their country and secure its vic-
> tory. But no such considerations seem to have touched
> the young composer (a neutral no doubt), the author
> responsible for this indiscretion, who has known how
> to find in Paris a committee willing to admit his work
> and a public to listen to, and perhaps applaud it. But
> we protest in vain.[10]

In 1920 the *Musical Times* was running a series on Modern British Composers written by Edwin Evans.[11] The first
article in the January issue, and the seventh in the series, was
a thorough five-page study of Berners with music examples.
Evans recognised that:

> As a composer, Lord Berners stands entirely alone.
> He not only represents a special feature in our musi-
> cal life but he combines it with a paradox. He has a
> sense of humour which corresponds to a national trait,
> but the manner of its expression is international. It is

5 Sir Eugene Goossens
(1893–1962), British composer
and conductor, descended from a
remarkable Belgian family of musicians. He was the brother of harp-
ists Sidonie and Marie and oboist
Léon Goossens, worked in the USA
and Australia, and was knighted in
1955.

The première of Berners' *Fantaisie espagnole* (then called *Spanish
Fantasy*) was given at the Proms
under Sir Henry Wood on 24 September 1919, and Goossens included
it in a significant concert given in
the Queen's Hall, London, on 7 June
1921. He launched his orchestra with
a programme that included the first
concert performance in London of
Stravinsky's *Le Sacre du printemps*.
See Eugene Goossens, *Overture and
Beginners: a Musical Autobiography* (London: Methuen & Co., 1951),
156–64. Two weeks later the programme was repeated without the
Berners. However, Goossens conducted it in a programme of British
music with the Berlin Philharmonic
in December of the following year.
Overture and Beginners, 318.

6 *Chesterian*, May 1919, 292.

7 Florent Schmidt (1870–1958),
French composer, pianist and critic.

8 Ernest Newman (1868–1959),
'the most celebrated British
music critic in the first half of the
twentieth century'. *The New Grove
Dictionary of Music*, 2nd edn, ed.
Stanley Sadie and John Tyrrell
(London: Macmillan, 2001).

9 Julien Tiersot (1857–1936),
pioneering French ethnomusicolo-
gist, folksong collector and writer.

10 *Chesterian*, February 1919,
259–60.

11 Edwin Evans (1874–1945), critic
who wrote for the weekly *Pall Mall
Gazette* and from 1933 the *Daily
Mail*. Based in London, he was an
enthusiastic and well-informed
promoter of Stravinsky and contemporary British and French
composers.

English fun with a Latin pungency, and the blend is sometimes a little perplexing … his works in this vein display a kind of tangential wit, at times ironic or even perverse …[12]

Evans found sentiment in the funeral march for the canary: 'If there be irony in it, we prefer to ignore it and hear only its poetry.' In 'Le Rire', the second of the *Fragments psychologiques*, Evans missed Berners' onomatopoeic reflection of the sound of people laughing. He noted that *Le Poisson d'or* is dedicated to Stravinsky; that the sheet music is embellished with handsome decorations by the stage-designer Natalia Goncharova (plate 20); and that the *Three Pieces* in their piano duet version have designs by Michel Larionov (plates 21, 22), who both worked for Diaghilev and his Ballets Russes.[13] Finally Evans pointed to the *Fantaisie espagnole* as Berners' most important work to date. Overall it is clear that Evans understood exactly what Berners was about, and recognised the importance of his work at this early date when the composer was thirty-six.

Evans drew attention to admiring comments about Berners at exactly the same time from Eugene Goossens, another advanced British composer. Goossens' article in the *Chesterian* opened with a list of composers, most of whom have stood the test of time:

> To the ranks of Ireland, Scott, Bax, Delius, Vaughan Williams, Bantock, Bridge and others whose work has infused new vitality into English music, and who have occasionally administered somewhat rude shocks to the delicate susceptibilities of our convention-loving public, we welcome yet another Englishman in the person of Lord Berners, more recent and more daring than any of his predecessors, a modernist whose work has already given rise to quite a storm of controversy.[14]

Goossens went on to attribute the character of these first works by Berners to his Continental environment, and recognised their harmonic texture as:

> … uncompromisingly modern – I had almost written brutally modern. But it is a stimulating brutality, that of an iconoclast who hacks and hews and blasts his way over the shattered relics of nauseating mediocrity – a very hot-gospeller of modernism. Yet withal, a real strain of deep emotion … for he can at will touch the whole gamut of human emotion, despite his often forcible methods of expression.

Goossens cited Berners' sources as Prokofiev, Ravel, Casella

12 Edwin Evans, 'Modern British Composers: VII – Lord Berners'. *Musical Times* 61, no. 923 (1 January 1920), 9–13. Evans also quotes from his own article in *Outlook*, 25 October 1919.

13 Natalia Goncharova (originally Gontcharowa) (1881–1962) and Michel (originally Mikhail) Larionov (1881–1964), who lived together then married in 1955, were leading figures in modernism in Russia, but they left in 1915, settled in Paris and became French citizens in 1938. By then they were neglected, but there was a revival of interest in their work in the early 1960s. Larionov drew cartoons of Berners, who made sketches himself of his friends at this period in Rome.

14 Eugene Goossens, 'Lord Berners', *Chesterian*, December 1919, 65–8.

and Malipiero, as well as his friend Stravinsky, but did not mention Schoenberg. He found the *Fragments psychologiques* 'the real Berners' with its 'amazingly vivid intensity ... unsurpassed by any contemporary piano music'.

Another fellow composer who appreciated Berners was Arthur Bliss:[15]

> The existence of a Berners is a very healthy tonic to a sick musical community. At all times a satirist is needed, especially when he can lay his finger unerringly on the fads and foibles of past and present fashions. There is no surer way of exposing futility than by ridiculing it ...'[16]

Three years later Bliss addressed American readers in *Modern Music*, the review of the newly formed League of Composers based in New York: 'Berners, it might be fancied, is most at home in the salon, whose rather languid brilliance he lights up with epigram and sally – he passes from one guest to another, picking the guard of each and lightly mocking the exposed weakness – a sometimes awkward but always salubrious visitor'.[17] Later that year in the same periodical, after listing the senior British composers, Edwin Evans related:

> Among the new men Lord Berners finds himself in the, to him no doubt, exhilarating position of the doyen, owing to his career having begun comparatively late ... His output is not voluminous but it is personal and significant, besides representing an angle of vision not unknown in other spheres of English artistic expression, but hitherto unaccountably missing in our music.[18]

These assessments show that Berners' music was understood to a remarkable degree by the more discerning of his contemporaries. Perhaps little has changed in response to his work – simply that its exposure has varied from time to time, but, significantly, at this stage he was not known as an eccentric.

Another yardstick is the representation of Berners in the various editions of *Grove's Dictionary of Music and Musicians* and it will be convenient to take these together. Edwin Evans wrote the entry for the third edition, where Berners has one column plus a short list of works. At this point his most recent work was the opera *Le Carrosse du Saint-Sacrement*, produced in Paris in 1924. Evans reported that 'the most frequently performed of his works is the *Fantaisie espagnole*, which seems to have secured a permanent place in the repertory'.[19]

By the time of the fifth edition of *Grove*, which appeared

15 Sir Arthur Bliss (1891–1975), Master of the Queen's Music, 1953. In 'What Modern Composition is aiming at', a paper read to the Society of Women Musicians on 2 July 1921, Bliss said: 'In England many names shine forth, of which the most conspicuous are Vaughan Williams, Holst, Goossens, Bax, Ireland and Berners.' Bliss went on to show that in England composers are individuals rather than groups such as the Russian Five or the Parisian Les Six. Thus 'Holst the mystic, Bax the romantic, Ireland the rugged, Goossens the exquisite, Berners the satirist, all add their quota to the stream of national music that looks like flowing with nobler current than that of any other country.' Arthur Bliss, *As I Remember* (London: Faber & Faber, 1970), 250.

16 Arthur Bliss, 'Reviews of New Music: Lord Berners', *Musical News and Herald*, 25 June 1921, 817.

17 Arthur Bliss, 'Berners and Bax', *League of Composers Review* [*Modern Music*] 1/1 (February 1924), 26–7 (also in *Bliss on Music*, ed. Gregory Roscoe (Oxford: Oxford University Press), 1991, 46).

18 Edwin Evans, 'Who is next?' *League of Composers Review* [*Modern Music*] 1/3 (November 1924), 3–6.

19 *Grove's Dictionary of Music and Musicians*, 3rd edition, ed. H. C. Colles (London: Macmillan, 1927).

four years after his death, Berners got three columns written by Kenneth Avery, who recognised that the *Three Funeral Marches* with their modern harmony 'led to the composer's becoming known as a musical humorist – a designation that has obscured the technical skill and the implications of irony in his works.'[20] In *A Wedding Bouquet* Avery found that the Gertrude Stein text 'fitted in perfectly with the patterns of the musical score' and that the work was 'generally recognised as one of the outstanding achievements in British ballet'. Avery thought Berners' later works had attracted less attention 'because of his activities in other spheres'. He then went on to list the two London exhibitions of paintings, and treated the novels and autobiographies sympathetically. He was generous to the last two ballets, *Cupid and Psyche* (1939) and *Les Sirènes* (1946), that 'gave the impression that the composer's work was still neat and delightful', although they were not regarded as a success at the time.

In the *New Grove* of 1980 Berners got two columns, including a list of works and partial bibliography.[21] The author, Ronald Crichton, was discerning, finding that 'Berners lived the life of an eccentric English gentleman' and traced 'irony, parody and repressed romantic feeling' in his earlier music and in the ballets 'a genuine gift for ... good straightforward light music'. By the time of my own article in the second edition of *New Grove* in 2001, Berners had achieved four columns, which included a list of works and bibliography.[22]

Going back to the 1920s, it is clear that Berners' first position was within the British tributary of modernism. At this time Chester put out what they called 'Miniature Essays' about each of their composers. These were small booklets in English and French with a good photograph, an example of manuscript and a reproduced cover design from one of the composer's works. In April 1922 Chester ordered 3000 copies of their booklet on Berners.

The anonymous six-page essay is admirably written and could hardly be improved on today. The writer confirms the impact of the *Three Funeral Marches*:

20 *Grove's Dictionary of Music and Musicians*, 5th edition, ed. Eric Blom (London: Macmillan, 1954).

21 *The New Grove Dictionary of Music and Musicians*, 1st edn, ed. Stanley Sadie (London: Macmillan, 1980).

22 *The New Grove Dictionary of Music and Musicians*, 2nd edn, ed. Stanley Sadie and John Tyrrell (London: Macmillan, 2001).

This first work at once created a stir in musical circles by the extraordinarily incisive individuality it revealed, and criticism, whether friendly or hostile, at any rate agreed unanimously in recognising the amazing maturity which gave this first effort ... the appearance of the work of a practised hand. No critic ... ventured to dispute its complete and masterly realisation.

He compares Berners and George Bernard Shaw, who kept up with Berners' music and would later stay at Faringdon:

Both are embittered by the knowledge of a world that is unable to live up to their exacting idealism, which consequently turns into cynicism; but both have the redeeming sense of humour that can turn the worst human weakness into a jest.

And the writer has complete understanding of the defining feature of Berners:

He is the only composer so far who has been completely successful in musical parody, and if he cannot be said to have actually invented this genus of music, there is no doubt that he was the first to profit by the tentative efforts of other composers in this direction, and to make of the parody a thing of definite artistic value.

The tone may be laudatory, but all Berners' music before the opera is discussed with virtually complete understanding.

From 1926 onwards his ballets and his activities as a writer, painter and eccentric enlarged this initial impact. However, in *British Music of Our Time*, a symposium published in 1946 and widely accessible as a Penguin paperback, J. A. Westrup provided a chapter on Berners, concentrating on the music.[23] Like Edwin Evans, Westrup realised exactly what Berners is about. He rightly refuted labels like 'the English Satie' and mere 'amateur', and appreciated the sallies of the satirist. However he was wrong to think that there is an element of improvisation – Berners' music was far too carefully calculated for that – but he may be right that his opera is 'obstinately harnessed to the text' with 'whole tracts of accompanied recitative'. 'A good production with first-rate acting might make the piece convincing but its success would owe comparatively little to the music.' Meanwhile *Le Carrosse* has not been staged in Britain, and, apart from the recording of the BBC production in 1983, has been represented only through the *Caprice péruvien*, a short orchestral selection put together by Lambert. When Westrup enlarged Ernest Walker's *History of Music in England* he described Berners as 'a romantic at heart who made his name largely by music of a satirical character, which employs romantic idioms only to make fun of them.' He felt that Berners had found his true *métier* in ballet.[24]

A year before the production of the opera, there was an interview with Berners, contributed by Georges Jean-Aubry to the *Christian Science Monitor*.[25] He visited Berners at his house in London 'in a room where I noticed some specimens of old painting, and where I noticed a clavichord', and was surprised when Berners offered to play him the whole

23 Sir Jack Westrup (1904–75), musicologist and conductor, Professor of Music at Oxford 1947–71.

24 Ernest Walker, *A History of Music in England*, 3rd edn, J. A. Westrup (Oxford: Clarendon Press, 1951), 352.

25 Profile and interview with Berners, *Christian Science Monitor*, 31 March 1923. Mary Gifford, *Lord Berners: Aspects of a Biography* (PhD thesis, University of London, 2007), table 9.

26 G. Jean-Aubry, 'Le Carrosse du Saint-Sacrement', *Chesterian*, June 1923, 244–51. Berners' opera was produced at the Théâtre des Champs-Élysées, Paris, on 24 April 1924. *The Times* called it: 'An unqualified success … Lord Berners' music makes the work an unalloyed enjoyment'. Lane, CD booklet Marco Polo 8.225155 (2000). The BBC broadcast was on 18 September 1983. That performance, in an English translation by Adam Pollock, with soloists and the BBC Scottish Symphony Orchestra under Nicholas Cleobury is recorded on Marco Polo, 8.225155 (2000).

27 Poulenc admired *Le Carrosse*; Francis Poulenc, *Correspondence, 1910–63*, ed. Myriam Chimènes (Paris: Fayard, 1991), 227. There is also a reference to Denise Duval, who worked closely with Poulenc, preparing the title role for the performance on 2 June 1948, 648, n. 7.

28 Philip Lane, unpublished biography (*c.* 1975) [henceforth Lane MS], 54–5. 'His taste was that of a very civilised man. He had a very acute sense of the ridiculous and of paradox. He was also a very sensitive and very kind man. I was then just beginning as a very young inexperienced colleague; he immediately noticed me, became interested and helped me through his friendship.'

29 'The last Rose of Summer' is an Irish tune with words by Thomas Moore: it appears in the opera *Martha* by Friedrich von Flotow (1812–83). Berners quoted the first line, with drunken adjustments, for the Sailor's return in the Polka in *The Triumph of Neptune*; he arranged Bach's Christmas chorale prelude *In dulci jubilo*, BWV729, for *A Bach Book for Harriet Cohen*, an anthology of piano arrangements by well-known composers ▸ ▸ ▸

work lasting over an hour. Berners commented: 'Although this is a comic opera, or, if you prefer it, a comédie musicale, I have laid aside the traditional overture or prelude, the utility of which I fail to see … My musical comedy is strictly between the rise and fall of the curtain. As regards style you will see that I have not adhered to the old tradition of different airs and scenes following each other.' He felt that Prosper Mérimée's story unfolds in too continuous and concise a manner to do anything else, and admitted that he had made cuts. Because he worked slowly, he said that *Le Carrosse* had taken him two years, but he did not 'think it would have been better had it been written more hurriedly.' It is surprising to discover that at that time Berners was studying Hindu theatre, and mentioned his plans for another opera on Sakuntala. *The Recognition of Sakuntala* is the best-known play by the Sanskrit playwright Kālidāsa. Perhaps the reception of *Le Carrosse* and its failure to achieve further productions, especially in England, was what discouraged him from continuing.

Jean-Aubry, whose poems Berners had set in his *Trois chansons*, also wrote an article on the opera for the *Chesterian*.[26] He spent most of the discussion – in rather quaint English – on the source of the text from Mérimée, another of whose stories gave rise to Bizet's *Carmen*. The story of *Le Carrosse* had previously been used as *La Périchole* (1868) by Jacques Offenbach. Jean-Aubry recognised that Berners' fluency in Spanish idioms qualified him ideally to deal with a comedy in a South American setting. He went further:

> Because he started his artistic career with productions of a small size and of a parodistic character, the author of the *Fantaisie Espagnole* is still regarded by certain 'weighty' music lovers as an amiable amateur only … A study of the score and orchestration of *Le Carrosse* will convince the most incredulous of the fact that Lord Berners' works are something quite different from the praiseworthy pastimes of an aristocrat.

At this stage Jean-Aubry was still awaiting the production in Paris, but his study of the piano score increased his 'admiration and sympathy for a composer whom I regard … as one of the foremost in England today, and one of the best qualified to convince the Continent that the musical powers of the English are not merely a paradox, as some of us are fond of saying'.

Berners maintained his musical connections with Paris that gave rise to performances. *Le Carrosse*, staged in 1924 and again in 1925, was given in a triple bill with Stravinsky's *L'Histoire du soldat*, and *La Chatte* by Henri Sauguet

(1901–89).[27] When Philip Lane asked Sauguet about Berners in the 1970s he replied:

> Son goût était celui d'un homme très civilisé. Il avait un sens très aigu de la drôlerie et du paradoxe. Il était aussi un homme d'un grand sensibilité et d'un grande bonté. J'étais alors de mon début un tout jeune confrère inexpérimenté; il m'a tout de suite témoigné de l'attention, ou l'intérêt et m'a aidé de son amitié.[28]

In December 1926 *The Gramophone* ran a symposium, and asked a number of well-known public figures about their favourite music and musicians. Many responses were drearily unimaginative, but Berners replied:

> My favourite song is 'The Last Rose of Summer'; my favourite composer Bach; my favourite tune is the third of Schoenberg's *Six Pieces*, because it is so obscure that one is never likely to grow tired of it (which you must admit is as good a reason for preferring a tune as any other); and if by 'singer' you mean any kind of singer then the one I prefer is Little Tich. But, on the other hand, if you mean merely concert singers, please substitute Clara Butt.[29]

It was December 1926 when Berners made his London debut with the first of his five ballets. *The Triumph of Neptune* was written for Diaghilev's Ballets Russes with choreography by George Balanchine[30] and a scenario by Sacheverell Sitwell, based on situations close to traditional English pantomime and depicted in coloured prints.[31] In January 1925 an article by Berners was published in the *Evening News* entitled: 'Happy Hampstead as a ballet! Why not? – Some Suggestions for Diaghilev.' He speculated that since Diaghilev had asked him rather than Rutland Boughton, Holst or Elgar to write the music that 'the kind of ballet he has in view is not to be a serious one, and that it will be satirical rather than romantic. He may even be intending to parody some of our most cherished national characteristics. And perhaps in this he is guided once more by his unerring instinct, because there is nothing an English audience seems to enjoy so much as seeing itself laughed at on the stage.'[32]

It was from this point that Berners addressed his British public – he had found himself as a ballet composer. His early miniatures were for Rome; *Le Carrosse* was for Paris, and now seems transitional; finally, through ballet he indulged his hedonistic temperament in a more conventional idiom that lasted the rest of his composing career, made him a natural film composer, and brought him into contact with all

► ► ►

(Oxford University Press, 1932); the Schoenberg piece is the third of *Sechs kleine Klavierstücke*, op. 19 (1911) from his free atonal period; Little Tich (Harry Relph, 1867–1926) was a versatile music hall comedian, short in stature and with six digits on each hand, who became a sensation in London and Paris; Dame Clara Butt (1872–1936) was the celebrated contralto. Elgar wrote his *Sea Pictures* for her, and she carried his *Land of Hope and Glory* far and wide. Sir Walford Davies (1869–1941), Master of the King's Music, also used the name of Schoenberg provocatively. His pioneering BBC talks *Music and the Ordinary Listener* began in 1926; when he was pressed by his radio listeners to broadcast the names of his favourite composers he gave: Bach, Beethoven, Billy Mayerl and Arnold Schoenberg. Peter Dickinson, *Marigold: the Music of Billy Mayerl* (Oxford: Oxford University Press, 1999), 9–10.

30 George Balanchine (Balanchivadze) (1904–83), Russian-American dancer and then influential choreographer who choreographed Berners' first two ballets: *The Triumph of Neptune* (1926) and *Luna Park* (1930).

31 *The Triumph of Neptune* was premièred at the Lyceum Theatre, London, on 3 December 1926 under Henri Defosse. The 45-minute work was a major success, and music from it was used again in *Le Boxing* and *Waterloo and Crimea*, both with Ballet Rambert in 1931. Philip Lane added more music for David Bintley's ballet *Mr Punch and the Street Party* (1979). The Suite has been regularly performed and recorded; the full ballet is on Marco Polo 8.223711 (1998).

32 Lane MS, 60–1.

the arts allied to the world of fashion in ways that he found so congenial.

Eight years later, when Berners' second ballet *Luna Park* was receiving its first concert performance in the Proms, there was a preview in the *Radio Times* from Sacheverell Sitwell, who had provided the scenario of *The Triumph of Neptune* for Berners and Diaghilev. Sitwell thought that Berners' reputation as a composer was now being compromised by his first London exhibition of paintings – and the books were yet to come. He thought Berners typically English in being active in more than one artistic medium, and cited William Blake and Sir John Vanbrugh as predecessors.[33] Sitwell saw 'plenty of able painters but a dearth of good composers', urging:

> Lord Berners must paint less and compose more … the hope of music in our country lies in his hands and in those of Constant Lambert and William Walton. This will be the more evident as time goes on and it is a pity if, during these years, Lord Berners does not add to his too scanty opus list … it will be the loss of one of the few opportunities given to English music in our century.'[34]

It is obvious that the Sitwells would value their immediate colleagues and friends. They were Walton's patrons; Lambert was part of the group; and they cannot have been much interested in music arising from provincial English folksong.

It was during the 1930s that stories of Berners' eccentricity became inseparable from everything else. One of the most discussed sallies was dying the pigeons at Faringdon. On 25 November 1937 Berners asked Stravinsky to thank his mistress, Vera Sudeikina, 'for having sent the colours for the pigeons. They are magnificent and add a tropical touch to this wintry country.'[35]

The inter-war years were Berners' heyday, when he could pursue all his activities untrammelled. But it could not last, and the negative impact of the war on Berners is discussed in several of the interviews in this book. An inevitable post-war landmark was his death in 1950 and the tributes that followed. *The Times* delineated his personality in now familiar terms: 'Versatility was his most evident characteristic, for apart from his gifts as a musical composer, novelist, painter and a collector of pictures, he was a dilettante of the Walpole or Beckford type, with a witty tongue and a taste for the bizarre.'[36] *First Childhood* suggested that the flippant and ironical manner 'in his writings, musical and other, was largely self-protective'. Finally: 'Lord Berners was a small, quiet man, with watchful eyes, a closely clipped moustache,

33 Sir John Vanbrugh (1664–1726), playwright noted for *The Relapse* (1696) and architect whose buildings included Castle Howard and Blenheim Palace.

34 Sacheverell Sitwell, 'British Composers at the Proms (5): Lord Berners', *Radio Times*, 11 September 1931, 556.

35 Igor Stravinsky, *Selected Correspondence*, ed. Robert Craft, vol. 2 (London, 1984), 157.

36 William Beckford (1759–1844), of Fonthill Abbey, the rich Lord Mayor of London, MP, novelist , collector and eccentric; and Horace Walpole (1717–97), of Strawberry Hill, MP, 4th Earl of Orford, collector and writer on a remarkable variety of subjects, known primarily for his posthumously published memoirs.

and a demure expression. The impression he gave was that of great sensibility, carefully guarded, and that his devastating wit in speaking and writing was a sort of sublimation of his boyish propensity of practical mischief.' *The Times* made no reference to the legendary anecdotes, but did report that the building of the Folly at Faringdon had been made possible 'only by an appeal to the Ministry of Health'.

Berners' old rival for over fifty years, Harold Nicolson, found it difficult to write his obituary without thinking that Berners himself was at his side 'laughing at some of the passages, parodying their style, adding fantastic variations of his own'. He summed up:

> Nobody who knew Lord Berners will forget him; he remains in the memory as a gay and, in a way, formidable person. He might have been happier had he lived in another age, but his curiosity was so vivid that he was unable to detach himself from the novelties of his own. His talents were so dispersed that he failed somehow to get his centre into the middle. He was a perhaps belated type of cultured eccentric, a gifted aristocrat. Yet his patrician qualities showed themselves in something more than contempt for vulgarity; they showed themselves in delicate consideration for the feelings of the friends he teased.[37]

On 16 February 1951 there was a concert of music by Berners on the BBC Third Programme conducted by his friend and colleague Constant Lambert, who died at the age of only forty-five the following August.[38] He also gave the preceding twenty-minute talk. A second concert was broadcast two days later. In his talk Lambert covered all the familiar aspects of Berners' public persona – everything that has attracted and amused people ever since. He cited the harmless dyes colouring the doves at Faringdon; various anecdotes such as how Berners tried to keep a railway carriage to himself by wearing dark glasses, beckoning people in and then reading *The Times* upside down; his fits of melancholia so that one night he exploded a paper bag in the night to frighten his guests who came out of their bedrooms in disarray. Lambert defended Berners against the charge of dilettante just because he had mastered more than one art form; and, when he conducted in America, Lambert enjoyed telling people that Lord Berners was not just a showbiz title like Duke Ellington and Count Basie.[39]

Lambert thought that *A Wedding Bouquet* 'lacked the brilliance of *The Triumph of Neptune*' and said that pieces like the funeral march for the rich aunt 'gave him the reputation of being a farceur and nothing beside. It was not until

37 Harold Nicolson, 'Marginal Comment', *Spectator*, 28 April 1950, 568.

38 Constant Lambert (1905–51), British composer, conductor and writer. (See plate 5.) He conducted Berners' last three ballets; wrote his influential study *Music Ho!* (1934); and dedicated his *Music for Orchestra* (1927) to Berners.

39 Berners wrote a letter himself to the *Daily Herald* on 21 November 1946: 'Now I am neither rich nor a dilettante. In my case, I would seem to be less of a dilettante than the writer of the article who doesn't know his facts.' Lane MS, 121; Gifford, *Lord Berners*, table 9.

The Triumph of Neptune, with its exquisite snow scene, that he began to be taken more seriously, and not until *A Wedding Bouquet* that people realised that, though his tongue was often in his cheek, his heart was just as frequently on his sleeve'.[40]

In 1934, when his *Music Ho!* was published, Lambert described Berners as a parodist, and added: 'It would hardly be an exaggeration to say that the Spanish national style was invented by a Russian, Glinka, and destroyed by an Englishman, Lord Berners; for after the latter's amazingly brilliant parody of Spanish mannerisms it is impossible to hear most Spanish music without a certain satiric feeling breaking through'.[41] This is an overstatement arising from Lambert's denigration of national schools of composers as artificial, especially the English variety. Nowadays it is difficult to view Berners in those terms after hearing the over-the-top parodies of Peter Maxwell Davies or John Adams.

A specifically musical estimate of Berners – with no reference to the legends of eccentricity – was provided by Colin Mason in the *Listener* in advance of the BBC concerts conducted by Lambert. He focused on a new definition: 'Lord Berners was always a miniaturist, and the miniaturist in music has never been so fortunate as his counterpart in literature or the other arts'. He cited Wolf and Chopin as composers who also had to overcome the disadvantages of working mainly on a small scale; saw Berners' ballet scores as 'sequences of miniatures'; and, like Westrup, judged that 'in ballet he found the metier that offered the happiest outlet for his musical personality and exposed fewest of his limitations'. However, Mason found Berners' earlier music more significant, although he wondered how to take its humorous side, and asked whether there is 'a Berners manner'. In this connection he mentioned 'the English Satie' label. In looking back at the advanced early works, Mason, like other critics, saw them hiding a repressed sentimentality that emerged later in the ballets. He recognised Berners' musical professionalism in spite of his enjoyment of a variety of other accomplishments. 'Although his works will occupy a very minor position in the history of music of our time, when they were written they attracted the attention of masters far greater than himself. For us today they are like cocktails – not satisfying for those hungry for the big things in music, but very pleasant occasionally for the musically well fed'.[42]

Similar things were being said about the work of Satie at that time. Then, gradually, the interest of Cage, Feldman and some of the avant-garde revealed Satie as more central than

40 Constant Lambert, 'Tribute to Lord Berners', BBC Radio 3, 16 February 1951.

41 Constant Lambert, *Music Ho!: a Study of Music in Decline* (London, 1934; Harmondsworth: Penguin, 1948), 67, 78, 123 & 139.

42 Colin Mason, 'Lord Berners: a Miniaturist in Music', *Listener*, 8 February 1951, 236.

had been suspected. It is the devotion of Gavin Bryars and other experimental composers to the cause of both Satie and Berners that implies an expanded relevance for Berners in the twenty-first century.

Only a month after Berners' death there was an obituary tribute from John Betjeman, who knew Berners well. He started off: 'Lord Berners was well known as a musician, painter and writer' then he considered the novels and memoirs:

> If the word 'light' were not used today as a term of opprobrium for whatever is understood and spontaneously enjoyed I would apply it to Lord Berners' novels. His two volumes of autobiography were light only on the surface. The second, describing his life at Eton, was I think the best book he wrote and one of the few school stories likely to last.

Betjeman confirmed what Berners' friends interviewed here would later say: 'There is little doubt that of the three arts he practised, he liked his music best. By that he hoped to be remembered.' Betjeman went on to describe life at Faringdon and its setting and concluded:

> Envious dry blankets who did not know him ... may regard him as a relic of a civilised age. They can think what they like, the dreary form-fillers. They can preach their dry economics or expound their comfortless faiths. They cannot be expected to understand the pleasure and thankfulness those people feel who had the privilege of his friendship.[43]

The appreciation of Berners in all his dimensions has long gone beyond those who knew him. But, of course, the label of eccentric remains. In his self-portrait as Lord Fitzcricket, in *Far from the Madding War*, Berners admitted this: 'He was astute enough to realise that, in Anglo-Saxon countries, art is more highly appreciated if accompanied by a certain measure of eccentric publicity.'[44] In 1980 Peter J. Pirie in *The English Musical Renaissance* dealt with Berners in one revealing sentence: 'a slight but attractive talent, more memorable as a great eccentric'.[45] Frank Howes, in his earlier study of the same subject, mentions Berners in a single sentence with a group of ballet composers.[46]

Although some of Berners' ballets had held the stage more or less continuously, the 1972 Purcell Room recital felt like the start of a revival. The first step was to persuade John Betjeman to take part. I had attended a reading he gave at the Institute of Contemporary Art in London, discussed the idea with him then, and wrote with more details on 19 June

43 John Betjeman, 'Lord Berners: 1883–1950', *Listener*, 11 May 1950, 839.

44 *Far from the Madding War*, 128 (1941); 408 (1999).

45 Peter J. Pirie, *The English Musical Renaissance: Twentieth-Century British Composers and their Works* (New York: St Martin's Press, 1980), 121.

46 Frank Howes, *The English Musical Renaissance* (London: Secker & Warburg, 1966), 318. Howes joined *The Times* in 1925, and was chief music critic 1943–60.

1972 saying that John Woolf of the Park Lane Group would like to put the concert on. His reply on 24 June was not encouraging:

> I'm afraid I'm never very good immediately after giving a lecture and I could not concentrate when I saw you. Now I can ... I am very glad there was quite a lot of interest in Lord Berners, but I fear I am so heavily committed with both writing and television work that I just cannot take on anymore for at least six months.

I sent him more details and asked what his fee would be. He replied:

> It's not the money, it's the time. We will have to wait until the beginning of next year before I know where I am.

Since the date of 8 December was already booked and I was anxious to keep to it, I appealed to Robert Heber-Percy, Lord Berners' heir. He spoke to Betjeman, and may well have mentioned Berners' hospitality to him and his wife for so many years. It worked, and Betjeman's next letter came on 24 July:

> I have entered the details in my diary for December 8th. Please drop me a line so that we can arrange a meeting here at drinks time, some time during that month. If you would like to make the selection we will discuss it together.

I sent some material in advance, and he responded on 21 November:

> I think it is very good. If I am to do an introduction to begin with, which may be a good idea, I would mention his house, his love of painting and his fundamental gloom. The poems I had forgotten about, and they are great fun. Sometimes they are halfway between Edward Lear and Harry Graham,[47] but a thing like 'Red Roses' is entirely on its own, and I think it would make a perfect end as you suggest.

I went to 43 Cloth Fair at 5.00 p.m. on 5 December. Betjeman opened the door himself and in one breath said: 'Come in it's this fucking laureateship I'm getting six hundred letters a week would you like tea or whisky it's malt!'

I had met Betjeman over lunch earlier than this, but he was so surrounded by television people that we had got nowhere. This time I had him to myself after his secretary left. I settled for tea rather than whisky; the discussion was constructive – as long as I was going to provide all the material; and, since it was raining heavily and he was concerned

47 Harry Graham (1874–1936), English writer of light verse.

about how to cope, I took him in my car to the Royal Opera House, Covent Garden.

At the Purcell Room concert on 8 December Betjeman duly delivered the readings in his inimitable style; my sister Meriel Dickinson and I gave all the songs; and Susan Bradshaw and I shared solos and one set of duets, the *Valses bourgeoises*. Robert Heber-Percy sent furniture and pictures from Faringdon to transform the stage of the Purcell Room. The occasion was covered by at least five newspaper critics: in those less Philistine days there were more of them, and they had more opportunity to attend concerts and space to write about them.

Ronald Crichton found the look of the Purcell Room 'a nice change from what we normally see there' and noticed 'quite an aroma of country house life'. He found Berners 'more parodist than satirist, and parodists love what they poke fun at ... There was a soft heart behind the quizzical monocle.' He realised that Max Beerbohm had understood Berners. The programme reproduced his 1923 drawing of Berners at the clavichord entitled: 'Lord Berners, making more sweetness than violence' (see plate 18).[48] Crichton went so far as to say that 'perhaps the best musician of them all was the Laureate, reading in his perfectly cadenced voice ...'[49]

Meirion Bowen also reacted to the occasion: 'an epoch and a society were brought back to life ... Among this gallery of eccentrics Lord Goodman looked a commonplace figure which is saying something ...'[50] But he felt that Berners had failed to 'tap the potential of an idiom spiced so astringently with the atonal sounds of Schoenberg and with the chromatic inflections of Debussy and Ravel. Perhaps life was too comfortable ...'[51]

Max Harrison took the music seriously, and was not overwhelmed by the audience. He thought Berners' pieces were 'brief, clever, to the point like successful party tricks. And they do work.' In the Lullaby from *Three English Songs* he found a 'repressed vein of romanticism which even the straight-faced foolery of 'Red Roses and Red Noses' cannot quite conceal.'[52]

For the composer Anthony Payne, who would later complete Elgar's Third Symphony, the occasion 'had the air of an official revival ... We may lament the fact that he divided his energies between composing, writing and painting and this division of labours did undoubtedly prevent him from making a definitive statement in any of the three arts, but whatever he did had the stamp of effortless individuality.' He also found that 'if Berners' style is a mask there is warmth beneath the mask.'[53]

It seems odd that critics found it difficult to accept what

48 Sir Max Beerbohm (1872–1956).

49 Ronald Crichton, 'Lord Berners', *Financial Times*, 11 December 1972.

50 Arnold Goodman (1913–1995), influential London lawyer and advisor to Harold Wilson's government who negotiated improved government sponsorship of the arts.

51 Meirion Bowen, 'Berners', *Guardian*, 9 December 1972.

52 Max Harrison, 'Lord Berners: Purcell Room', *The Times*, 9 December 1972.

53 Anthony Payne, 'Betjeman Gives Reading of Berners' Wit', *Telegraph*, 9 December 1972.

Berners actually did rather than what he might have done if he had not been so versatile. Christopher Norris caught the BBC broadcast, thought that a 'worthy revival was spoiled by an over-developed sense of social occasion' but got through to the music: 'The concert did prove impressively how much of Berners' more serious music can be rescued from the period appeal of its surface charm.'[54]

An even more interesting tribute came from the composer Michael Nyman, later to become widely known as a kind of English minimalist and for film scores such as *The Piano* (1993). He also heard the broadcast, knowing nothing of Berners, and responded: 'I am forced to ask why the post-Berners generation (he died in 1950) has had to be deprived of this fascinating, original and wayward music.' Nyman appreciated Berners' stylistic diversity, and asked: 'Was Berners, then, just (just?) a gifted, instinctive, somewhat whimsical, eclectic musician, unable to find a "consistent" style (the ultimate sin of a composer)? Instinctively one feels that the pre-1920 piano pieces are the "true" Berners. They are certainly independent and individual, written in an unclassifiable variant of the atonality which was then current ...'[55]

I was in touch with Betjeman again and sent him a copy of the LP recording *A Portrait of Lord Berners*.[56] He responded on 15 February 1979:

> I think the record of Gerald Berners wholly delightful. He would have liked it too. Thankyou so <u>very</u> much for sending it. As well as being a <u>very</u> kind man he was <u>very</u> modest. I think he cared for his music more than any other of his accomplishments, and that is why he would have liked the record and its sleeve of Faringdon [his painting for the Shell poster – see plate 55].
>
> Well done. Yours ever,
>
> too many 'verys' in this letter [handwritten and underlinings][57]

As the editions of the *Collected Music for Solo Piano* and *Collected Vocal Music* neared completion I asked Betjeman if some of what he said at the Purcell Room with some sentences from the letter above could be used as a preface to each volume and he readily agreed. When the volumes were sent to him he commented on 5 July 1982: 'I think the production of the two-volume edition of Gerald Berners' songs and piano music is perfect and worthy of Gerald's genius.'[58]

An international dimension was added at the 13th Autunno Musicale at Como on 8 September 1979, when Berners' music reappeared in Italy. With the support of the

54 Christopher Norris, 'Radio and TV', *Music and Musicians*, February 1974, 31.

55 Michael Nyman, 'Last Week's Broadcast Music', *Listener*, 27 December 1973.

56 *A Portrait of Lord Berners: Songs and Piano Music*. Meriel Dickinson (mezzo); Bernard Dickerson (tenor); Susan Bradshaw, Peter Dickinson, Richard Rodney Bennett (piano). Unicorn LP RHS355 (1978). All first recordings, later available on CD Symposium 1278 (2000) along with historic transfers, including Berners as pianist.

57 Berners' painting of Faringdon Folly (1936) was used as a poster advertising Shell petroleum products. See *The Shell Poster Book*, introduction by David Bernstein (London: Hamish Hamilton, 1992); *Faringdon Folly* (1936) number 64 of 92. Jack Beddington at Shell commissioned some of the most prominent British artists to contribute to his remarkable series. See plate 55. There was no Shell Guide to Berkshire cited by Mark Amory, *Lord Berners: the Last Eccentric* (London: Chatto & Windus, 1998), 152.

58 *The Collected Music for Solo Piano*, ed. Peter Dickinson (London: Chester Music, 1982; 2nd edn 2000); *The Collected Vocal Music*, ed. Peter Dickinson (London: Chester Music, 1982; 2nd edn 2000).

British Council, there was a recital of songs and piano music, a round-table with Sir Harold Acton, Robert Heber-Percy, Gavin Bryars and Jack Buckley, and an exhibition. This was in communist-run northern Italy, so concerts were free, and people came and went as they pleased on the edge of the lake.[59]

By the time of the centenary in 1983 there was more interest in Berners than in 1972, when the Purcell Room recital was not quite sold out. The Wigmore Hall programme, again promoted by the Park Lane Group, was full on 25 September, and so there was a repeat at the Purcell Room on 16 October. This time John Betjeman was not well enough to take part, and Timothy West gave a wider range of readings, which I again chose. Meriel Dickinson and I were responsible for the more-or-less complete songs and solo piano music. Robert Henderson felt it was 'a rare and notable virtue' of the programme that it 'never overplayed its hand'. In the early piano works, 'beneath their amusing anti-romantic surface there is both a conscientious and sophisticated mind at work'. The programme was 'an amiable, witty and affectionate centenary portrait of a man who was not only a distinctively picturesque figure in the musical life of his time but, whatever his gifts as composer, writer or painter, earned himself a lasting place in the gallery of English eccentrics'.[60] Earlier, in a preview, Henderson had concluded that 'Berners is best viewed whole; not just as composer but as novelist in his sequence of social comedies and author of two elegant volumes of autobiography, and as painter in mild imitation of early Corot, of whose work he owned a fine collection'.[61]

Ronald Crichton reviewed the centenary offerings from BBC Radio 3, which included the first opportunity to hear *Le Carrosse* in England. He remarked on the Spanish colouring and the 'remarkable assurance with which the self-styled amateur Berners handles voices and orchestra for operatic purposes – spitefully fast or unctuously slow, the voices ride naturally on the instrumental commentary. One can't think of another English composer who could have done this. But in no real sense is *Le Carrosse* an English opera'.[62]

Gillian Widdecombe also admired the opera as 'the most impressive thing I have heard so far … an amazing piece for 1923'. She felt Berners was badly served in sharing BBC Radio 3's *Composer of the Week* with Lambert, whose music was 'similar but more substantial'. She came close to summing up: 'For Berners and his friends, novelty was exciting, and frivolity was no less creative than seriousness. It was fun to champion the arts, and to dabble in all of them.'[63]

Michael Hurd also responded to the opera as 'a very deftly turned piece that might well be effective in the theatre, even

59 Pioneri Sconosciuteri della nuova musica: Lord Berners. Salone Villa Olmo, 8 September 1979. Meriel Dickinson (mezzo), Susan Bradshaw and Peter Dickinson (piano). Other pioneers represented in the festival were Grainger and Sorabji.

60 Robert Henderson, 'An Evening with Lord Berners', *Daily Telegraph*, 26 September 1983.

61 Robert Henderson, 'The Bubbling-over Berners', *Daily Telegraph* 10 September 1983.

62 Ronald Crichton, 'Lord Berners Centenary/BBC Radio 3', *Financial Times*, 20 September 1983.

63 Gillian Widdecombe, 'Lord of Music and Mischief', *Observer*, 25 September 1983.

if it is a little short on action ... Berners, it would seem, was a born man of the theatre'. But Hurd regarded Berners as 'no more than a pleasant footnote in the history of British music' and concluded that had Berners 'remained Gerald Tyrwhitt it is doubtful if we would be celebrating his centenary at all. His gift for making his life a newsworthy fantasy has remained useful to the end. – even now it is this that has caught the limelight.'[64] Twenty-five years later, Berners' artful use of publicity – if that is what it was – seems ahead of its time. Nowadays the media provides a barrage of detail about celebrities regardless of what it is they are supposed to be famous for. Look at the careers of John Cage or Andy Warhol – not to mention the idols of pop. However, writing in 1998, Hurd recognised that: 'Though wealth and social status conspired with a certain emotional diffidence to allow Berners to pose as a dilettante, there can be no doubt that his musical achievements were those of a true professional.'[65] Meirion Bowen remembered the Purcell Room concert in 1972 but still found Berners 'a splendid dilettante'. He 'attracts attention mainly as a clever miniaturist and as a deflater of all and sundry'.[66]

Simon Mundy got it right – it could hardly be put better – in asserting that Berners' dabbling in composition, writing and painting

> was accomplished enough to put many professionals firmly in their place. It is an extraordinary attitude of the present day to assume that if a man does one thing well he is an expert and is respected, if he does three things well he is dismissed as an amateur and treated with lofty condescension. Lord Berners had the further disadvantage of nobility ... Perhaps now his centenary has awakened the curiosity of a generation that never knew the gossip-column view of Berners, his real achievements and not just his eccentricity will be remembered.

Michael Ratcliffe, in a feature in *The Times*, focused on Berners' versatility and thought he was best remembered for *A Wedding Bouquet*, where he had also designed the costumes and sets. He discussed *Far from the Madding War* in some detail as 'a hard bright jewel from a dark hour ... beneath the jokes is a desperate sense of futility at the pointlessness of the war'. The novel 'is much tougher than Firbank or Beerbohm ... and closer to Peacock and Waugh: it may be enjoyed for its own sake and as a kind of companion prologue to Waugh's *Put out more Flags* (1942), a comparison with which it has nothing to fear. It is a find, a lost classic, and a perfect way to begin the savouring of Lord Berners.'[67]

64 Michael Hurd, 'Civilising the Wealthy', *Times Literary Supplement*, 14 October 1983.

65 Michael Hurd, CD booklet notes: Lord Berners – Songs Piano Music; Ian Partridge (tenor), Len Vorster (piano); Marco Polo 8.225159 (2000).

66 Meirion Bowen, 'Berners' Centenary', *Guardian*, 26 September 1983.

67 Michael Ratcliffe, 'Lord Berners, that Most Versatile Peer', *The Times*, 3 September 1983. It was Waugh's *Put out more Flags* that took off Auden and Isherwood as Parsnip and Pimpernel following their departure for the USA in January 1939. But the novel has a convoluted plot and a multiplicity of characters that makes Berners seem the essence of simplicity.

It was unusual for a centenary tribute to end with a fanfare for one of Berners' novels. When they originally came out they were well received, but since then the literary establishment has ignored Berners completely. I remember questioning the distinguished poet John Heath-Stubbs about his writings: he knew something about them, but rated them as 'very slender'. Soon after the centenary Stephen Banfield's two-volume *Sensibility and English Song* was published. He felt Walton's *Façade* had brought 'a welcome breath of fresh air into the English drawing room', but that Berners 'brought an even fresher one'. He recognised his parody and satire, and found his song output to be 'striking and significant for its range and diversity'. In the second of the *Three English Songs*, 'The Lady Visitor in the Pauper Ward' to a poem by Robert Graves, Banfield detected 'music of social criticism: a new voice in English music' and went on to discuss Britten from this point of view.[68]

A notable exception to the silence about Berners' books, until the 1998 reprints, is a thorough article from Julian Cowley in 1995 under a revealing title: 'The Neglected Satirical Fiction of Lord Berners'.[69] He started with Nancy Mitford's characterisation of Berners as Lord Merlin in *The Pursuit of Love*, and soon diagnosed: 'Arguably, Berners' addiction to pranks has been largely responsible for the neglect of his work.' Cowley compared his novels with the savagery and breakdown of Waugh's satires and the social detail satirised in Anthony Powell, but: 'Berners' writings are closer to fables, stylistically simple, yet embracing the improbable in order to shed light on the familiar. The portentousness of modernism does not suit his temperament; the more playful aspects of the European avant-garde inform his tales of change, loss and cultural impasse.' Cowley considered the fiction in some detail without reference to the then unpublished French and German volumes of autobiography or Berners' play *The Furies*. In *The Camel* he perceptively saw the animal itself as inhabiting 'a fictional space like a disjunct figure on a Magritte canvas' – an example of the kind of incongruity that appealed to Berners and does not have to be explained. However, the camel can be connected to the East, and it is perhaps a reflection of dedicatee Penelope Betjeman's interest in India. Cowley neatly connected the brightly coloured flies released in *The Romance of a Nose* with the multi-coloured pigeons at Faringdon, and found that the image 'hovers in the midst of the exquisite, the hilarious and the grotesque. Those uncomfortable categories have perhaps conspired to exclude Gerald Berners from serious attention as composer, painter and writer ... His fiction employs dislocatory strategies of romance, fantasy and parody as a means of challenging the

68 Stephen Banfield, *Sensibility and English Song: Critical Studies of the Early Twentieth Century* (Cambridge: Cambridge University Press, 1985), 378–82.

69 Julian Cowley, 'The Neglected Satirical Fiction of Lord Berners', *Journal of Modern Literature* 19/2 (Fall 1995), 187–200.

philistinism and complacency of a society persistently subordinating creativity to authority and routine' – and one result was war. In that sense Berners was providing a kind of social criticism.

The historian and Shakespeare scholar A. L. Rowse came to know Berners at Oxford during the war through David Cecil, and wrote a whole chapter about him in a book of memoirs, which came out after the centenary.[70] He regarded *First Childhood* as 'the delicious volume of autobiography which is the best of his books', but undermined his case by admitting that he had not read *The Camel*, which Harold Acton apparently called 'a rococo pastiche of a Victorian moral tale with macabre undertones'. Rowse considered *Count Omega* to be 'a rather nightmarish fantasy' reflecting the manic-depressive side of Berners' make-up. But he remembered *Far from the Madding War* because he was with Berners in Oxford when it was written, and was well aware of the thinly disguised characters. Mark Stein summed up for the youngest generation: 'He was far more than a patrician eccentric, great wit and popular socialite. He was true Renaissance man, whose music, books and paintings demonstrate far more than just a great sense of humour. His technical skill is obvious and even his worst self-indulgences show great originality.'[71]

Following the attention given to Berners in his centenary year of 1983, there were various landmarks during the 1990s. This was when several new recordings came out, and Wilfrid Mellers responded to *A Wedding Bouquet* by finding it less close to Stein than Virgil Thomson's operas.[72] He saw Berners as 'a quintessential English Eccentric', and summed up by finding him 'a remote survival from a very old England who disappeared, like Lewis Carroll's Cheshire Cat, into the thin air of a wide grin, a crazy joke (often in a foreign language), and a cosmopolitan musical stylisation.'[73]

By 2000 there were enough recordings for Berners to be Composer of the Week on BBC Radio 3 to mark the fiftieth anniversary of his death – on his own and not shared with Lambert as in 1983. Major events took place in 1998/9 – the publication of the biography by Mark Amory and the republication of *First Childhood* and *A Distant Prospect* in the USA and the UK along with the *Collected Tales and Fantasies*. The volumes of Berners' own writings were presented without any editorial or biographical material so a new generation of readers had to find its own bearings. The American response was revealing, although Berners' admirers in the later 1930s had included Bernard Herrmann (1911–75), who would later write the classic scores to the Alfred Hitchcock films, when he was on the staff at CBS radio. And before that Marc Blitzstein (1905–64), whose 1929 lectures included:

70 A. L Rowse (1903–1997), *Friends and Contemporaries* (London: Methuen, 1989), 47–74.

71 Mark Stein, 'Centenary of Lord Berners – a Brilliant Man', *Shropshire Magazine*, April 1983.

72 Virgil Thomson (1996–1989); *Four Saints in Three Acts* (1934), *The Mother of Us All* (1947).

73 Wilfrid Mellers, 'Visionary Gleams', *Musical Times*, October 1996, 17.

If Bliss is the bad boy of England then Lord Berners is the Puck ... a delightful combination of Anglo-Saxon and Latin. His music is extremely witty, droll and keen; he has little use for profundity, although it is quite possible that his philosophy of life, if he has any, strikes the note of depth through the indirect shaft of satire.[74]

Richard Dyer, reviewing *First Childhood* and *A Distant Prospect* in the *Boston Globe*, set the scene:

America has not forgotten Lord Berners because he was never known here ... What makes the books memorable is the clarity of Berners' unforgiving memory, his sense of character and eye for detail, his judgement, his wit, his voice, his slant. The familiar story is told from a point of view that still sounds fresh and modern more than sixty years later – and it is bracingly free from self-pity ... he creates entertaining artifice by facing down uncomfortable facts.[75]

David Finkle in the *New York Times* found more than meets the eye in Berners:

Although he must have hoped that his works would be regarded as benign mockery by both peers and Peers, Berners also clearly meant to point a well-manicured finger at the gloomy detachment that lurks beneath this sort of comedy. Today's readers, without *Debrett's* at their elbows, may miss out on some of the fun, but should still delight in the humorous texts as they unfold – and get a second kick from their bitter, bracing aftertaste. That's because Berners, like Max Beerbohm (an obvious influence), excels at a particularly British sub-genre: melancholic whimsy.[76]

Twenty years earlier, responding to the Unicorn LP, Donald Ritchie, in San Francisco, began optimistically: 'Lord Berners was one of England's finest composers.' Then he too considered why the Americans had never heard of him. He found obstacles in Berners' eccentricity, his ironic humour and his versatility, but he ended up by regarding him not as 'the English Satie' but rather plausibly as 'the Ronald Firbank of music'.[77] Then Ritchie expanded the legends by quoting Consuelo Vanderbilt, who apparently remembered Berners – a new slant – as playing a harmonium whilst being chauffeured in his car![78]

The Amory biography brought Berners to a wide audience outside the musical world: it has been described as a best-seller. Noel Malcolm summed up:

74 Information from Howard Pollack, whose biography of Blitzstein is forthcoming.

75 Richard Dyer, 'Revisiting the Life of Lord Berners', *Boston Globe*, February 1999.

76 David Finkle, 'Twitting the Twits', *New York Times*, 24 October 1999.

77 Donald Ritchie, 'The Return of the Eccentric Lord Berners', *San Francisco Sunday Examiner*, 15 July 1979. Ronald Firbank (1886–1926), primarily a novelist with a highly individual style. Berners was Firbank's literary executor. See also interviews with Daphne Fielding, Chapter 6, p. 68; Lady Betjeman, Chapter 12, p. 109; and Lord David Cecil, Chapter 14, p. 125.

78 Consuelo Vanderbilt (1877–1964), American heiress, first wife of 9th Duke of Marlborough.

> The real legacy of Lord Berners is threefold: his music
> ... his marvellous childhood autobiographies ... and his
> life itself. The last of these, alternately silly, sparkling
> and touching, has waited nearly fifty years for a biogra-
> phy to do it justice.[79]

Reviews went over the usual stories without adding much to
the established canon, although Alan Hollinghurst wrote a
carefully considered estimate in the *Times Literary Supplement.*

> There is often an element of revenge in Berners' humour
> – on neighbours, friends, bores – and the satirical por-
> traits in his novels led to a good deal of prevaricat-
> ing correspondence; he wanted both to offend and to
> remain in the right. He preserved copies of different
> drafts of letters, which suggests a peculiar mixture of
> self-doubt and calculation. The effort of shutting out
> despair, regret and guilt with oddity and frivolity made
> him look selfish and silly to some, to others not quite
> human, though that may have been part of his charm;
> Siegfried Sassoon found him 'consistently inhuman
> and unfailingly agreeable'.[80]

Noel Annan in a substantial article in the *New York Review
of Books* saw Berners as part of the tradition of the English
'vogue' novel, with antecedents in Thomas Love Peacock and
Aldous Huxley, although Berners used this form as fantasy of
the kind found in Firbank and H. H. Munro (Saki).[81] Annan
asked if a Berners revival was on the way with, apparently,
no awareness of what had been achieved for his music. He
preferred *Far from the Madding War* to *First Childhood*:

> The talk is astonishingly faithful to the Oxford gos-
> sip of those days: you can hear the exact tone of voice
> in which the witticisms were delivered. There is also
> an almost serious theme, namely that war consists in
> destroying everything of beauty, which is why Emme-
> line's war work consists of picking apart a rare and
> valuable fourteenth-century piece of German tapestry.
> War, in fact, should prevent anyone taking anything
> seriously.

79 Noel Malcolm, 'The Lord of
Many Talents', *Sunday Telegraph*,
15 March 1998, 15.

80 Alan Hollinghurst, 'An
Unconveyable Aesthete', *Times
Literary Supplement*, 20 March
1998, 18–19.

81 Noel Annan (1919–2001), 'The
Camel at the Door', *New York
Review of Books* 46/15, 7 October
1999.

Annan saw this novel as fitting in with Cyril Connolly's magazine *Horizon* with 'the same determination not to glamor-
ise the war and to proclaim the supremacy of personal relations and art above politics'. Like Michael Ratcliffe, Annan
compared *Far from the Madding War* with Waugh's 'devas-
tatingly serious' *Put out More Flags*, but unfavourably. He
quotes Waugh as regarding

the whole world in which he and Berners moved – its jokes, its malice, its relentless desire to be amusing and amused – with an Augustan conviction of original sin. The friends of Berners were so agreeable, so loyal, so charming, but they were aboriginally corrupt. Their tiny relative advantages of intelligence, taste, good looks, and good manners, he said, were quite insignificant.[82]

Waugh overstated his curmudgeonly case. Berners made some sketches in justification of Firbank which relate to his own situation as shown in the interviews which now follow:

Ronald Firbank is frivolous par excellence. Frivolity combined with beauty, humour and fantasy. One should not expect to find in his work any weighty sociological or philosophical judgements, any more than one would in the books of Edward Lear … There is a good deal to be said for frivolity. Frivolous people, when all is said and done, do less harm in the world than some of our philanthropisers and reformers. Mistrust a man who never has an occasional flash of silliness.[83]

Berners once wrote: 'There is a legend that Our Lord said "Blessed are the Frivolous, for theirs is the Kingdom of Heaven" and that it was suppressed by St Paul.'[84]

82 Berners and Waugh had a difficult relationship. Amory, who edited *The Letters of Evelyn Waugh* (London: Weidenfeld & Nicolson, 1980), diagnosed: 'Perhaps one seemed too fierce, the other too silly; for different reasons, neither was an easy friend.' Amory, *Lord Berners*, 142.

83 Berners Archive, notebook 67A/Bryars, complete. Amory, *Lord Berners*, 93–4, quotes.

84 Berners Archive, notebook 5/Bryars.

CHAPTER 3

Sir Harold Acton

Interview with Peter Dickinson on 28 May 1983 at La Pietra, Florence

THE FAMILY of Sir Harold Acton (1904–94) had connections with Italy for several generations, and it was his father who bought La Pietra around 1900. The villa, approached through a long drive of cypresses, became legendary for its art collection, scrupulously maintained by Harold Acton following the death of his father in 1953, and eventually left to New York University.

Acton's first visit to England was when he was sent to a prep school. Some of his contemporaries at Eton, such as Lord David Cecil, soon became allies in his fight against the philistines – Aldous Huxley taught there – and at Oxford he was of the same generation as Evelyn Waugh, Graham Greene, Anthony Powell and Cyril Connolly. Waugh dedicated *Decline and Fall* to Acton. After going down he started to publish poetry, and his first novels were influenced by Ronald Firbank. His Italian interests were reflected in his biography *The Last Medici* (1932) and later on in studies of the Bourbons of Naples.

Acton spent most of the 1930s in China, lecturing at Peking National University on English poetry – 'the happiest years of my life' – and he published translations of Chinese poetry.[1] He served in the RAF during World War II, after which he wrote *Memoirs of an Aesthete* (1948) and *More Memoirs of an Aesthete* (1970). *Nancy Mitford: a Memoir* (1975) was dedicated to her sisters – Diana, Debo and Pam. He was knighted in 1974 for services to the British Institute and to Anglo-Italian relations, and in 1986 he was made an honorary citizen of Florence. The broadcaster Russell Harty said: 'The thing he does best is being Sir Harold Acton. Exquisitely mannered, precise – some would say fussy – a most diverting gossip, the perfect host, a gentleman always in dark English tie and suit even in the most sultry Florentine summer.'[2] His recreations listed in *Who's Who* include 'hunting the Philistines'.[3]

PD When did you first meet Gerald Berners?

HA I met him when I was quite a young boy really. I had just gone to Eton and I was visiting in Rome with my father, who took me to see Berners' studio, which was full of modern paintings such as Giacomo Balla,[4] and there were huge bowls of coloured water with tin goldfish in them, which used to stir. There were all sorts of gadgets such as marionettes and peculiar things that struck a boy as extremely unusual. He himself was never very talkative. He just waited for one's comments. You could see he was anxious to surprise one. There were hidden jokes: something might pop out of a cushion or anything. It had a curious atmosphere of its own which he had created.

1 Maureen Cleave, 'Acton in Aspic', *Observer Review*, 21 February 1982.

2 'Mandrake', *Sunday Telegraph*, 23 September 1984, quotes Acton: 'When they did a television series with Russell Harty the whole television company was here. Very agreeable but they made the servants roll with laughter because they were wandering about the place half naked: these hairy Scottish electricians with no shirts on were very funny to look at.'

3 See Alan Pryce-Jones, Obituaries: Sir Harold Acton, *Independent*, 28 February 1994; Peter Quennell, 'The Sage of Florence', *Guardian*, 28 February 1994; John Ezard, 'Harold Acton, Connoisseur and Philistine-Hunter, Dies Aged 89', *Guardian*, 28 February 1994; 'Sir Harold Acton', Obituary, *The Times*, 28 February 1994. Also Derek Robinson, 'Hunting the Philistines – with Sir Harold Acton', *Listener*, 20 & 27 December 1979, 841–3, and George Armstrong, 'Sir Harold in Italy at 80', *Guardian*, 5 July 1984.

4 Giacomo Balla (1871–1958), Italian futurist painter and sculptor mainly based in Rome.

5 The Marchesa Luisa Casati (1881–1957): 'In Italy, especially in Rome, Venice and Capri, this fabulous beauty devised the most exotic spectacles with herself as their dazzling cynosure. She was the D'Annunzian Muse incarnate. Wisely, she seldom uttered: ordinary sentiments from the lips of so chimerical a creature were inconceivable: they would have struck a discord. The companions of her choice were albino blackbirds, mauve monkeys, a leopard, ►►►

One of the most noticeable things was a large photograph of the Marchesa Casati, a very striking lady much painted by all the well-known painters of the period from Boldini to Augustus John.[5] She was a close friend of his, also very interested in eccentric things. She had Moorish servants feeding leopards from her house – very strange.

He was then in the British Embassy and the Ambassador was Sir Rennell Rodd, a remarkable poet, whose first book of poems *Rose Leaf and Apple Leaf* had an introduction by Oscar Wilde, which he tried in later years to suppress. It was always rumoured that one of his sons, Peter, who married Nancy Mitford, used to buy up copies and sell them to his father for pocket money.[6] Berners, then called Gerald Tyrwhitt, was Honorary Attaché at the Embassy. That's when I first met him. And I saw him fairly often when he came to Florence in his huge Rolls-Royce with a porcelain turtle in it and a little spinet which he used to play while being driven.[7]

PD Did you see him do that?

HA No, I saw the car – a very large, capacious old Rolls-Royce. He was rather shy about his playing really. He'd sit down and play something he was going to perform later on – I heard fragments of *The Triumph of Neptune* on the piano. But I missed a great many years when I would have seen him normally, because I lived in Peking from 1932 to 1939. When I came back he would very kindly invite me for weekends in that delightful house at Faringdon full of Victoriana mixed with surrealist paintings by Dalí and extraordinary cushions with portraits of Queen Victoria on them.[8] There were funny things on the chimney-piece. He had a squeaking pig, I remember, which closely resembled a mutual friend. It was Violet Trefusis, who was extremely greedy and had a very pig-like side![9]

PD I'd like to go back to those years in Rome. Do you remember Casella?

HA I never met him, but he was Gerald Berners' teacher wasn't he?

PD Casella and Berners were both writing rather advanced music in the World War I years but it's hard to sort out who influenced who.

HA I should have thought Casella influenced Gerald Tyrwhitt. Didn't he play some of Gerald's compositions?[10] I remember going to the Teatro dei Piccoli in Rome to a performance of some fairy story with music by Gerald and which was very highly praised by Casella.

PD There were marionettes dancing?

HA Yes: magnificent marionettes. I saw several performances

►►► a boa-constrictor, and, among Englishmen, Lord Berners.' Harold Acton, *Memoirs of an Aesthete* (London: Methuen, 1948), 37. Her legendary extravagances caused her to go bankrupt in 1932; she spent the last years of her life in penury in London, where she died. Gabriele d'Annunzio (1863–1938) was the flamboyant Italian writer, soldier and nationalist politician influenced by Nietzsche. Debussy set one of his plays, *Le Martyre de San Sébastian* (1911) – Berners possessed a vocal score. Giovanni Boldini (1842–1931), internationally known society portrait painter: Augustus John (1878–1961), British painter and graphic artist.

6 James Rennell Rodd (1858–1941), 1st Baron Rennell (1933), diplomat, writer and archaeologist, Ambassador at Rome (1908–19).

7 See interview with William Crack, Chapter 4, p. 58.

8 Salvador Dalí (1904–89), Spanish artist widely known for his eccentricity, primarily associated with Surrealism. In 1929 he moved to Paris, spent 1940–8 in the USA, then returned to Spain at Port Lligat.

9 See Diana Mosley, *Loved Ones: Pen Portraits* (London: Sidgwick & Jackson, 1985), 102–4, for confirmation of the pig and the story of the joke engagement between Berners and Violet Trefusis (1894–1972), writer and lover of Vita Sackville-West.

10 Alfredo Casella did perform Berners' *Three Funeral Marches*. See Chapter 2, p. 24.

11 Fortunato Depero (1892–1960), the Italian futurist painter, writer and designer, created what he called *Balli plastici*, with puppets instead of dancers. The première of *L'uomo dai baffi* (The Man with a Moustache) was at the Teatro dei Piccoli, Rome, on 15 April 1918, repeated eleven times. The programme states that Berners had orchestrated his *Trois petites marches funèbres* and *Trois fragments psychologiques* for small orchestra (flute, clarinet in A, oboe, bassoon, piano, two violins, viola, cello and bass). In fact the full score in Berners' hand consists of 'Le Rire' (*Fragments psychologiques* no. 2), then all three Funeral Marches, and finally an untitled movement Berners later called *Portsmouth Point: Symphonic sketch after a drawing by Rowlandson*, which anticipates Walton's use of this title. The piano arrangement was first published in Berners, *The Collected Music for Solo Piano* 2nd edn, ed. Peter Dickinson (London: Chester Music, 2000). On 11 June 1918 Berners wrote to Stravinsky: 'The other day some pieces of mine, scored for small orchestra, were played at the Teatro dei Piccoli. This was the first time I heard an orchestra perform my music, and I was pleased by the sonority. (I sound like Casella – but he would have said "very pleased".)' Igor Stravinsky, *Selected Correspondence*, ed. Robert Craft, vol. 2 (London: Faber & Faber, 1984), 150. Berners corresponded with Stravinsky in French.

12 Sergei Pavlovitch Diaghilev (1872–1929), enormously influential ballet impresario, whose Ballets Russes used the finest dancers, composers, painters and designers. Berners' *The Triumph of Neptune*, with a scenario by Sacheverell Sitwell and choreography by Balanchine, was premièred at the Lyceum on 12 December 1926. The history of the Ballets Russes was one of constant intrigue and financial problems. Diaghilev must have been relieved to find that Berners was not temperamental – and he probably didn't have to pay him. See Richard

– they did the whole of Rossini's *La Cenerentola*, and I must say I enjoyed it more as done by the marionettes than I ever did when it was done by human beings! I seem to remember a little orchestra in the marionette theatre. It must have been 1915 or 16.[11]

PD   What did people think of this strange music?

HA   They thoroughly enjoyed it. It was the moment when futurism was in the air in Italy and there were futuristic magazines very well produced. Illustrated with De Chirico, Balla, Bocioni and Prampolini. Berners was very much in with those people. He had his British Embassy side, but also a Bohemian side.

PD   I'd like to follow up his connection with several forms of the arts.

HA   When I met him he was young, but he always seemed rather middle-aged to me because he was bald. He wore a monocle, which was part of his equipment, and was very formal in his dress – dark city suits. He was by no means remarkable in appearance. What was striking was his studio with the Balla paintings and Balla himself. The paintings were hung on wires and if you gave a tug they would move. They used to say: 'La casa di Balla tutto balla!' The painter was one of Gerald's chief friends at that time.

PD   Was Berners affected by Diaghilev?

HA   I think he was very much so. He was always a devotee of the Russian Ballet, a ballet addict. The sort of music he composed also appealed to Diaghilev. There's nothing to touch Diaghilev in my opinion. New York City Ballet is very fine; Ballet Rambert has its virtues, but nothing to compare.[12]

PD   The New York City Ballet has the same parentage with Balanchine, who choreographed the first two Berners ballets.[13] Is that a link with the Russian tradition?

HA   I don't know much about Petipa and all those: you really ought to speak to Richard Buckle, the big authority on Diaghilev.[14]

Buckle, *Diaghilev* (London: Weidenfeld & Nicolson, 1979). Harold Acton: 'In the beginning of 1914 the Russian Ballet was at its zenith and its influence was felt all over Europe. The great galas of colour organised by Diaghilev were being imitated even in private entertainments: fancy-dress balls and *tableaux vivants* became sumptuous and spectacular to a degree unrealised

since'. *Memoirs of an Aesthete* (London, 1948), 37.

13 George Balanchine (Balanchivadze) (1904–83), Russian-American dancer and then influential choreographer who choreographed Berners' first two ballets: *The Triumph of Neptune* (1926) and *Luna Park* (1930).

14 Buckle, *Diaghilev*.

PD We're talking to Ashton too.

HA He's a very fine choreographer. Didn't he do *A Wedding Bouquet*? I never saw that, unfortunately. Wasn't there a spoken part?

PD It was spoken by Constant Lambert only as a wartime economy, but it was composed for chorus, and that is surely how it should always be performed.[15]

HA I hear there was wonderful harmony between him and Gertrude Stein. I knew her fairly well, better than I knew Gerald Berners. I met her in Florence when I was very young indeed. Her brother Leo lived here. Eventually she quarrelled with him because he claimed that she had monopolised his ideas. They were daggers drawn towards the end. It was Leo Stein who started buying the Picassos actually: he had a big collection of Renoir.

PD Did Berners take Gertrude Stein seriously?

HA He never took anything very seriously. No, he never did. He did read certain German philosophers – I think Schopenhauer must have influenced him. Nietsche at one time.[16] He was, curiously enough, a devotee of Ibsen and was familiar with all his plays.[17] His literary taste was full of unexpected things – very peculiar.

PD What about Berners' own writings?

HA The two volumes of autobiography are by far the best. There's a certain social interest to see how people lived in the last days of the Victorian era. He had these rather narrow Protestant forbears, with grandmother Lady Bourchier [actually Lady Berners], an extremely Calvinistic lady, who took her religion very seriously with prayers morning and night.[18] Everybody had to suffer from it. He tells that very well in *First Childhood* – he was very amusing about her. I think one of the gems of *First Childhood* is about the folding screen with all these marvellous birds of paradise and objects that he saw on it. They'd been cut out from various magazines and books, which had been ruined by his mother and aunt, and varnished over. In later years he saw that screen and saw no birds of paradise but nothing but hunting scenes. There were birds of paradise, but the child had selected the exotic, the orchids, and hadn't noticed the hunting scenes. All through his life it was a business of selection.

In his *First Childhood* he tells how the visual aspect of music appealed to him far more than the sound. His cousin Emily used to bore him terribly with her singing. He didn't like the sound of music: he liked the look of it. That's an extraordinary thing isn't it?

PD He wrote an article about the visual appeal of music.[19]

15 For confirmation of this, see interview with Sir Frederick Ashton, Chapter 11, p. 100.

16 Arthur Schopenhauer (1788–1860), the German philosopher, whose recognition of the world's irrationality and whose advocacy of the arts as one way of overcoming the frustrations of the human condition, would have appealed to Berners. Schopenhauer is mentioned in Berners' poem 'Spring Thoughts', Chapter 19, p. 155.

Frederick Wilhelm Nietzsche (1844–1900), German philosopher and poet. When reading in German at Dresden, Berners said that Nietzsche was one of his first discoveries (*Dresden*, 37) and he relished his bound copy of *Also sprach Zarathustra*. When he was based at Weimar he found he was not far from Nietzsche's house, inhabited after his death by his sister. The family Berners was staying with did not approve of Nietzsche. One of them had seen his face at the window – 'his eyes were terrible and the general effect was sinister'. (*Dresden*, 92).

17 When he was in Weimar Berners developed a craze for Ibsen and saw a production of *Ghosts* (1881). He then read more of his plays and started writing one himself. 'The subject of my play was the story of a married woman who fell in love with another man, upon which her husband went mad ...' (*Dresden*, 115). This sounds like an anticipation of his later mockery of conventional marriage.

18 *First Childhood*, 35–45.

19 See also *A Distant Prospect*, 73.

20 *A Distant Prospect*, 75–6.

21 3 Foro Romano.

22 'Did you know that I changed my name – I am no longer Tyrwhitt! This thanks to my aunt – or, rather, to the death of my uncle, whose title I have now inherited. Unfortunately, though, it seems that this and plenty of taxes are all that I have inherited.' Stravinsky, *Selected Correspondence*, vol. 2, 153.

23 See interview with Sir Frederick Ashton, Chapter 11, p. 102, n. 12.

24 *The Romance of a Nose* was translated into French by Marie Canavaggia, and came out in paperback as *Le Nez de Cleopatra*, Fenêtres sur le Monde no. 3 (Paris: La Jeune Parque, 1945). *The Camel* was translated into French by Jean Barrée as *Le Chameau* in *Les Œuvres libres: revue mensuelle ne publiant que de l'inédit* no. 60 (Paris: Librairie Arthème Fayard, 1951). This paperback appeared with six other authors little known today. Barrée describes: 'la substance de ce conte ou les événements se succèdent et s'imbriquent comme dans un roman policier, et que Lord Berners narre avec malice et le charme qui font de lui l'un des auteurs favoris de l'élite anglaise'. 43. [... the substance of this story where the events follow on and impact on each other like a thriller, and Lord Berners narrates with malice and the charm that make him one of the favourite authors of the English élite.] *The Camel* also appeared earlier in Swedish: *Kamelen: en berättelse av Lord Berners* (Stockholm: Hugo Gebers Forlag, 1937)

25 Two poems by Berners were published in the darkest days of the war in *Horizon: a Review of Literature and Art* vol. 6, no. 31 (1942), 5–6. These were 'The Performing Mushroom (To Professor Jebb, author of *Inedible Fungi, The Toadstool and all about it* etc, etc)' and 'Surrealist Landscape (To Salvador Dali)'. These were the first items in that issue and the first two of a group of poems, followed by Dylan Thomas, Norman Cameron and Gavin Ewart. *Horizon* was

It's a nice connection because of his mixing of the arts. It fits doesn't it?

HA   It does, but it's very unusual. I never heard of anybody else who liked the look of Chopin – or Wagner? I love the description of his longing for the score of Wagner's *Das Rheingold*. Then his father, with whom he didn't have very much in common, gave him a nice tip, and he could afford to buy it. Rather touching all that.[20]

PD   He was devoted to Chopin. Do you remember him playing any?

HA   I only remember him playing his own things, thumping them out. He wasn't a very fine pianist. I very seldom met a composer who was. William Walton, whom I knew very well, was not exactly a fine pianist. But I think Berners blossomed in Rome. Something in Italy helped him to expand because he seemed rather an introvert at times, very buttoned-up.

PD   One's accustomed to this connection between England and Italy – the writings of Forster, the Sitwells, your own background. Was it like that for him?

HA   I think he had a great feeling for Rome in particular, where he had a beautiful house overlooking the Forum, marvellous and devoted servants.[21] In those days life was so much simpler for those who could afford the good things of life. As Gerald Tyrwhitt he wasn't as well off as later on, after he inherited the title.

PD   In a letter to Stravinsky he talked about inheriting debts.[22]

HA   Well, to Stravinsky one had to be very careful talking about money because he was extremely grasping. Everybody who had any dealings with him, including the Princess de Polignac,[23] found that he was extremely keen on adding noughts to cheques! It was his due as, I think, the greatest composer of his period.

PD   Did you know that Berners wrote a play?

HA   No. To tell the honest truth I wasn't really a great admirer of his fiction.

PD   Why did his novels sell well enough to go into further

edited by Cyril Connolly (1903–74) and financed by Peter Watson, who was its art editor, and features as Lizzie Johnson in Berners' privately printed novella *The Girls of Radcliff Hall* (c. 1935). After the publication of *Far from the Madding War* John Lehman asked Berners to write about Blenheim Palace for *Penguin New Writing*, but he refused saying: 'I could write a story about its inmates but that, I think, would be as unacceptable to your magazine as to them ... The idea of having to be accurate and critical appals me.' Mark Amory, *Lord Berners: the Last Eccentric* (London: Chatto & Windus, 1998), 192.

editions and even translations?[24] They were well reviewed and received even as something of a literary event.

HA I don't think they were literary events. At that time I was in the Air Force, but I was writing for *New Writing*, edited by my friend John Lehman, and there was *Horizon*, edited by Cyril Connolly.[25] At the beginning of the war Berners was going through an extreme phase of melancholia. I remember lunching with him, and, like most people, he was very depressed. He couldn't see any solution of any kind, and was rather desperate. He went in for a lot of psychoanalysis and tried various treatments.

He recovered, living in Oxford and seeing all those eccentric dons and their wives – Sir John Beazley was very eccentric indeed. Lady Beazley may have inspired *The Romance of a Nose* because she had a very pronounced one. She also had a little incipient moustache which she used to cover with cream to make it grow because her husband liked moustachioed ladies and even had a collection of photographs of bearded ladies! I think she would have grown a beard if she could! She was a great friend of Berners.[26] Then there was a Spaniard called Gregorio Prieto, who did quite a good drawing of him at that time.[27]

PD With a cap on?

HA Yes. We who are bald like to hide our baldness, so he always had a cap or a bowler hat or something of that kind! [*Laughs.*]

PD Did he have much to do with the University?

HA He was a friend of Maurice Bowra[28] and had quite a few friends in the colleges, such as David Cecil. During the war I was in the Far East, and it was only just after that I stayed once or twice at Faringdon. On one occasion John Betjeman was staying too. He was on the top of his form and we had a delightful time. Berners wasn't a great talker – not what they call a conversationalist. He would say sharp comments very much to the point.

PD Presumably he wasn't part of groups like those around *Horizon* and *New Verse*?

HA Completely outside.[29]

in demand as a fashionable portrait artist. See Obituary, *Independent*, 17 November 1992, 12.

28 Sir Maurice Bowra (1898–1971), classical scholar, Fellow of Wadham College, Oxford, from 1922 and Warden from 1938. Also served as Professor of Poetry and Vice-Chancellor of the University.

29 This is still arguable. Reviews of *First Childhood* were very favourable. Desmond MacCarthy, in BBC broadcast review: 'I could chatter for twenty minutes about this excellent and entertaining book ... Lord Berners is a musician of repute, a painter, a connoisseur, a figure in the social world of London; but he is also an exceedingly neat, witty, candid writer.' Compton Mackenzie in the *Daily Mail*: 'Autobiography of the very finest quality. Having enjoyed in the course of reading it the loudest and longest laughs I have enjoyed in the last two years, I am quite incapable of making any critical observations. I found the book enchanting from cover to cover.' Beverley Nichols in the *Sunday Chronicle*: 'I wish I had more space to appreciate this book. It is a very delicate and subtle work of art.' Constant Lambert in the *Sunday Referee*: with the exception of *The Home Life of Herbert Spencer*, I can honestly say that *First Childhood* is the funniest book I have ever read ... Lord Berners can be witty without ever being facetious or arch; and he can be serious by implication without ever being pompous or sentimental. Above all he is a master of understatement.' [All quoted on the dust jacket of *The Camel* (1936)]. On 26 June 1936 Aleister Crowley (1875–1947), prolific writer and diabolist, wrote to Berners: 'I have rarely enjoyed a book so much as your *Memoirs of Infantile Paralysis*. To speak plain truth I do not know another book which even describes the spirit of childhood. In comparison *Alice in Wonderland* is shoddy.'

26 J. D. Beazley (1885–1970), authority on Greek vases, single-minded perfectionist of few words, married to a fiercely protective Viennese wife who played Chopin memorably. Harold Acton, *Memoirs of an Aesthete* (London: Methuen, 1948), 139–42.

27 Gregorio Prieto (1897–1992), the Spanish-born artist and writer, made at least two drawings of Berners that have been used on CD covers. Prieto's first one-man show was in Madrid in 1919, then he came to know the cubists and surrealists in Paris. During the war he lived in England, until 1949, where he was

30 Robert Byron (1905–41) writer on travel and architecture, aesthete, contemporary of Acton at Oxford.

31 The Folly was erected in 1935 and it was designed by Lord Gerald Wellesley (1885–1972), 7th Duke of Wellington, diplomat, soldier and architect. See Robert Heber-Percy's explanation, Chapter 9, p. 72.

32 Jean-Baptiste-Camille Corot (1796–1875) French landscape painter who sketched from nature. He lived in Paris but travelled abroad including three visits to Italy. He believed in reproducing 'as scrupulously as possible' what he saw in front of him. See interview with Robert Heber-Percy, Chapter 9, p. 86, and plate 30.

33 John Sutro (1904–85), multi-talented contemporary of Acton at Oxford, with a passion for railways. See Harold Acton, *Memoirs of an Aesthete* (London: Methuen, 1948), 124–5.

34 The Grosvenor Gallery was opened in London in 1877 and became associated with the aesthetic movement, which was satirised in Gilbert and Sullivan's *Patience* (1881) as 'A greenery-yal-lery, Grosvenor Gallery, / Foot-in-the-grave young man' – a reference to the pale complexions of some figures in paintings.

35 Ronald Firbank (1886–1926) novelist, aesthete and eccentric. See Berners' personal reminiscence of Firbank in Ifan Kyrle Fletcher, *Ronald Firbank: a Memoir* (London: Duckworth, 1930), 145–50. 'On encountering Firbank for the first time [at a performance by the Russian Ballet], I was a little disconcerted both by his appearance and his general demeanour, which seemed to be attracting a good deal of attention. His ▶ ▶ ▶

PD Do you think Berners had any influence on John Betjeman, who also had a sense of humour?

HA John Betjeman has his own sense of humour and was very original indeed. I should say that in certain ways in architecture he was influenced more by Robert Byron[30] in his love of Victorian things – Victorian Gothic. Perhaps John Betjeman influenced Gerald Berners to build that folly on the hill outside Faringdon. Gerald Wellesley, who became Duke of Wellington, designed it. The neighbours didn't appreciate it very much, but now I think they do.[31] It takes time in England for people to like something! [*Laughs.*] It's taken time for Gerald Berners to be appreciated to the extent that he is now. He was always treated as an amateur, which was really a pejorative term in England. It should not be, because it really means that you love what you are practising. Whether he was painting or composing or writing he enjoyed it very much. I feel that writing is the weakest of his talents.

PD What about his painting?

HA He was very much under the influence of Corot as far as I can see.[32] Extremely unlike the sort of things he chose to buy such as Dalí or Balla, the futurist. You'd have expected him to try and express himself in some futuristic way instead of which they're really very conservative, conventional views, charming settings, pine trees in a style very much of the early Corot, when Corot lived in Rome. I think as such they're very charming, but I don't think they're in any way remarkable.

PD He used models. At least one of his pictures of Venice seems to be based on a Corot he possessed [see plate 30]. In his music and in his writings he uses models. Is this a kind of parody?

HA I think he was a born parodist really. He was thinking of parodies all the time – one felt a little alarmed that he might parody one's conversation. I never heard him actually mimic anyone, unlike my friend John Sutro,[33] who used to imitate everybody. Berners used to notice things, listening with a very sharp ear. His pointed comments punctuated and stimulated conversation. He was also gastronomically expert. Even in the period of post-war restrictions he produced magnificent meals.

PD Since he applied artistic criteria to living, was he an aesthete?

HA I should say he was. Not a conscious one, but he was a natural aesthete – one who loved art, in the old meaning of the term. Not of the greenery-yallery Grosvenor Gallery sort.[34]

PD Not as exaggerated as Firbank, of course?[35]

HA Firbank was a great friend of his. Firbank died in Rome and – this is a very Bernersian thing – he buried him in the Protestant cemetery. He didn't know he was a Roman Catholic and they had to move him to the Catholic cemetery. Firbank was extremely eccentric in appearance – and don't you think his writing is very eccentric?

PD I love that moment in *Valmouth* where he says the dance band struck up an *au delà* laden air. Lord Berners? Scriabin? Tchaikovsky?[36]

HA I think Berners was sorry for him. He realised that he was in an advanced state of tuberculosis and was dying. But he didn't know he would die so soon – he was only about forty. But he was a lost figure. You would see him walking along the street like somebody walking out of some sort of hallucination. Very strange.

PD In the second volume of your memoirs you said about Berners: 'Had he been less versatile he would have been less charming but more profound.'[37] Would you still say that now in his centenary year?

HA Yes, I would. That was a careful judgement.

PD You also said: 'He was an inspired amateur whose talents conspired against each other.'[38] Is that a detraction?

HA I think he'd have been a better musician had he stuck only to music, and not painted or written. I think his gifts were really those of a musician: other things distracted him. To have many different sides is very English, isn't it? Had he concentrated more he might have been a great musician. You couldn't call him that.

PD Stravinsky is reputed to have told Edward James, quoted by Nancy Mitford in about 1951, that he thought Berners was the most interesting of English composers.

HA That I can well believe. Interesting. But that doesn't mean he had created anything that is of the first rank.

PD After his avant-garde period around World War I he turned to ballet, where he could design his own sets. Did he flourish in this multi-media scene?

HA I think he did.

PD In your memoir of Nancy Mitford you call Berners 'a composer, painter and writer of whimsical originality. He was also an epicure.'[39]

HA Well that's true. He was really an epicure in everything. Whimsical he certainly was. Blowing soap bubbles in a restaurant full of people! That's not general is it? The idea of watching soap-bubbles floating about over different tables in

▶ ▶ ▶

incoherence (which I attributed to intoxication) I found decidedly embarrassing: in those days I was still young enough to resent being embarrassed. A few days later I met him again in Piccadilly – inappropriately enough outside the Army and Navy Club. I feared another difficult encounter, and so, shouting at him "You are my favourite author!" I hurried on.' In his reminiscences of Firbank, Berners describes how he arranged Firbank's burial in the Protestant Cemetery in Rome, realised it was a mistake because he was a Catholic, but did not know when writing his memoir that Firbank's sister put matters right. Brigid Brophy, *Prancing Novelist: in Praise of Ronald Firbank* (London: Macmillan, 1973), 94 n. 2.

36 See interview with Lord David Cecil, Chapter 14, pp. 116 & 125.

37 Harold Acton, *More Memoirs of an Aesthete* (London: Methuen, 1970), 35.

38 Acton, *More Memoirs of an Aesthete*, 37. But Acton quoted with approval from *Reflections on History* by the Swiss philosopher Jacob Burckhardt (1818–1897), Eng. trans. (New York, 1943): 'In learning a man should be an amateur at as many points as possible, privately at any rate, for the increase of his own knowledge and the enrichment of his visions. Otherwise he will remain ignorant of any field outside his own special area and, perhaps individually, a barbarian. The amateur, because he loves things, may find points at which to dig deep in the course of his life.' *More Memoirs of an Aesthete*, 278–9.

39 Harold Acton, *Nancy Mitford: a Memoir* (London: Hamish Hamilton, 1975), 53.

a crowded restaurant. I call that whimsical! Perhaps it's more than whimsical.

PD   Surrealist?

HA   He was very interested in Dalí.

PD   In the same memoir of Nancy Mitford you said that you suspected that she regarded him as her mentor, consulting him about her writing.

HA   Yes. She submitted her manuscripts to him for his judgement. He was a very good critic. I submitted the first volume of my *Memoirs of an Aesthete* to him, and he made a few suggestions, which I followed.[40]

PD   What sort of suggestions?

HA   I seem to remember that when I was a little boy I had a 'best girl', Francesca Braggiotti,[41] and Berners didn't like that expression at all. He said I should call her 'inamorata'. They were good suggestions and I followed them.

PD   He would have thought 'best girl' was American?

HA   I'm half American and very happy to be so!

PD   He's been used by some writers – as Lord Merlin by Nancy Mitford and much less happily as Titty in Harold Nicolson's *Some People*.[42]

HA   No, horrid. I think *Some People* is very amusing, but apart from Arketall, about Lord Curzon's valet, which I think is brilliant, the rest of it seems to be extremely unfair. Cruel to poor Ronald Firbank, who didn't deserve Lambert Orme, as he calls him. Obviously Firbank had his naïve friendly side; he was extremely shy and was genuinely sorry that he couldn't keep the appointment to go on the Bosporus with Harold Nicolson. So he sent him some flowers. Well, I'm sent flowers here, and I'm very pleased when I am. But Nicolson seemed to think this an extraordinarily humiliating and ridiculous thing to do.[43] Then there are other reasons too – they disliked each other. He found that type of aesthete too flabby for him.

PD   The Lord Merlin portrayal is rather nice?

HA   Oh yes, but Nancy was really fond of Gerald Berners.

PD   I wonder whether, in *Far from the Madding War*, one should see some kind of symbolism about somebody destroying a work of art in wartime. Or is that making it too serious?

HA   The novels were little light skits that he was writing to amuse himself and a few friends. I don't think he took himself at all seriously as a writer. He was taken far more seriously by the critics. He was pleasantly surprised by their praise.

40   Harold Acton, *Memoirs of an Aesthete* (London: Methuen, 1948).

41   Francesca Braggiotti (1902–98), actress and ballet dancer.

42   Harold Nicolson, *Some People* (London: Constable & Co., 1927; Folio Society, 1951).

43   Nicolson, *Some People*, 51–2.

But he was a composer first and foremost; then the paintings were a natural expression of himself. He loved scenery, and his descriptions of it in *First Childhood* are charming – the neo-Gothic mansion on the top of the hill at Arley with the river below. I think he noticed scenery. A lot of people don't. They go through it in the train, just talking, and they don't look out of the window. He noticed everything.

PD Do you remember anything about his connections with fascism? He may even have had lunch with Hitler in the mid-thirties.

HA That I didn't know. You must ask Lady Mosley about that! [*Laughs.*] I think she might have arranged it.[44]

PD How did he react to Mussolini?

HA I don't think he reacted at all. He was totally non-political.

PD Some of his friends and colleagues have now died.

HA Constant Lambert would have been invaluable. I think he is a very good composer. The Betjemans were very close friends of Gerald Berners. There was an occasion when they were all together. The Sitwells, Berners and Willy Walton gave an enormous bouquet of flowers to Tetrazini.[45] 'From the Poets of England' was the inscription. This was taken up by Scott-Moncrieff, who wrote a poem about them in a paper called *The New Witness*.[46] One of the lines was: 'Gerald Berners, Gerald Berners, Oh where does this desert blossom as the rose?' People were indignant – they had no sense of humour – that these 'Poets of England' should have presented a bouquet to Tetrazini.[47] It was done half as a joke, because she was a most grotesque lady who went on having endless farewell concerts and her voice went higher and higher. She was a very good *opera seria* singer in the great tradition. They were very close to the Sitwells, but there was a shade of irritation when it came to Sacheverell Sitwell talking about Berners: he didn't care for his practical jokes in conversation, which got on his nerves. He thought he was overrated as a writer. There was a definite break I thought.

PD But the context of the Sitwells, who were also outside the literary establishment ...

HA Totally outside.

PD ... that context was affected by Diaghilev.

HA Diaghilev was the *deus ex machina*.

PD Was Lambert the same kind of musician as Berners?

HA I would bracket them together. Lambert had great possibilities had he lived on, but unfortunately had certain weaknesses, which are shared by many English composers.

44 See interviews with Lady Mosley, Chapter 10, p. 92, and William Crack, Chapter 4, p. 59.

45 Luisa Tetrazzini (1871–1940). Celebrated Italian soprano at her peak in the years before World War I. She made many concert tours, appearing in London for the last time in 1934.

46 C. K. Scott-Moncrieff (1889–1930), best known for his translations of Proust.

47 The 'Poets of England' (*Daily Express* 22 December 1921, Mary Gifford, *Lord Berners: Aspects of a Biography* (PhD thesis, University of London, 2007), table 9) were the three Sitwells, William Walton, Aldous Huxley, Berners, Alan Porter (1899–1942: literary editor of the *Spectator*, poet and critic, left for New York in 1929, finally lecturer at Vassar College from 1932 until his death) and Augustine Rivers (whose name may have been a spoof). See Amory, *Lord Berners*, 74. Gifford, table 9.

48 Sir Lennox Berkeley (1903–89) had dinner with Berners in London, probably in 1933, and afterwards Berners introduced him to his publisher J. & W. Chester. See Peter Dickinson, *The Music of Lennox Berkeley*, 2nd edn (Woodbridge, Boydell Press, 2003), 45–6.

49 2 Carlisle Square, 24 January 1922; Aeolian Hall, 12 June 1923; Festival of the International Society for Contemporary Music, Teatro Rozzi, Siena, 14 September 1928.

50 *London Calling* by Sir Noël Coward (1899–1973) opened on 4 September 1923. The skit on the Swiss Family Whittlebot did involve the sister Hernia and two brothers called Gob and Sago; it started Coward's attack on modern poetry, exemplified by that of Edith Sitwell, who had taken such offence. Cole Lesley, *The Life of Noël Coward* (London, 1976; Penguin 1978), 87–8. Beverley Nichols saw it. *The Sweet and Twenties* (London: Weidenfeld & Nicolson, 1958), 48–54.

51 Arthur Johnson, BBC producer.

Not by Lennox Berkeley evidently.[48] Lambert was very fond of the bottle. He was a most distinguished reciter of English poetry, particularly of Edith Sitwell – I've never heard *Façade* recited so beautifully. It was metrically so perfect with Walton's music. I heard a rather remarkable performance recently given by the Lindsay Kemp Company – they gave it in Pisa and Prato. Poor Willy Walton was to have been there, but he died just about a month before. But Lady Walton was there with her mother. It was very pathetic in a way to have this lively sparkling early composition, which was performed in Siena not long after it was written. I went to the first performance in London, apart from hearing it in the house of the Sitwells, who lived in 2 Carlisle Square, Chelsea.[49] The Aeolian Hall performance was attended by a rather, let's say, 'smarty' audience. Noël Coward was there, and he had the bright idea of parodying it. In one of his early reviews an extremely funny Australian comic actress called Maisy Gay took the Sitwell role reciting this nonsense verse composed by Noël Coward. The skit was called *The Poems of Hernia Whittlebot* and was taken extremely seriously by Edith Sitwell as a deep insult. The Sitwells all rallied around her with endless scenes, and I think Gerald Berners thought it all very ridiculous and was outside that. There was a slight feeling between him and the Sitwells that he was not loyal enough. They used the word 'loyal'.[50]

PD Wasn't it a kind of Berners leg-pull, the sort of thing he sometimes tried to engineer?

HA Yes, he enjoyed it.

AJ [51] When Berners wrote some of the most advanced music by any British composer in his years in Rome, why is his writing and painting so conventional?

HA I think it's the residue of his very conventional ancestry – the aunts and people who went sketching. A sort of compulsive thing, but I don't think he had any real genius for painting. It was very charming and certainly appealed to the average collector. I think his paintings were all bought.

PD They were, so it's hard to trace them. Have you got any?

HA No. The walls of this villa are packed with paintings. There's no room for anything new! [*Laughs.*]

CHAPTER 4   # William Crack

Based on interviews with Gavin Bryars on 20 July 1980
and with Peter Dickinson on 25 April 1983 at Faringdon

THE INTERVIEW here is a conflation of what William Crack
(1893–1985) told Gavin Bryars and me. Crack's daughter Sylvia has
told me that her parents kept a public house called The Lamb near
Bury St Edmunds, Suffolk, and her father was in the army in World War
I. When she was a child her family lived in Lowndes Mews and for a
short time in Berners' house at Halkin Street. She remembers him as
'a funny little man with an odd walk and a monocle'. In his final will, made
on 13 April 1950, Berners left £2,000 each to two of his servants: Frederick Law and William Crack. Robert Heber-Percy inherited the rest.
Berners painted Crack's portrait at least twice, but, unlike the paintings
he exhibited, these are not signed. (See plate 23.) However they show
that Crack was a handsome and imposing figure, serious enough to
disapprove of some of his employer's antics: Berners' friends called
him 'blue-eyes'.

PD   Did you have to pass any kind of test to get the job of
Lord Berners' chauffeur?

WC   He didn't try me out. I was recommended to him, really.
It was in London that I got the job, and we used to go backwards and forwards to Rome every year. We went all over
Europe – Salzburg and Munich where the festivals were. We
went to the Munich Festival for a month the year after the
First World War then on to his house in Rome. The year
afterwards we started going to Salzburg every year.

PD   What was the journey like then?

WC   Mostly we took the car from London to Newhaven. In
those days you'd drive it onto a platform then a crane would
lift it over onto the boat and put it on the deck. Our car was
too big to go underneath. We had to empty the petrol tank –
the AA would see to it. In those days you'd get punctures on
the road and carried two spare wheels. If you got more than
two you'd have to mend it on the road. It used to take six or
seven days to get to Rome. The roads weren't like they are
now.

[Now talking to GB]

WC   When I first worked for Lord Berners I was living mostly
in London. He had a flat at 40 Half Moon Street, near Shepherd's Market, and I used to keep the car at Hampstead. Then
he and Gerald Robartes[1] bought a house in Chesham Place

1 Gerald Agar-Robartes Clifden,
7th Viscount. A. L. Rowse saw himself as a link between Berners and
Clifden, 'old friends who saw little of
each other in later life'. *Friends and
Contemporaries* (London: Methuen,
1989), 55–6. See Mark Amory, *Lord
Berners: the Last Eccentric* (London:
Chatto & Windus, 1998), 38.

2 Benito Mussolini marched on Rome on 28 October 1922, and installed a fascist government two days later.

3 Crack actually said harpsichord. Some people talked of a piano played during journeys. Legends persist, but in fact the instrument was a clavichord made by Arnold Dolmetsch (1858–1940). Following my enquiry, Dr Brian E. Blood wrote to me on 15 August 1983 to confirm this: 'Dr Carl Dolmetsch knew Lord Berners through their joint interest in the breeding of pheasants. Dr Dolmetsch remembers the collection, by the Berners Rolls-Royce, of a small four-and-a-half octave clavichord which slid into a space lined in velvet beneath the front seats of the car.' Berners himself confused things by letting Lord Fitzcricket say: 'When travelling on the continent he had a small piano in his motor car ...'. *Far from the Madding War*, 128; *Collected Tales and Fantasies*, 408. However, as a girl, Lady Pamela Knyvett Berners remembers travelling to Rome by car with Berners – the chauffeur was not Crack – when he had a kind of toy piano (or the spinet Harold Acton mentioned) which he did play when being driven, and he may also have played it on summer evenings in the gardens. (Interview at North Creake, Norfolk, 6 October 2007.) The drawing of Berners at his clavichord made by Sir Max Beerbohm (1872–1956) and captioned 'Lord Berners making more sweetness than violence' was first published in Beerbohm's *Things New and Old* (London: William Heineman, 1923), plate 12. (Included amongst long-forgotten figures were: H. G. Wells, Arnold Bennett, Aldous Huxley, Rudyard Kipling, Osbert and Sacheverell Sitwell.) In a letter to me of 3 July 2007, Uta Henning has pointed out that the Dolmetsch clavichords carried the inscription inside the lid 'plus fait douceur que violence', taken from a fable of Jean de la Fontaine (*Phébus et Borée*, Book 6, Fable 3), but going back to Aesop, 6th century BC, which must be the source of the Beerbohm caption.

which they shared. After I was married Lord Berners bought a garage in Lowndes Mews, and I lived in the flat above. Then they sold Chesham Place, or the lease ran out, and he bought the house in Halkin Street.

We were in Rome when Mussolini took over in 1922.[2] He surrounded the city and we couldn't go out for three days. The fascists would pull you up in the street if you didn't wave your hat when they marched by. As a precaution I locked the car away and took the float out of the float chamber so the fascists couldn't steal it!

I took him to Rome the first year I joined him in an old Lancia car with only two wheel brakes, and I had to drive over the Alps. We came back along the coast – Florence, Spezia, Genoa, Monte Carlo, and then right the way back to Paris, where he used to stay at the Ritz ... It was a lovely drive but we were unfortunate with that car. It had a cracked chassis in Rome and then, near Paris, the shaft broke in the axle and the back wheels came off on the road. We had to get somebody to tow us to a garage and put everything on the train. The car was ready in about three days. Before that he had a Fiat and an Italian driver. Lord Berners never learnt to drive himself though he took a lot of interest in cars.

GB Did he buy the Lancia in England?

WC Yes: it cost about £1,500. After that he bought a Rolls, probably 1921, and he had a specially designed body. Park Ward was the builder: it was called a false cabriolet and you could lift the top off and fold it back. Underneath the front seat of the car there was a tool box – with a Rolls they give you every spanner that you'd need for every nut on the car. He had a place made there to put the [clavichord]. I used to take him down there while it was being made by Dolmetch at Haslemere.[3] It hadn't got any legs on. You just pulled it out and carried it. We used to take it out when we were on the road, or in hotels, to take up to his room to do a bit of practising.

PD So he didn't play it while driving along?

WC No, he couldn't get at it. [*Laughs.*]

In *Dolmetsch: the Man and his Work* (London: Hamish Hamilton, 1975) Margaret Campbell said Berners supported Dolmetsch for a civil list pension in 1937. In his diaries Siegfried Sassoon remembered Berners had a 'clavichord on the table' on which he played Bach, Stravinsky and sketches of his opera. In her biography of Firbank Brigid Brophy discussed what instrument Berners had in his car. She asked Walton, and had a letter back saying it was a clavichord; he added 'it was not there permanently – he was transporting it to Rome'. *Prancing Novelist: in Praise of Ronald Firbank* (London: Macmillan, 1973), 94 & 118.

[*Now to* GB]

WC The Italian Automobile Association had a show at the Villa Borghese, and I got first prize for elegance. There was a photograph in the *Corriere della sera*, a tiny blue rosette for me and a gold medal for Lord Berners.

He had a manservant in Rome, Tito Mannini, who used to do the cooking, and there was also a maid. Lord Berners had a garage built at the side of 3 Foro Romano – before that I had to use a public garage at the Via Varese, where he had his previous house: there was a pool at the back with fish in.[4]

In 1922 we went to Munich for a month for the Festival and stayed at the Continental Hotel. We met little Willy, the Kaiser's son, who used to stay there. I've also been within four or five yards of Hitler. Sir Oswald and Lady Mosley ... her sister [Unity] used to go with Hitler. Lord Berners went to lunch with Hitler, not at the Braunhaus but at a restaurant in Munich.[5] I had to wait for him outside surrounded by all the police. When Hitler arrived he had his two guards. I used to take Lady Mosley – she was Mrs Guinness then[6] – to the Braunhaus where Hitler's place was.[7]

GB Lady Mosley sends her best wishes and so does Lady Diana Cooper.

WC They all dressed up rough once – at least they thought it was rough – and went to the market in the Caledonian Road. She [presumably Lady Diana] found she hadn't any money, and asked me to lend her £5. She paid me back – took me some time to get it! The year I got married she did *The Miracle* with Max Reinhardt at the Salzburg Festival, and my wife helped to dress her and look after her. I've got a photograph of her standing in front of the car with Reinhardt and his secretary, Rudolph Kommer.[8]

One year, after Salzburg, we went right through the Dolomites to Venice, where the Coopers had a flat. There was a carnival and they all went: I volunteered to go as a sort of page and stand on the stairs. But when they got there they were not allowed in with masks on. Royalty were present and no-one was allowed to wear a mask in front of royalty.[9]

We nearly always came back via Paris, where we might stay for a week.[10] The valets, maids, couriers and chauffeurs used to eat in a couriers' room at the Ritz, sitting at a long table. There would be seventy to a hundred down there for lunch or dinner – two sittings and marvellous food.

Lord Berners was very good with his staff. When we went out he'd always make sure I had somewhere to stay.

GB How many people did he have working for him?

4 8 Via Varese: Berners bought 3 Foro Romano in 1928. Amory, *Lord Berners*, 80 & 110.

5 Presumably the Osteria Bavaria. See Diana Mosley, *A Life of Contrasts* (London: Hamish Hamilton, 1977), 122–3.

6 She married Sir Oswald Mosley in 1936.

7 This testimony in his interview with Gavin Bryars is so important that the transcript is verbatim. Crack also told Gavin Bryars: 'If I'd had a pistol I could have shot him and stopped the whole war before it started couldn't I?' For further evidence see interview with Lady Mosley, Chapter 10, p. 92.

8 Max Reinhardt (1873–1943), Austrian-American director and actor who founded the Salzburg Festival with Richard Strauss and Hugo von Hofmannsthal in 1920. *The Miracle*, starring Diana Cooper (1892–1986), ran internationally for some twelve years. They would have been at Salzburg in 1923 when Berners' *Valses bourgeoises* for piano duet were performed at the Festival of the International Society for Contemporary Music.

9 This was a costume ball given by the Baroness d'Erlanger, wife of cosmopolitan financier and composer Baron Frédéric D'Erlanger (1868–1943), and Lady Colebrooke at Teatro La Fenice on 27 August 1926. It was Crown Prince Umberto whose presence put a damper on the proceedings. He didn't want to dance, so no one else could, and masks were not allowed. The young and then virtually unknown Cecil Beaton was there, and confided to his diary his first impression of Berners: 'a ridiculous-looking man – like a particularly silly taylor's dummy'. Hugo Vickers, *Cecil Beaton: the Authorized Biography* (London: Weidenfeld & Nicolson, 1985), 74.

10 On 24 April 1924 Berners' opera *Le Carrosse du Saint-Sacrement* was premièred at the Théâtre des Champs-Élysées along with Stravinsky's *L'Histoire du soldat* and Henri Sauguet's *La Chatte*. Crack saw it.

WC Here in Faringdon he had a butler, footman, two house-maids, cook and kitchen-maid and five or six in the garden. He used to have a butler in London but he didn't live at Faringdon until after his mother died. I nearly left him in 1930 when the slump was on. My wife and I had to leave the London establishment, so he just had a butler and somebody in the kitchen. Then when things got better I went back to the garage and everything turned out all right.

GB So he came back to Faringdon permanently after his mother died in 1931?

WC That's right. It was always his house, but he let his mother have it for her lifetime. After he inherited he had a house at Stanley in Shropshire which he sold. I went up there once or twice. It was in bad condition and needed a lot doing to it. Water had to be pumped up to the house.[11]

GB Do you remember his mother well?

WC Oh, yes. She was very nice. She once came out of the front door, saw he'd got 'GB' on the car, and asked him why he put his initials there! She married a second time to Colonel Ward Bennitt, who was a funny old chap with a monocle. He never used to think we did enough work – that sort of thing. Their chauffeur told me that. They wouldn't put me up when I first came down here. They wouldn't have anything to do with chauffeurs, so I had to stay with the butler [in a cottage in the town]. The staff lived in the house on the top floor. She was a Foster and had a cousin who lived at Apley Park – Captain James Foster.

GB How did Berners get on with Colonel Ward Bennitt?

WC I wouldn't know – I don't expect he did. Perhaps that's why he didn't come down here so much.

GB When his mother was alive how often would he come to Faringdon?

WC Weekends. For a week occasionally. Not every weekend, then we'd be four months abroad. He was usually in England at Christmas. We used to go all over the place, but I never went to Ireland or Greece: he went by train and boat.

GB Do you remember his mother's chauffeur?

WC She had two. The first one was a coachman called Watkins, when they had horses and carriages, then he took over with their first car, a Daimler. After Watkins died Barrett came from Newbury in 1923. They had a butler called Smith. Lord Berners had a butler called Marshall. I think he got himself into trouble: he'd done a bit of fiddling and he used to drink quite a lot.[12] Mrs Nelson was the cook in London.

PD What were the painting expeditions like?

WC He always used to go out painting in Italy – he was a

11 See Chapter 1, p. 8.

12 Robert Heber-Percy told Gavin Bryars that Marshall claimed to have spent fourteen years with Lord Berners and was recommended by him. In fact, Crack said, his tenure was only five or six years, and when Marshall went on to his next job a grand lady from Sussex telephoned to say: 'What do you mean by recommending this man? He drinks like a fish!' Herbert Marshall advertised for a new job in *The Times*, 17 February 1933. Mary Gifford, *Lord Berners: Aspects of a Biography* (PhD thesis, University of London, 2007), table 9.

good painter. He used to have a girl in Rome who sat for him, and I sat for him too – the two portraits of me were done at Foro Romano. I'd have to sit there for hours and used to read books. He'd go out from Rome to Frascati, Castel Gandolfo, round the lakes where the Pope lives,[13] Lago di Nemi, Sorrento and Naples. Once when out painting we nearly got run in when two motorcyclist policemen thought we were spies!

PD He must have enjoyed having a good time?

WC I've taken him to many different people. On my job in those days you were out half the night waiting at parties such as Lady Cunard's.[14] I once took Sir Thomas Beecham to Venice then on to Rome. I remember the conductor Constant Lambert. They didn't talk to me. I used to take them about.

GB I've heard that he sometimes used to wear masks when he was in the car.

WC He had a lot of masks but he never used to put them on outside – at least I never saw it when driving.[15] Funny thing, when we were out somewhere driving, he'd put on a different hat when going through a town. And he always used to smoke a lot of cigars.

Faringdon is quite small compared to some of the big houses like the Duke of Sutherland's, where they used to treat us very well. You'd be called in the morning with a cup of tea and that sort of thing. There was a big long table, and forty-five of us sat down to meals. In some places they put chauffeurs up, and in some they didn't.[16] During the twenty

15 Crack said the same in his interview with me:

> PD Another legend was that he would wear masks when being driven along. Did he actually do this?
>
> WC I don't really remember. I was driving and wouldn't see what they were doing in the back of the car. I know he had masks, but I never saw him actually wear one.

However, Lady Pamela Knyvett Berners remembers as a girl a journey to Rome when Crack was not the chauffeur, and Berners would entertain her. One of his stunts was singing popular songs to some kind of keyboard instrument with the window open, both of them wearing masks. The peasants were terrified and could be seen crossing themselves! (Interview, North Creake, 6 October 2007.) She also recalls Berners swearing about the traffic in front of her, which used to upset Crack, and her father thought Berners was a bad influence. Beverley Nichols said: 'In the back of the motor-car there was a strange object; a white, hideous mask, the mask of an idiot, fashioned by Oliver Messel ... This mask was part of his lordship's travelling equipment.' *The Sweet and Twenties*, 162–3. Oliver Messel (1904–78) artist and stage-designer: Olive Mason in *The Girls of Radcliff Hall*.

13 See Berners' paintings, plates 34, 35.

14 Maude Alice Burke (1872–1948), known as Emerald, American-born widow of shipping magnate Sir Bache Cunard, prominent London society hostess during the 1930s. Friend of Edward VIII and Wallis Simpson and mother of Nancy Cunard. James Lees-Milne recalled Berners' cryptic differentiation between parties given by Lady Colefax and those given by Lady Cunard: 'The first was a party of lunatics presided over by an efficient, trained hospital nurse: the second a party of lunatics presided over by a lunatic.' *Prophesying Peace: Diaries, 1944–45* (Norwich: Michael Russell Publishing, 2003), 24. Cecil Beaton was kinder: 'As a young man I used to warm myself in my friendships with older people; when Emerald took notice of me I felt I had not lived in vain. I thought I had never

seen a more amusing-looking little parakeet in her pastille-coloured plumage ... she presented herself with such artistry that she seemed to be the embodiment of her own wit and gaiety. No one else remotely resembled her.' 'Follies of the Famous', *Sunday Times Weekly Review*, 26 August 1973, and *The Strenuous Years, Diaries, 1948–55* (London: Weidenfeld & Nicolson, 1973). But Beaton recognised that she was devastated when, after their long affair and her support for his enterprises, Sir Thomas Beecham abruptly married Betty Humby. Sybil Lady Colefax (1874–1950), wife of Sir Arthur Colefax, indefatigable society hostess, co-founder of the interior decoration firm Colefax and Fowler. Berners used to refer to her as 'the coal box'. Beverley Nichols knew both of them: see *The Sweet and Twenties* (London: Weidenfeld & Nicolson, 1958).

16 The Duke of Sutherland at Dunrobin Castle in Scotland. Crack also mentioned many other visits to Gavin Bryars – Montegufoni, when Sir George Sitwell was still there; Mrs Keppel, near Florence; Marchesa Casati near Sorrento; Lady Wimborne, Walton's friend, at Ashby St Leger; Max Reinhardt near Salzburg; Vita Sackville-West at Sissinghurst; the Duke of Wellington at Stratfield Saye; Gerald Agar-Robartes in Cambridgeshire; Mario Pansa in Rome, whose family had a house near Reggio on the road to Milan; Max Beerbohm at Rapallo; Lady Juliet Duff at Wilton; and Edward James in Sussex.

years I was with Lord Berners we went to Rome every year, sometimes twice, but the last time was 1938. We'd booked for 1939 – I've still got the AA papers upstairs – but the war came.

I was with Lord Berners for five or six months when he was in Oxford early in the war, then I left. He did something to do with blood transfusion but I don't know much about him after that. In 1940 I went to training school in Southampton and got bombed out, and then I was with Vickers for four years. After the war was over Lord Berners couldn't afford to keep me, so I went into the Military College of Science as a fitter. I jacked the car up, left it in the garage and put it ready. I used to see him occasionally, but he never seemed quite the same, and I think he wasn't in very good health.

PD   What did people think of him in Faringdon?

WC   I don't think he was here much really. He got on all right and was very good to the people here.

PD   They didn't think he was crazy?

WC   I didn't mix much with the people in those days. You see at weekends we used to go all over the country staying at different places. I wasn't at home all that much.

PD   Were there funny things that happened?

WC   Once we were stopped by police in Germany for speeding and Lord Berners told me to make out that we didn't know what they were talking about. They wanted to fine us and he said: 'Cannot understand.' They got fed up and let us go!

PD   When you got into scrapes like that it must usually have been helpful that he actually could speak the language?

WC   I think he could speak four languages. But the funniest thing was when we were going along the road from Florence to Rome, approaching a railway crossing and they shut the gate just as we got there. [*Laughs.*] He was going to throw a stone at the woman at the gate! I told him not to – we might have got run in or anything! They kept you waiting sometimes half an hour for a train to go through in those days.

CHAPTER 5

Edward James

Based on interviews with Gavin Bryars

EDWARD JAMES (1907–84) was a rich patron and collector who supported Dalí and Magritte. He inherited the West Dean estate in West Sussex from his father, but in 1964 donated it as a centre for arts and crafts. It remains a success, but James disapproved of the way it was run, and in the late 1970s told George Melly, who was co-authoring his memoirs: 'I didn't sign away a fortune so that middle-class couples could enjoy a rather cheaper holiday, as if they were in an hotel in Torquay.'[1]

After Eton, James went to Christ Church, Oxford, where he was a contemporary of Evelyn Waugh, Harold Acton and John Betjeman, whose work he supported, but he was eccentric and aspects of his life turned out to be as surreal as the painters he admired so much.

In 1931 James married the celebrated Austrian dancer-actress Tilly Losch (1907–75) but they parted in a scandalous divorce three years later. After this James was ostracised and left England. But in 1998 Melly looked back at the evidence: 'I am convinced James was telling the truth when he said Losch married him believing him to be gay and planning to divorce him on these grounds for a great deal of money. In those days a gentleman was expected to accept his role as the guilty party. James didn't. He counter-sued, on the grounds of serial adulteries and abortions, handled his own defence and won – "the act of a cad". For this society didn't forgive him.'[2]

In 1937 James published his novel *The Gardener who saw God*,[3] and as the war came he moved to Mexico, where he lavished large sums of money on building his fantastic surrealist paradise called Las Pozas near Xilitla in Mexico.

On 3 November 1977 Gavin Bryars spoke to Edward James on the telephone. It was during this conversation that James recalled having been at a party in Hollywood, in about 1950, when Stravinsky was present, and he was asked who he considered the best British composer. James expected him to say Walton or Britten, but, remembering his old friend, he replied: 'Lord Berners'.

hearing with several well-known rips named as co-respondents. In those days divorce courts were open to the public and London society had flocked to hear their friends giving spicy evidence ... The star turn had been Adele Astaire, who was Tilly Losch's best friend. She spoke as freely in the witness box as she would have to close friends during a night out at the Embassy Club. The judge's wig almost rose on his head as he listened to her wisecracks, and there was so much laughter that the court had to be called to order over and over again.'

3 An English Lord appears who has a Gothic castle in Berkshire, but the resemblance to Faringdon is slight and cloaked in surrealist fantasy. 'In his extensive grounds and gardens, on the elms of his park and among the fountains of his pleasure lawns, the surrealist peer had lavishly practised and installed the theories and emblems of the new movement; grand pianos carved in marble might be seen perched in the upper branches and colossal poached eggs of painted alabaster swam or seemed to swim like nenuphars in the pools ... One was so trapped by the trompe-l'œils on every hand and worried by the entanglements of wire and coloured enamels designed by Joan Miro which swung along the heads of the hedges ...' *The Gardener who Saw God* (London: Duckworth, 1937), 268–9. The new gardener had been told his lordship was mad, but found he talked sense about horticultural matters. Then he noticed that the head of the enamel and platinum tiepin 'which held the good lord's sober, grey silk tie tidily in place ... represented a miniature poached egg'. But James' Lord had a habit of singing snatches of operatic arias from Musorgsky and Rimsky-Korsakov at the top of his voice when walking through the gardens – something Berners might not have done (272–3).

---

1 Edward James, *Swans Reflecting Elephants: My Early Years*, ed. George Melly (London: Weidenfeld & Nicolson, 1982). (*Swans Reflecting Elephants* is also the title of a painting by Dalí from 1937.) All went smoothly in this collaboration, but when Auberon Waugh attacked the book in the *Evening Standard* Melly got the blame, and James turned against him.

2 George Melly (1926–2007), 'Strange Reflections', *Daily Telegraph*, Arts and Books, 11 April 1998. See also Daphne Fielding, *The Face on the Sphinx: a Portrait of Gladys Deacon, Duchess of Marlborough* (London: Hamish Hamilton, 1978), 84–5, who remembered a house-party at Faringdon: 'Edward James had just divorced ... Tilly Losch. It had been a long and sensational

A Meeting with Gavin Bryars

Bryars visited Edward James on 31 May 1978. He relates:

4 Email to Peter Dickinson 14 February 2007.

5 First published as *Percy Wallingford and Mr Pidger* (Oxford: Basil Blackwell, 1941); *Collected Tales and Fantasies* (1999). Berners inscribed a copy of this paperback to Constant Lambert: 'To Constant from Gerald "En zee esklabusteten eenden Tetz mit klinkoftenfelt" Feb. 1942'. This seems to be an untranslatable private joke.

6 Washington Treaty (1921) between the USA, British Empire, France, Italy and Japan.

7 Cecil Beaton (1904–80) saw Berners in a nursing home in 1945, when he was missing the spring at Faringdon, and wrote: 'Pathetic Gerald! When he returned to Faringdon life was made no easier for him. He was not even allowed his breakfast in bed. It was not long before, in desperation, he turned his face to the wall.' *The Happy Years: Diaries, 1944–48* (London: Weidenfeld & Nicolson, 1972), 130. The entry about Berners occurs in Beaton's diaries in the year 1947. Hugo Vickers has described the outcome following its publication: 'Heber-Percy seized his opportunity and knocked Beaton down outside Peter Quennell's house. Shortly afterwards, Beaton, aged seventy, suffered a severe stroke. I can remember the Mad Boy, by then the sole incumbent of Faringdon, laughing gleefully about this incident without a jot of remorse.' *Spectator*, 26 August 2000.

8 See interview with Lady Mosley, Chapter 10, p. 90.

9 According to Mark Amory, Stein was not quite so officious: *Lord Berners: the Last Eccentric* (London: Chatto & Windus, 1998), 169–70. *A Wedding Bouquet* was given at Sadler's Wells Theatre, London, on 27 April 1937. The choreography was by Frederick Ashton; the young Margot Fonteyn danced the drunk Julia; and Constant Lambert conducted.

I spent a whole day with him at Monckton, the Edwin Lutyens lodge, redesigned by Dalí, on what was left of his estate in West Sussex. It was impossible to record our conversations as we were in and around the house that contained the original sofa in the shape of Mae West's lips designed by Salvador Dalí and many paintings by Magritte. We walked through the thousand-acre arboretum containing his collection of rare trees and rare pheasants. It was a very hot day, and we swam nude in the heated pool which we came across in the middle of the woods. It was under a glass dome, entirely circular and hemispherical like a large bowl, so there was no real bottom. It was kept permanently at exactly the temperature of the water in which James swam in Mexico. I wrote my notes immediately afterwards, like transcribing a dream on awaking. This visit provoked a comment which, to me, represents the highest praise. Robert Heber-Percy told me that Edward called him just after I left to ask: 'Who was that eccentric young man you sent to see me?' Being termed an eccentric by Edward James, in conversation with Robert Heber-Percy, is quite something ... and I wasn't even trying![4]

From Gavin Bryars' Notes on his Visit

Edward James said he met Berners shortly after he had inherited the barony in 1918. This was at the house of James' aunt, Mrs Arthur James, who was later caricatured by Berners as Mrs Pontefract in *Percy Wallingford*.[5] Physically Berners was the same all his life, although he became a bit balder later. He was short, dapper, well dressed, with a quiet slightly gravelly voice. His laugh was a combination of a chuckle and clearing the throat.

Like Berners, Edward James had been a diplomatic attaché in Rome (1929), and was put on indefinite leave for his error in sending a ciphered signal to the Prime Minister, Ramsay MacDonald, about three keels being laid by Mussolini at the port of La Spezia. James's signal referred to thirty keels by mistake. Since the message was received on a Friday, the Prime Minister had gone to Chequers, and so had to be brought back to London. If Italy had really laid thirty keels they would have been violating the treaty to limit naval armaments.[6]

James remembered a jealous triangle when Berners,

Robert Heber-Percy and Peter Watson were together in Venice in 1932. Some of this was reflected in *The Girls of Radcliff Hall*, in which Watson was Lizzie. James knew that Heber-Percy had punched Cecil Beaton in 1977 because of what Beaton had written in his diary.[7] But James, like Lady Mosley, confirmed that Heber-Percy had in fact looked after Berners very well.[8]

Like Berners' novels, James' *The Gardener who saw God* has elements of the *roman à clef*. Lady Cunard appears as Lady Judas Iscariot – Christopher Sykes' name for her – but she also comes in under her own name to disguise the other portrayal.

James alleged that at the performance of *A Wedding Bouquet* Gertrude Stein hogged all the applause, bumping Berners back into the wings with her 'big bum'.[9] He claimed that, since the text consisted of bits and pieces from Stein, the words were really Berners' too. James thought Stein lived off her reputation for having known all the French artists, and that she made feeble attempts at profundity. He said Picasso would fly into a rage if anyone mentioned her name during the last thirty years of his life.[10]

James was once annoyed about something, and showed Berners an angry letter which he had written. Berners told him: 'My father always said one should never trust a man with a grievance.'[11] James realised that he was merely airing his grievance, so he didn't send the letter. He had the impression that Berners admired his father a lot. Although there was always a distance in his talk about his father, there was at the same time admiration – and humour, as the autobiographies show.

James used to stay at Berners' house in Rome, and once spent a month there on his own, but he found Berners' man-servant and caretaker Tito unbearably rude. Apparently, when Berners was away, he used the front of the house as an antique shop and resented intruders.[12]

When Berners visited James he used to stay at West Dean rather than Monkton – his visits included post-war Christmases in the 1940s. James often visited Faringdon after his divorce, when almost everyone turned against him. Berners maintained his friendship unchanged. James thought this was brave and characteristic, and compared it with his similar loyalty to the Mosleys [during World War II, when they were sent to prison].[13]

10 Harold Acton was in Paris at the time of the liberation in 1944; he and Picasso went to see Gertrude Stein: 'Picasso hugged Gertrude like a beloved bolster. "Et mon portrait?" [of Stein, painted in 1906] he asked with a sudden note of anxiety, as if it were a lucky talisman … It was there waiting for him and he examined it minutely. "Ah, it is finer than I had dreamt", he said, embracing her again.' Harold Acton, *More Memoirs of an Aesthete* (London: Methuen, 1970), 171–2.

11 Cited also in *The Château de Résenlieu*, 70.

12 Lady Mosley remembered: 'Gerald's cook, Tito, bred canaries which sang all day and kept him company when Gerald was in England and he was alone in the house. An enemy opened all the doors of the cages and the canaries flew away into the Forum where they perched singing and twittering on bushes and trees. There was no food that day; Tito was in the Forum from morning till night coaxing and whistling to his birds. They all came back and even seemed pleased to find their familiar cages once again. Tito made delicious things, in particular there was a cake, hard chocolate outside and inside sour cream, sponge, rum and candied cherries which I have often thought of since but never achieved.' *A Life of Contrasts: an Autobiography* (London: Hamish Hamilton, 1977), 109–10.

13 As Lady Mosley said in a letter to her sister Deborah, Duchess of Devonshire, on 16 May 1961: 'friends are friends even when they don't agree about politics'. *The Mitfords: Letters between Six Sisters*, ed. Charlotte Mosley (London: Fourth Estate, 2007), 353.

CHAPTER 6

Daphne Fielding

Interview with Peter Dickinson on 14 May 1983 at Faringdon House

THE HON. Daphne Vivian (1904–97) was the elder daughter of the 4th Baron Vivian and Barbara Fanning. She was much admired and moved in literary circles getting to know Harold Acton and Evelyn Waugh, who dedicated *The Ordeal of Gilbert Pinfold* (1957) to her. She married Henry, Viscount Weymouth, later the 6th Marquess of Bath. Their first wedding in 1926 was secret because his parents disapproved. After they relented there was a formal wedding the following year. The Baths divorced in 1953, when she married Major Alexander Fielding DSO, who had served in the Resistance in Crete. For some years they lived abroad and she wrote her reminiscences, *Mercury Presides* (1954), following with a novel, *The Adonis Garden* (1961) about which Evelyn Waugh said: 'It is as though Norman Douglas, Nancy Mitford and Ernest Hemingway had sat down tight to a paper game.'[1] Daphne Fielding wrote biographies of Rosa Lewis (*The Duchess of Jermyn Street*, 1964, with a foreword by Evelyn Waugh); Lady Cunard and her daughter (*Emerald and Nancy*, 1968); and Gladys Deacon, Duchess of Marlborough (*The Face on the Sphinx*, 1978). The Fieldings divorced in 1978, and she went to live in America with Ben Kittridge, returning to Gloucestershire after his death. In *Mercury Presides* Daphne Fielding mentions Berners, a near neighbour, as 'a mixture of sweetness and malice. He was a gourmet, and used to describe the excellent meal that one was about to eat in an hour's time so deliciously that one's gastric juices were at once on the move.'[2] There was a sign in the grounds at Faringdon which said: 'Beware of the Agapanthus'! Her third son, Lord Christopher Thynne, remembers:

> I met Lord Berners only once when I was a schoolboy. My father and I went to have lunch with him at a pub where we were in a private room. My father said he thought the room was quite nice but Berners insisted that the colours clashed. They seemed to argue about it and in desperation Berners turned to me for confirmation. At the age of about ten I had no idea what a clash of colours meant but I did realise that Lord Berners probably knew more about such things than my father.[3]

1 'Daphne Fielding', Obituary, *The Times*, 16 December 1997.

2 Daphne Fielding, *Mercury Presides* (London: Eyre & Spottiswoode, 1954), 129–30.

3 Telephone call to Peter Dickinson, December 2006.

4 Alice B. Toklas (1877–1967), Stein's near life-long companion.

PD Do you remember anything Lord Berners said about Gertrude Stein?

DF Only telling me about the food and describing Gertrude and Alice.[4] He made one absolutely long to know people, and generally when you met them they weren't as good as his description: he'd conjured them up already.

PD Was that part of his generosity because he was kind, wasn't he?

DF Oh terribly kind, and yet with a hidden sting that could come out quickly, but not viciously, if anyone he liked was criticised – such as Doris Castlerosse, who was unique as the last of the *poules de luxes*.[5] At once he carried a banner for her, but there would be a stab there.

PD What about him as a writer?

DF I stayed here at Faringdon a lot. I was married in 1927 and was having my first baby when we lived nearby at Wantage. I was sewing an enormous quilt, and Gerald would read out chapter by chapter. That was most peaceful and blessed. One didn't have to talk but went on with the tatting. He read *The Camel, The Romance of a Nose, First Childhood* and *A Distant Prospect*.[6] Then he read *The Girls of Radcliff Hall* – lampoons of school-girl stories such as Angela Brazil or L. T. Meade as a *roman à clef* with real people in it.[7] He told me who all the people were. Utterly fascinating.[8]

PD What was his voice like?

DF A nice timbre, good pauses, led you on to what was coming – made you juice up! [*Laughs.*] He used to do that about food too. He'd always tell you what you were going to have for dinner some time in the afternoon and described it.

PD Could you place his work in terms of other writers?

DF Max Beerbohm a little bit. The caricature and sense of humour are comparable.

PD Are the memoirs better than the novels?

DF They're what I like best. He got pictures of childhood that one could compare with one's own and know it was true. I think the novels like *The Camel* and *The Romance of a Nose* were slight compared to the autobiographies.

PD As an author yourself, what future do you see for his writings? How will the young react?

DF I think they'd be well received now after a gap.

PD But today we don't know the people on whom some of the writings are based or the context.

DF *The Girls of Radcliff Hall* would have no importance because they wouldn't even have heard of Angela Brazil or L. T. Meade. Who is there now? Enid Blyton perhaps.[9] Nothing exists like the model: the mould is broken.

PD Is he like L. P. Hartley?[10]

DF Yes. I met them together. Berners is livelier with more fantasy.

PD Firbank?

5 Lady Castlerosse (1901–42), first wife of Lord Castlerosse, later 6th Earl of Kildare.

6 For an earlier account of these readings, see Daphne Fielding, *The Face on the Sphinx: a Portrait of Gladys Deacon, Duchess of Marlborough* (London: Hamish Hamilton, 1978), 2–3.

7 Angela Brazil (1868–1947), pioneer writer of entertaining girls' stories; L. T. Meade (1854–1972), Irish-born Elizabeth Thomasina Meade, prolific writer of girls' stories.

8 The list of characters Daphne Fielding gave to me is shorter than the one provided by John Byrne in his edition of the book, but it coincides exactly. Byrne's list is based on one written into the copy of the book owned by Cyril Connolly. Lizzie Johnson (Peter Watson); Daisy Montgomery (David Herbert); Miss Carfax (Berners); Cecily Seymour (Cecil Beaton); Olive Mason (Oliver Messel); Miss MacRogers (Jimmy Foster, or Sir Michael Duff); May Peabody (Robin Thomas); Vivian Dorrick (Doris Castlerosse); Millie Roberts (Robert Heber-Percy); Madame Yoshiwara (Pavel Tchelitchev); Mademoiselle Gousse (Christian Bérard); Helena of Troy (Jack Wilson). Berners, *The Girls of Radcliff Hall*, ed. John Byrne, designed by Simon Rendall (London: Montcalm and The Cygnet Press [750 copies]; North Pomfret, VT: Asphodel Editions [250 copies], 2000), 95–6. The original preface, not included in this edition, is Appendix 1, p. 165.

9 Enid Blyton (1897–1968), highly successful author of children's stories.

10 L. P. Hartley (1895–1972), novelist best known for *The Go-between* (1953). Hartley reviewed *The Camel* in the *Sketch*: 'Lord Berners has a genius for finding grotesque juxtapositions, and for startling us with an incongruity so violent as to be really frightening.' Quoted on back pages of *The Camel* (1941).

DF   Oh, yes, now you remind me. He gave me my collection of Firbank and would read that aloud – *Valmouth*, *Prancing Nigger*, *The Flower beneath the Foot* and his favourite was *The Eccentricities of Cardinal Pirelli*.[11]

PD   The cardinal who dies at the end of the story chasing a choirboy round the church! That was just his kind of humour wasn't it?

DF   Yes. [*Laughs.*] Strange fantasies.

PD   How did this connect with his life?

DF   I look upon Gerald as the king of dilettantes, and he was able to afford it. He also was very kind and encouraged younger people. He inspired me like anything. I think it was because of him that I took up my pen. Because he was a true critic who wouldn't say something was good if it wasn't, one wanted to please him very much and one got the truth.

PD   You mention him as a dilettante – Stravinsky called him 'an amateur in the best sense'[12] – but do you think he spread himself too much?

DF   Painting must be the most enjoyable thing of all, but one always imagines Gerald alone practising or wearing funny masks in the car to surprise people. He'd do it when he was being driven alone. I've not been with him when he did it: I'd have been too embarrassed![13] [*Laughs.*]

PD   Why do you think he wanted to disconcert people? Was he lonely and needed to make some kind of relationship.

DF   I think he was lonely, until he found close friends. Although he was so popular, treated as a lion and hunted by people like Lady Colefax and Lady Cunard, he always went but I think he enjoyed weekend parties with a few friends.[14] He was so exquisite about everything he did – the food, the flowers, the books you had in your bedroom, the biscuits in the tin …

PD   And Robert has kept this up.

DF   That's the wonderful thing. Gerald would be so pleased. One absolutely feels he lives in this house and is very conscious of his presence.

PD   I agree with you. That's a very strong feeling I've had over more than ten years. But what is it that causes us to feel that Gerald Berners is in his house?

DF   The objects he collected. It's a wonderful mixture of some of the Victorian paintings, the stuffed birds – unique.

PD   I wish this programme was going to be on television to catch all these details.

DF   Can't you do it on television? There was a wonderful

11 See interviews with Sir Harold Acton, Chapter 3, p. 53, and Lord David Cecil, Chapter 14, pp. 116 & 125.

12 'I met Gerald Tyrwhitt – he was not yet Lord Berners – in Rome in 1911 … His remarks about music were perceptive; and though I considered him an amateur, but in the best – literal – sense, I would not call him amateurish, as we now use the word. When we knew each other better, he began to come to me for criticism and advice in his composition.' Igor Stravinsky and Robert Craft, *Memories and Commentaries* (London: Faber & Faber, 1960), 83.

13 See interview with William Crack, Chapter 4, p. 61.

14 'I am inclined to think that these were the last days of the great London hostesses who preferred quality to quantity and ostentation, and I would choose Lady Cunard and Lady Colefax as their leading representatives. Both could blend politicians with poets, painters, novelists, economists and musicians, but they were very different.' Harold Acton, *More Memoirs of an Aesthete* (London: Methuen, 1970), 30.

concert at the Purcell Room with furniture from Faringdon on the stage, and John Betjeman read and had a bottle of champagne. It was a tremendous success and very much remembered.[15]

PD John was fiddling with the cork of a champagne bottle whilst I was trying to play the Polka from the film *Champagne Charlie*. I could see him out of the corner of my eye. It was a terrible moment. I only relaxed when he put it down and I could see that he wasn't going to open it – and it was a BBC broadcast![16]

DF I shall never forget it.

PD I think Margot Fonteyn[17] thought there wasn't enough from the ballets.

DF I thought it represented Gerald's many facets.

PD Have you any anecdotes about him?

DF Did you know he wrote a funeral dirge for his mother when he was about ten? His mother was very pleased with the genius of her son. At every children's party he went to she'd ask him to play her funeral dirge! [*Laughs.*] He was devoted to his mother, but that was his [party piece].

PD Did he play it to you?

DF No. But I wrote about it in the book I wrote about Gladys Marlborough, whom Gerald introduced me to.[18]

At about the same time – this is what he told me – he used to enthral other children by pretending to be a wizard, which indeed he was. He used to put on a white dressing gown and had a huge white hare that he said was his familiar; incense was burnt off-stage by some child accomplice; there was a ringing of bells, and all the other children were bewitched! [*Laughs.*]

15 *An Evening of Lord Berners* with Sir John Betjeman, Meriel Dickinson, Peter Dickinson and Susan Bradshaw, Purcell Room, South Bank, 8 December 1972.

16 BBC Radio 3, 12 December 1973, repeated 20 April 1975.

17 Margot Fonteyn (1919–91), one of the greatest ballerinas of the twentieth century. She danced Julia in *A Wedding Bouquet*, and also appeared in *Cupid and Psyche* and *Les Sirènes*.

18 Fielding, *The Face on the Sphinx*, 2–3. Berners was fascinated by Gladys Deacon (1881–1977), the American heiress, who married the 9th Duke of Marlborough in 1921. They parted ten years later.

CHAPTER 7

Professor Derek Jackson

Based on a meeting with Gavin Bryars in Paris on 27 May 1980

DEREK AINSLIE JACKSON (1906–82) was the son of Sir Charles Jackson, barrister, landowner, art collector and authority on English silver. Derek was very close to his twin brother Vivian, and was devastated when he died in 1936 in a sleigh accident after the horses bolted. After Rugby, Jackson went to Trinity College, Cambridge, where he took a first in Natural Sciences. He was then invited to undertake research in spectroscopy at the Clarendon Laboratory, Oxford, notably on the determination of nuclear magnetic spin, now used for MRI scans.

Jackson was appointed a university lecturer in 1934, and became Professor of Spectroscopy in 1947, the year he was made a Fellow of the Royal Society. Both his university positions were unpaid, but fortunately he had always been rich enough to subsidise his own research. He was addicted to hunting and horse-racing and rode three times in the Grand National.

In 1940 he entered the RAF where he became an enormous asset through the application of his scientific expertise to radar. He flew regularly to test his schemes, which were outstandingly successful – he was awarded the DFC, AFC and OBE for valour. After the war he lived partly in Ireland, to avoid punitive taxation, and travelled and worked in America before settling at the Aimé Cotton Laboratory in France, where he continued his work in atomic spectroscopy and was made a Chevalier de la Légion d'Honneur.

He was married to Pamela Mitford, his second wife, for fifteen years and he was a close friend of her sisters the Duchess of Devonshire, and Lady Mosley.[1] His sixth wife was Marie-Christine Reille, with whom he lived in Lausanne.

1 See Diana Mosley, *Loved Ones: Pen Portrait* (London: Sidgwick & Jackson, 1985). The portraits are of Lytton Strachey and Carrington, Violet Hammersley, Evelyn Waugh, Professor Derek Jackson, Lord Berners, Prince and Princess Clary and Sir Oswald Mosley. Lady Mosley's representation of Jackson as arrogant and dictatorial is so unflattering that when John Cary reviewed the book ('Discreet Charms of the Aristocracy', *Sunday Times*, 24 March 1985, 45) he found him 'by far the least engaging Loved One' and concluded that 'compared with Jackson almost anyone would seem tolerable'. Cary took a phrase from Oswald Mosley's book, *Fascism* (1936): 'the parasite who creates the barrier of social class' and surprisingly found it 'an accurate description of several Loved Ones – most notably Lord Berners'. Mark Stein was more charitable and concluded: 'Lady Mosley has been a hate-figure since 1940, but have people vilified someone who doesn't really exist? She makes a rather disappointing right-wing monster.' 'A Mellowed Mosley's Labour of Love', *The Times*, 22 March 1985. See also Catherine Stott, 'The Mitford who Became a Mosley', *Sunday Telegraph*, 17 March 1985.

2 See interview with Lady Mosley, Chapter 10, p. 92.

From Gavin Bryars' notes on the meeting

Jackson recalled that he first met Berners in about 1930, and that he used to stay at their house, Rignell, north of Oxford. He remembered Berners composing at his grand piano. They enjoyed talking about their work to each other even though neither had any technical knowledge of the other's field.

Berners liked dogs and had a Dalmatian at that time.

At Oswald Mosley's Olympia meeting in 1934 Berners was arrested along with Jackson's brother Vivian.[2] Apparently Vivian's gold watch was confiscated, and he was furious when the police insisted on describing it as a watch made with yellow metal!

Berners' closest friends included Diana Mosley, the

Betjemans, Clarissa Churchill, Lord David Cecil and Gerald Wellesley, the architect who designed the Folly and who became Duke of Wellington.

Jackson frequently stayed at Faringdon, especially when he had leave in Oxford during the war, and remembered being there with the Lygons and the Betjemans.

Berners liked a good Beaujolais but was not particularly interested in special vintages.

Jackson stayed at the house in Rome only once, and thought Berners had let Lord Beauchamp have it for a time.[3]

Jackson and Berners both enjoyed the theatre, and they used to visit Stratford together. Jackson agreed with Lord David Cecil that Berners remained like a schoolboy – he felt that way himself and regarded it as the only way to keep age at bay. There was no pomposity with Berners. He was a great man, and Jackson would say that about very few people.

Sometimes Robert Heber-Percy would misuse words, which amused Berners. On one occasion he was annoyed about something and said that he had 'taken unction'. These incidents led Berners to dedicate *First Childhood* to Heber-Percy, 'whose knowledge of orthography and literary styles has proved invaluable'!

Jackson said that both he and Berners were against the war. This did not mean they supported Hitler or his policies – quite the reverse – but they felt the war was a mistake. Jackson observed that 'people who are strongly in favour of the war are in inverse relationship to those prepared to fight it.'

3 William Lygon, the 7th Earl of Beauchamp left England in 1931 to avoid prosecution. This was another example of Berners supporting his friends regardless of what they had done or what people thought of them.

CHAPTER 8

Lady Dorothy Lygon
& Robert Heber-Percy

Interview with Peter Dickinson on 25 April 1983 at Faringdon House

LADY DOROTHY LYGON (1912–2001), known to all her friends as Coote, was the fourth child of the 7th Earl of Beauchamp of Madresfield Court in Worcestershire. She knew Evelyn Waugh, and aspects of her family emerged in his novel *Brideshead Revisited* (1945), which epitomised the period. When the openly gay Lord Beauchamp had to leave the country to avoid prosecution in 1931 the family was left at Madresfield. It was around that time that Lady Dorothy first met Berners, when Phyllis de Janzé brought him to stay at Madresfield.[1] During World War II Lady Dorothy served with the WAAF in Italy, and after various spells abroad she became an archivist at Christie's. She knew Berners well, and in 1985 married his heir, Robert Heber-Percy: they parted soon after, although she moved to a house nearby and they remained friends. She was chairman of the Berners Trust until her death and supported all its activities. Mark Amory recalled: 'It was possible to tell at a glance across a crowded room that she was a good person.'[2]

Robert Vernon Heber-Percy (1911–87; see plates 11, 12, 49, 50) was the youngest son of Algernon Heber-Percy of Hodnet Hall in Shropshire. He was brought up to country pursuits, at which be excelled. On Berners' death he became his heir, maintaining the legendary high standards at Faringdon House. He too was a generous host, and from the early 1970s onwards he supported the endeavours of those who helped to make Berners' work, especially his music, more widely known.

Heber-Percy met Berners in 1932, became his friend and companion, and was soon known as 'the Mad Boy' through his at times outlandish behaviour, although he helped to run the estate at Faringdon as well as an undertaker's business. He married Jennifer Fry in 1942 (divorced in 1947), and their daughter Victoria is the mother of Sofka Zinovieff, who inherited Faringdon on her grandfather's death.[3]

Apart from his antics, such as throwing a tankard out of an upstairs window in Salzburg or being carried prostrate into the Hotel Excelsior in Florence, Heber-Percy liked to tease, as these interviews show. This could mean bending the facts for sheer amusement or taunting people who were too serious – like me. So he told me that a whole wall of Berners' books and papers had been closed off for good when he constructed the flats at Faringdon and built partition walls.[4]

1 Phyllis de Janzé (1894–1943). See plate 4.

2 Mark Amory, 'Lady Dorothy Heber-Percy', Obituary, *Independent*, 20 November 2001. See also 'Lady Dorothy Heber-Percy', Obituary, *Telegraph*, 17 November 2001.

3 'Don't Look Back', Sofka Zinovieff talks to Sara Wheeler, *Telegraph Magazine*, 8 May 2004.

4 Richard Brain, 'Obituaries: Robert Heber-Percy', *Independent*, 3 November 1987; 'Robert Heber-Percy', *Daily Telegraph*, 31 October 1987.

PD How did Berners come to build Faringdon Folly in 1935?

RHP It wasn't part of the estate then – a timber merchant bought it and was going to cut the trees down. There didn't seem to be any reason why he shouldn't. Gerald bought it and then I took him up there. Quite a lot of village people were walking about, and he announced: 'I think it would be rather nice to have a tower here.' It was immediately reported in the town. The council forbade it, and an admiral objected to it too. Then Gerald was very angry because he'd bought the trees to save them. That he shouldn't be allowed to build a tower there was absolutely insufferable. So he got the Minister down; we gave him lunch and he gave us his blessing. Then Gerald had to build it, although it had only been an idea in his head. It was about 110 feet high. He wanted it Gothic, and chose the only architect who loathed Gothic – Gerry Wellesley.[5] Gerald went off to Rome, and Gerry built it Classical up to nearly 100 feet. When Gerald came back he was furious at its being classical, and insisted on the top bit being Gothic – the last ten feet. It was a present for my 21st birthday.[6] My birthday is on the 5th of November, so he had a fireworks party. I was very irritated because I'd wanted a horse! It was used before the war. The boy scouts wanted money, so they had it open and charged threepence to go up.

PD   How did the locals take to it finally?

RHP They don't remember they ever disliked it – they're proud of it.

PD   How did Berners get on with the town? I've seen a photograph of him crowning the Rose Queen.

RHP They liked him very much, and they now adore his memory because they never saw him! He used to wear a mask of a frightening-looking pig when going through the town and glare at them.

PD   You mean he was driven in the Rolls by the chauffeur …

RHP And sat in the back wearing a mask gently looking out.[7] He was a lot abroad but the vicar used to come up and ask for funds for things. Gerald would say: 'I'm afraid I can't – much as I would like to. My parents always told me never to associate myself with anything that might be a failure.' Then he'd write them a large cheque and they'd go! [*Laughs.*]

DL   When did he put the carillon into the church tower?

RHP That was for my birthday – but as I was tone-deaf I didn't recognise they were my great-grandfather's tunes.[8]

PD   He had a spectacular house in Rome?

RHP No. 3 the Forum. It had its own gate into the Forum.

DL   There was a large drawing room on the first floor with an enclosed balcony – you could sit out there in almost any weather – which looked straight over the Forum. When Mussolini was doing any sort of grand parade he used to get on his white horse there and start riding off.

5 Lord Gerald Wellesley (1885–1972), 7th Duke of Wellington, diplomat, soldier and architect.

6 5 November 1935 was actually Heber-Percy's twenty-fourth birthday. He gave the Folly in trust to the town after Berners' death.

7 See interview with William Crack, Chapter 4, p. 61.

8 Bishop Reginald Heber (1783–1826), Bishop of Calcutta, who wrote the words for many popular hymns such as 'Holy, Holy, Holy' (*English Hymnal*, ed. Ralph Vaughan Williams (1933), no. 162) and also one of the tunes set to 'From Greenland's Icy Mountains' (Calcutta – *English Hymnal*, no. 547.)

9 See Appendix 5 for details of the Stravinsky manuscripts and proofs Berners possessed.

10 On 13 May 1916 Berners wrote to Stravinsky: 'I am overjoyed to learn, through Madam Khvosh-chinsky, that you will consent to see me and give me some guidance if I come to Switzerland for a few days. I fear that I will be a nuisance to you; nevertheless, I do not hesitate to accept your kind offer, for a half hour of conversation with you will undoubtedly mean more to me than a century of [lessons with academics]'. Igor Stravinsky, *Selected Correspondence*, ed. Robert Craft, vol. 2 (London: Faber & Faber, 1984), 135. In a letter to his mother from Rome dated 16 July 1919 Berners said he was going to spend two days in Lausanne 'to see Stravinsky to show things'. In another letter, dated only 8 August, Berners wrote to his mother from Lausanne: 'Spent the day with Stravinsky. He is very pleased with my latest compositions and says I have made great progress.' Mary Gifford, *Lord Berners: Aspects of a Biography* (PhD thesis, University of London, 2007), table 3. So Berners was still showing his work to Stravinsky. Later Stravinsky said: 'A great lover of art and a cultured musician, Berners became in succession a composer and a painter. Diaghilev commissioned him to write the music of the ballet *The Triumph of Neptune* (1926), which was a great success. I very much enjoyed his company, his English humour, his kindness, and his charming hospitality.' Igor Stravinsky, *An Autobiography* (1936) (New York: Norton Library, 1962), 57.

On 29 June 1937 Stravinsky wrote to his publisher: 'Yesterday my friend Lord Berners, the English composer, visited me; his ballet *A Wedding Bouquet* just had a very big success at the Sadler's Wells Theatre in London ... I have always been devotedly sympathetic to his music ...' *Selected Correspondence*, ed. Robert Craft, vol. 3 (London: Faber & Faber, 1985), 251–2.

PD Mussolini was admired for organising things, but what did Berners think of him?

RHP He liked his mistress – she used to come to the house. I don't think he took any notice.

PD He loved Italy, like so many English people?

RHP I think he liked the Campagna and painted a lot there. He led a tremendously social life.

PD It was in Rome that Berners became the most advanced English composer in history up to that time.

RHP He met Casella and Stravinsky.

DL My father took the Foro Romano for two winters, and there were some manuscripts of *Petrushka* done for the piano. So I imagine that Berners and Stravinsky were in Rome at the same time.[9]

RHP Yes they were. Gerald definitely took lessons from Stravinsky.

PD That's unusual, because Stravinsky hardly taught, but he admired Berners and says so in his writings.[10]

RHP He used to come and stay here. Once, in London, Gerald had to go out to a dinner and I was left with Stravinsky. Quite difficult, but he was very sweet and nice.

PD What did Berners and Stravinsky talk about?

RHP I don't know what language they spoke – I didn't listen.

DL Probably in French.

RHP He spoke French, German and Italian, and made jokes in French – very dangerous!

DL And got away with it.

PD What was the story about you giving a party here?

RHP I had some hunting neighbours to the house. I'd warned Gerald, so he said he wouldn't come in. We were all sitting talking, and I was longing for them to go really. A silence was induced and suddenly the door opened and Gerald came in on all fours carrying a big hearth-rug over his head. He took a book and went out again – nobody ever said a thing! [*Laughs.*] They then left – hurriedly!

PD Was he drawing attention to himself?

RHP He was trying not to – I think he thought nobody would notice. [*Laughs.*]

PD How did Berners become so versatile when his family background can't have encouraged it?

RHP I haven't the faintest! [*Laughs.*]

PD In *First Childhood* he calls himself a sport in the biological sense.

RHP I used to take him out hunting.

DL   He rode *Passing Fancy*, didn't he, a horse Robert ran in the National?[11]

RHP Yes. When I first came here and we had a lot of horses, Sachie, Georgia, Edith and Reresby [Sitwell] came, all dressed in riding clothes to lunch – just as a tease. [*Laughs.*]

DL   He was rather superstitious, wasn't he? He always used to stamp a white horse.

RHP When you were in the car with him and passed a white horse he'd sometimes stamp it and then he say: 'You can't talk now. When I've stamped a hundred horses I get my wish.' When I tackled him seriously one day he said: 'I do it when there are bores in the car. It stops them talking.' [*Laughs.*]

DL   If he saw a feather lying on the ground he'd stick it in the ground and wish. Every day he used to walk round the lake. Robert observed this thing about the feathers, so early one morning he went round the lake scattering a whole bagful of them. Gerald's walk took three times as long as usual because he had to stick them all in and wish!

RHP He wasn't really superstitious: it struck him that it would be apposite to do it at that moment.

PD   Which of his accomplishments did he value most?

RHP He took his music seriously – not his painting, or his writing.

PD   The books went through more than one edition; they were translated; they were well reviewed.

RHP He didn't take himself as a serious writer.

DL   I think music was the most serious thing for him. After music I don't know which he thought most important – painting or writing.

RHP I think both equally.

DL   He had a very light touch about everything.

PD   Do you remember the books taking off actual people?

RHP Definitely. There was a lady called Lady Fitzgerald, an immensely rich jewess who came into *The Camel* – with orchids and things. He thought she was a figure of fun.[12]

PD   Do you remember about Walton and *Count Omega*?

RHP I remember him taking an injunction out against Gerald to stop the book being published. Gerald took an injunction out against him for trying to force his way into his books!

PD   They both went to lawyers?

RHP They really did.

DL   Did they stay friends in spite of it?

RHP Civil.[13]

11 *Passing Fancy* is mentioned in *The Times* (25 January and 9 March 1937) as racing at Leicester and Wolverhampton. Gifford, *Lord Berners*, table 9. Deborah Mitford, later Duchess of Devonshire, wrote to her sister Jessica on 2 April 1937: 'Lord Berners had a horse in for the first time in his life and the Mad Boy said to us before the race: "If it falls at the first fence Gerald will be broken-hearted". And it did! Wasn't it *awful*. But luckily he is very short-sighted and he thinks it was the second fence so all is OK.' *The Mitfords: Letters between Six Sisters*, ed. Charlotte Mosley (London: Fourth Estate, 2007), 86. (There are further references to Berners which the indexer has missed: 216, 243, 738, 793, 803.)

12 Presumably Lady Bugle of Slumbermere Hall, married to Sir Solomon Bugle, who made his money in buttons. The vicar said he hoped he wouldn't put any of them into the collection box. *The Camel* (1936), 65; *Collected Tales and Fantasies*, 80.

13 For details see Chapter 1, p. 18.

CHAPTER 9
Robert Heber-Percy

A memoir by Sofka Zinovieff
and an interview with Peter Dickinson

Remembered by his Granddaughter, Sofka Zinovieff

I FIRST went to stay with Robert Heber-Percy, my grandfather, when I was seventeen. This was nearly three decades after the death of Gerald Berners, but it was quickly apparent that his influence was still strongly felt at Faringdon House. The flock of multi-coloured pigeons circling over the roof, the oversize family portraits in the orangery, the chandelier outside the front door, the pewter tankards of champagne and the elegance and eccentricity of fellow visitors all summoned up another age, an unknown country. It was an astonishing experience for a teenager, and I have since wondered whether Robert might not have seen in my amazement and delight some of the same reactions he had as the Mad Boy, also barely out of his teens, when Berners first took him to Faringdon almost half a century earlier. I imagine that Robert was having his last boyish laugh when he decided to leave the house to me – a half-Russian anthropology student, who had grown up in bohemian London and knew nothing of upper-class country pursuits.

If Robert had been an improbable companion for a mild-mannered, cosmopolitan, sensitive intellectual and artist like Berners, he was also an unlikely grandfather. He himself appeared benignly bemused by having a granddaughter in the house for occasional weekends, while some of his guests could barely contain their surprise: 'We didn't even know you had a child, let alone a grandchild!' one visitor exclaimed when she was introduced to me. Certain older friends, however, knew the story about my grandmother's fish-shaped, wicker handbag, which lay undisturbed on a chair in the drawing room. It had allegedly been there since 1944, when Jennifer, Robert's wife, left for good, along with their infant daughter, Victoria.

Robert remained provocative, unpredictable and sybaritic even in his last years; the handsome, fearless daredevil who had captured Berners' imagination refused to grow old gracefully. He still drove his car like a maniac – the stonework to the front steps was frequently half-destroyed from misjudged returns home, presumably after good lunches – he smoked furiously, dropping ash all over his beautiful suits, and he teased mercilessly. However, it was entirely evident that he had devoted himself whole-heartedly to Faringdon.

There was a surprising tenderness, seriousness and loyalty in his relationship to the place, which was perhaps influenced by his own rural upbringing, but also reflected a respect and deep appreciation of what his partner of eighteen years had achieved there.

While much of the wonderful furniture and paintings remained from Berners' era, Robert continued improving the house and gardens in his own way; it was never a museum or mausoleum. There were still the exotic stuffed birds under glass, music boxes and the expanding collection of clockwork animals and toys, but it was often hard to tell whether things were a recent addition, or had been there since the glory days of the 1930s. The antique stone wyverns overlooking the swimming pool seemed a Berners touch, except that they were recent arrivals brought on an open truck, their angry demeanour surely provoking local onlookers almost as much as Berners' supposed forays with masks. And if some of the odd signs nailed to trees were apparently from the pre-war days, others were added: 'Do not throw stones at this notice' was somewhere near the dogs' cemetery, where one small, undated tombstone was inscribed: 'Towser: A short life but a gay one'.

Food was always exquisite at Faringdon, in a way that I imagine owed a debt to Berners' meticulous style and good taste. Rosa Proll, Robert's fiercely loyal Austrian housekeeper, served vegetables from the garden that were so small that eating the embryo carrots, broad beans, asparagus or new potatoes felt like cruelty. There were mushrooms picked in the park, peerless summer puddings constructed from the fruit cages' harvest, and if a pike was caught in the lake, it was transformed into dainty quenelles with a creamy sauce. Perhaps the most memorable of feasts, at least when I was still a schoolgirl, resulted from the rule that 'Ladies take breakfast in bed'. Rosa would bring up a tray with a huge scented magnolia bloom nestling amongst a delicate set of gilded porcelain. I remember sitting in the 1930s crystal-columned four-poster, drinking my coffee and looking around until my gaze landed on a portrait in an ornate frame. The young man with a high, domed forehead, sleek hair and sensuous lips could only have been Robert, and the painting was evidently by Berners, though it was quite different from his muted landscapes and classical scenes of Rome. At the time it seemed a good way of starting to understand the mysterious paradoxes of what lay between Gerald Berners and Robert Heber-Percy and their life together at Faringdon. And now, over twenty years after Robert's death, it still hangs there as a reminder.

SOFKA ZINOVIEFF is the author of *Red Princess: A Revolutionary Life*, a biography of her Russian grandmother, and *Eurydice Street: A Place in Athens*, a memoir of her life in Greece.

Interview with Peter Dickinson on 14 May 1983 at Faringdon House

PD   When did you first meet Lord Berners?

RHP   I met him at Michael Duff's house, Vaynol.[1] It was the first time I had met civilised people. People thought I was funny and didn't regard me as an outrageous child. I don't know why I'd got it into my head that he was a South African gold magnate. Then people told me he knew about art. I thought I knew about art – I knew about Cecil Alden, who did drawings of funny dogs. So I asked him: 'Do you like Cecil Alden?' Gerald looked amazed, and I didn't understand. I went back to Michael Duff and said: 'Lord Berners doesn't know anything about art – he doesn't know about Cecil Alden!' It was as crazy a juxtaposition as you could find.[2]

PD   Did Lord Berners give you your nickname?

RHP   I was called the Mad Boy. I think Georgia [Sitwell] gave me that ...[3] I didn't know what he died of – he just died having been ill for a long time. He had this doctor who came twice a day. The murderer! I'd been warned against him, but Gerald liked him and they became great friends. He never sent a bill, and when I wrote as executor he said: 'It was such a pleasure and a privilege knowing Lord Berners that I don't want to send a bill in at all.' A nice story.

PD   Did he feel he'd done what he wanted to do?

RHP   No. He used to repeat endlessly: 'If I hadn't been asked out to lunch every day I'd have written better music. If I'd been poor I'd have written much better music.'

PD   He knew too many people?

RHP   Had too much money and had too much his own way. He was always besotted by nice invitations.

PD   People wanted to come to him.

RHP   They did ... He gave a great deal to people. He was an enchanting host.

PD   Would it have been better if he'd concentrated on one thing?

RHP   He wouldn't have had *foie gras* so much! He took tremendous trouble. I did the meals and was the liaison between the cook and him. He used to sit in bed and order the meals, and say: 'I think *foie gras* is very nice to start with.' He would always end with a thing called Pudding Louise, a case with boiling *marrons glacés*, boiling raspberry jam, and ice-cream on top. It was a killer!

PD   Is it true that he'd have food of one colour going right through the meal?

1 Sir Michael Duff (1907–80), 3rd baronet, Vaynol Park, North Wales. Duff wrote a novel, privately printed, called *Parable of a Parasol*, where Heber-Percy features as Robert Oddman.

2 Cecil Alden (1870–1935), illustrator known for sporting and animal prints, often funny.

3 Georgia Doble (1905–80), wife of Sir Sacheverell Sitwell, 6th baronet.

4 It was Stravinsky who said, about his visits to Faringdon: 'Meals were served in which all the food was of one colour pedigree; i.e, if Lord Berners' mood was pink, lunch might consist of beet soup, lobster, tomatoes, strawberries ...' Igor Stravinsky and Robert Craft, *Memories and Commentaries* (London: Faber & Faber, 1959), 84.

5 Spike Hughes tells of how Constant Lambert (1905–51) wanted to produce 'an album of Schoenberg waltzes, gavottes, and other essays in what the composer is pleased to call "dance forms", put them on the market with a pretty 1890 cover on them and then sit back and watch the fun'. Hughes goes on: 'Lord Berners ... has an even more mischievous scheme which is to include without warning a couple of Schoenberg waltzes in a programme by Lanner, Waldteufel and the Strausses.' *Opening Bars: Beginning an Autobiography* (London: Pilot Press, 1946), 265. Berners did publish his own *Valses bourgeoises* for piano duet with a Victorian cover taken from *Les Jeunes Desmoiselles: Quadrille for the Pianoforte* by Camile Schubert (D'Almaine & Co's Edition of Camile Schubert's Works no. 4, undated). The *Valses bourgeoises* were played at the festival of the International Society for Contemporary Music at Salzburg in 1923.

RHP No, that's rubbish.[4] Up to the war he organised the meals, and after the war I did. When I first came and there were guests here he went round every bedroom to see that things were right …

PD Constant Lambert has said that he was deeply serious about his music, and after the main guests had gone then they'd play and talk about the music. Do you remember that pattern?

RHP I probably went to bed too … He did a lot of serious stuff that I was left out of, luckily. Probably he realised that my brain wouldn't take it in.

PD Was he happiest in the ballet world?

RHP He was happiest with Constant: he loved him. He was the greatest fun, terribly witty. Their sense of humour went very well together. I just remember terrible things like at the end of Constant's life, when Gerald was ill, driving Constant down, and we stopped at every pub for him to have a drink. We were meant to be at Faringdon by about eight, and got there at half past ten. Gerald had gone to bed. The whole thing was tragic.[5]

PD Did Lord Berners actually meet Hitler?

RHP He had lunch with Hitler.

PD Why?

RHP Because he was invited.

PD Did you go?

RHP I was asked for coffee afterwards.

PD Do you know what they discussed?

RHP Yes, I do. They discussed his composer – Diana Mosley will know his name – and Hitler said he wasn't much good and he'd like Gerald to write a March for him. Gerald, I think, knew this composer, and said: 'Perhaps he isn't very much good.' And Hitler said: 'I thought of sending him up in an aeroplane.' Gerald changed immediately and was absolutely furious and very upset. Then I came in so we got away.[6]

to BBC producer Arthur Johnson, 1983). Lady Pamela Knyvett Berners' recollection in 2007 of what she was told at the time was that Berners' party was at one table and they were asked to join Hitler's. Berners told her mother that 'The bugger had peculiar eyes.' One way Berners could have met Hitler was through Unity Mitford, who had stalked him and first met him at the Osteria Bavaria on 9 February. See *The Mitfords: Letters between Six Sisters*, ed. Charlotte Mosley (London: Fourth Estate, 2007); also David Pryce-Jones, *Unity Mitford: a Quest* (London: Weidenfeld & Nicolson, 1976). A friend of Unity's might have arranged a meeting, but Lady Mosley denied this. (See interview with Lady Mosley, Chapter 10, p. 92.) William Crack has confirmed that he took Berners to a restaurant in Munich – presumably the Osteria – when Hitler was there with his guards. (See interview with William Crack, Chapter 4, p. 59.) John Betjeman remained sceptical, and wrote to his wife on 28 September 1935: 'Apparently it is all rot about Robert and Gerald lunching with Hitler. They merely happened to be in the same restaurant. We must cross-examine them very thoroughly on what Hitler said to them.' John Betjeman, *Letters, vol. 1: 1926 to 1951*, ed. Candida Lycett Green (London: Methuen, 1994), 155. Salvador Dalí, an inveterate fantasist writing forty years later, said: 'I did not personally know Adolf, but theoretically I might have met him in private on two occasions before the Nuremberg Congress [15 September 1935]. On the eve of the Congress my intimate friend Lord Berners asked me to sign my book *The Conquest of the Irrational* in order to give it personally to Hitler, as he saw in my painting a Bolshevik and Wagnerian atmosphere, especially in the way I represented cypress trees …' *Diary of a Genius* (London: Pan Books, 1976), 137. See Mark Amory, *Lord Berners: the Last Eccentric* (London: Chatto & Windus, 1998), 134–5.

6 Berners sent a postcard from Munich to Heber-Percy at Faringdon on 5 September 1935: 'Thanks for telegram … I hope all is well at Faringdon. Did you find any visiting cards? If so please post here as soon as possible. Sorry you had such a lousy journey back. Lucky you had little Ham to keep you company. It was lovely meeting Hitler. Will write you a nice letter shortly. Love Gerald.' Gavin Bryars suggested: 'It could be, of course, that Robert had been in Munich and that the journey referred to was Munich–Faringdon. That may be inferred by the fact that Robert must have known by some other means the address in Munich to send visiting cards since there is none here.' (Bryars' note

PD   He did write a fascist march. Did you know?[7]

RHP We went to Tom Mosley's meeting in Olympia, which broke up in disaster, rows and fights and things. We went with Vivian Jackson as well. There were police charging on horses. Gerald had got away from us and was talking to one of these communists outside and said: 'I'm afraid the *Internationale* is no good. It's really badly composed.' And the man agreed with him. Gerald said: 'I'll write you a better one.'[8] Then we were arrested and taken to the police station. Vivian was stripped of all his valuables and they wrote down 'one nickel cigarette case'. Vivian said: 'You don't know platinum when you see it, you ignorant bastard!' [*Laughs.*] We were all put inside in a cell with a lot of communists, then we were rescued. We came in front of a magistrate the next day, Vivian still seething with rage, and he said: 'Do you know they didn't even call me sir!'[9]

PD   Was Berners put inside too?

RHP Only for a short time.

PD   Berners once told an interviewer for the BBC radio programme *Woman's Hour* that he never used one side of the double staircase at Faringdon because it was unlucky. What is the story?

RHP It's not a story at all. One side of the banisters was weak!

PD   What about Lord Berners wanting to keep a railway compartment to himself?

RHP That was rather a flop because he used to get into railway trains with his luggage. Then he'd stand at the window beckoning to people to come in whom he'd never seen or heard of. They rushed on! But one lady firmly got in and sat down and said: 'Oh, I know you, Lord Berners, I'm going to have this seat!'

PD   And reading his newspaper?

RHP There was somebody at the Carlton Club he didn't like, so he said he read *The Times* upside down because he couldn't read!

PD   Was it true that he'd take his temperature in a train compartment?

RHP Probably – and said he'd got scarlet fever!

PD   What about the bang in the night?

RHP When he was depressed and was talking about suicide he had Sacheverell and Georgia Sitwell staying. When they'd all gone up to bed and there was suddenly a tremendous bang. They all came rushing out of their rooms thinking Gerald had done it. He was just standing there and had taken

7 Lady Mosley asked him to write it – see her interview, Chapter 10, p. 92.

8 The *Internationale* has words written by Eugène Pottier in 1870 and melody by Pierre Degeyter in 1888.

9 Heber-Percy actually referred to Derek Jackson, confusing him with his twin brother Vivian (1906–36).

a paper bag and blown it up and gone bang! Georgia had been sent an enormous box of chocolates by Oswald Mosley, whom she was having a walk-out with. She said to Berners: 'What am I going to do with this box that Tom's given me? I can't bring it into the drawing room. Will you say you've given it to me?' Gerald said: 'No, I won't!' [*Laughs.*]

Diana [Mosley] was staying here with her eldest son Jonathan and a school friend. They all went out for a drive with Gerald, and the car had a puncture. Gerald was no good at cars, and neither were the boys, so Diana sent them for a walk in the fields and hailed a motorist, who stopped. He changed the wheel and did everything. Just as Diana was thanking him for helping the three of them came back. She was furious with them for arriving at the wrong moment and said: 'You could have waited a few minutes!' Jonathan said that Lord Berners said he was ready for tea! [*Laughs.*]

PD   Was it when he was in Rome that there was a misprint in a report about floods in Venice?

RHP When he had just inherited and was leaving the Embassy he was a handed a letter to reply to. It was from the Venetians complaining about a report in an Australian newspaper saying that Venice used to be a luxurious place but now it is full of nothing but beggars. Gerald was told to write back and smooth things over. He wrote back and said it was a misprint – for 'beggars' read 'buggers'! [*Laughs.*]

PD   Berners said his problem was that a psychiatrist had found a dead bird in his unconscious. Did he see a psychiatrist?

RHP I'm sure he did, but took it with a pinch of salt.[10] The big thing was when he tried to find God. So he sent for all the Oxford people, the rabbis, Catholics, and so on and they all came trooping out here like a shot, terribly excited about having a new convert. I came in afterwards and said: 'How did it go Gerald?' He said: 'They keep telling me that God loves us and I said: 'Is that any reason to love God?'[11]

Penelope [Betjeman] had become a Catholic and was an ardent proselytiser. She rang up one day and asked to see Gerald, but I had to say he wasn't very well and I'd ask him. He said: 'I don't mind Penelope as long as we have none of that God nonsense!' That set her back a bit. [*Laughs.*]

PD   Did he do anything for the local church?

RHP He put in the carillon. Then we had a new curate here. I met him and he said: 'I'm longing to meet Lord Berners. I know I shall get on very well with him.' So I said: 'Yes. Why?' He said: 'I was a curate in Chelsea where I used to meet all the artists and go and see them in their bed-sits and cook on gas rings ...' That was the end of him. [*Laughs.*]

10 'At times I have come to the conclusion that my character is utterly contemptible. This conviction reached such a pitch that I resolved to have recourse to psychoanalysis. Four times a week I visited an amiable Viennese Jewess, a pupil of Freud, and lay on a sofa in a small room in the Woodstock Road and was invited to say anything that came into my head (free association), evoke early memories and recount my dreams. (The first discovery I had was that I had a dead bird inside me ... walking with my nurse in the fields I came across a dead swallow. It was my first sight of death.) It transpired that most of the delinquencies of my character were due to the abnormal conditions of my early home life.' Amory, *Lord Berners*, 181.

11 Compare this with what Berners said about his grandmother: 'I didn't flatter myself that Lady Bourchier [Berners] was in the least fond of me. It would have been unreasonable, as Spinoza says of God, to expect that, even if I had loved her, she should love me in return.' *A Distant Prospect*, 108. 'We may regard his lifelong pursuit of beauty in every form as his religion.' A. L. Rowse, *Friends and Contemporaries* (London: Methuen, 1989), 72–3.

PD   Was it William Morris' daughter who particularly objected to the Folly?[12]

RHP When the fuss about the tower was going on a Miss Vivian Lobb wrote to the local newspapers saying that she had heard that Lord Berners was installing a siren to go off every two hours and which would waken the sick and dying. She signed herself Vivian Lobb. Gerald, who knew her very well, wrote that it would be better if Mr Vivian Lobb ascertained his facts before writing letters which looked as if they emanated from the brain of a crazy spinster!' That was the end of that! [*Laughs.*]

Lord Berners had no telegraphic address, and when I started a farm I needed some note-paper – or is it writing paper? I can never remember which. Nancy Mitford would tell us![13] I had to have a telegraphic address and Gerald said: 'Make it neighbourtease!'

PD   Did you actually do it?

RHP Yes. People running a farm don't generally get telegrams anyway! [*Laughs.*]

PD   What do think of Nancy Mitford's portrait as Lord Merlin?

RHP I think she loved him. They were very good friends.[14]

PD   She has this character, the daughter, who makes a silly marriage, then the family get angry and Lord Merlin buys her a house in Tite Street.

RHP That was Diana – in between marrying Guinness and Tom Mosley.

PD   So Nancy based that on how Berners treated her sister?

RHP Yes. I don't think he was out of pocket for long.

PD   Do you remember that story about the boa?[15]

RHP No, but I remember when a boa-constrictor was brought to Faringdon by Luisa Casati, the famous marchesa. It was when Lord Berners' mother was alive, and Mrs Tyrwhitt said: 'Wouldn't it like something to eat?' Luisa said: 'No, it had a goat this morning!' Mrs Tyrwhitt came to see Gerald and said: 'It does seem so inhospitable.'[16] [*Laughs.*]

PD   Harold Nicolson's representation of Berners as Titty in *Some People* is less realistic than his treatment of Firbank.

RHP Titty is nothing like him. Firbank was pretty horrid and took the mickey out of Harold. Gerald and Harold were at the Embassy in Constantinople, and Harold was always complaining that there were no aesthetes to talk to. But Firbank came and stayed in Constantinople – he was slightly more than Harold meant to deal with, but he felt he must ask him

12 May Morris (1862–1938), daughter of William Morris (1834–96) who is primarily associated with the Arts and Crafts Movement, lived with Vivian Lobb.

13 Nancy Mitford, ed., *Noblesse oblige: an Enquiry into the Identifiable Characteristics of the English Aristocracy* (London: Hamish Hamilton, 1956). She mentions Faringdon Folly, 56.

14 After Berners died Nancy Mitford wrote to Robert Heber-Percy: 'Please let me come to Faringdon. Nobody knows what he meant to me.' Mary Gifford, *Lord Berners: Aspects of a Biography* (PhD thesis, University of London, 2007), table 4.

15 Lord Merlin, in *The Pursuit of Love*, finds Linda reading 'Dieu que le son du cor est triste au fond des bois.' This is the final line of *Le Cor: Poèmes antiques et modernes* (1820) by Alfred de Vigny. Merlin adds: 'I had a friend, when I lived in Paris, who had a boa-constrictor as a pet, and this boa-constrictor got itself inside a French horn. My friend rang me up in a fearful state, saying: "Dieu, que le son du boa est triste au fond du cor."' Penguin edn, 145.

out for a picnic on the Bosporus. The whole of the Embassy came to see them off. Harold stood there by the man with the boat and another man with all the picnic things. No sign of Firbank. Then a boy came carrying an enormous sheaf of lilies and they handed them to Harold with a note saying: 'The day is too beautiful, don't let's spoil it all!' The Embassy never stopped ragging him about it.[17]

PD   Berners took off Nicolson in *Far from the Madding War* as Lollipop Jenkins?

RHP Harold wrote complaining, and Berners said: 'If you go on trying to shove yourself into my books I shall take out an injunction against you!'

PD   But wasn't that about Walton and *Count Omega*?

RHP He did it with both. The caricature didn't please either of them. Willie more than anybody.[18]

PD   Did you know that the vicar and his wife in *The Camel* were based on the Betjemans?

RHP It was very far-fetched.

PD   Berners must have relied on his driver William Crack a great deal.

RHP We were going out to lunch once, and the chauffeur took a wrong turning and we got lost, and went further and further away. Gerald said: 'William, I'm an old man and I've left you a lot of money in my will. I do think you might go the way I want sometimes!'

   The chauffeur didn't like driving abroad and once on the way to Rome we drove into a herd of cows. The horn of one of the cows just dented the mudguard slightly. William said: 'Nasty foreign cows. English cows wouldn't have done that!' [*Laughs.*]

PD   What was Edward James like?

RHP He was just a lot of trouble. He always made a bog of arrangements. He took Gerald's house in Rome, where there was a good couple to look after him, and claimed his mail had been stolen. He was endless trouble.

PD   How did Professor Jackson fit in?

RHP We knew him through the Lygons. He had an astonishing brain – best I've ever met. He drank a great deal and owned the *News of the World*, which was left him. He was invited to Madresfield and went hunting, never having ridden a horse before. Then he took up racing a great deal and rode in the Grand National. Won quite a lot of races. He had six wives!

PD   It's not easy to find anybody who's seen enough of Berners' paintings to say anything about them.

16 See interview with Sir Harold Acton, Chapter 3, p. 47, also Osbert Sitwell, *Laughter in the Next Room* (London: Macmillan, 1949), 181, where this story is confirmed and followed by a rare glimpse of Berners' mother.

   She remained, for a sensitive but conventional old lady, singularly unruffled under every circumstance. The hunting field and country pursuits claimed her interest, but her son's friends from London could not surprise her. From one evening I remember a scrap of conversation – she was engaged in solving a crossword puzzle.
   'What do you do', she asked me suddenly, 'when you are dealing the cards at bridge?'
   'Put the ace up my sleeve.'
   'Quite a wit, Mr Sitwell', she replied.

Lady Aberconway also remembered Mrs Tyrwhitt: 'He was devoted to his old mother, but couldn't resist training his parrot to walk across the room in front of her chair with his bowler hat covering the parrot with the brim almost sweeping the floor. Nevertheless this strange sight of a self-moving hat didn't seem to surprise Gerald's mother.' Christabel Aberconway, *A Wiser Woman?: a Book of Memories* (London: Hutchinson, 1966), 124–5.

17 Compare this with Sir Harold Acton's version, Chapter 3, p. 54.

18 Nicolson wrote a long letter of complaint to Berners on House of Commons notepaper on 18 December 1941 but wrote again to apologise for his 'bad humour' on 23 December. Gifford, *Lord Berners*, table 4. See Chapter 1, p. 78, for extracts from letters with Walton.

RHP There's not much to say about the paintings except that they're charming.

PD What was the most important thing to Berners?

RHP Music – undoubtedly.

PD His life and his friends were important too?

RHP I think he knew always exactly what he wanted his life to be. He was a fairly penniless young man – he had what his mother gave him, which wasn't very much – then he inherited a great deal. There were three large estates with huge houses in Lincolnshire, Leicestershire and Norfolk. When his mother wrote to him and said he must come back, he said: 'I'm not coming back; I'm studying under Stravinsky; tell them to sell the places and send the books and pictures here.' Of course, train-loads of books and pictures came which were put in the stables. When I came here I wanted the stables for some horses. So Gerald said, 'Do exactly what you like with them', so I put them in the hell-hole – only rescued them twenty years later.

PD I didn't realise that he had to make a decision about so much property.

RHP Absolutely straight. His mother wrote to say that one of his uncles had a mistress who was living it up drinking champagne and having wild parties in Leicestershire. He wrote back to say that any friend of his uncle, whom he never knew, must be very good. If she was living it up, the place would be sold in a couple of months and it didn't matter. He just got out of it.

PD What was the difference between Berners' three places – Faringdon, London and Rome?

RHP There was no difference. Any room of Gerald's would be in the same muddle. He had a very good cook in London and also in Rome. When I came to live at Faringdon I was looked after by the caretaker and his wife. Then when Gerald started to come here a lot he brought a cook down.

PD How did Cecil Beaton fit in?

RHP He didn't!

PD He was caricatured in *The Girls of Radcliff Hall*?

RHP He bought all the copies, which is why it's so rare now, because he comes out so badly in it. There were only about a hundred printed: he bought about fifty and burned them.[19]

PD Why did Berners mock him?

RHP I don't know, I really don't. I think Gerald must have written it before I had a row with Cecil. He does make him a ridiculous character.

19 *The Girls of Radcliff Hall* was privately printed at Faringdon under the *nom de plume* of Adela Quebec. Although apparently a schoolgirl story, it is a precise *roman à clef*. For the identification of characters, see interview with Daphne Fielding, Chapter 6, p. 67. Hugo Vickers reviewed the book's first trade publication (ed. John Byrne (London: Montcalm and The Cygnet Press, 2000) in the *Spectator* (26 August 2000): 'Beaton was always said to be the one who hated this book the most, feeling more socially insecure and less well-off than others in the group. When researching my biography of him [*Cecil Beaton* (1985)] I was certainly misled by Robert Heber-Percy into believing that Beaton had destroyed most of the copies. I am sure that the editor [of *The Girls of Radcliff Hall*], John Byrne, is right in his postscript to suggest that Heber-Percy … was more likely, and better placed as a resident of Faringdon and the boyfriend of Lord Berners, to have disposed of the copies.' See also interview with Lady Mosley, Chapter 10, p. 94.

20 Lady Diana Cooper (1892–1986), celebrated actress married to the politician and writer Duff Cooper, the prominent opponent of Chamberlain's appeasement who became Ambassador to France in 1944 and later Viscount Norwich.

PD   Berners gave an inscribed copy to Diana Cooper: 'To Diana with love from Gerald'.

RHP He didn't terribly like her. I remember going with her and Duff to a cinema. Gerald was absolutely bloody to her all evening, and as I came back I said: 'Why were you so bloody to Diana?' She was then about sixty. Gerald said: 'She's gone on too long!' Now she's ninety![20] [*Laughs.*]

PD   There was a feature about Berners and his music in *Gay News*, but in *Résenlieu* he talks about the landlady's daughter as if he's really falling in love with her. Is it possible?[21]

RHP I wouldn't have thought so. I mean he liked the company of women, but I don't think he ever fell for anyone particularly. He never talked about sex – so I don't really know.[22]

I think he liked people who behaved badly. He loved Doris Castlerosse, who was complaining she'd got no money. She really spent twenty times what Gerald spent in a year. I heard him say to her: 'Doris, if there's anything I can do to help I will.' She came over and kissed him, which was very surprising, because he didn't like being kissed, and said: 'Dear Gerald, anything you could do wouldn't last me two days!'[23]

PD   Liking people who behaved badly fits in with surrealist incongruity or putting moustaches on the family portraits. Do you remember that?

RHP Yes, I do. When I inherited there were a lot of hideous Victorian portraits. I thought I might as well send them to the new Lady Berners as a present. Then I went to look at them and they'd all got moustaches or he'd lowered their dresses down to their navel so I knew I couldn't send them!

PD   You mean he'd really painted in oil on top?

RHP Yes.

PD   Didn't he have enough family sense to want to preserve ...

RHP None. He had no family sense at all. He said: 'There have been only two distinguished Lord Berners – the one who translated Froissart and myself.[24] I see no reason why it won't be another four hundred years before there are any more.'

PD   That shows he knew his own worth, but what do you think about the interest in Berners with another generation? Did you dream of this even when he died?

RHP No. I didn't think about it. I knew his worth, and I didn't mind if anybody else did.

PD   But when I first met you about twelve years ago you didn't use to reply to enquiries.

21 'I believed that in France an amorous adventure, an affaire de cœur, was thought as important as, in England, the pursuit of manly sports, that if a young man thrown into the company of a young and attractive girl did not promptly fall in love with her he would be accounted a poor creature indeed. Thus it came about that I fell in love with Henrietta. If there was some degree of self-conscious effort in the summoning up of my passion, it was helped by the season and the environment, by the soft summer climate, the fragrance of flowers that filled the air as if with the incense of love's fever. However, in spite of these violent emotions it was a case of *si jeunesse savait* and my love was innocent and chaste ...' *The Château de Résenlieu*, 58–9.

22 'I do not suppose there had been much sex in his life: when he was approaching sixty he told me, that it was all over, and "a good thing, nothing but a nuisance".' Rowse, *Friends and Contemporaries*, 72, also 56.

23 Doris de Lavigne (1901–42), first wife of Viscount Castlerosse, later 6th Earl of Kenmare. Robert Heber-Percy was cited in her undefended divorce case, *The Times*, 18 December 1937. Gifford, *Lord Berners*, table 9.

24 *Lord Berners: a Selection from his Works*, ed. with an introduction by Vivian de Sola Pinto (London: Hamish Hamilton, 1936). John Bourchier (1467–1532/33), 2nd Baron Berners, was a member of an influential English family of the late Middle Ages. He was Chancellor of the Exchequer under Henry VIII, and in 1520 was appointed Deputy Governor of Calais, an English possession. His signature was attached to Henry VIII's divorce petition sent to Pope Clement VII in 1530. As an author he was primarily known for his translations of the Chronicles of Jean de Froissart undertaken at the command of Henry VIII.

RHP I didn't reply because I knew I'd give a wrong reply. That's slightly worse than giving none.

PD   Do you remember the exhibitions of paintings?

RHP They were held by Mr Reid in the Reid-Lefèvre Gallery. He was a very nice man who used to come down with some Corots that he'd discuss with Gerald. I went out of the room probably. Gerald would have one on trial for about a month to see if he liked it, and then they'd do a deal. Mr Reid wasn't like an art gallery now, where they shove it at you: he really minded what happened to the pictures. I suppose one thing Gerald didn't understand was about money. He always thought he was immensely poor – and convinced me that he was poor too, which was very clever! I used to be a hooligan and I'd break objects by knocking them down. I'd admit it and Gerald would say: 'It doesn't matter. It was given me by a dear friend who's dead.' After about a dozen things had gone I thought he'd got a hell of a lot of friends who'd died! [*Laughs.*] It was just to try and make me more careful.

PD   So he bought his Corots from the Reid Gallery, where he exhibited his own paintings?

RHP Yes. I don't know that he bought all his Corots there, but some certainly: they were only about £30.

PD   He really copied from Corot?

RHP When he was starting to paint he did.[25]

PD   Did he use writers as models in the same way?

RHP In the war he fell on Dickens, and he was always spouting about Nietzsche.

PD   That seems incredibly unlikely.

RHP I can remember something Nietzsche said: 'The higher you fly, the smaller you seem to those who cannot fly.'

PD   Did Berners quote that?

RHP Yes – at me! [*Laughs.*]

PD   Did Berners speak his own poem at the opening of Dalí's London exhibition?

RHP I only remember him opening it. Dalí was in a diving suit with a mask on. They couldn't get it off and struggled – it took up half the time.[26]

PD   What did Berners think of the exhibitionism of Dalí?

RHP He liked it. Dalí was a sweet friend and lived here for about three or four months – solidly. That's a long time to have anybody in the house! I was very fond of him, but I thought three or four months was a bit much.

PD   Do you remember the openings of the exhibitions?

RHP They were occasions with all the people that ought to

25 Amory, *Lord Berners*, 107, points out that Sir Robert Chiltern in Act 1 of Wilde's *An Ideal Husband* (1895) says: 'Corots seem to go with music, don't they?' He keeps his Corots in the music-room, but when Lord Goring is asked if he is going there, he retorts: 'Not if there is any music going on.'

26 Dalí's first London exhibition was at the Zwemmer Gallery, 24 October – 10 November 1934.

be there. The paintings were sold. I've only got about one that's signed. If he hadn't finished them he didn't sign them.

PD   Was he a kind of Sunday painter like Winston Churchill? Did they meet?

RHP They once stayed in the same house and went out painting together. Churchill was annoyed, threw his canvas away and started on another one. So Gerald picked it up, painting over, and started on it himself.

PD   To do all the things he did, Berners must have been very hard-working. What was his average day like?

RHP I think he was called at 8.00, with his tea, then he came down to breakfast about 9.00. I don't remember a day in his life when he did nothing. When he was ill he couldn't do anything. We tried occupational therapy, which I'd heard about, with a nice lady who tried to teach him knitting – and, after three times, just gave it up! [*Laughs.*]

PD   What about his connection with films?

RHP Cavalcanti was very nice. He came down here for a weekend, was charming to Gerald and built up his confidence. Gerald didn't think he could do the score for *Halfway House*, but I thought it was a very good thing for him to do – he enjoyed it.[27]

PD   Do you remember the song 'Come on Algernon' at the time?

RHP Only since you've been doing the music. I remember 'Red Roses and Red Noses' very well. Then I remember him playing the piano – about Penelope Betjeman. He used to quote Walter de la Mare's poem, *The Listeners*:

> 'Is there anybody there?' said the Traveller,
> Knocking on the moonlit door;
> And his horse in the silence champed the grasses
> Of the forest's ferny floor …

Then Penelope's voice came in: 'Yes, me, Penelope Betjeman. Have you ever been here before?' Then he used to turn round and hit the piano with his bottom![28] [*Laughs.*]

PD   What do you remember about the song 'Red Roses and Red Noses'?

RHP I just liked it.

PD   Why did he have an obsession with noses? There's Cleopatra's nose too in *The Romance of a Nose* (1941).[29]

RHP Maybe he didn't know himself.

PD   What about the ballets?

RHP I remember going to rehearsals and things. First nights followed by supper parties.

27 Alfredo Cavalcanti (1897–1982), Brazilian-born film director who in 1934 joined the GPO Film Unit, where he worked with Britten and Auden on *Coal Face* (1935) and *Night Mail* (1936). He joined Ealing Studios in 1940, and two of his feature films had scores by Berners: *The Halfway House* (1944), and *The Life and Adventures of Nicholas Nickleby* (1947). *Champagne Charlie* (1944) included two numbers by Berners. For details of these films, see interview with Sir Richard Rodney Bennett, Chapter 16, p. 142.

28 A version of this story, based on an earlier interview with Heber-Percy in 1976, appears in Bevis Hillier, *John Betjeman: New Fame, New Love* (London: John Murray, 2002), 17.

29 On 6 October 1910 Berners wrote to his mother from Constantinople mentioning an 'amusing series of dinner parties: one for bores, second for the people with red noses, third for all pregnant ladies. Indignation expected if guests work this out.' Gifford, *Lord Berners*, table 2, 86.

CHAPTER 10

Lady Mosley

Interview with Peter Dickinson on 28 June 1983 at 14 Sloane Court East, London SW3

1 Brian Masters, 'The Other Diana: Still Hated, after Fifty Years in Exile', *Night and Day, The Mail on Sunday Review*, 2 January 1994, 40–5. For a detailed account of the Mitfords, see Jonathan Guinness with Catherine Guinness, *The House of Mitford* (London: Hutchinson, 1984); Mary S. Lovell, *The Mitford Girls: the Biography of an Extraordinary Family* (London: Little, Brown & Co., 2001); and *The Mitfords: Letters between Six Sisters*, ed. Charlotte Mosley (London: Fourth Estate, 2007). See also Jan Dalley, 'Beauty and the Blackshirts', *Guardian Saturday Review*, 11 September 1999; 'Je ne regrette rien: Valerie Grove meets Diana Mosley', *The Times Weekend*, 27 April 2002; 'The Hon Lady Mosley', Obituary, *The Times*, 13 August 2003; A. N. Wilson, 'The Diana I knew', *Daily Telegraph*, 13 August 2003; Andrew Roberts, 'Diana Mosley, Unrepentantly Nazi and Effortlessly Charming', *Daily Telegraph*, 13 August 2003.

2 Harold Acton, *More Memoirs of an Aesthete* (London: Methuen, 1970), 184.

3 Anthony Masters, 'A Day in the Life of Lady Mosley', *Sunday Times Magazine*, 4 December 1983.

4 Diana Mosley, *Loved Ones: Pen Portraits* (London: Sidgwick & Jackson, 1985), 117. See Desmond Guinness, 'At Home with a Musical Eccentric', *Irish Times*, 23 May 1975, where he recalls his first visit to Faringdon as a child. Berners' unsigned painting of Faringdon House from across the lake is reproduced. He did at least two versions. See plate 29 for the signed painting.

5 Letter of 7 May 1987.

6 Sir Thomas Beecham (1879–1961) is supposed to have said: 'The English may not like music, ▶ ▶ ▶

THE HON. Diana Freeman-Mitford (1910–2003) was the third of the six famous Mitford sisters, daughters of the 2rd Baron Redesdale. In 1929 she married the Hon. Bryan Guinness, later the 2nd Baron Moyne, but divorced and married the fascist leader Sir Oswald Mosley in 1936. The previous year Diana had been to Germany with her sister Unity, who was in the grip of the obsession with Hitler that finally destroyed her. Unity contrived to meet him and introduced the dictator to her sister. Diana was bowled over to such an extent that she never recovered from this mesmerising first impression, and remained loyal to him as a person regardless of what he did. When the Mosleys married secretly the wedding took place in the drawing room of the Goebbels' house in Berlin, and Hitler gave them flowers and a photograph of himself in a silver frame. All this has overshadowed almost everything else about the Mosleys, who have been widely reviled.[1] But at a personal level things were different. Like many others, Harold Acton succumbed: 'All the Mitfords exerted a fascination purely English, clear-eyed, rose-petalled, instantaneous, which no caprice could shiver … no political difference could alter my affection for the radiant Diana.'[2] Because of their affiliations and Oswald Mosley's position as head of the British Union of Fascists the Mosleys were imprisoned or under house arrest for most of the war and, after a spell in Ireland, went to live in France in 1951. Here they came to know the exiled Duke and Duchess of Windsor, and as a result Lady Mosley wrote *The Duchess of Windsor* (1980). She published her own memoirs as *A Life of Contrasts* (1977) and followed it with *Loved Ones: Pen Portraits* (1985), which contains a long chapter about Berners. Like him she 'always felt truly European and … equally at home in Germany, France, Italy or England'.[3]

In *Loved Ones* Lady Mosley mentions a concert including some of Berners' music that was put on by her son Desmond Guinness. This was at Castletown House near Dublin on 12 June 1975, and was given by Meriel Dickinson (mezzo) with me (piano).[4] Some of Lady Mosley's published material about Berners resurfaces in her interview here. She came to the Berners Centenary Concert at the Wigmore Hall on 25 September 1983 and said later: 'It is wonderful the way you and your sister don't just talk about his music, but perform it and encourage others to do so. *He* would be delighted, that I'm sure of. He enjoyed painting but looked upon himself as a composer. One sees the whole man in his music – jokes but underlying sadness, with horrible depression as it were lying in wait for him.'[5]

It is important to emphasise that Berners was in no way a fascist, but it still seems extraordinary that some of his friends were in contact with the perpetrators of some of the most evil crimes in history, even though little of what we now know would have reached pre-war social circles. Ironically, as well as costing millions of lives, Hitler's wars were to hasten the end of the privileged world in which Berners and many of his friends lived.

DM I met Gerald when I was twenty-two and he forty-eight, and we instantly became great friends and remained so until he died about twenty years later. He was an absolutely perfect friend, not outwardly very affectionate because that was not his way. As far as music is concerned I correspond exactly to what Sir Thomas Beecham said of the English in general. 'They simply love the sound it makes but they know nothing about music.'[6] The first time I got to know him well was staying with the Hon. Mrs Ronnie Greville at Polesdon Lacey in 1932, when he motored me down in his Rolls-Royce. Mrs Greville had a wonderful cook, and Gerald was as greedy as I was. It was a link between us from the beginning. Also her unusual cattiness appealed strongly to him. He caught her voice when he repeated remarks she had made about a woman friend of us both: 'I'm very fond of a kitten but I'm not so fond of a cat!' I'm not sure Mrs Greville can ever have been a kitten![7] From the time of that visit I saw Gerald Berners continually. I stayed with him often at Faringdon and at Halkin Street when I had no London house. Two or three times I spent several weeks with him in Rome, where his house looked on the forum. He was the ideal companion and knew the city and the Campagna, where he used to paint in company with the Princess Marie Murat.[8] He had been *en poste* there as a young man. He knew exactly what to show one, adored beauty and allowed one to discover it for oneself – something older people can hardly ever do for the young. His jokes never failed to amuse the Romans. Not always easy to please, they delighted in the company of Lord Berners.

I should like to speak not so much of the composer, author, painter but about his genius for friendship and his wonderful loyalty. In 1940 at the end of the phoney war my husband was arrested and put in prison. There was no charge and therefore, of course, no trial. He had been advocating a negotiated peace while France, Britain and the Empire were intact. Gerald knew our point of view about the tragedy of European war by which England win or lose would be reduced in power and influence to the position it in fact has now. I don't think he was in the least interested in the Empire. But he was a complete European, and anyone could see from the outset that for Europeans to fight each other was disastrous for Europe. In any case, after my husband was arrested, in a moment of maximum panic in England caused by the fall of

▶ ▶ ▶
but they absolutely love the noise it makes.' *Beecham Stories: Anecdotes, Sayings and Impressions of Sir Thomas Beecham*, compiled and ed. Harold Atkins and Archie Newman (London: Robson Books, 1978), 29. Beecham made two recordings of *The Triumph of Neptune* (see Discography).

7 The Hon. Mrs Ronnie Greville was a famous hostess at Polesdon Lacey, Surrey, in the years following the death of her husband in 1908; her guests included royalty. George VI and Queen Elizabeth spent part of their honeymoon there. When Mrs Greville died in 1942 she bequeathed the house to the National Trust. There are various versions of a story that Berners told about Mrs Greville's butler. He was so drunk one evening at a dinner party that she gave him a note: 'You are drunk. Leave the room.' The butler simply put the note on a silver salver and handed it to the most pompous and probably distinguished person at the table. Mosley, *Loved Ones*, 97. A. L. Rowse remembered rather more. The butler 'staggered across and carefully placed it before the abstemious Sir John Simon', the foreign secretary who appeased Hitler. *Friends and Contemporaries* (London: Methuen, 1989), 193. Cecil Beaton recalled: 'Mrs Ronnie Greville was a galumphing, greedy, snobbish old toad who watered at her chops at the sight of royalty and the Prince of Wales' set and did nothing for anybody except the rich.' 'Follies of the Famous', *The Sunday Times Weekly Review*, 26 August 1973, and *The Strenuous Years: Diaries, 1948–55* (London: Weidenfeld & Nicolson, 1973). Beverley Nichols recalled that he once heard Mrs Greville tell a bishop at lunch that she was leaving her money not to the poor but to the rich. *The Sweet and Twenties* (London: Weidenfeld & Nicolson, 1958), 82.

8 Marie Murat (1876–1951), Princesse de Rohan-Chabot, later married diplomat Comte Charles de Chambrun.

France, Gerald came to spend a day with me. There was no Rolls-Royce: he struggled over in a couple of buses. He was living at Oxford, and several dons, he told me, begged him not to go to see me. It might compromise him in some way. It is hard to recapture now what that sort of panic is like. Gerald was not by nature particularly bold or adventurous, but he paid not the slightest attention to these timid dons. He came to see me. When I too was arrested he wrote to me the moment he heard it on the wireless. I only got the letter many weeks later because two a week was all we prisoners were allowed to receive, and I asked that my two should be one from my husband and one from my baby's nurse.

When I did get Gerald's letter it was covered in pin-holes which meant it had been sent by the prison censor to the Home Office. This is what he said: 'What can I send you? Would you like a little file concealed in a peach?' [*Laughs.*] It was so like him! He visited us in prison, bringing luxuries, and was sad that he was not allowed to give us his presents himself: they had to be opened and censored. When we were released and living under house arrest in an uncomfortable inn he came to stay, and when I wanted to get a house in Berkshire and went to look at it he gave me luncheon at Faringdon. Of course, I was in a police car with two policemen to guard me, and as he saw me off with these two uniformed men sitting in front he said: 'You're the only person now who has a chauffeur and a footman on the box!' [*Laughs.*] While I was in prison he sent me his books as they came out. After the war he continued to paint and to write: I don't think he composed much more music. He told me he wanted to do one more thing and that was to make a new delicious scent. He discovered from friends in Paris, notably the dress-maker Madame Schiaparelli, that making scent involved the use of something with an appalling smell.[9] I think it is secreted in the civet cat. In the end I dissuaded him and said: 'Imagine if you drop it at Faringdon you'd have to leave the house for weeks!'

Like so many very amusing clever witty people Gerald suffered from depressions. He had a bad heart – an illness which makes one pessimistic and gloomy. He often came to stay with us after the war at a house we had in Wiltshire and we tried to cheer him up. Once when he was there I had to go up to London for the day. When I got back he was on the doorstep: 'What did you do? Whom did you see?' I told him that I'd had lunch with Evelyn Waugh, who said he prayed for me every day. This made Gerald quite cross, and he said: 'God doesn't pay any attention to Evelyn!'[10]

After he took to his bed I went over to Faringdon as often as petrol rationing would allow. It is impossible to exaggerate

9 Elsa Schiaparelli (1890–1973), celebrated Parisian fashion designer who worked with artists such as Dalí, and whose creations were worn by famous beauties such as Daisy Fellowes.

10 Mosley, *Loved Ones*, 130. Berners was keen on gossip. When he was at the British Embassy in Rome he got to know Florence Baldwin, whose husband had caught her with her lover in her bedroom and killed him in a famous case of *crime passionel*. As Daphne Fielding relates: 'When he felt they had established sufficiently intimate terms, he ventured a question: "Do tell me, Mrs Baldwin, a little more about your husband." Florence looked him straight in the eyes and said: "He was a very good shot."' Daphne Fielding, *The Face on the Sphinx: a Portrait of Gladys Deacon, Duchess of Marlborough* (London: Hamish Hamilton, 1978), 37.

how perfect Robert Heber-Percy and Hugh Cruddas[11] were to him in those last dark days. (I put that because of what Cecil Beaton put in his diary, which is so unfair. Cecil evidently went and found him alone which, obviously, he sometimes was, and put in his diary that they did nothing for him.) They were gold, perfect and made life possible.[12] I think that his extraordinary loyalty was something people wouldn't realise he had.

[*End of prepared statement*]

PD   It does come out from what people have said to us. They talk about him, too, as an eccentric. Was he?

DM   I think he was fairly eccentric – not the ordinary normal peer by any means. When people asked him if he went to the House of Lords he used to say: 'No, I did go once and my umbrella was stolen by a bishop so I've never been again!' [*Laughs.*]

PD   Was he a gossip?

DM   Oh, tremendous: he adored gossip. He was very up and down in his moods. He could be talkative and gay at lunch, keeping everybody happy, then he'd be very down the whole afternoon probably. Then if somebody came to dinner he'd whizz up again. He really was a sort of depressed person but you had to know him rather well to see it. Once I said to him: 'Don't worry, you'll come out of it: you always do.' And he said: 'My mother had the same depressions and she died in the middle of one!' There was nothing left for me to say.

PD   His parents weren't particularly sympathetic to the kind of person he became.

DM   No. I think one sees that in the memoirs.

PD   Where did he get all these artistic interests?

DM   People have so many genes. In his ancestry there must have been people more like him than his parents were.

PD   What do you think mattered most to him?

DM   I think his music came first, intellectually, and he was very proud of the fact that Stravinsky thought so highly of it. Then after that, really and truly, friends and fun and talk.

PD   Did he take his novels seriously?

DM   I think he was delighted when they were a success. The best, I think, was *Far from the Madding War*. I wouldn't say he took them all that seriously.

PD   What about *First Childhood* and *A Distant Prospect*?

DM   I think they're beautifully written. You see he had enormous taste in everything he did – perfect I should say.

11 Friend of Heber-Percy who lived at Faringdon for a time. Prisoner of war in World War II, estate manager to Gavin, Lord Faringdon at Buscot Park.

12 Lady Harrod told Gavin Bryars: 'Cecil was a very spiteful character – I'm quite certain that Robert didn't neglect Gerald.' For further confirmation, see also Mosley, *Loved Ones*, 130–1. Sacheverell Sitwell wrote to Robert Heber-Percy after Berners' death: 'What amusing and lovely times we have all had. How well you looked after him.' Mary Gifford, *Lord Berners: Aspects of a Biography* (PhD thesis, University of London, 2007), table 4. The historian A. J. P. Taylor was at Berners' funeral: 'I went to Berners' cremation, one of the only two Oxford people there. Tinned music was played which Gerald would not have liked at all. Afterwards, Robert Heber-Percy, Gerald's friend to whom indeed Gerald had bequeathed his Faringdon House, greeted me and then turned to Isaiah Berlin, the other Oxford person present, and said: "Very good of you to come Maurice". I thought this very funny. Gerald would certainly have done so.' A. J. P. Taylor, *A Personal History* (London: Hamish Hamilton, 1983), 200. In fact Heber-Percy would not have met Berners' Oxford friends very often, especially after Berners became ill. To confuse Isaiah Berlin with Maurice Bowra at such an occasion was forgivable.

13 *The Daily Express*, 19 April 1934, 6. William Hickey's column contained a reproduction of eight bars of Berners' manuscript marked 'con brio'. The caption was: 'Original MS of opening bars of latest composition by Lord Berners – a Fascist March'. The rest of it has not survived, although I played what there was at the centenary concerts in 1983. The same column that day in 1934 had further news about Berners:

> DIED of jealousy aged 15: JOHN KNOX, emerald bird-of-paradise belonging to LORD BERNERS. Berners' luncheon guests are asked to wear half-mourning.
>
> BERNERS' newest project is the building of a 'folly' on a high hill near his Berkshire home, Faringdon: a tall, isolated ecclesiastical-looking tower in the middle of a clump of trees. Tower will be about 100ft high: of brick faced with stone; probably Gothic: square at the base, octagonal at the top, where there will be a room with a view. Great point of the tower is that it will be completely useless.
>
> ARCHITECT of Berners' folly is Lord GERALD WELLESLEY – once congratulated by a wit on being only living architect on whom a style of architecture had been named. 'What is that?' he asked. 'Why, the jerry-built style'. Wellesley took this totally unjustified aspersion in good part.

14 Mosley's British Union of Fascists held a rally at Olympia's Grand Hall on 7 June 1934. It was given considerable publicity, and free tickets could be obtained from the *Daily Mail*. L. W. Bailey was there ('I Witnessed a Mosley Riot', *The Times*, 6 March 1998), and has confirmed that Mosley modelled his tactics – black shirts and salutes – on Mussolini rather than Hitler. 'There was obviously a concerted effort by left-wing individuals and movements to be there. As a result a substantial proportion of the ▶ ▶ ▶

PD Did the war explain his depressions?

DM Only partly, because the gloom that sometimes came over him was endemic really. I think he always had it.

PD Do you remember that the *Daily Express* printed the music to the opening of his *Fascist March* in 1934?[13]

DM Oh yes. I asked him to write it and he did. He did it in Rome.

PD What was it used for?

DM Not very much, because I don't think it had words. The idea was to have a march and I said: 'You could write us a lovely one.'

PD Were those the early days when Mussolini was thought to be quite a good thing?

DM I think he thought so. Then he went to the Olympia meeting, the famous one when there was all the row.[14] He dined with me before it, but I wasn't well enough to go, and it's been a regret to me ever since that I never saw it with my own eyes. I've never been able to get to the bottom of what happened there – people tell such different stories. Gerald and Robert went and Vivian Jackson, who got himself arrested by what they call the Cossacks, the mounted police, and Gerald had to go and bail him out!

PD Robert says that Gerald Berners had lunch with Hitler. Can it be true?

DM It isn't true, I'm afraid. Did he say so?

PD Yes he did!

DM You see he stayed in Munich when my sister Unity and I were there, and we spent every day together. We went to the place where Hitler sometimes came for lunch, but in fact he didn't come while Gerald was there. I don't object to your saying he did if you want to, but it's not true.[15]

PD I think it's important to separate fact from legend.

DM He was terribly funny about Unity's extremism. He brought it all out and questioned her more and more about it – we laughed like mad! He wrote a little poem in German to amuse her about a great enemy of hers there:

> Rotraut Sperk, du kleine Nette,
> Bleib' bei mir im Ruhebette.
> Du bist ein schönes Gotteswerk,
> Du alleliebste Rotraut Sperk[16]

Rotraut Sperk was a real person whom my sister couldn't bear!

It's so difficult for anybody young now, because in those

days it never occurred to us what was going to happen later. So the fact that he went to Munich and enjoyed himself doesn't mean that he was a fascist. It's become so overlaid with legends.

PD You didn't feel that history was in the making while you were there?

DM No, absolutely not. Hitler was in the making, but the great fascination with him was that he was the person who was making the news. It was far more interesting to talk to him than someone like Winston, who was outside everything at that time. I did see him occasionally and I was very fond of him, but Hitler was something different. One felt that something was going to happen, and I'm afraid it did.

PD Do you remember much about Berners' relationship with your sister Nancy and their writing?

DM He was really my friend in the beginning. Then in the war he made great friends with her, and she stayed at Faringdon whilst she was writing *The Pursuit of Love*.[17] She either read aloud to him or he read bits as it went along. He did write to me about that and said how good it was. Faringdon was wonderful because it was complete peace and quiet, delicious food and everything perfect. It's so hard to write in your own house where the telephone keeps ringing.

PD Was she affected by his books that had been published for some time?

DM I should imagine so a bit – very much so by his jokes, which were rather similar to hers. Also by Evelyn.[18] I think she was very original, but the fact that *The Pursuit of Love* was the first mature book she wrote rather points to Gerald having had quite a big influence over her. It was her first best-seller, and after that everything was a best-seller.

PD That's a lovely portrait of Berners as Lord Merlin – nicer than Harold Nicolson's treatment.[19]

Jonathan Guinness: 'the Nazi press, in its endless stories of lascivious Jews seducing poor and innocent Gentile girls, very often had them doing it on a daybed.' Rotraut Sperk was the leader of the Nazi girl students. *The House of Mitford*, 344.

17 Nancy Mitford (1904–73). Mosley, *Loved Ones*, 126. See 'Nancy Mitford: an Outstanding Writer', Obituary, *The Times*, 2 July 1973. Harold Acton, *Nancy Mitford: a Memoir* (London: Hamish Hamilton, 1975), 53–4. Mitford's appreciation of Faringdon is documented in 'Faringdon House', *House and Garden*, August–September 1950, which is also an obituary tribute to Berners. It ends: 'Faringdon was solid and elegant and so was Lord Berners. So great was his sense of elegance, fantasy and humour that the solid quality of his talents, and above all the immense amount of hard work he did all his life, are sometimes overlooked, though a moment's reflection would show that without great talent and hard work he could not, as he did, write and paint like a professional, in addition to shining as a composer of music.' Faringdon House, during the ownership of Robert-Heber Percy, has often been the subject of articles. See Mark Girouard, 'Faringdon House, Berkshire', *Country Life*, 12 & 19 May 1966.

18 Evelyn Waugh (1903–66). See Mosley, *Loved Ones*, 52–69.

19 Lord Merlin is a delightful character in Mitford's *The Pursuit of Love* (1945), but he is also mentioned in *Love in a Cold Climate* (1949), which is dedicated to Berners. The blimpish philistine Uncle Matthew in *The Pursuit of Love* was worried about asking Lord Merlin to their ball: 'If we ask that brute Merlin to bring his friends, we shall get a lot of aesthetes, sewers from Oxford, and I wouldn't put it past him to bring some foreigners.' Penguin edn, 41. Harold Nicolson, *Some People* (London: Constable & Co., 1927).

▶ ▶ ▶

audience was hostile. There were also, however, a number of respectable right-wingers who sensed here a possible bulwark against the growing menace of communism.' After enduring extensive heckling, Mosley lost his temper; the result was described as the worst riot seen in Britain for thirty years; and the British Union of Fascists lost credibility and most of its support. (*The Times* report, 14 June 1934).

Jonathan Guinness claims that Berners' *Fascist March* was played at that meeting, which seems unlikely. *The House of Mitford*, 344.

15 William Crack, Berners' chauffeur, was there – see interviews with him, Chapter 4, p. 59, and Robert Heber-Percy, Chapter 9, p. 79.

16 'Rotraut Sperk, you nice little thing, Stay with me on the daybed. You are a lovely work of God, darling Rotraut Sperk.' According to

DM Of course, Harold Nicolson's relationship with Gerald Berners was almost stormy. Gerald couldn't resist making jokes about Harold, and he didn't like it.[20]

PD What was the atmosphere surrounding that first book *The Girls of Radcliff Hall*?

DM He wrote it in Rome. While I was staying with him he got up very early and used to come up and sit on my bed and read bits out of it. It was so funny with him being the headmistress, but you've got to know the people.

PD Apparently Cecil Beaton burnt some copies? Is that true?

DM I don't know.

PD That's what Robert told us. Again it's part of the legend – apparently he was so angry he burnt any copies he could get his hands on!

DM I think it's quite possible.[21]

PD People have said that Lord Berners used to wear masks when being driven in his car. Was that true?[22]

DM I don't know whether he did or not. [*Laughs.*] He used to say he wore tinted spectacles because his eyes were so kind. If anyone saw them he'd be a prey to beggars![23]

PD That's probably how the story started. Do you remember the building of the Folly?

DM Yes, it's Gerry Wellesley, afterwards Duke of Wellington, isn't it? So pretty. Funnily enough it was called Folly Hill before he built the Folly. I think I know the reason, because our little Temple in France is what they call a folly – it was built for one of Napoleon's generals, hence Temple de la Gloire. Apparently, some learned French person told me, it doesn't mean somebody who does something a bit mad, it means something where there's foliage – and therefore it's in the country and surrounded by trees. That's exactly the case in Folly Hill.

PD Do you remember his painting of the Folly that became a Shell poster? [See plate 55.]

DM Yes.

PD What do you think of his paintings?

DM They're very charming and I think he was tremendously influenced by Corot – in fact it's obvious. He loved Corot so much and collected him. He did lovely paintings in the Campagna. The stories of him and Marie Murat are so wonderful. She was living with the French ambassador, and in the end the Pope insisted on them getting married. So they did and she became Marie de Chambrun. She'd lived with

20 An advertisement in the Personal Column of *The Times*, 21 December 1936: 'Lord Berners wishes to dispose of two elephants and one small rhinoceros (latter house-trained). Would make delightful Christmas presents.' Questions began to be asked: a newspaperman telephoned Faringdon House. Lord Berners answered himself, and pretended to be the butler. 'Actually, I haven't seen the rhino myself, sir, but it's often about the house. It's quite gentle I'm told. The weather was getting too cold for the elephants, so I'm glad they've gone. They went on Saturday. I understand Mr Harold Nicolson has bought one and Lady Colefax the other. I hope they have good homes.' When approached, Mr Nicolson said grimly: 'I have NOT bought an elephant! I do not intend to buy one! I do not want an elephant and I have nowhere to put an elephant! This looks like a joke. I have known Lord Berners for twenty-five years, but I don't feel friendly to him this morning.' Lady Colefax was equally indignant: 'Of course I haven't bought an elephant from Lord Berners or anyone else!'

21 See interview with Robert Heber-Percy, Chapter 9, p. 84.

him for years when he was Ambassador in Constantinople, and a very shy young man came in the drawing room when she was there alone and said: 'Je m'addresse à la maîtresse de maison?' She replied: 'Maîtresse – oui. Mais je ne m'occupe pas la maison.'

One story used to make me laugh so much. Gerald used to go for a sort-of cure at Richmond, and the Reynolds Albertinis used to ask him for luncheon. One day Mr Reynolds Albertini told him that he'd had a siesta the day before, and when he woke up and looked out of the window the whole lawn was white. So he rang the bell and said to the footman: 'What is all that white out there?' The footman said: 'It's the 'ail, sir.' 'What? One small bird did all that?' 'I didn't say the owl but the hail, sir!' [24] [*Laughs.*]

PD How do you think Berners could appeal to the young these days?

DM There's every reason why he should, because what he did was extremely good in its own way. Of course, he wasn't an abstract painter, but you might say a clever exponent of the school of Corot.

PD Could you compare him with Constant Lambert?

DM Constant wasn't half as amusing as Gerald. He was a charming person but he wasn't someone who made you scream with laughter the way Gerald did.

PD How did he speak?

DM He spoke in a very short rather gruff way. He seldom laughed himself, but when he did it was like a terrific sneeze. Haw-haw-haw, rather low. Otherwise he sort-of giggled to himself a little bit. It used to amuse my husband so much when he shouted all over Faringdon 'Robert! Robert!', like an old colonel. There was a touch of that in Gerald, which was so unexpected.

PD Somebody said he looked like a businessman.

DM No, he was very neat, beautifully dressed.

He was so funny too the way he brought himself down to the level of little children. When he used to stay with us there were the strip-cartoons in the *Daily Mirror* and my children, then aged about seven and eight, said: 'Where's the *Daily*?', wanting the strips, and Gerald would say: 'Those children have taken the daily!'

Then there was a friend of ours who'd had many lovers and they got younger and younger. One day Gerald was lunching in the Ritz and she came in with her little boy who was at a private school aged eleven and he said: 'This time you're going too far!' [*Laughs.*]

My sister Pamela and her [then] husband Derek Jackson

22 'Ronald Firbank was coming to lunch with me one day in Rome. It was shortly after the publication of *Prancing Nigger*. Thinking I heard Ronald approaching the house, a sudden impulse seized me to put on a Negro mask and surprise him by appearing at one of the windows. However, it was not Ronald after all. And a small boy who happened to be passing on a bicycle looked up and was so frightened that he fell off and was run into by a motor. He was luckily unhurt but a crowd collected. At this juncture Ronald himself arrived, and when I explained to him what had happened he said: "That will teach him to concentrate in future." Ifan Kyrle Fletcher, *Ronald Firbank, a Memoir* (London: Duckworth, 1930), 84–5. In *Loved Ones*, 125, Lady Mosley recalled that Lord Lambton told her that he once asked Berners about the masks, and that he had said: 'They made a great impression in France and Italy but in England people thought it was the squire out for a drive!'

23 Lord Merlin in *The Pursuit of Love* says: 'Oh, the spectacles – I have to wear them when I go abroad. I have such kind eyes, you see, beggars and things cluster round and annoy me.' Penguin edn, 143.

24 Mosley, *Loved Ones*, 113.

were great friends of Gerald's. They were mad about two little long-haired dachshunds they had. Gerald used to say:
'The trouble with the Jacksons is that they've got bow-wows
in their bonnet!'

He had jokes around the house at Faringdon. For example,
there'd be a dust jacket on one of the books by your bed saying: 'This is the hottest thing written in the last twenty years
– sex, crime, violence ...' Then when you opened it – it would
be the Bible! And he had a printed notice on the stairs which
he'd got from somewhere: 'MANGLING DONE HERE'.[25]
[*Laughs.*] You must admit he was eccentric!

PD Do you remember his connection with the Sitwells, who
were also eccentric and involved in all the arts?

DM He was very fond of them, and loved the stories about
Sir George, their father. Sir George was very punctual and
Sashie and Osbert weren't always. They were supposed to be
meeting to eat in a restaurant and they came in, and when
Sir George was annoyed he used to make a sort of buzzing
sound. He was annoyed and he was buzzing, and he said to
Osbert: 'I'm just deciding which table to settle on.' He made
a sound exactly like a bluebottle!

PD Did Berners know about the trouble Sir George caused
his children?

DM Oh, completely because they never stopped talking and
writing about it. But Sir George was a charming old man to
meet. Gerald was very fond of one Sir George story. There
was an enormously deep well at Montegufoni. When he was
showing visitors around in order to show the depth he would
light a piece of straw and drop it down the well so you could
see it go down, down, down. One day Osbert said to Sashie:
'I wish father would light his beard and throw himself down
the well!' (laughs)

Another aspect of Gerald was his great love of everything.
We discovered that the Empire cinema started its programme
at ten in the morning, so Gerald and I used to go at ten and
then go back to Halkin Street for lunch – fairly debauched![26]
[*Laughs.*]

PD With hardly anybody in the cinema?

DM Nobody except us!

PD What did he like to see?

DM Everything: he was very uncritical.

PD Then he wrote film scores himself.

DM I didn't know that. Is it true he didn't write much after
the war?

25 This was one of several notices
that Nancy Mitford mentions as
at Merlinford. She also said: 'As
Lord Merlin was a famous practical
joker, it was sometimes difficult
to know where jokes ended and
culture began. I think he was not
always perfectly certain himself.' *The
Pursuit of Love* (Penguin edn), 40–3.

26 Berners' London house was
3 Halkin Street, SW1.

PD He did a little piece for Penelope Betjeman's Nativity Play called *The Expulsion from Paradise* in 1945.

DM That was so funny. He telephoned me and said: 'It went off wonderfully. Penelope was God the Father, and she chased the children out of the church.' 'Out of the church? I should have thought she would have chased them into it!' 'Oh no', he said. 'They were Adam and Eve and this was the Garden of Eden.' Typical Penelope! But he seemed to become more of a writer in his later years.

PD He also wrote about his time in Résenlieu and Dresden as a young man.

DM He had lovely stories about Dresden, when they were learning German. He used to go to the theatre with the woman who looked after him or taught him German. He used to prefer to go to Ibsen and Strindberg but she always went out with her nose in the air and say: 'Ich ziehe vor ein elegantes Salonstück!' [I prefer an elegant drawing-room comedy] [27] [*Laughs.*]

PD He thought the Germans were rather funny?

DM He thought the whole world was funny. What he thought funniest of all in the language line was Dutch. He used to say that 'Oh death, where is thy sting' was in Dutch: 'O tot wo ist sein stichel?' [28]

PD Did you go to the ballets?

DM Yes, *A Wedding Bouquet*, and I saw a good deal of him while he was doing it – and Gertrude Stein. It was typical of him to choose Gertrude Stein. There's no doubt that he loved what was fashionable at the moment. That was the charm of Schiaparelli too. He was fascinated most about where fashionable life bordered on artistic life.

PD Did he take Stein seriously?

DM No, never. But he thought it was fun, amusing and she was a clever old woman. Her collection of pictures was remarkable, but I think he thought the writings were real rubbish.

PD There's so much of them too.

DM Agony! They had to pretend at the time to think that Alice Toklas was also rather wonderful, but she really was a most fearful bore!

I do remember *A Wedding Bouquet*, what the scenery was like and how the bouquet came down at the end. Of course, he was a great admirer of Diaghilev, as anyone must be. It was so interesting, if you're my age, to see the wonder of the Diaghilev ballets – and then the *dégringolade* that happened so quickly after his death. I think Diaghilev had an immense

27 Mosley, *Loved Ones*, 111.

28 Lady Mosley seems to have slipped into a kind of German here. The Dutch Authorised Version (1618–19) for Corinthians I, chapter 15, verse 55 is: 'Dood, waar is uw prikkel? Hel, waar is uw Overwinning?'

influence over him, and so had Stravinsky. He once said to me that Stravinsky was the only genius he'd ever known. Nobody who has only seen ballet since Diaghilev can imagine the excitement of what it was then.

PD   And George Balanchine, who choreographed Berners' first two ballets, continued that tradition.

DM   I think Cuevas did good ballets, and Boris Kochno, who did some rather wonderful ballets with Edward James and Tilly Losch.[29]

PD   What was the connection with Edward James?

DM   I once spent Christmas at Faringdon, and Edward was there, also Gladys Marlborough. In the Christmas pudding Gerald put nothing but thimbles and buttons, so that nobody got a ring or anything nice, like sixpence! [*Laughs.*] So typical.

PD   He was a gourmet?

DM   His food was so wonderful, even in the war.

PD   Do you remember when Stein and Toklas came to lunch, but when Stein declined all the courses, Toklas explained: 'Gertrude doesn't eat Tuesday'?

DM   [*Laughs.*] Alice B!

PD   What's your final recollection of him?

DM   His being such a loyal friend, when it was almost dangerous. It's so important because it's so rare. He was always there if one was in any trouble. It isn't as if he was one of these very bold people who'd stick his head into a wasp's nest.

PD   So it cost him an effort?

DM   It was just a wonderful quality he had.

29 Jorge Cuevas Bartholin (1885–1961), who ran the Grand Ballet du Marquis de Cuevas; Boris Kochno (1904–90), Russian dancer and writer, Diaghilev's companion and collaborator, who provided the story for Berners' second ballet *Luna Park*; Tilly Losch – see introduction to interview with Edward James, Chapter 5, p. 63.

CHAPTER 11

Sir Frederick Ashton

Interview with Peter Dickinson on 3 August 1983
at 8 Marlborough Street, London SW3

S IR Frederick Ashton (1904–88; see plates 5, 7) was born in Ecuador and went to school in Lima, Peru, before continuing his schooling in England. When he was twelve or thirteen he saw Pavlola dance, which was a crucial experience, and he later had his first lessons from Léonide Massine. Ashton was a dancer and choreographer with the Ballet Rambert 1926–33; with the Ida Rubinstein Company in Paris, 1929–30; and he was founder-choreographer of the Vic-Wells Ballet (later the Royal Ballet) in 1933, and director of the company, 1963–70. He was widely celebrated as one of the greatest choreographers of the twentieth century, whose work defined the classical style in English ballet. His honours included the CBE (1950), the Légion d'Honneur (1960), knighthood (1962), CH (1970), OM (1977) and several honorary degrees. He choreographed the last three of Berners' five ballets.[1]

1 See Julie Kavanagh's detailed study, *Secret Muses: the Life of Frederick Ashton* (London: Faber, 1996). Also Ashton quoted by Brian Connell in, 'Sir Frederick Ashton: the Boy from Lima who Made Good', *The Times*, 20 March 1978: 'I don't believe that by setting out to be profound you necessarily are profound. You can do something quite light which may be more profound if you look into it.' Ashton would have applied that to Berners too.

2 C. B. Cochran (1872–1951), impresario and producer responsible for many of the most popular theatrical productions of the interwar period. Berners' *Luna Park* was premièred at the Palace, Manchester, on 4 March 1930, and included in Cochran's *Revue of 1930* at the London Pavilion and dedicated to him. It was the second of Berners' ballets with choreography by George Balanchine.

3 *Foyer de danse* was given by Ballet Rambert, Mercury Theatre, London, 9 October 1932. Benjamin Britten was there, and thought it 'very amusing'. *Letters from a Life:the Selected Letters and Diaries of Benjamin Britten, 1913–1976, vol. 1: 1923–1939*, ed. Donald Mitchell and Philip Reed (London: Faber, 1991), 282.

4 Opera by Virgil Thomson (1896–1989), words by Gertrude Stein (1874–1946), scenario by Maurice Grosser, Avery Memorial, Hartford, Connecticut, 8 February 1934.

PD Do you remember when you first met Gerald Berners?

FA A Cochrane review contained a ballet about freaks called *Luna Park* with music by Berners.[2] I wanted to use that music for something at the Ballet Club, and I did a kind of Degas thing called *Foyer de Danse*, and so I must have gone to see him about that in Halkin Street.[3] He was very accommodating and said just go ahead. I think he came to see it and was quite pleased. In that way we started a collaboration.

PD It's almost fifty years since you choreographed *Four Saints in Three Acts*.[4] Was that your first connection with Gertrude Stein?

FA Yes, but I didn't know her then, because she didn't appear at all. It was purely through Virgil Thomson and Maurice Grosser.

PD You are a link between *Four Saints* and *A Wedding Bouquet*. How did Berners get involved with the sets and painted backcloth?

FA He pretty well thought it all out himself. He'd been in contact with Stein and Constant Lambert, and I came in later. I think Berners always intended to do the scenery and costumes himself.[5] Constant helped with the spoken rather

5 Berners saw a carpet, made by an old woman in Virginia, at Gertrude Stein's house at Bilignin, made a drawing from it, and decided to use it as backcloth to *A Wedding Bouquet*. Gertrude Stein, *Everybody's Autobiography* (London: Heinemann, 1938), 192.

than the sung choral version of the text, and recited it himself.[6]

PD The recent revival of *A Wedding Bouquet* has rightly gone back to full use of the chorus. How did Berners feel about the use of speaking voice?

FA I think he didn't mind because it was wartime and it was very expensive to have a whole chorus. But some people liked it because they could hear the words. Gertrude Stein, I remember, was upset because you couldn't hear the words enough when it was sung.

PD What do you feel about the choice between sung and spoken text?

FA It depends on the aptness, so to speak, of what you're doing. I liked it personally with the chorus better than with the words. I find the narrator becomes too dominant and too distracting. From my point of view, when it's sung, you can concentrate more on the choreography, and you can see what it's all about rather than having somebody flinging their own personality at you rather too strongly.[7]

PD I was delighted to hear the chorus because it's got good tunes.

FA Yes, marvellous tunes. I used to call him a governess for waltzes because it sounded like a frustrated governess pounding away at an upright piano! [*Laughs.*] That's the impression I used to get from them.

PD There's that photograph taken at Faringdon with Lambert at the piano, Berners looking on and you in the foreground. [See plate 5.] Do you remember?

FA Yes, I do. There are also photos where Berners was dressed in a kind of oriental thing with a hat on. I went to Faringdon quite a lot, especially when we were doing *A Wedding Bouquet*. Then Stein came over for it. That was my first contact with her.

PD Were you disappointed with her?

FA Oh not at all. You couldn't be disappointed! As a couple [with Alice B. Toklas] they were so extraordinary.

PD Do you think Berners took her seriously as a literary modernist?

FA Probably up to a point. I think he was amused by it. He liked anything turned upside down. The fact that it didn't make sense appealed to him.

PD Was Berners of professional standard as a designer?

FA Oh yes. He was a professional in every way. He was called an amateur, but he worked very hard: if you wanted anything changed he would do it in a highly professional way.

6 See Richard Shead, *Constant Lambert* (London: Simon Publications, 1973), 162: 'It was perhaps as well that Miss Stein was never present at the wartime performances, for Lambert did not regard her text as sacrosanct and was apt to interject comments of his own. On one occasion the dancer playing the maid was taken aback to hear the words "Webster your shoes are creaking!" issuing from Lambert's stage box.'

7 See John Percival, 'Travesty of Ashton's work', *The Times*, 10 November 1989, where he criticises the use of Anthony Dowell as speaker, and finds the expressive voice of actor Derek Jacobi even worse. He concludes: 'Can it be that, not much more than a year after Ashton's death, the Royal Ballet is forgetting how to do his works?' This was the 53rd performance of *A Wedding Bouquet* at Covent Garden by the Royal Ballet since 17 February 1949. When it was given on 11 March 1983 chorus was used. 'An Incandescent Marriage of Two Minds: Ashton ballets', *The Times*, 11 March 1983.

He presented his music professionally, and it was the same with designs.

PD Some people say that he was an amateur in his writing and painting, but better in his music, while the ballet brings several things together.

FA Of course, he had so many talents really, with his writing, his painting and the extraordinary things that he did.

PD Do you remember Berners' backcloth for *A Wedding Bouquet* based on a carpet Gertrude Stein had?

FA I thought it was supposed to be her house at Bilignin, but I don't remember exactly.

PD It's very characteristic of his oil paintings. Have you got any yourself?

FA No. I've been very stupid all through my career. I've never got anything out of anybody! [*Laughs.*] It's true. It never occurred to me to ask for a design from anybody. I could have got one out of Derain even. Unless they gave me one, I never touted for it.

PD How important are the five ballets which are central in Berners' output – two choreographed by Balanchine and three by you?

FA I don't know about important. It depends on what their lasting quality will be. Of the ones that I did with him *A Wedding Bouquet* has stood up best.[8]

PD *Cupid and Psyche* came just before the war in 1939.[9] Wasn't it booed?

FA Yes it was. We made a mistake by taking a serious subject, and towards the end we guyed it. I can't remember clearly but I think the end was a sort of festival of the gods. Jupiter and his wife Juno came in, and I treated him like Mussolini. [They saluted.] Funnily enough, Gerald brought Bernard Shaw to see it, and he said: 'You've made the same mistake I did. You can't take a serious subject and halfway through change your whole attitude. It never works.' I remember Shaw saying that to me as he was getting into his taxi.

PD You had stunts like Cupid whizzing up on a wire at the end?

FA Yes, it was quite elaborate. Gerald paid for the scenery and the costumes.

PD Which he hadn't designed?

FA No. It was Francis Rose, whom Gertrude Stein used to call a genius.[10] Nobody else seemed to!

PD Cupid was invisible, which must have been quite hard for a dancer.

FA It was. It's a stupid story because she mustn't see him, yet

8 P. W. Manchester, *Vic-Wells: a Ballet Progress* (London: Gollancz, 1946), 36–7: 'On 27 April 1937 Ashton could chalk up another success … *A Wedding Bouquet* … It was all terrific fun, in which both audience and dancers joined … Mary Honer … as the bride … was abysmally silly, the incarnation of a giggle … Robert Helpmann's bridegroom … captured exactly the spirit of burlesque … June Bray made another hit as the tippling Josephine … as the dog Julia Farron received her first press notices. Only Margot Fonteyn struck a false note … with an incongruous tragic element out of place in this heartless frolic.' Ninette de Valois, as the maid Webster, made her last appearance as a dancer in this ballet.

9 See plates 6, 7, 8, photographs taken at the 1939 première.

10 Sir Francis Rose (1909–79), painter and designer. See his autobiography *Saying Life* (London: Cassell & Co., 1961).

11 Manchester, *Vic-Wells*, 43 & 57: 'The Ashton-Berners ballet *Cupid and Psyche* was given on 2 April 1939. It was a complete failure, in which Ashton's invention seemed to have deserted him entirely. He was able to do nothing with a story which one would have expected to have had a great appeal for him. He conceived Venus as a vulgar little chit from the chorus of a non-stop revue, and his Jupiter marched about the stage making fascist salutes and hiccupping violently … the one really resounding flop of his career.'

12 *Les Sirènes* opened with the Sadler's Wells Ballet at the Royal Opera House on 12 November 1946. Choreography was by Ashton and costumes and sets by Cecil Beaton. Mark Amory quotes a letter from Roy Douglas (1907–) indicating that he did most of the orchestration and was not credited: *Lord Berners: the Last Eccentric* (London: Chatto & Windus, 1998), 226. Beaton recalled: 'Gerald was beginning to suffer from the illness from which he died, and was, no longer, at the height of his powers. His perverse and comic music … was not in the serious mood of the moment when post-war ballet enthusiasts were looking for something more significant. The ballet soon faded from memory.' Cecil Beaton, *The Happy Years: Diaries, 1944–48* (London: Weidenfeld & Nicolson, 1972), 96. However, Constant Lambert described *Les Sirènes* as Berners' last and 'in my opinion, most brilliant work … an Edwardian pastiche which wonderfully combines slapstick and sentiment.' 'The Uncommon Man: Lord Berners', *Strand*, April 1947, 62–3. Both *Cupid and Psyche* and *Les Sirènes* are recorded with the RTE Sinfonietta/David Lloyd Jones, Marco Polo DDD 8.223780 (1995).

you have to do *pas de deux* and all that kind of thing! I can't remember how we got by with it.[11]

PD   What was *Les Sirènes* like just after the war in 1946?[12]

FA   By then Gerald was a bit in decline. He wasn't entirely with it, which made it rather difficult. At first it was all right, but by the time it came to be staged he was a little bit waffly. The war had upset him terribly. He felt it was the loss of his world and everything that he liked – frivolity and a light touch towards everything. The war upset his way of life too.

PD   He was really a European?

FA   He was very European and fond of his contacts with the Princesse de Polignac and Mrs Reginald Fellowes, and he liked a foreign element.[13]

PD   Did you see him in Italy?

FA   No, I didn't know him then.

PD   *Les Sirènes* had eighteen performances, but *Cupid and Psyche* only three.

FA   Only three? Then the war came I suppose.

PD   It's not been revived?

FA   No.

PD   Do you think, from a dance point of view, that the music of the last two ballets is as good as *Wedding Bouquet*?

FA   No. I think *Wedding Bouquet* is the best, and perhaps *The Triumph of Neptune*, which has some good music in it.

PD   How does Berners compare with other composers you've choreographed, such as Bliss or Lambert?

FA   It's difficult to compare. He had so much his own idiom – it was a much lighter approach than Lambert or other composers of that time. Berners was a law unto himself: unique in a way.

PD   Berners seems closest to the world of ballet. You can even feel Delibes?

FA   I think so, because he enjoyed the ballet. He studied Tchaikovsky and Delibes when he was doing things, and took his cue from them. I remember one weekend when Stravinsky was there. He used to play things to Stravinsky, who would make suggestions to him.[14]

PD   Can you remember any particular occasion?

FA   Once Stravinsky sat down at the piano and played the Valse lente from *Sylvia* and said: 'Oh, comment c'est ravissante!', which was very surprising when one thought of what his own music was like![15] He and Gerald would spend time together.

   At Faringdon it was very lively indeed. You had a mixture of very sophisticated Continental people, upper-class

English people, and then artists. The Betjemans were there quite a lot and, before sitting down, Penelope would say: 'Gerald, what's the pud?' [*Laughs.*]

PD Can you remember any examples of his schoolboy sense of humour?

FA No, I can't. That's the sort of thing I'm bad at. I remember him and Robert having rows and throwing things at each other!

PD Did you ever read his books?

FA Yes. I read *The Romance of a Nose* and *The Girls of Radcliff Hall*. I think I read them all.

PD Do you know why he wrote *The Girls*?

FA I think he took *The Well of Loneliness* by Radclyffe Hall and was guying that. It was trying to make out that Lesbianism was something very high minded – a kind of women's lib very early on. Have you ever read it?

PD I tried.

FA That's what I mean – impossible isn't it?[16]

PD Did you realise that Berners' spoof was based on actual people?

FA Sort of, yes. I may have known some of them.

PD *The Girls* was a private publication, but *First Childhood* and *A Distant Prospect* became widely known.

FA I seem to remember that amongst the books by the bedside at Faringdon you had what looked like a Bible or a classic like *The Mill on the Floss*, but inside it was a pornographic book!

PD You worked very closely with Lambert. How does he compare with Berners?

FA He was a more serious musician. I don't think Gerald ever strained himself to be profound or to make a real musical statement in any way. He was perfectly happy to entertain. Maybe in the back of his mind he may have had more serious things, but that was not what came through.

PD Did they have the same sense of humour?

FA Very much so. The collaboration was not torture, but all fun and amusing, being at Faringdon and living extremely well with wonderful food.

PD Harold Acton has said that if Berners had tried to do less he'd have been less versatile but more profound.

FA I don't agree. His talents were light all the way through. I don't think if he'd stuck to his painting he'd have been a better painter. He had a light talent.

PD Do you think he found himself in the ballet scores rather

13 The American Winnaretta Singer, Princesse de Polignac (1865–1943), was heir to the Singer sewing machine fortune, and a generous and influential musical patron. Her niece Daisy Fellowes (1890–1962) 'possessed exactly the fashionable elegance that Berners admired': Amory, *Lord Berners*, 172.

14 Berners wrote on his copy of the score of the piano duet version of *The Rite of Spring*:

> Shall I compare thee to a porcupine
> Or, with some quaint comparison,
>   [declare
> The armadillo's hide no match for thine
> Nor alligator scales so wild and rare
> As the cortex that doth guard thy brain

[For the rest of this, see Poems, Chapter 19, p. 162.]

15 Leo Delibes (1836–91); his ballet *Sylvia* was produced in Paris in 1876.

16 Radclyffe Hall (1883–1943). *The Well of Loneliness* (1928) was banned as obscene, with copies removed from the shops after a court judgment. The subject of lesbian love was topical in 1928, with further novels by Virginia Woolf, Compton Mackenzie, Elizabeth Bowen and an anonymous lampoon called *The Sink of Solitude*. However, *The Well* was available in Paris after the ban, was republished in England in 1949, and by 1974 it featured on the BBC Radio 4 programme *Book at Bedtime*. Berners was using the associations of the scandal, but the cover of the first edition of *The Well* and his hastily assembled *The Girls* are similarly severe. *The Well* apparently sold a million copies and was translated into at least a dozen languages. The heroine has constant anxiety about her sexuality; she generously arranges to lose her final lover to a man; so that, if this is a moral tale, it was not the sort to appeal later to gay liberation movements. Beverley Nichols called *The Well of Loneliness* scandal 'one of those deplorable examples of mob hysteria which periodically make the British people so ridiculous in the eyes of the rest of the world.' *The Sweet and Twenties* (London: Weidenfeld & Nicolson, 1958), 107.

than in the more experimental pieces he wrote around World War I?

FA   I would say so, but then the ballet reaches a bigger audience. The earlier work is more specialised.

PD   Did you know he wrote film scores?

FA   No.

PD   Did you come across the song 'Red Roses and Red Noses'?

FA   Only at your Purcell Room recital in 1972. At *Riverside Nights* there was a dancer called Penelope Spencer who danced the *Funeral March for a Rich Aunt*. It was very successful in the revue.[17]

PD   Did the music sound like jubilation?

FA   Yes, it did. You see he worked hard. He didn't just wait until he was inspired. Sometimes at Faringdon you could hear him playing the piano when one was still in one's bedroom.

PD   What interest do you think future generations will have in Berners?

FA   Who can say? He could suddenly become a cult figure. The young might take him up. It depends on how he's presented to them. I think that could easily happen.

PD   Would it matter if he became a cult figure?

FA   I think he'd have liked it. He quite liked publicity, having his name in the papers, with everybody talking about his eccentricities. But I often wonder how deep the eccentricity really was or how much it was played on.

PD   So he draws attention to himself like that, but his work is more restrained?

FA   I think he was too sane to be really eccentric. He knew what he was doing. He wasn't a profound eccentric.

PD   Not like Salvador Dalí?

FA   Would you say that Dalí was eccentric? Also played on. I think a real eccentric isn't that aware – they just are eccentric. I'm sure Dalí was aware of the effect he was making all the time. It was the same with Gerald to a lesser degree – and not so famous.

PD   Berners was attracted to surrealism.

FA   Anything extraordinary would have attracted him. He was very good at constructing a ballet. He could do a good *pas de deux* in a Tchaikovsky or Delibes way. He understood about lengths, and what he did was agreeable to the ear. He was good at timing. If I said something was too long he would cut it. Every note wasn't sacred. With Britten, when I wanted cuts in *Death in Venice*, he would cut two bars, which was no good at all![18] Gerald was more realistic.

17 Penelope Spencer (1901–93). *Riverside Nights*, Lyric Theatre, Hammersmith, reviewed in *The Times*, 12 April 1926.

18 *Death in Venice*, Britten's final opera, with choreography by Ashton, premièred at Snape Maltings, 16 June 1973. A well-thumbed manuscript copy of Berners' Polka (1941) has an improvised cover made from turning inside out and upside down the cover of the first edition of Britten's set of piano pieces *Holiday Tales* (1935) – later called *Holiday Diary*. In 1942 Berners compiled his own Desert Island Discs – not for the BBC programme – and said: 'Of the moderns I prefer Stravinsky, Bartók and of the younger English composers Benjamin Britten. At the risk of seeming priggish I say that I like all music that is good of its kind and I am not impressed, like so many of the English music critics, by pretentious emptiness.' Amory, *Lord Berners*, 241.

CHAPTER 12 Lady Betjeman

*Interview with Peter Dickinson on 15 May 1983
at New House, Cussop, Hay-on-Wye, Hereford*

THE HON. Penelope Chetwode (1910–86) was the only daughter of Field Marshall, 1st Baron Chetwode, who was Commader-in-Chief of the British Army in India. As Penelope Chetwode she wrote books on travel such as *Two Middle-aged Ladies in Andalusia* (1963) – the other was a mare – and *Kulu: the End of the Habitable World* (1972). She met John Betjeman when he was working for the *Architectural Review*. He didn't impress the Chetwodes, but she married him in 1933 and they lived in Berkshire, where they came to know Lord Berners. She was passionate about horses; her half-Arab grey gelding Moti entered the news when it was photographed at tea in the drawing room at Faringdon and painted by Berners. She became a Catholic in 1948, which made difficulties with Betjeman's Anglicanism, and later they lived apart. She was devoted to India, and thought it wonderful to travel in old age 'because men don't pester you any more'. She died on what was planned as her final expedition to the Himalayas.[1]

PD   I'd like to go back to the 1930s. Do you remember when you first met Lord Berners?

PB   I have absolutely no recollection at all. We went to Uffington in 1934 and rented a farmhouse there for £36 a year. Gerald and Robert were living four miles away. It was such fun having them so near, and John and I both owe Gerald a tremendous amount, because we met so many fascinating people through him. He was always asking us to lunch and dinner. He used to come to our village concerts. He even used to play the harmonium when I sang in a Methodist choir at one point.

PD   I can't imagine him playing the harmonium!

PB   He played it beautifully. Robert used to come, and I think he even preached a sermon at one of the Methodist things once. I was very interested in Methodism at that time, and we had great friends, the village store-keepers, Mr and Mrs Norton. On Sunday afternoons the Nortons, their daughter and I used to go round singing hymns – I was descant – at the various village chapels – Black Bourton and Ashbury. Gerald used to come round and play the harmonium.

PD   What was his attitude to religion?

PB   He was fascinated by it, and he always used to say to me that he thought religion was a talent like music or painting.

1 'The Hon. Lady Betjeman', *The Times*, 16 April 1986. 'Lady Betjeman's last trip: Richard Boston on an entertaining exchange', *Guardian*, 16 April 1986.

Either you have got it or you haven't. He'd like to have had it, but he hadn't.

PD   When you first met him were you aware of him as a composer, writer, or painter?

PB   Before I met him I'd always heard of him from my aunt Juliet Duff,[2] who used to live at Vaynol – we used to stay there a lot – but entirely as a composer. The legend was that he played a piano in his car. Then, when we went to Faringdon we used to see him painting – very much in the style of early Corot.[3] His wonderful collection of paintings included several early Corots. The one he did of me was from a photograph – a still from a BBC film about film critics. John was a film critic at the time.

PD   What about the painting he did of the horse?

PB   When we married my father sent my Arabian horse back from India. People said the whole house revolved around a horse called Moti. He was a great personality in our lives. I had a lovely cart we used to drive around – often to Faringdon and to Kelmscott to tea with May Morris.[4] Moti was terribly domesticated and used to come into the house at Faringdon. Gerald loved having him in the house, and he was photographed having tea with us. I always think he was the origin of that advertisement for whisky – 'You can take a white horse anywhere.' So many photographs of him in the house at Faringdon were published. Gerald used to have meets of the hounds often: Robert and I used to ride with the Old Berks.

PD   Did Berners ride?

PB   In that generation everybody was brought up to ride, but by that time he didn't like it. He wasn't interested, but I've got a photograph of him in breeches. At one period Robert bought a very old flea-bitten grey cob – all its legs were wobbly – because he thought it would be nice for John to have a quiet horse. Gerald very occasionally used to go out hacking with Robert, but then completely gave it up. I borrowed it for John, and used to take him out on it. I've told this story before. One day we went up into the Downs and got into a field with a lot of yearling bullocks that all rushed after him. They were very inquisitive but weren't going to hurt him. He cantered up the hill shouting out: 'You've brought me here to kill me!' I laughed so much I nearly fell off. Then I chased the bullocks away, so that was all right, but he didn't ride after that.

PD   Why was Berners attracted to Corot?

PB   I've no idea, but he loved landscape and beauty of all

2 Lady Juliet Lowther, wife of Sir Michael Duff (1907–80), 3rd baronet of Vaynol Park, where Berners first met Heber-Percy.

3 Jean-Baptiste-Camille Corot (1796–1875), French landscape painter. Among the Corots owned by Berners was *Venise, Le Grand Canal vu du quai des esclavons, 1828* (plate 30), which clearly affected Berners' own paintings of Venice – see plates 31, 32, 33.

4 Daughter of William Morris (1834–96); Kelmscott Manor, Oxfordshire, was one of William Morris's houses.

kinds. Perhaps he found wonderful calm in the landscapes of Corot. He seemed to concentrate on early Corot.

PD   *The Camel* is dedicated to you and John.

PB   It was always supposed to be John and me – it's about a clergyman and his wife, isn't it? I was supposed to go around doing my parish visiting on a camel. All Gerald's books are really fantasies.[5]

PD   Do you think he took himself seriously as a writer?

PB   I honestly don't know. People used to say that if he hadn't been a rich man he would have concentrated on music and become a very famous composer. As it is, he is quite a famous composer today, but he'd probably have been as famous as his great friend Stravinsky. They say he dissipated his talents by doing too many different things. I don't really agree with that. I believe he is considered a very good musician, less good as a painter and writer. I find his books very readable, especially *A Distant Prospect*. The ridiculous book *The Girls of Radcliff Hall* was really only understandable if you knew all the characters. I don't suppose it would be the least amusing to you today because you wouldn't have known the people concerned.

What was so fascinating in the 1930s was all the people he had to stay. For instance, Bernard Shaw and his wife – dim, deaf and a complete nonentity compared with him! We all went afterwards to the Great Tithe Barn at Great Coxwell, and Shaw said the last time he'd been there was with William Morris. Then Dalí used to come and stay with his wife Gala – God, she was an attractive woman. I remember sitting next to him at dinner. He liked to shock you, and never stopped talking about fur-lined wombs!

PD   Berners liked to shock people. Did it come from Dalí?

PB   No, I think he was naturally rather mischievous. His great butt, of course, was the poor old Coalbox – Lady Colefax.

PD   Do you remember the Sitwells coming to Faringdon?

PB   The Sitwells were cousins of my mother's – Osbert wrote quite a lot about her in one of his autobiographical books. Edith I never met. Sachie used to come quite a lot with Georgia. There was one unfortunate woman with a rather grand name who was mad, and we all rather cruelly played up to her. Gerald used to pull her leg. It was in his nature – a sense of humour, I suppose.

One thing I'd like to say is that he was the most incredibly well-read man I've ever met, with an amazing literary memory. I think he'd read all the great novels in German, French, Italian and English. I remember once we were talking about

5 Berners, *The Camel* (1936), in *Collected Tales and Fantasies* (1999). A friendly camel appears from nowhere on the vicarage doorstep and develops a relationship with the vicar's wife, Antonia, comparable to Penelope Betjeman's love for her horses. The vicar is too amiable towards the local Catholic priest for his wife's liking – that prefigures the conflict between the Betjemans that resulted in her converting to Rome. The vicar becomes jealous of the organist – he thinks he is having an affair with his wife but the organist is actually gay – and murders him, then shoots himself. All this interrupts the village fête, but Berners' final sketch shows Antonia on her camel going off like a Hollywood couple into the sunset. Some months before *The Camel* came out Berners gave his own explanation to Clive Bell: 'Incidentally I've got a book coming out in May. It is a "fantastic" tale and is called "The Camel". It is about a camel that arrives unexpectedly and mysteriously at an English country vicarage and causes considerable inconvenience to the vicar and his wife, in spite of its being in a sense a mystical camel. I think it is very funny and I hope you will too.' And later: 'I am so glad you enjoyed *The Camel*. I have squared the police but not Mr Cecil Beaton who is threatening me with a libel action for having taken his name in vain.' (Undated letters from 1935–6 now in the library of King's College, Cambridge CHA/1/64.) In a letter to E. S. P. Haynes, who had reviewed one of Berners' books in *Truth*, Berners said: 'one mustn't always doubt things merely because they are improbable.' Bertram Rota catalogue 239 (Winter 1985–6), item 89. See Appendix 2 for his unpublished foreword to *The Camel*.

Goethe and I'd been trying to read *Werther* in German: he'd not only read it but remembered all the characters in it.[6]

PD   In that sense he was a kind of European?

PB   He was probably the most cultivated man I've ever met. He knew all about Renaissance painting – you could discuss anything like that with him in great detail.

PD   Wasn't he kind too?

PB   He was terribly kind to his friends, although his sense of fun did sometimes entail him being rather cruel. He was merciless with snobs because he was the least snobby person you could possibly wish to meet.

PD   It seems he may have had lunch with Hitler. Did you know anything about that?

PB   No I didn't, but he was a very great friend of Diana Mosley – I should think she arranged that.[7] Gerald wasn't in the least political – he simply wasn't interested in politics any more than John or I was. He wouldn't have had the slightest Nazi trace in him. I think in those days I'd have gone to lunch with Hitler if I'd been asked – just out of curiosity. I never remember discussing politics at Faringdon at all.

PD   Berners came across Mussolini in Italy. Did you ever go to the house in the Forum?

PB   Yes, it was wonderful because John and I were going to Italy. He hated going abroad, but he thought he ought to see the churches in Rome – it turned out he didn't like them. The first time we stayed in a pension and John got flu, which he always did as soon as we got abroad! Robert somehow arranged that we should be moved to Gerald's house. John found the American tea-room, and used to go and sit and read *The Times*, like my father did in Rome. He thought the Roman churches were all façades. I suppose they are, all squashed into the buildings behind. He loved Tivoli and said: 'This beats Okehampton!'

Robert and I went to stay two or three times in that lovely house. Gerald had a wonderful cook, whose *soufflé de fungi* was famous. Gerald was a tremendous gourmet: I never had such wonderful food. Although Gerald couldn't cook himself, he would always discuss dishes with his cook, and say if he'd done them well or badly.

PD   When John Betjeman did the readings at our Purcell Room concert in 1972 it became very noticeable from the way he read that Berners' humour was close to his own. Did Berners influence him?

PB   We both adored Gerald and admired him very much for

6 Johann Wolfgang Goethe (1749–1832), *Die Leiden des jungen Werthers* (The Sorrows of Young Werthe, 1774).

7 But see interview with Lady Mosley, Chapter 10, p. 92.

his culture and kindness, but how John was affected in his personality and his work I couldn't say.

PD Does it surprise you that there is this amount of activity for Gerald Berners' centenary?

PB No, not in the least, because he was one of the great characters of the first half of the century, especially because of his music. I'm very glad that he's having the recognition that he got partly in his lifetime – but he's getting more now. Of course, he was terribly depressed by the war, thought it was the end of everything, and moved to Oxford, but I saw very little of him then, and I can't remember anything about the books.

PD Do you remember about the connection with Firbank?

PB He often used to talk about Firbank, who hated noise and used to shut himself up. I think Firbank is a wonderful writer, very subtle.

PD Berners is in that tradition but simpler?

PB I think he was influenced by Firbank.[8]

PD What about Gertrude Stein?

PB She was another character we met through Gerald. I think she and Alice B. Toklas stayed at Faringdon. Toklas was a most extraordinary character, who looked very gipsy and dark-skinned. I found Gertrude Stein extremely forbidding, very unattractive: I couldn't make headway at all. I got on well with Toklas because we were both mad on cooking. We used to discuss recipes, and I think I gave her one for her cookery book. Anyway, Gertrude didn't mean much to me – nor did her work.

PD Do you think Berners took her seriously?

PB I don't know. He was an extraordinary man because he was very much in the fashionable world of London at that time, but he had a lot of friends who were very serious like Stravinsky and Shaw who were not in the least interested in London society.

Constant Lambert I adored – he had a most attractive oriental wife – and was often at Faringdon.[9]

PD You implied that if Berners wasn't rich he might have been a more serious composer. But isn't it possible that he did do exactly what he wanted to do?

PB I'm only saying the *on dit* about Gerald – that he would have been a world-famous composer if he hadn't spent so much time doing other things. The books and painting were his amateurish side, whereas his professional work was his music. He would probably have produced more music had he not had so many distractions.

8 See interviews with Daphne Fielding, Chapter 6, p. 67, and Lord David Cecil, Chapter 14, pp. 116 & 125.

9 Constant Lambert married his first wife, Florence Chuter, in 1931. Their son, Kit (1935–81), was a rock 'n' roll entrepreneur, and first manager of The Who.

We knew him mostly through country life round Faringdon. I hardly ever went to London – I hated London society and smart life. Our chief social life in the country was with Gerald and all the people we met through him, which was fascinating. He had that lovely lake at the bottom of the park where we all used to go and swim – so much nicer than this vulgar craze for building swimming baths! I don't think Gerald swam himself. Our lives were mixed up in those days – Gerald and Robert, people like Diana Mosley, Nancy Mitford, Daphne Fielding and all the famous people we'd never have met except for Gerald. We were very privileged to have known him. Robert and I got on terribly well over riding and hunting: John and Gerald used to sit at home. But Gerald used to come driving with us in the pony cart and was always frightfully funny about all the neighbours. He liked people who entertained and amused him. He used to call some of them dry blankets, as opposed to wet.

PD   Berners wrote some music for your play *The Expulsion from Paradise* in 1945.

PB   It was simply a nativity play in the little church at Farnborough, the one near Wantage – before I became a Catholic – and I asked him to write an overture to it. It was difficult to play on the harmonium, and I cannot think how our village organist Miss Dearlove managed it! The next year we did it in our loft. Lady Redesdale came with one or two of the Mitford girls.[10] After she was seated the solicitor's wife came up the ladder in an enormous brown fur coat. Lady Redesdale said in a loud voice: 'How like Penelope to have a real ox!' We didn't have any harmonium in that, because there wasn't one.

PD   Did he play it himself?

PB   I don't think so, but he may have played it over on the piano. Gerald wrote to me and said he'd tried to express the fact that the expulsion from paradise was very unfair.

PD   What about the Folly?

PB   I remember that local people said the money would have been better spent on local charities. It was designed by Gerry Wellesley. As soon as it was built we all went up regularly – people staying there were taken up to the top of the Folly from which you got a lovely panorama. I was heartbroken when I heard it was pronounced unsafe.[11]

10 Sidney Bowles (1880–1963), wife of 2nd Baron Redesdale, mother of the six Mitford sisters.

11 In 2007 the Folly was open to the public once a month.

CHAPTER 13

Lady Harrod

Interview with Peter Dickinson on 14 May 1983 at Faringdon House

W ILHELMINE (Billa) Cresswell (1911–2005) was born into a Norfolk family and became an architectural conservationist widely known for her work throughout the county; she was personally responsible for saving many churches from demolition. She knew writers in London, such as Nancy Mitford – Fanny in *Love in a Cold Climate* is partly based on her – and she herself wrote *The Shell Guide to Norfolk* (1957) with the Rev. Charles Linnell, in the series edited by John Betjeman, and *The Norfolk Guide* (1988).[1] In 1938 she married Roy Harrod (1900–78), the eminent economist who was knighted in 1959. He held Oxford posts at Christ Church and Nuffield College, and was a personal adviser to Churchill during World War II. Lady Harrod told Gavin Bryars that she met Berners before the war through her oldest friends, Penelope and John Betjeman.

PD You probably remember Lord Berners best when you were together in Oxford during the war?

WH He lived in St Giles with a landlady called Miss Alden, who was rather tough.[2] I don't think she made his life hell or anything, but he wanted to do what she wanted. He was depressed in those days because he hated the war so much. All the things that Gerald loved were being destroyed. He was very amusing, and all the Oxford people – also stuck and bored – were glad he was there.

I remember we once went to *Gone with the Wind*[3] at the cinema, and it seemed to go on for hours and hours. When we came out I remember Gerald saying in a very exhausted voice: 'The next film they're going to make is the Bible, and it's going to last for two days!' [*Laughs.*] He was like that – there were lots of jokes of that sort.

Once he came into my house – I think we used to leave the door open – rushed up to the drawing room and said: 'I've opened the wrong door and I've killed an old lady!' It was my mother-in-law who was sitting downstairs and used to shriek when anybody came into the room. We rather wished he had! [*Laughs.*]

We used to talk a great deal about food. Whatever cook they had at Faringdon the food was absolutely superb, with Gerald saying how to do it. You could guarantee that you couldn't have a bad meal at Faringdon. In the war there wasn't any food, and Oxford was particularly bad.

PD Did you get the impression he was working in Oxford?[4]

1 'Lady Harrod: Redoubtable Norfolkwoman who worked energetically to save her county's churches from dereliction', Obituaries, *The Times*, 12 May 2005.

2 22 St Giles. Lord David Cecil remembered: 'They are pretty little houses in St Giles. As I remember, it was a late eighteenth/early nineteenth century house and he had a sitting room on the ground floor. There was a bow window – pleasant rooms.' (Interview with Gavin Bryars). Lady Harrod told Gavin Bryars on 8 February 1980 that Robert Heber-Percy had Miss Alden out to tea: apparently she accused him of having aged at a time when she herself was almost 100! A. L. Rowse remembered that 'Gerald's landlady ... from a good old-fashioned Oxford town-family, was quite a character: her hair simply wouldn't grow grey and in her knowing way she thought Robert was Lord Berners' illegitimate son.' *Friends and Contemporaries* (London: Methuen, 1989), 65.

3 The single novel by American author Margaret Mitchell (1900–49), published in 1936, which was a bestseller, a Hollywood film (1939) and won a Pulitzer Prize.

4 He did some work for the blood transfusion service and catalogued books at the Taylor Institute.

WH He did write certain books there didn't he?

PD Did you read them?

WH Yes, he gave me them all: some of them are very good and very funny, but I don't like fantasy. There's one about a camel, which I didn't like very much.

PD Did you hear his music then?

WH No, not at all. I wasn't very musical. The highbrow musical ladies, like Mrs A. J. P. Taylor [Margaret Adams, his first wife] must have done. She was very keen on culture and frightfully boring about it, like those sorts of people are. She went to see Gerald one morning to talk about music, and she got out of his house and was walking quite a long way down the road, and Gerald ran after her carrying with him that golden cockerel that you saw on the sideboard in the dining room at Faringdon. He called out: 'Margaret, Margaret, wait a minute! I want to show you my cock!' [*Laughs.*]

PD How did you hear about this?

WH Certainly she didn't tell us. Gerald must have done.

PD Do you feel all his activities come together?

WH I was very unsophisticated about the arts at that time, and didn't know much about his music or his painting. I just thought he was a very amusing man. I knew about Faringdon before the war, full of wonderful things as well as jokes. I understood about the jokes, but not the serious artistic side. I'm rather ashamed now to think that I didn't recognise his music and his paintings. Mind you, one didn't hear the music, so one didn't have much chance, and one just saw what paintings happened to be at Faringdon.

PD Did he see much of the dons at Oxford?

WH I've been wondering about that, and I don't know that he did. My husband liked him very much, and I don't doubt that he asked him to dine in Christ Church, but many of the dons were away during the war. I don't think the right people were there at that time.[5]

Afterwards André Gide came to get an honorary degree at Oxford. The Vice-Chancellor at the time was rather shocked at the idea, and rang up Enid Starkie, the French don at Somerville, and said: 'This fellow Andre Gide is coming for an honorary degree. Will you entertain him and have him for dinner? I hear he's a very queer fellow.' And Enid said: 'Do you mean queer in the modern technical sense?' [*Laughs.*] And the Vice-Chancellor said: 'Oh, I don't know.' And Enid did have him to stay in Somerville, poor man. Then Gerald asked him out to Faringdon for lunch on the Sunday.

5 The historian A. J. P. Taylor remembered: 'Frank Pakenham (later 7th Earl of Longford) had an incorrigible taste for airy talk and collected a group to discuss the future of the world ... Among those who attended was Gerald Berners, one of the few friends I would gladly recall from the dead ... His little novel *Far from the Madding War*, although now no doubt forgotten, gives incomparably the best picture of wartime Oxford ... The coming of war had driven Gerald to a mental breakdown ... He came to dinner with us every week or took us to the George Restaurant, where he was greeted obsequiously as my Lord, while the Duke of Leeds at a neighbouring table was ignored. Of our conversation I remember nothing except that we laughed all the time.' *A Personal History* (London: Hamish Hamilton, 1983), 155.

We all came, and it was wonderfully exciting and successful. Thrilling to meet Gide.[6]

PD   Who were some of the people who came to Faringdon?

WH   They were just the ordinary people we all knew like the Betjemans, the Mosleys, the Pakenhams and the Cecils. I expect there were many others I don't know about.

PD   The visitors' book is fantastic!

WH   It must be. We came fairly often to stay here and I remember bringing my children during the war. The house was upside down because there were soldiers in it. The beautiful red bed was in the drawing room, and my little boys slept in it. I was terrified they'd wreck it in some frightful way, but they didn't.

PD   Knowing the Mitfords as he did, do you think he had an ambivalent attitude towards fascism? He wrote a *Fascist March* in the 1930s.[7] Was he unpatriotic in any sense?

WH   Absolutely no sense at all. The point was we were all very fond of the Mitfords. We all, including my husband, who was very far from being a fascist, knew and enormously admired Tom Mosley. My husband thought he was a very clever man, and if only he hadn't taken a wrong turning he could have been a great leader and a help to this country. But he did take the wrong turning – we all thought that. But we all still liked him both before and after his prison and everything else. We used to go and stay with them in France, and we all loved Diana. Tom was very clever and attractive, and I think Gerald put the politics absolutely aside and just loved them as friends. He used to go and see them in prison, and he once took Diana some lovely Floris bath essence, and when he arrived the wardress said: 'Oh, Lady Mosley will be absolutely thrilled!' [*Laughs.*] The wardress had got the measure of everybody.

Gerald was very imaginative and knew what people were like. He was a funny man in a way because, although he wasn't very quiet, he was very un-ebullient, gentle and in a low key. At one point we thought he was in love with a very pretty young woman, and I remember saying to my sister: 'We think Gerald might marry.' And she said: 'Lord Berners, but he's exactly like Groucho Marx: he couldn't marry anybody!'[8] [*Laughs.*]

PD   He wasn't of the generation to be openly gay.

WH   Absolutely and utterly not, and perhaps he wasn't even. Not the sort of thing you would associate with him. You'd think he was the most amusing and original man you'd ever met. You wouldn't have thought of that other aspect. He wasn't at all a show-off like Lytton Strachey.[9] But it doesn't

6 André Gide (1869–1951) received his honorary degree from Oxford in 1948. Lady Harrod told Gavin Bryars that the Vice-Chancellor was Richard Livingston, Master of Corpus Christi. She said that some people had refused to entertain Gide because of his reputation, so Dr Starkie, the specialist in Gide studies, took him to dine at her own college, Somerville – a women's college until 1992.

7 See interview with Lady Mosley, Chapter 10, p. 92.

8 Lady Harrod told Gavin Bryars that the young lady was Clarissa Churchill (1920–), niece of Winston Churchill, who married Foreign Secretary Anthony Eden in 1952. He was Prime Minister 1955–7 and later Lord Avon. See Clarissa Eden, *A Memoir*, ed. Cate Haste (London: Weidenfeld & Nicolson, 2007). Berners' letter of 10 October 1941 thanks her for sending some chocolates: 'Robert and I fell upon them as cannibals might fall on a missionary.'

9 Lytton Strachey (1880–1932), biographer and critic, member of the Bloomsbury Group. Author of *Eminent Victorians* (1918), *Queen Victoria* (1921), *Elisabeth and Essex: A Tragic History* (1928).

matter. People have gone on too boringly much about all that.[10]

PD   Wasn't he a vanishing breed, rather like the Sitwells, in having the time and the opportunity to be sophisticated in many different ways?

WH   I think he was, and much of his depression at Oxford was because he was suddenly put out on a limb, cut off from the things that had always surrounded him – beauty, luxury, servants and the way of life. You couldn't have that in the war: it wasn't there. I think he was a vanishing breed. I don't know many people like that now.

PD   You always came to Faringdon with the drive swept and the pigeons dyed different colours?

WH   It was always like that. I once went to the island of San Francesco in the lagoons off Venice, where there were some Franciscan monks – and coloured chickens. We asked the monk who was showing us round why the chickens were coloured and he said: 'Just for fun.' I don't know where Gerald got it from, but it's awfully pretty.

PD   He liked disconcerting people through his music and his novels but not his paintings?

WH   His paintings are much more serious. There was one lovely disconcerting thing. There was a well-known snobbish lady whom he asked to lunch on a postcard saying: 'Do come to luncheon on Sunday the P. of W. is coming.' She got wildly excited and thought it was the Prince of Wales, came dashing down in her best clothes, and when she arrived Gerald said: 'Do you know the Provost of Worcester?'[11] [*Laughs.*] It was about Lady Colefax, who was funny and nice, and I liked her.

AJ[12]   Could Berners actually cook himself?

WH   I don't know, but he knew exactly how it ought to be done. However, I found in one of my old cookery books something called 'Consommé Berners', which was just Marmite with grated carrot in it! In the middle of the war, when there wasn't any food, it looked better.

One wasn't allowed to have a car during the war, but you could hire one for a certain number of miles. So he used to hire a car for part of the journey from Oxford to Faringdon, and then hire another one to go on. That was fun. Faringdon was the most magical place in England.[13]

---

10   Referring to the period around 1900, Berners wrote: 'The subject of homosexuality was one which was strictly taboo in those days. By many it was hardly believed in, and I was told that some people when informed of what Wilde had "actually done" declared that such a thing was not possible. I, who had been to a public school, knew that it was, but for a long time I imagined that it was a form of vice confined to public schools and only very rarely practised by adults and then only by foreigners.' *The Château de Résenlieu*, 74.

11   According to a letter from Sir Isaiah Berlin to Gavin Bryars on 6 April 1979, the Provost of Worcester was the Rev S. J. Lys.

12   Arthur Johnson, BBC producer.

13   Faringdon House was rented by Berners' mother in 1910; Berners bought it after he inherited the title in 1918; in 1931 he moved in after both his mother and her second husband, Colonel Ward Bennitt, had died. Berners started his visitor's book at the end of 1933. In the following year there were seventy-four guests, and in each of the next two a hundred. Mark Amory, *Lord Berners: the Last Eccentric* (London: Chatto & Windus, 1998), 139–40.

CHAPTER 14 Lord David Cecil

Interview with Peter Dickinson on 15 May 1983 at Red Lion House, Cranborne, Dorset

LORD David Cecil (1902–1986; see plate 10), literary critic and biographer, was a younger son of the 4th Marquess of Salisbury. His ancestors included some of the most enlightened and influential politicians in British history – William Cecil, Lord Burleigh, and Robert Cecil, 1st Earl of Salisbury, both of whom served under Queen Elizabeth I, and Robert Cecil, 3rd Marquess of Salisbury, who was Queen Victoria's favourite Prime Minister. Lord David Cecil was educated at Eton and Christ Church, Oxford, and married Rachel, daughter of Sir Desmond MacCarthy.[1] After fellowships at Wadham College and New College he was appointed Goldsmiths' Professor of English Literature (1948–69) at Oxford. His many books include *Early Victorian Novelists* (1934), *Jane Austen* (1936), *The Young Melbourne and the Story of his Marriage with Caroline Lamb* (1939), *Hardy the Novelist: an Essay in Criticism* (1942), *Lord Melbourne, or the Later Life of Lord Melbourne* (1954), *Max* (1964), *The Cecils of Hatfield House: a Portrait of an English Ruling Family* (1973). He was awarded the CH (1949), the CLit (1972) and several honorary doctorates.[2]

PD   I'd like to talk about Lord Berners in any way you think relevant, but particularly about his writing. I don't know how much you know about music.

DC   I'm very fond of music indeed and have always been, but I don't play an instrument; I can't read music; I can't call myself in a high degree musical, except that it's always been one of my great pleasures.

PD   Did you know any of Berners' music?

DC   Only after I got to know him. I know Gerald's music but not intimately. I know more about his writing.

PD   Do you remember him playing at all?

DC   Yes, he did when I went to stay at Faringdon. I didn't know him nearly so long as the other people you've been seeing. I must have met him at various times in the inter-war period, but I never got to know him at all well.[3] What really made the friendship was the Second World War. I'd been a don before, but had a time in between, and I went back to New College, and Gerald came to live in Oxford during the war. He became a great friend of me and my wife Rachel. But I'd seen much less of him than Penelope Betjeman, who'd known him for a very long time.

In Oxford we were cut off from the war, although a lot

1 Sir Desmond MacCarthy (1877–1952), literary journalist on *The New Statesman* and then the *Sunday Times*. Cecil edited *Desmond MacCarthy: the Man and his Writings* (London: Constable, 1984).

2 'Lord David Cecil: Eminent Man of Letters', Obituary, *The Times*, 3 January 1986. See also A. L. Rowse, 'Lord David Cecil', *Friends and Contemporaries* (London: Methuen, 1989), 1–45.

3 Cecil thought he might have met Berners before the war, when they were both staying with Lord Alington, whose friends often mixed the worlds of art and fashion. Apparently Alington, known as 'Naps', had had an affair with the American actress Tallulah Bankhead (1902–69). One night he was dining out at a restaurant with his wife when Bankhead came in. As she passed he looked away but, after a few moments, she left her table, came over to him and asked in a husky voice: 'What's the matter, darling? Don't you recognise me with my clothes on?' Francis Rose remembered Alington as part of a 'group of a few remarkable men, in a period of decay between two wars'. He was 'a born courtier ... not profound or intellectual; beautiful objects, fashion, and hunting meant more to him than really serious art. He was not frivolous or a snob, and had enchanting manners, was charmingly reckless with money, and there was always at least one beautiful woman in love with him'. *Saying Life: the Memoirs of Sir Francis Rose* (London: Cassell & Co., 1961), 83.

of government offices moved there, so people who had the same kind of tastes and interests got to know each other. That went on through the war and afterwards.

We went to stay at Faringdon after the war, and I had a very memorable weekend there with Max Beerbohm, whose biography I afterwards wrote.[4] The party consisted of myself, my wife, my father-in-law Desmond MacCarthy, and Max and his wife Florence. I'd already met Max before but we got to know each other better, and it was in consequence of that he bequeathed to me the task of writing his biography – some years later.

PD   I don't know how clear the books are in your mind?

DC   One or two I know much better than others.

PD   How does he fit in as a writer?

DC   I think he was an extraordinarily gifted man. In whatever he took up – music, which was obviously chief, or writing or painting – he had a natural facility. It was as an amateur in the good sense of the word that he did it for his own pleasure, and it wasn't very heavyweight. But it's professional in the sense that it's very accomplished. He easily achieved an accomplishment that most people get only after quite a struggle. In writing that showed very much. I think he was an admirable stylist and writer of light easy accomplishment.

PD   He was Firbank's literary executor, but he was obviously not as avant-garde. How would you place his tradition?

DC   You could see from reading what he wrote about himself that he was the kind of person who would appreciate Firbank. But I wouldn't say he was very like Firbank, who was a very odd, original, quirky talent. Rather delightful, but it's very much its own thing. Some of Gerald's stories, which I know less well, may be Firbankian, but I don't feel he'd have written any differently if Firbank had never lived.

PD   Would you separate the autobiographies from the novels?

DC   Yes, I would – in my own mind. I'd put him first of all as an autobiographer.

PD   There are two essays about his time in France and in Germany.

DC   I'm so glad, because he read aloud a lot of them to me and my wife. I remember him reading *Résenlieu*. I always wonder why they never got published – they were awfully good.[5]

This I will say. I think our age – the last fifty or sixty years – hasn't been outstanding in poetry, with exceptions. And – this is more disputable – I certainly think it isn't equal in

4 Sir Max Beerbohm (1872–1956), critic and caricaturist, author of *Zuleika Dobson* (1911), married the American actress Florence Kahn. Cecil's biography was *Max* (London: Constable, 1964) and he also edited *The Bodley Head Max Beerbohm* (London: Bodley Head, 1970).

5 *The Château de Résenlieu* (2000); *Dresden* (2008), both New York: Turtlepoint Press and Helen Marx Books.

fiction to the hundred years before it. But I think we've made quite an achievement in what I call the literary documentary. Things of real life, but done in such a way that they are genuine works of literary art. I don't want to put his claims too high – Gerald was rather lightweight – but I think he did that beautifully. Those two books about childhood and Eton are very good.[6] The last sixty years have seen a lot of good things – autobiographical, biographical, travel, war experience – very unlike Gerald's. Making a work of literature founded on fact but not just a record was a very happy climate for somebody like him to write in. On his own scale he did it as well as you could do it.

PD What you say about autobiography does apply to the novels, which are based on people he knew, often as take-offs of actual people. The composer in *Count Omega* could be related to Walton. Can you extend what you are saying to these?

DC The awful thing is I feel rather shy saying all this to you because I don't remember them well enough. Many of the great novels of the past were inspired by real people, and I don't know if Gerald did that more than other people, or whether he did it better. I think everything he did had distinction.

PD Do we need to know who his characters are based on? What appeal is there for the next generation who didn't know his friends and context?

DC Your guess is as good as mine! All literature except the very greatest is fairly feeble – more than authors like to think – the more it depends on relating to a particular society. This, alas, is true, even if it's very good.

PD How would you compare him to the Sitwells, a lot of whose work seems dated and related to their particular period?

DC I personally admire the two autobiographical studies of Gerald's more than anything of the Sitwells. However I thought they could write delightfully, and I admired a lot of Edith's poetry. Osbert, whom I knew quite well, was a most entertaining and likeable man, but his autobiography was too flamboyant. Berners had a graceful, easy, understated accomplishment that appeals to me more.

PD When you were living in Oxford, and Berners was living at 22 St Giles, there was a production of his play *The Furies* in 1942. Did you happen to see it?

DC No! Fancy my not having seen that!

PD The Eumenides were three social ladies who kept

6 *First Childhood* (1934); *A Distant Prospect* (1945).

chasing the hero who preferred a woman they regarded as a tart and brought her in and married her – a very Berners situation!

DC Very. I've just said to you how intimate we were and I don't remember that.

PD It was at the Oxford Playhouse.[7]

DC I can well imagine the whole situation. I often went to the theatre with him. What I do remember is some music he wrote for a pantomime at the Radcliffe Hospital.

PD Called *Cinderella*?

DC Yes. He wrote a very nice dance for them.

PD The Polka.

DC I remember Rachel and me going to the opening performance.[8] It was done by the medical students – a jolly all-male affair, gay and cheerful. What gave it a cachet was this charming light music. My impression is that they asked him, not at all expecting him to say yes, but he was delighted to do it.

PD Those years in Oxford saw several novels getting into print.

DC For my particular interest and taste the autobiography was much better. I thought he did the others very well – you can hear his voice now and again in his particular brand of semi-fantasy – but those are not the books I've returned to.

PD The novels went into several reprints; some of them were translated; reviews were good, such as one from Compton Mackenzie. Is that a kind of success?

DC Although I knew a lot of writers I'm not sure how good a barometer I am about the literary world in that way. You were never surprised to find somebody who had read them and liked them but not a great many people. In all those ways, in the wholly good sense of the word, he was an amateur. What the word originally meant before it implied you weren't skilful – he did the thing for love. He had neither the limitations nor the sort of attention paid that would go with a thorough professional writer.

PD Such as Somerset Maugham or Evelyn Waugh?

DC Exactly. And Somerset Maugham must have been one of the most widely read and highly paid writers in the world.[9] That's what I mean. People would ask: 'Is Berners a composer, a painter or a writer?' But he was known to be a personality.

PD He was a polymath but was he an aesthete?

DC I've never known anyone like him in those ways. An

---

7 *The Furies*, Playhouse, Beaumont Street, Oxford, 1 June and that week, 1942. J.N.B. reported in the *Oxford Magazine*, 4 June: 'A versatile amateur well known in Oxford has found yet another outlet for his talents. The world premiere of Lord Berners' first play was received … with acclamation. A distinguished audience hugely enjoyed themselves.' The *Oxford Times* added: 'Lord Berners, who wrote *The Furies* in Oxford and at Faringdon especially for the Oxford Repertory Players, cleverly relied on the interplay of mature characters to produce the action of a sophisticated comedy.' A. L. Rowse was there: 'He was always working at something. At one time he wrote a play, in which we all lent a hand, Robert [Heber-Percy] bringing in furniture for the stage from Faringdon – did Daisy [Fellowes] produce the curtains?' *Friends and Contemporaries*, 72.

8 He just said to Rachel and me: 'I've written a Polka for this pantomime: do come.' (Interview with Gavin Bryars, 24 April 1980.) The first performances were given by the Tynchewyke Society (now known as the Tingewick Society) at its Christmas Pantomime at the Radcliffe Infirmary on 29 and 30 December 1941. Afterwards the Polka, scored by Ernest Irving, was used in the Ealing Studios film *Champagne Charlie*. (See interview with Sir Richard Rodney Bennett, Chapter 16, p. 142.) The original version for solo piano, recorded by Peter Dickinson along with a historic recording of Berners himself playing it, is available on Symposium 1278 (2000), and it has been orchestrated by Philip Lane on Marco Polo 8.223711 (1998).

9 Somerset Maugham (1874–1965), playwright and novelist, who travelled widely and settled in France in 1926.

aesthete? It's a doubtful word, but to me is a word of praise. It's become a word of contempt: I never know why. That's a person who lives for art. Gerald's chief interest and pleasure – and he lived for pleasure in the nicest way – was the pleasure he got from art. An aesthete would have a more solemn philosophy about where the truest values lie. I never talked to him about that sort of thing, and I didn't think of him like that. I think he was more an artist, a born artist in many dimensions. What was unusual was this facility he seemed to have quite instinctively. I am very keen on actual use of English – style – and I looked again at *First Childhood* the other day and thought how awfully well he writes. It's so natural and yet it's so civilised, with such a sense of the value of words and the right way to end a paragraph and all that.

PD Didn't he apply this kind of aesthetic discrimination to all avenues of life? To cuisine, living, collecting?

DC It was all in a light vein, and that was the charm. He was meant for happy times. In the war he was very good at adapting himself, but he was dreadfully depressed when I first got to know him. It was not a time for him to be living in. If somebody had tried to build him up with some more tragic or solemn philosophy of life it would have been no good. He couldn't respond to that. He was quite modest but at moments perfectly wretched. He managed by being in Oxford to make friends. Any pleasure that was going, he made the most of it. We had quite a nice life in Oxford: no raids even. It was a curious enclave.

PD Was he prone to depression, like many amusing people?

DC There must be people who can tell you more. I wasn't in that sense intimate with him, but I remember going to a service in Christ Church Cathedral quite early on. I'm a practising Christian, but I was surprised to see Gerald there. I think Penelope or somebody had persuaded him to go. I could see he was bewildered by it, not hostile or anti, but – this is a memory and he said nothing to me – it was like something that didn't take. The church was part of my life, but it didn't mean much to him.[10]

PD Perhaps he never got over that evangelical grandmother?

DC Exactly – it might put anybody off! [*Laughs.*] But I don't think it was just that he felt some gloomy memory of his grandmother, but that his way of living had to have its light side.

I'm not quite sure with music. I remember going with him to a concert at the Sheldonian, where a new orchestral piece

10 'I wouldn't call him anti-religious because that would have meant him taking religion seriously in a way. I think his generation, the people who had his taste, very easily felt that. They had this rather grim nineteenth-century evangelical approach thrust down their throats ... he kept going as best he could. In a way it was very brave.' (Interview with Gavin Bryars.) Berners wrote to Cecil probably in 1940, when he had first gone to Oxford. He said he was trying to find God but not succeeding, even though he was going to Pusey House at 8.00 every morning and Penelope Betjeman had had a mass said for him at Uffington. But Berners also enclosed a photograph of Anna Lea Merritt's painting *Love Locked Out* (1889), which depicts a naked Cupid outside the doors of a mausoleum – Merritt's husband had died within three months of their marriage. Berners adjusted the caption to read 'Locked Out' and placed 'W.C.' above the door!

11 Lord and Lady David Cecil were photographed together with Berners and Walton outside the Sheldonian, probably after this concert. (See plate 10. The photograph was probably taken for the *Oxford Post*, 26 November 1941: Mary Gifford, *Lord Berners: Aspects of a Biography* (PhD thesis, University of London, 2007), table 9.) A. L. Rowse also remembered the concert: 'Gerald and I went along to hear Walton's Violin Concerto; Gerald's brief "Well played" to him after made me wonder whether there wasn't a slight touch of envy at the far greater success the former Christ Church choirboy had achieved.' Rouse came across a woman don he knew who had deliberately stayed outside during a performance of the 'Eroica' Symphony because 'One simply can't put up with middle-period Beethoven: only the last quartets.' Rowse told Berners, who simply said: 'But the *Eroica* has everything'. *Friends and Contemporaries*, 60. However, in 1922 in Munich, according to Siegfried Sassoon, Berners said: 'Nothing will induce me to go and hear the Ninth Symphony.' Mark Amory, *Lord Berners: the Last Eccentric* (London: Chatto & Windus, 1998), 78. Thanks to scrutiny of the archives at the Bodleian Library, Oxford, by Peter Ward Jones and Ian Taylor, it is possible to establish that the planned performance of Walton's Violin Concerto in Oxford suffered various mishaps. It was announced for 20 November 1941 with the LPO but replaced by the Brahms because the parts had not arrived. On 12 February 1942 Henry Holst played the concerto with the LPO conducted by the composer. Other sources are wrong. The rest of the programme was Ireland, *A London Overture*; Beethoven, *Eroica*; and Delius, *Brigg Fair*.

by William Walton was being played.[11] We all applauded it, but afterwards we had one of the symphonies of Beethoven, and then Gerald turned to me and: 'I'm afraid Beethoven's better!' [*Laughs.*] I don't want to make him out as too frivolous and light, because Beethoven in any mood is grand stuff. He entered into that.

PD   I wouldn't have thought he was that keen on Beethoven.

DC   Nor would I. It wasn't his characteristic taste, but on the other hand he had obviously been completely responsive to the Beethoven.

PD   He was dismissive of Walton – the *Count Omega* situation. Do you remember their solicitors becoming involved when Walton thought Berners was going to put him into one of his novels? Apparently there was something similar with Harold Nicolson.[12]

DC   He comes into *Far from the Madding War* rather unfavourably. He's 'Lollipop' Jenkins! It's a little skit. It isn't a seriously satirical portrait. You could say it's a comic character slightly inspired by memories of Harold Nicolson.

PD   Nicolson is one of several writers who have tried to give an idea of Berners – Titty in *Some People* is partly based on him. How does this compare with Berners' own technique?

DC   I think that's very comparable, an example of what I was saying – the kind of thing that was very well done in this period.

PD   Lambert Orme in *Some People* was based on Firbank.

DC   I know. Some of them are even closer – almost the most amusing is Lord Curzon's valet, Arketall. I've been told that was done direct from life. I think Gerald can be compared to the Harold Nicolson who wrote that book – his other books are of a different kind. It's not the same, but came from the same period and in a broad sense the same social world.

PD   They were together in Constantinople.

DC   They'd all have known each other and the other people they talk about.

PD   Is there a comparison with Nancy Mitford, who based Lord Merlin on Berners?

DC   It's *The Pursuit of Love*, isn't it? When reading it I never thought it was the sort of thing poor Gerald wouldn't have liked. He wasn't at all touchy, you know – at least not in my experience.

PD   But could be quite cruel in his humour?

DC   That was of the period too. You couldn't call it kindly humour, but it's not ill-tempered. It's mischievous – that's the word I'd use. He was very boyish. I ought to have said that earlier. That's one of the words I would use to describe him more than any other. He was a great contrast to his own appearance because he looked much older than his age. He retained a great deal of the lively entertaining boy, not even a youth.

PD Schoolboy pranks?

DC Jokes, yes: like all those coloured pigeons at Faringdon. I wouldn't say he never grew up because that's patronising. He kept pretty young. Whatever the boy Gerald had been was there right through his life.

It was a delightful friendship that began late in his life and was great fun. If something amusing had happened, the telephone would ring at quarter past nine and Gerald would say: 'You'll be amused to know what happened last night.' That was so unlike the war, the whole atmosphere, somebody who, as it were, had got his nerve back. I'd say: 'Do come in this evening. Rachel and I would love to see you.' Then there would be lots of gossip.

Then I'd read something of my own. I wrote a book called *Two Quiet Lives*: the first was a study of Dorothy Osborne, the romantic love-letter writer of the Charles I period.[13] She suffered tremendously from scruples that she was loving against her family's wishes. I remember reading it to Gerald and thinking it wasn't the sort of subject I would connect with him, but he was very appreciative and nice. He said: 'Oh how people make problems for themselves!'

PD Many people say how kind he was.

DC Very – and he was utterly unsnobbish. He'd take equal trouble with anybody who was there. He wasn't exactly a great mixer. I connect him with certain people at Oxford, but with anybody he got on with he was only too delighted to like and be liked. He'd known all these brilliant people, such as Stravinsky, Picasso and Diaghilev, and there he was with all of us in this little Oxford world, and you'd never have known it. He might talk about them, but there was no question of his not being just as willing to appreciate things.

PD Do you remember anything he said about Gertrude Stein? He did the ballet *A Wedding Bouquet* to her text in 1937.

DC I know – I saw it.

PD I don't think he took her seriously.

DC When I looked at her work again I found it was impossible. I've never been a Stein fan. She was a big personality – I heard her speak in Oxford once. It was knock-about stuff you know![14] [*Laughs.*]

12 In *Far from the Madding War* 'Lollipop' Jenkins comes to Oxford as a distinguished visiting speaker. 'On leaving the playground of the university and embarking on the more serious activities of political life he continued to fulfil the promise of all that had been expected of him. In the course of an unchequered career he had been in turn author, journalist and MP and now he was all three at once ... Yet as he approached middle age his more thoughtful friends began to suspect that something was going a little wrong. Although outwardly the rose retained its rubicund exterior intact, they scented the presence of the worm.' *Madding War*, 88–91, *Collected Tales and Fantasies*, 393. See also A. L. Rowse, 'Lord Berners', *Friends and Contemporaries*, 56–7: 'Gerald went on teasing Harold Nicolson and Rye Vita as he called Vita Sackville-West ...'

13 *Two Quiet Lives: Dorothy Osborne and Thomas Gray* (London: Constable, 1948).

14 Cecil heard Stein lecture in Oxford: 'I asked her some questions and she answered very effectively. Not at all annoyingly but she put one in one's place in a sort of genial, hearty way.' (Interview with Gavin Bryars.) In *Far from the Madding War* Emmeline reads a hilarious passage of Stein parody to Dr Pocock, who is in bed with flu and has soon had enough, 116–17; *Collected Tales and Fantasies*, 403–4.

PD There's an industry of Gertrude Stein studies now in America!

DC Desmond MacCarthy wrote a thing about her that is awfully amusing. He thought it was completely bogus, thinking she had discovered a new way of using language. He said she mustn't think she's the only person who writes like that, and quoted a passage by a less conscious artist that was equally good. Then he provided a section from my wife's typewriting manual and it's absolutely indistinguishable! [*Laughs.*]

PD Berners would have liked that.

DC He liked my father-in-law awfully – he was a wonderful talker and they got on very well.

PD Do you remember Berners' paintings?

DC I liked them very much. I don't possess any; it's years since I've seen any; but I thought they were interesting because they didn't quite fit in with Gerald's reputation for pranks and follies. But actually his art isn't like that, although some of his stories are. His style is light and lively but classical, really, good English. I felt the same with the landscapes that are quiet and sensitive, and didn't show off in any way.

PD Clive Bell, who wrote the foreword to one of the London exhibitions, said: 'Here is exquisite painting.'[15] That was a professional judgement.

DC I would accept all that, but I haven't a very vivid memory of the pictures, except that I always liked them.

PD Cecil Beaton did the sets for some of Berners' ballets. Is that an interesting connection?

DC It's all got this relation to the ballet in a way. Looking back on all that period, there were different groups, as there always are in the arts, but there was one that was centred round the Diaghilev Ballet, whether as photographer, composer or something different. It made this enormous mark. Any art form that was light and sparkling, international, sophisticated, consciously or not was related to this phenomenon of the Diaghilev Ballet.

PD This was something that combined the different arts so Berners could design his own sets ...

DC I think Diaghilev sounds an odious man, but he was a real genius because he really thought of all this. It began before World War I with *L'Oiseau de feu* and *Petrushka*, when he employed composers but also distinguished artists.[16] Such people had never been thought of for doing that kind of thing before. You can't exaggerate the sensation created around 1910–1914, when I was only a schoolboy. It was Diaghilev

15 Clive Bell (1881–1962), art critic associated with the Bloomsbury Group.

16 Stravinsky's *Firebird* (1910) and *Petrushka* (1911), both premièred in Paris.

who joined all these things together. The dancers faded into insignificance, relatively, but he united them all.

PD It's been said that he didn't associate much with the dons in Oxford.

DC Well he associated with me, Isaiah Berlin,[17] Maurice Bowra[18] – three dons – and knew Roy Harrod,[19] who worked in London, but Lady Harrod was there. That was the university world. I would have said that his great friends in Oxford were as much dons as anything else. But the whole place was breaking up because they were all taking part in the war in one way or another. He knew people to do with the Playhouse – especially one actress he admired – and he liked going to the theatre and went often.

I remember very well going with him alone to a revival of *The Admirable Crichton* by J. M. Barrie, who was a very out-of-fashion playwright at the time.[20] We both said we'd never seen this play, which was a great success in its day, and thought it was awfully good. We were amused to find that it had that rather cloying sentiment of Barrie, but not so much as generally. It was very entertaining, and acted well enough. Gerald was in his late fifties and, although he had been quite avant-garde in some aspects, I think he was quite old-fashioned in the techniques he liked in writing for the theatre. Not like a person interested in odd experiments at all. He had rather a traditional taste, and this was a very well-made play by old standards – good openings, good curtains, good parts for the actors and all that. I think that was the kind of play he enjoyed when he was much younger, and it was refreshing for him to see one again.

PD Which may have been why he wrote his own play, unless he was reacting to T. S. Eliot's *The Family Reunion* [1939]?

DC It's bad that I don't remember Gerald's play, since I do remember the pantomime, concerts and going to the theatre with Rachel too. He was very fond of Rachel, and dedicated *Far from the Madding War* to us both.

PD What's the significance of the heroine, Emmeline, who unravels a priceless tapestry as war work?

DC It was a complete invention. The only thing was her looks. There was a very pretty daughter of one of the heads of colleges. I think she gave him the idea. He wrote it to take his mind off the war as a general 'send-up' – to take a modern phrase! It was written in what was then called the phoney war, before anything much had happened. It was like Gerald's sense of humour, where Emmeline's task was described as difficult and disagreeable, which is what war work should be. It didn't seem much use, but from what he could see much of

17 Sir Isaiah Berlin (1909–97), influential political philosopher, born in Riga into a Jewish family who moved to England in 1921. He went to Oxford and largely remained there becoming Chichele Professor of Sociology and Political Theory and subsequently the founding President of Wolfson College.

18 Sir Maurice Bowra (1898–1971), classical scholar born in China, where his father worked for Chinese Imperial Customs. He went to Oxford, where he became Warden of Wadham College. He also served as Professor of Poetry and Vice-Chancellor, and was a partial model for Mr Samgram in Waugh's *Brideshead Revisited* (1948).

19 Sir Roy Harrod (1900–78), eminent economist, who held Oxford posts at Christ Church and Nuffield College, and was personal adviser to Churchill during World War II. He married Wilhelmina Cresswell in 1938.

20 Sir James Matthew Barrie (1860–1937), highly successful dramatist, who reached a wide audience from *Peter Pan* (1904) onwards. *The Admirable Crichton* was a comedy of 1902.

the war work wasn't much use either. She wasn't a character satirised from life. It was just a joke. People weren't being killed in London then. It was a distraction. I did meet one or two rather priggish people who said: 'What an odd book to write in wartime!' But I didn't think so.

PD Comparable to putting moustaches on the family portraits perhaps?

DC Yes, but not even as mischievous. I think he just enjoyed doing it. If he'd heard people objecting he would not have said: 'These are the people I'd wanted to annoy.' It was written just for the fun of it, really. I enjoyed that book very much. I'd have thought that had dated, depending on knowing the place and the people.[21]

AJ[22] Do you remember *The Camel*? Penelope Betjeman said that it's not only dedicated to her and John, but the vicar and his wife are based on them.

DC She's in *Far from the Madding War* all right. She's Lady Caroline Paltry – a comic but quite affectionate picture unmistakeably inspired by her. Berners comes in himself undisguised as Lord Fitzcricket.

PD Including his head 'shaped like a diabolical egg'!

AJ It's a rather melancholy self-portrait?

DC Yes, it is. I do think there was something a little melancholy because to be essentially rather boyish and living in the nicest possible way for pleasure and then to find yourself in Europe in the mid-twentieth century isn't a very happy thing to happen.

PD Do you see any influence of Berners on John Betjeman?

DC I wouldn't, quite honestly, but if John told me he had been influenced by Gerald I would take his word. They are very much people who enjoy each other's work, because they find the same things amusing – the comic grotesque. Betjeman had this passionate curiosity and interest in what other people might think was commonplace English life, which he successfully brought into the realm of poetry. Places such as old North Oxford have become part of poetry largely because John has written about them.

PD Betjeman, like Nancy Mitford and Berners, had a fascination about what people did and exactly what they said – 'U' and 'non-U' usage.

DC It's their habits and mannerisms. I wouldn't have said any of the three were interested psychologically in people. Why should they be? This is not against them, but what they're interested in is what in the eighteenth century would have been called manners. Gerald has more of straight fantasy,

21 Cecil told Gavin Bryars who he thought were the models for some of the characters: Caroline Paltry (Penelope Betjeman), Lord Fitzcricket (Berners himself), 'Lollypop' Jenkins (Harold Nicolson), Provost of Unity (Maurice Bowra – some of his devastating remarks, but he did not have a white beard and was neither old nor a recluse), Emmeline Pocock (appearance and position taken from Janet Gordon, daughter of the President of Magdalene, George Gordon, partly perhaps Clarissa Churchill, later the Countess of Avon), Mr Jericho (Isaiah Berlin – amusing description of his conversation) and Mrs Postlethwaite (a don's wife about whom scandals were constantly being told). Lady Mosley told her son Jonathan Guinness that what Lord Fitzcricket says in the novel is 'almost word for word' what Berners was saying at the time. Jonathan Guinness with Catherine Guinness, *The House of Mitford*, 2nd edn (London: Phoenix, 2004), 502.

22 BBC producer Arthur Johnson.

rather like Firbank, whereas Mitford and Betjeman in their different ways have their feet on the real world.

PD The feet of some of the characters in Firbank are actually dancing to the music of Lord Berners![23]

DC The thing about Firbank is that he's deliberately silly. People who love him can stand any amount of that – personally it amuses me for about a page!

PD It can be obscure too?

DC The conversations are perfectly futile and that's the point of them! [*Laughs.*] One woman said to another: 'I must take off these earrings; they tire me.' A typical Firbank remark – quite funny but idiotic! This is where he's a great contrast to a writer like Max Beerbohm, who is equally light-hearted and entertaining, but is very clever.

PD Do you know the Beerbohm drawing of Berners at the clavichord captioned 'Lord Berners making more sweetness than violence'? [See plate 18.]

DC That's very good. They appreciated each other very much. I did enjoy that weekend at Faringdon. It was the only time I heard Beerbohm talk. He was a delightful talker, but a very quiet one: he had to be brought out. Gerald was very good at that. It was partly Gerald who helped to produce one of the most amusing remarks I've ever heard anyone make. Max had rather a pose about how he was very old and right out of things. Lady Cunard was discussed, and Berners said she was now seventy but absolutely the same, with nothing altered. Max paused and said: 'I'm very sorry to hear that.' Everybody thought he was going to say: 'How splendid!' [*Laughs.*] That's very un-Firbankian, very intelligent.[24]

PD Do you think that a public that enjoys Waugh's *Brideshead Revisited* as a TV serial could respond to Berners?

DC They ought to. I'm glad he's being revived, because he really deserves it. I tried to persuade Oxford University Press to reprint *A Distant Prospect* as well as *First Childhood*. I thought it would have a greater general interest than *Far from the Madding War*.[25] I don't know what you think.

PD I think you're right. However, the two novellas together – *Percy Wallingford* and *Mr Pidger* – seem to strike a more brilliant level than any of the single novels.

DC I should think that's true.

PD There's realism in *Percy Wallingford* where the successful schoolboy disintegrates in adult life and kills himself: and also in *Mr Pidger* there's the wrangling between the couple whose dog causes the uncle to disinherit them because

23 *Valmouth* (London: Grant Richards, 1919; Harmondsworth: Penguin, 1992), 86: 'But with quick insight the *maître d'orchestre* had struck up a capricious concert waltz, an enigmatic, *au delà* laden air; Lord Berners? Scriabin? Tchaikovsky? On the wings of whose troubled beat were borne some recent arrivals.'

24 Cecil tells this story more fully in *Max*, 462, when Beerbohm, Desmond MacCarthy and the Cecils were staying at Faringdon in December 1946. 'Lord Berners mentioned Lady Cunard, with whom Beerbohm had spent an unenjoyed weekend long ago in Edwardian days. "I haven't seen her for years", he said, with an innocent air. "Has she changed at all?" "No", answered Lord Berners warmly. "It's wonderful, she's exactly the same." Max did not answer for a moment; then, still looking innocent, "I am very sorry to hear that," he said.' The visit was obviously a success, since Berners wrote on 21 January 1946 encouraging the Beerbohms to come again. The pretext for the letter was to enclose a *Daily Mail* photograph of a person called Henry James who was reported as having suffered 'a crack on the back of the head'. Knowing Beerbohm's respect for the great writer, Berners knew he would find this amusing.

25 Berners, *First Childhood; and, Far from the Madding War*, with a preface by Harold Acton (Oxford: Oxford University Press, 1983).

he can't stand dogs. Then the man throws the dog out of the window of the train as they go away, having lost their inheritance.

DC What I also thought about *A Distant Prospect* is that it's an awfully good picture of Eton. It's not the Eton I was at – I went there in 1915 – but it was quite like enough. A lot of it was left. It rather irritated some of the old-fashioned Eton masters, but it was really quite true and very amusingly done.

PD The turn of the century must have been a terrible time for a creative person in Berners' social context. His mother would shut the piano ...

DC Awful, I think. I was always interested in the arts more than anything else, and I was always encouraged. My mother later said that the one thing a parent can do is to find out what a child is interested in and encourage it, unless it's something harmful.

Finally I would like to say that I was very fond of Gerald, and he was very delightful. I was always rather touched because he lived in this very sophisticated world – some of the people were pretty awful by my ideas – but it had never affected him, and he remained so friendly, able to enjoy himself and be amused and that kind of thing. I would like people to realise how loveable he was.

He had panics, by the way. Like a lot of people who've always been well off, he was very frightened of being poor as he got older. But it never made him in the least mean. He was always generous in taking one out to meals. He had this slightly touching side. Just after the war a slightly more sophisticated restaurant opened in Oxford that looked like the pre-war ones, with red curtains and Italian waiters. Gerald was so pleased – in a boyish way. One felt how he'd missed such things.

At the end of an interview with Gavin Bryars, Lady David Cecil joined in:

DC Faringdon told one something about him. It wasn't very grand or highly organised – it's a charming house. It was comfortable and there were a number of luxuries, but it wasn't like some of the houses I've stayed in. It had a touch of the boy who'd inherited it, and a touch of the undergraduate and the bohemian. It made it rather nice: I loved going there.

RDC The food was very good, delicious. And, of course, no war austerity because they had the farm.

DC   It was a bachelor's house.

RDC It was sort of luxury but rather uncomfortable. Very pretty room but not quite like a bedroom. You'd have nowhere to hang your clothes, and probably a writing bureau or something to put them in, and you'd find it stuffed with all sorts of things.

DC   Would you say he was a happy man?

RDC Yes, but he also worried a lot until he resigned himself. I think he was rather happy then.

DC   Well I would say he wasn't meant for tragedy or drama. Quite unsuitable – as if he'd been asked to write a requiem!

RDC He was quite abstemious, which was a surprise; he was physically old for his age; and he had a rather reddish face, but never drank much. He took snuff, and may have smoked an occasional cigar.[26] He loved jokes, like a boy. He didn't go into things, and I don't think we talked much about the war.

DC   Oh no, certainly not.[27]

RDC He was very worried when Robert was called up, but he came back fairly soon. He used to wear dark spectacles and wore spats. I suppose that was old-fashioned, because you wore spats when we first married.

DC   I recommend them – they were the most wonderful way of keeping your feet warm!

RDC Gerald used to wear white spats.

DC   That was ornamental – I never ran to white spats!

26 James Lees-Milne went to tea with Lady Cunard on 26 October 1944. Berners was there and asked them to sniff a white powder which he said was cocaine. 'It smelt of menthol, and I liked it, but Emerald did not, complaining that it burnt the membrane of her nose.' James Lees-Milne, *Prophesying Peace: Diaries, 1944–45* (London: Chatto & Windus, 1977), 125.

27 In *Dresden* (117) Berners considers German and French dislike of the British, which he had hardly noticed: 'I had the habit of turning a blind eye to things I didn't wish to see. There are certain advantages to our peace of mind in being unobservant or indifferent. We at least remain innocent and happy until the crash comes. And when the crash does come, it is just as bad for those who had foreseen it as for those who hadn't.' The final paragraph of *Dresden*: 'That Christmas in Weimar was one of the passages of my youth that remained imprinted in glowing colours on my memory and often during the periods in which we were at war with Germany when Christmas came round it used to come back to me arousing most inappropriately a revival of affection and a feeling of regret.'

CHAPTER 15

Gavin Bryars

Interview with Peter Dickinson on 4 August 1983 at the BBC

GAVIN Bryars (1943–) read philosophy at Sheffield University but became a jazz bassist and a pioneer of free improvisation. His early pieces *The Sinking of the Titanic* and *Jesus' Blood Never Failed Me Yet* achieved great popular success. His output includes three operas, a large body of chamber music, several concertos and much choral and vocal music, often for practitioners of early music. There are many CD recordings, including those on Bryars' own label GB Records. During the 1970s he taught in art colleges, and his first published work on Berners was in *Studio International*.[1] He undertook considerable research on Berners for an intended book, but abandoned this because of the demands of an international career as a composer.

PD How would you describe Berners' paintings?

GB There's quite a wide range. They start from paintings and drawings done when he was a child; there are a lot of watercolours from when he was at Eton; and a larger number that he painted when he first went to France when he was seventeen. He painted the château and the landscape at Résenlieu. He did a number of pastiche paintings – quite a respectable way of learning – including a watercolour version of Turner's *Fighting Temeraire*.

His letters to his mother from school at Cheam and Eton are decorated with lots of little drawings. Even the back of the envelope may have an express train, or a narrative sequence of drawings rather like an early comic strip. Fictitious things like Jules Verne stories. Some of the watercolours are very pretty. His mother, although she's often derided as having no artistic sensibility whatsoever, was quite a talented watercolorist who did similar pictures. With some of the early pictures it's hard to tell which is which. Hers say 'Julia' at the bottom and his say 'Gerald' – that's often the only way of knowing. A bit later he begins to paint more seriously and he also did decorative covers for his manuscripts, such as the funeral march for the canary, *Chinoiserie*, the first of *Three Pieces for Orchestra*, and the *Dispute between the Butterfly and the Toad*. There's a later one for 'Red Roses and Red Noses' too.[2]

He painted more actively from 1926/7 – there's an account of Diaghilev reproving him for painting when he should have been composing music. Beverly Nichols wrote about his early essays in painting when he was copying – often pictures he owned.[3] He copied a Corot, also a Polemberg. Berners was a

1 'Berners, Rousseau, Satie', *Studio International: Journal of Modern Art*, November/December 1976, 308–18. (Four paintings and the Shell poster are reproduced in black and white.) As in this interview Bryars compared the work of Berners and Satie, and argued convincingly that 'its "amateur" nature is its strength … the independence of spirit and confidence in the quality of their imagination, and the range of work that imagination generated, are themselves sufficient reason for prizing the "amateur" status above that of the competent professional'.

2 This watercolour from the original manuscript of 'Red Roses and Red Noses' forms the cover design to *The Collected Vocal Music*, 2nd edn, ed. Peter Dickinson (London: Chester Music, 2000). The watercolour of the canary's funeral appears on the cover of *The Collected Music for Solo Piano*, 2nd edn, ed. Peter Dickinson (London: Chester Music, 2000).

3 Beverley Nichols (1898–1983), *The Sweet and Twenties* (London: Weidenfeld & Nicolson, 1958).

collector of paintings, but not in the modern sense of collecting for investment. He bought paintings he was fond of which
represented an acute taste – he owned a Matisse, a Derain,
a Max Jacob and apparently the largest collection of Corots
outside the Louvre. His taste was for early Corot, especially
Italian landscapes around Rome. The first Corot he copied
was a Venetian scene.[4] These were now oils that have a more
professional quality, technically more accomplished. By 1931
he had enough paintings to justify an exhibition at the Reid-
Lefèvre Gallery. Then in 1936 he had a second one.

It's fair to say that his exhibition probably happened
because of his fame in other areas. I don't think his paintings would have attracted a one-man exhibition if he'd been
a plumber from Balham!

PD Nevertheless Clive Bell said in the preface to the catalogue: 'This is exquisite painting'?

GB Yes – and drew attention to Berners' debt to Corot. A
reviewer, Herbert Fuerst, thought that Berners improved on
Corot. When you look at Corot and then at the Berners copy
you find that in some ways Berners' composition is more sta-
ble, symmetrical and balanced. The colours are different – he
had a fondness for russet browns and dark greens. You see
very little red. Although he was taking a nineteenth-century
model he was adjusting it to a different state of composition.

PD So this is a serious strand right through his output from
childhood?

GB Yes. The last piece of visual work I know of was a drawing in 1949, the year before he died, but he was not as active
as in the late 20s and early 30s.

PD He was a modernist in his music during World War I, so
why was his painting so tame by comparison?

GB I don't think it necessarily was. In some respects his taste
in painting was more conservative than his taste in music.
But by the mid-1930s his taste in music had shifted too. He
wasn't painting actively at the time when he was a musical
modernist. So in a sense his artistic development is like a
relay race – one thing is winning for a time then another
takes over. By the 1930s his sensibility was more restrained.

PD With the ballet scores his music is much milder?

GB In some ways: in other ways not. Because his music is
more mild it's sometimes that bit more subversive perhaps.

PD Berners writes ballet music that is functional; Ashton has
told us how practical he was about making cuts; he looks like
a composer doing a job of work effectively and not obtruding.
How is that subversive?

GB That isn't subversive if that's all he was doing. What

4 When he was at Résenlieu Berners recalled: 'In the library I discovered some volumes of an art journal
containing reproductions of the
pictures of Corot, Rousseau, Daub-
igny. In the drawing room there was
a small picture by Harpignies of a
green valley with a stream and a line
of poplars. These pictures became
my guiding stars.' *The Château de
Résenlieu*, 37.

you've described is the surface appearance of his work. That's a respectable activity and there have been many composers who work in that way – many now forgotten, such as Gavin Gordon, who achieved a certain amount of fame with ballet music.[5]

PD Many great composers have fulfilled a need. If I'm only describing the surface of the ballet scores, tell me what I'm missing.

GB I think it's not necessarily the case that by the 1930s Berners stops being a modernist. What he does is to apply the kind of edge we see in the earlier more abstract work with some of the same characteristics to work which appears to be light and occasionally frivolous. That seems to be quite a clever deception, something which appears to be light and often isn't. There's a dark side to some of the works from 1930 onwards. *A Wedding Bouquet* has a number of sinister elements to it, both in terms of its narrative and the way he approaches things musically. One has here a situation where a composer is apparently writing something very pleasant and easy to listen to, and at the same behaving in an unorthodox way. I think he still is subverting certain kinds of musical practices even in the later ballets.

PD You mean the kind of waltzes he uses in *A Wedding Bouquet* as something to do with parody?

GB Parody is there all the time. If you look at the waltzes he wrote throughout his life you see what they have in common – the second of the *Three Pieces*, the *Valses bourgeoises*, the waltzes from *The Triumph of Neptune*, *A Wedding Bouquet* and *Les Sirènes*. The waltzes in the ballets appear in a theatrical context, where the audience is paying less attention to the music than in a concert performance, but the same kind of actions are going on in the music.

PD You could apply that approach to the music of Satie, who also moved to ballet later in life.

GB One can draw comparisons between Berners and Satie at many levels. They were both taken up by Diaghilev – Satie with *Parade*, Berners with *The Triumph of Neptune*.[6] At a similar stage in their creative careers they both developed doubts about their ability: both were, in principle, self-taught and went back to study sixteenth-century counterpoint.[7] That's a remarkable similarity in terms of their understanding of their own musical equipment. There are other correspondences, such as their habit of writing pieces in groups of three, their satirical edge, and their preoccupation with towers. The principal difference, of course, is their respective wealth. In an oddly inverted way that makes them similar.

5 Gavin Gordon (1901–70), Scottish actor and singer, wrote the score for *The Rake's Progress* (1935), choreographed by Ninette de Valois, premièred by the Vic-Wells ballet at Sadler's Wells and periodically revived.

6 Erik Satie (1866–1925), *Parade*, 'Ballet réaliste sur un thème de Jean Cocteau', sets and designs by Picasso, choreography by Léonide Massine, Ballets Russes, Théâtre du Chatelet, 18 May 1917.

7 Berners studied sixteenth-century counterpoint with Sir Thomas Armstrong (1898–1994), then organist of Christ Church, and impressed him with his understanding of Palestrina. His copy of *Contrapuntal Technique* by R. O. Morris has a funny pencil sketch of an indignant woman on one of the endpapers.

Berners had enough money to pursue a free artistic career, whereas Satie, unlike Stravinsky, despised money, and was free too. So their wealth or lack of it meant that they ended up in a similar situation – money was not a concern for either of them.

PD That's nice. Satie's servants were imaginary: Berners' were very real.

GB Berners' tower was real: Satie's imaginary. Berners was living out Satie's fantasy world. He was dubbed 'the English Satie' in a book by Cecil Gray.[8] We needn't take it too seriously because Berners wrote on the title page of his own copy: 'the silliest book on music ever written'. Then he annotates many pages in the copy later, though interestingly not the page where he is compared to Satie. Gray rambles on about Stravinsky representing the spirit of the age, the *Zeitgeist*. Berners just put a line through it and wrote: 'balls'![9]

PD What do Berners' writings consist of?

GB Apart from the published novels and autobiography there is *The Girls of Radcliff Hall* for private circulation; there are letters, notebooks from childhood onwards, plays, poems, anecdotes and essays. There are seventy-three notebooks stretching from the mid-1920s until virtually the day he died. There was hardly a day when he didn't work in some way – either painting, writing music or prose. In some ways it could be argued that people who do that can often duck problems that arise in one of the genres. If you're in a tricky spot with a piece of music you can slip off and write an essay instead. But I don't think that was necessarily the case with Berners – who seems, incidentally, to have generally worked early in the morning.

The published writing is quite extensive – the five novels, two volumes of autobiography and then further essays based on his time after Eton, in Résenlieu and Dresden. There's no evidence he intended to write more about his life. The autobiographies are extremely entertaining, factually quite accurate. But when Berners writes in his forties about his childhood he transposes on to his childhood his attitudes as a middle-aged man. He writes about himself, for example, as an artistic child not very interested in country pursuits. But the evidence from his mother's diaries and his letters to his mother shows a different picture. We have him hunting, fishing, canoeing, and swimming. When he was in Constantinople he swam the Bosporus and kept horses on the Asian side. He was vigorous and athletic. He was not a sickly wan child of the *Secret Garden* variety.[10]

PD Robert Heber-Percy has confirmed that he liked hunting even in the Faringdon days.

8 Cecil Gray, *A Survey of Contemporary Music* (London: Oxford University Press, 1924). In a chapter on 'Minor Composers' he writes: 'Why, indeed should we go abroad for things we can turn out just as well at home? In the same way that Parry and Stanford provided us with second-rate Brahms, Cyril Scott provides us with imitation Debussy; Holbrooke and Bantock have followed Strauss, and in the music of Goossens, Bliss, and Berners we find our English Ravel, Stravinsky and Satie.' 251. The Belgian painter E. L. T. Messens apparently mentioned the name of Berners to Satie, who became irritated and said: 'He's a professional amateur. He hasn't understood.' In James Harding, *Erik Satie* (London: Secker & Warburg, 1975), 188; also Robert Orledge, *Satie Remembered* (London: Faber & Faber, 1995), 182.

9 Gray wrote: 'The history of any and every art conclusively shows that the artists who most completely express the spirit of their respective ages are not by any means the greatest, but, on the contrary, are nearly always of the second rank.' *A Survey of Contemporary Music*, 127.

10 *The Secret Garden* (1909), the most popular novel by Frances Hodgson Burnett (1849–1924) with many stage and screen adaptations.

11 *An Egyptian Princess* by Gerald Tyrwhitt, privately printed. See Appendix 8. No. 11, Abanazar's Song, an onomatopoeic study in laughter – compare this with 'Le Rire', the second of the *Fragments psychologiques*. Stephen Banfield, in *Sensibility and English Song: Critical Studies of the Early Twentieth Century* (Cambridge: Cambridge University Press, 1985), 378–82, finds laughter motifs in several other works.

12 Edmund Kretschmer (1830–1908), German organist and composer mostly based in Dresden, where he held major church posts. Obituary: *Musical Times*, 1 October 1908, 652. In *Dresden* (47) Berners relates: 'Whatever may have been Professor Kretschmer's merits as a composer, at all events he looked like a very distinguished one, and in addition he was a charming old gentleman … His study, where I had my lessons, was a most inspiring room with faded laurel wreaths tied up with scarlet ribbons on the walls: there was huge grand piano, a mask of Beethoven and bookcases filled with scores and books on music. I felt that anyone possessing such a room could not fail to be a genius … Diplomacy faded for the moment into the background and I almost made up my mind to brave parental displeasure and devote my life to music.' In *Dresden* Berners said he had three lessons in orchestration 'brought to an end by the untimely arrival of my mother in Dresden', but Mary Gifford shows that his letters to his mother about the costs of these suggest that he had at least sixteen. Gifford, *Lord Berners: Aspects of a Biography* (PhD thesis, University of London, 2007).

13 Berners' *English Music* (notebook 32) starts:

There is a legend firmly rooted in the minds of foreigners that the English are an unmusical race. They are willing to give us points for literature, architecture, painting and all the commodities of comfort, but they deny that any good musical thing can come

out of England. They read our books, buy our motorcars and are dressed by our tailors, but they do not seem to listen to our music. Of course there have been isolated exceptions … and we read in the newspapers that when Sir Somebody Something's cantata for ladies' voices was

performed in Berlin it met with warm applause or when Doctor Somebody Else's oratorio *Zion's Trumpets* was given at a concert arranged by the League of Nations in Geneva, the audience (consisting almost entirely of politicians) rose to their feet and cheered.   ▶ ▶ ▶

GB   I can believe that.

PD   We've seen how important his painting and writing were to him. What about the music?

GB   *An Egyptian Princess* is the earliest surviving piece of music.[11] We know of a march he wrote when he studied with Kretschmer in Dresden.[12] He was unfortunate in his choice of teachers.

PD   What did he study with Kretschmer?

GB   Pastiche composition, orchestration. He took Kretschmer very seriously, writing home to his mother that he was a well-known composer and professor who'd written operas.

PD   What else survives of the juvenilia?

GB   We know of him arranging music for a Christmas pantomime at the Embassy in Constantinople. Then we come to the music published by Chester starting with the *Three Funeral Marches*.

PD   By then he was the most advanced English composer up to that point in history?

GB   Between the *Lieder Album* and the *Funeral Marches* we have the *Dispute between the Butterfly and the Toad*, which I would put at 1914–15. I think it misleading to ever call Berners an English composer. He was, of course, an Englishman, but had a low opinion of the idea of English music. We see him parodying English composers mercilessly with Emmanuel Smith in *Count Omega* and Francis Paltry in *Far from the Madding War*. He wrote a short essay on English music which is quite scathing about the way it is promoted abroad. He refers to Professor so-and-so's oratorio called *Zion's Trumpets*. That's his image of English composition. So he doesn't see himself as an English but rather as an international composer.[13]

PD   Everybody's confirmed that he made fun of everything so you wouldn't expect him to take English music seriously either. But you're objecting to him as an English composer?

GB   The point I'm making is that he wasn't actually composing in England but in Rome. That's a different artistic milieu from Vaughan Williams, Holst or others of that kind.

PD He seems to have been close to Casella?[14]

GB Yes, though there's little evidence for Casella having taught Berners. He showed his work to Casella as he did to Stravinsky – as advisers. By the time Berners was on friendly terms with them he was already writing in his modernist style. The annotations in Casella's hand on the score of *L'uomo dai baffi*, the pieces he wrote for the futurist marionette theatre in 1918, show that Casella was making adjustments – but as a conductor, much as Lambert might do in *A Wedding Bouquet*.

PD Do you see the *Funeral Marches* and the *Fragments psychologiques* as remarkably original? What are Berners' sources?

GB The early music has evidence of considerable originality, and I think Stravinsky was right to point to Berners as being one of the best English composers of the century. He didn't produce a lot of work, but what he did produce was remarkable. Fortunately Berners gave us some clues about his origins and produced a chronology – Chopin, Bach, Wagner then, quite importantly, Richard Strauss.[15] When Berners was studying in Dresden he attended one of the first performances of *Elektra* and saw as many Strauss operas as he could. He bought the vocal scores. Then there was Debussy, who also had an effect on him. A little later he became aware of Schoenberg and Stravinsky, which is a sequence he himself gives. The Schoenberg would have been the *Six Little Pieces*, op. 19, and *Erwartung*, op. 17, of which he had a full score. Perhaps the *Six Little Pieces* have a relationship with the last of the *Fragments psychologiques*.[16] There is certainly a connection with Stravinsky in the piano writing.

Those are more like inspirational sources than direct musical material. It's a puzzle where composers get their ideas from, but often it's by listening to other music and seeing where they go from there. That seems to be the way Berners went about it. He studied this music and tried to understand what kind of procedures were going on, then turned whatever he heard there to his own advantage. That's where evidence of his originality comes in. His music doesn't sound like Strauss, Schoenberg or Stravinsky although there's an occasional touch of Debussy in the slower piano pieces like *Le Poisson d'or*.

This did reflect the climate of artistic activity in Rome at that time. One would be hard pressed to say that Berners was taking ideas from Casella or even Malipiero. In some ways one could point to the obverse of that. In 1920 Malipiero wrote a set of three piano pieces called *Omaggi* where each one is parodistic: 'To a Parrot'; 'To an Elephant'; and

► ► ►

Berners saw all this from the other side of the Channel, and added: 'Debussy once said to me: "You English composers always seem to write with one eye on Brahms and the other on the cathedral towns."' See Oscar A. H. Schmitz, *Das Land ohne Musik: Englische Gesellschaftsprobleme* (Munich, 1914); trans. H. Herzl as *The Land without Music* (London: Jarrolds, 1925). The book is not about music, but states: 'The English are the only cultured race without a music of their own.' And Bernarr Rainbow, *The Land without Music: Musical Education in England, 1800–1860, and its Continental Antecedents* (London: Novello & Co., 1967).

14 See interview with Professor Fiamma Nicolodi, Casella's granddaughter, Chapter 17, p. 143.

15 Berners' few signed copies of books and scores surviving in the early 1970s are included in the list of his library of scores in Appendix 7.

16 Schoenberg: *Erwartung*, op. 17 (1909, full score published in 1916, not staged until 6 June 1924 at the Neues Deutsches Theater, Prague); *Sechs kleine Klavierstücke*, op. 19 (1911). Berners said: 'The violent interest I took for a time in Schoenberg was I fancy the interest of an explorer. He had opened up for me the new territory of atonal music but this territory, that at one time seemed almost a promised land, had proved itself infertile, an enclosed, dry, rocky academic valley with no issue.' Mark Amory, *Lord Berners: the Last Eccentric* (London: Chatto & Windus, 1998), 83.

17 Gian Francesco Malipiero (1882–1972), prolific Italian composer. *Omaggi* was published by J. & W. Chester in 1921. Berners dedicated his *Fantaisie espagnole* (1919) to Malipiero.

18 Giacomo Balla (1871–1958). Berners would have liked the witty approach exemplified by his paintings such as *Dynamism of a Dog on a Leash* (1910).

19 In a letter to Stein on 17 May 1938 Berners acknowledged receipt of the text of *Dr Faustus*, but on 3 December 1939 he wrote: 'What I want to say is, and it makes me very sad to say it – that all inspirational sources seem to have dried up: I can't write a note of music or do any kind of creative work whatever, and it's not for want of trying and I don't believe I shall be able to as long as this war lasts. I feel confronted by the breakdown of all the things that meant anything to me ...' Donald Gallup (ed.), *The Flowers of Friendship: Letters Written to Gertrude Stein* (New York: Octagon, 1953), 330 & 346. *Dr Faustus* was produced in 1951 at the Cherry Theatre, New York, with music by Richard Banks. In August 1992 the play was given at the Edinburgh Festival by the Hebbel Theatre of Berlin, with music by Hans-Peter Kuhn. The producer was Robert Wilson, who has worked with Philip Glass. This makes a link between the Stein operas of Virgil Thomson and the non-narrative operas of Glass. Martin Hoyle, 'Beautifully Drilled Puzzle Pieces', *The Times*, 27 August 1992: 'Gertrude Stein conceived these variations on a Faustian theme as a libretto for Lord Berners ... One can only speculate whether collaboration with the quirky composer with his gift for deadpan parody ... would have produced a work to rival the Walton-Sitwell *Façade*. Probably not, for reasons literary as well as musical.'

'To an Idiot'.[17] This is very close to the conceptual satire of Berners' *Three Funeral Marches*. So it's a two-way process in a particularly vigorous artistic climate when the futurist manifestos were proliferating from 1911 to 1912. Some were in English – one of the first came out in the *Daily Mail*.

Berners was also a friend of the futurist painter Balla[18] and owned a number of his pictures which were in his apartment in Rome. He was in the Diaghilev circle, and through that met Larionov and Goncharova, who were to decorate his scores. Berners responded to this climate of artistic activity, in many ways as an equal partner. It would be naïve to say that everyone took a cue from Stravinsky or fed off the futurist manifesto.

PD After this period in Rome Berners' music becomes less dissonant, even the opera.

GB I think the opera is important as a transitional piece, never heard in this country until the BBC broadcast (1983). Berners was predominantly a composer of miniatures, but *Le Carrosse* is his longest single work. It represents a partial shift in musical language, although it's close to some of the songs. As with the ballets and films, although these are more functional, there is a more accommodating kind of music for a different public.

PD What impact can we expect Berners to have on later generations?

GB I find him very interesting as a model, apart from the music itself. Any composer whose music has merit will, at some stage, attract attention. There's the perennial difficulty about how composers get heard. Berners' music wasn't heard much from the end of the Second World War until the early 1970s, when you revived the songs and piano music. But the *Three Orchestral Pieces* and the *Fantaisie espagnole* are tremendous. The *Fantaisie* is a skilful orchestral exercise rather like late Rimsky-Korsakov, an orchestral showpiece that could bring the house down.

PD Did Berners spread himself too thin?

GB Quite the reverse. I think if he'd spent more time on his music he could have become a duller composer. He did just the right amount of everything. Berners was very interested in cooking – he knew just how to concoct a successful recipe. He knew how to organise his time and focus attention on different artistic activities. My own feeling is that he did just the right amount of everything – my principal sadness is that he died too soon. If he'd lived into his eighties I don't think he would have become a boring old man!

PD Didn't the war upset his creative balance?

GB Absolutely. He wrote a very sad letter to Gertrude Stein at the outbreak of the war. They'd worked together on *A Wedding Bouquet*, and after its success they became good friends and planned another collaboration, *Doctor Faustus Lights the Lights*. It was discussed in the press, designs were drawn up and Berners began writing music for it. Then he told Stein he couldn't do anything and suggested Virgil Thomson, an acute observation. But she preferred Berners, and so nothing was done until it became a play with incidental music long after Berners died.[19]

It's important to bear in mind the credibility he had for other composers. Stravinsky took him seriously; Bliss, Goossens and Sauguet did; Lambert especially. Sorabji – one of the greatest British composers – took him very seriously.[20] Milhaud and Goossens did the first performance of the *Valses bourgeoises* as a piano duet. Berners was friendly with all the members of Les Six. A diary entry in December 1920 simply says: 'Dined, Les Six'. Shortly after that he went to see the play of *Le Carrosse*, which he then wrote as an opera. His peers had a high regard for him, which tends to be forgotten when people think of him as a dilettante who flitted on and off the musical stage and, when he got in trouble, daubed a few pictures or drafted a few novels. He was a very serious composer, and at the end of his life his greatest anxiety was that he should be remembered as a composer. He felt that was what he did best. John Betjeman has confirmed that he wondered what would become of his music.[21] Nevertheless he did other things supremely well too. There are touches in his writing which equal Evelyn Waugh or Ronald Firbank.

PD Are there differences between the writer of autobiography and the novellas?

GB There are fictionalised elements in the autobiography just as there are autobiographical elements in the fiction. He blurs the distinction. *Far from the Madding War* is keyed into the life Berners was leading in Oxford in the war. The characters appear disguised and some of them are composite – even the portrait of himself as Lord Fitzcricket has an element of the Sitwells in it at one point. In the autobiographies the names are changed – his grandmother is Lady Bourchier instead of Lady Berners. The houses are given different names. The various schoolboys and even the school have their names changed, partly because he was scathing about some of the masters.

First Childhood was one of the earliest things he wrote, but the very first was *The Camel*, which overlapped. It was partly inspired by reading Dashiel Hammet, who was recommended by Gertrude Stein.[22] Like a number of writers,

20 Kaikhosru Sorabji (1892–1988) lamented: 'The one contemporary English composer who has produced a really successful and accomplished stage work is Lord Berners with his delightful little comédie musicale, *Le Carrosse du saint-sacrement* and, as one would expect, he is never mentioned.' And: 'the delightful, amusing and brilliantly clever *Fantaisie Espagnole* of Lord Berners had a great reception on its first performance some years ago, so much so that one would have thought an early repeat assured ... Each time it is played, it has the same emphatic success, but appears as far as ever from assuming its quite justifiable place in the regular repertoire.' Kaikhosru Sorabji *Around Music* (London: Unicorn Press, 1932), 34 & 104.

21 John Betjeman, 'Lord Berners: 1883–1950', *Listener*, 11 May 1950, 839.

22 Dashiel Hammett (1894–1961), American writer of detective stories. Stein recommended *The Maltese Falcon*: see letter from Berners to Stein, 1 March 1936, in Gallup, *The Flowers of Friendship*, 313.

especially of detective fiction, he wrote his first piece while he was ill in bed. The elements are blurred in *The Girls of Radcliff Hall*.

PD Is that interesting if you don't know who the characters are based on?

GB I can see reasons why those who are portrayed in *The Girls of Radcliff Hall* might prefer to wait until they're long since gone before it appears, but there's nothing dreadful even if one knows who the people are. If one doesn't, it reads as a very good pastiche of an Angela Brazil story, many of which also have undercurrents of lesbianism.[23]

PD We've talked about how he entered the professional world of music, but what about literature?

GB He was a close friend of Evelyn Waugh and an even closer friend of Ronald Firbank. It was Berners who buried him in the wrong cemetery in Rome, assuming that he would want to be buried alongside Keats, and only discovering later that Firbank was Catholic. Firbank changed a line in *Valmouth* as a result of hearing Berners' music. At a party in the novel the orchestra starts playing a capricious waltz and Firbank tries to identify the composer. 'Is it Tchaikovsky? Is it Scriabin?' Those were the only two composers mentioned when an excerpt from the story was first published in a magazine. But when the book was finally published he adds to that 'Lord Berners'.[24] By then Firbank had heard the *Three Orchestral Pieces* played as an interlude for Diaghilev's ballet,[25] and the second is the *Valse sentimentale*, which Firbank had identified quite rightly as a very creepy sinister waltz. Firbank entrusted Berners, too, with his final manuscripts.

One can see certain elements in Berners' writings that relate to Firbank, especially some of the unpublished short stories. He borrows heavily on Henry James and to a certain extent Ibsen – and Max Beerbohm too, who was a friend in Berners' later life. He was close to the professional world of literature. Berners read a number of his works in manuscript to David Cecil to see how he reacted. His play *The Furies* was put on in Oxford in 1942.[26] It is a light frivolous piece, a bit Noël Cowardish, but with elements of Firbank, such as the setting in Haiti. There's a late play too – a translation of a piece by Voltaire called *Saul*, which he did at the end of his life in 1949 and showed to William Plomer.[27] As a child he wrote a play that he showed to his mother, who thought it was morbid and that he should write something lighter. Professional writers have envied the easy style that Berners had with his beautiful limpid phrases.

PD Did he make drafts in the notebooks?

23 Angela Brazil (1868–1947), pioneer writer of schoolgirl stories.

24 See interview with Lord David Cecil, Chapter 14, p. 125.

25 The 1919 London season which ran from 30 April to 30 July at the Alhambra Theatre.

26 See interview with Lord David Cecil, Chapter 14, p. 117.

27 William Charles Franklin Plomer (1903–73), South African-born poet and novelist, who came to England in 1929. He corresponded with Berners in his final years and was Britten's librettist for *Gloriana* and the three church parables.

GB The style is there straight away, and it was often a question of simply polishing up an adverb, altering the punctuation or putting one sentence before another. But he did always write first, in pencil, in a notebook before putting anything into the world – even the most apparently casual letter.

PD You see him as a perfectionist in every way?

GB Yes: a real craftsman.

CHAPTER 16   Sir Richard Rodney Bennett

Interview with Peter Dickinson on 4 August 1983 at the BBC

SIR Richard Rodney Bennett (1936–), one of the most versatile British composers of his generation, has also been involved with jazz as a pianist and singer. He was a pupil of Howard Ferguson and Lennox Berkeley at the Royal Academy of Music, then spent two formative years in Paris studying with Pierre Boulez. From his late teens he developed another career as a successful composer for films although he almost invariably kept his serious and commercial music poles apart. Some of his film scores are classics, several of which have gained awards: he was made a CBE (1977) and knighted in 1999. For some years he has lived in New York.

PD When did you first come across anything about Lord Berners?

RRB As a little boy I used to read avidly about modern music and modern writers. I'd read about Lord Berners and he sounded extraordinary, and I'd also read about Miss Stein. When I found out that they'd written a piece together called *A Wedding Bouquet* I jumped at it and got the music when I was about fourteen – and was thrilled. I bought the vocal score, played what I could, and it wasn't until years later that I actually saw the piece.

PD Did it disappoint you after all that build-up?

RRB I know I enjoyed it. I don't think I was disappointed at all. Maybe if I hadn't known his early music and how extraordinary it was, I might not have been that fascinated with *A Wedding Bouquet* apart from the Stein words and their strange world.

PD How does Berners fit in with British music?

RRB Outside. He's a very odd musical character. There were a lot of strange composers in English music working away, particularly in the 1920s. They weren't accepted and they didn't fit into any school. Berners was perhaps the most distinguished of them.

PD What sort of strange composers?

RRB I was thinking of Bernard van Dieren and Sorabji,[1] most of whom are disappointing when you get close to them. But Berners is not disappointing: he's a very strange genuine eccentric in the best sense.

PD How is the eccentricity expressed in the music?

[1] Bernard van Dieren (1887–1936), Kaikhosru Sorabji (1892–1988).

RRB Most of it is very jokey, looking sideways on at people – I don't mean frivolous – but with a very brisk unsentimental colourful eye. And, of course, harmonically he was remarkable. I've always wondered if there were early works of his which were more conventional, or whether he came out fully grown with that more or less atonal style.

PD He wrote that music when he was living in Rome during World War I: do you think he could have written it in England?

RRB I doubt it very much. And, of course, Continental influences, unless they were Brahms or whatever, were very unpopular in England. I remember Elisabeth Lutyens saying that one of the reasons that she had such a hard time as a young composer was because her influences were Bartók, and later on Schoenberg and Webern – and that was not the thing to do.[2] Berners was writing some years earlier, and what he was doing must have seemed quite mad to people who weren't sophisticated and intelligent.

PD How far do you think he was affected by Diaghilev and the atmosphere surrounding the Ballets Russes?

RRB I think Diaghilev had a great deal to do with it, and I think he influenced Constant Lambert as well – another curious figure in English music, very aware of what was going on across the channel and particularly of Stravinsky.

PD How would you compare Berners and Lambert?

RRB Lambert's music is more tonal; his influences were largely literary; and he used jazz – another thing that was unfashionable in classical music circles in the 1920s. I doubt if Berners was influenced by the same kind of jazz as Lambert – black music. I like those curious figures that were flourishing quite independently of the main stream.

PD It isn't jazz, but do you see an aspect of popular music in Berners?

RRB There's a certain brass-band-at-the-end-of-the-pier funny quality about his music. It comes out in pieces like *The Triumph of Neptune* – very much Pollock's model theatres. These are not conventional influences on 'serious' English composers.

PD It's an anticipation of Walton?

RRB Absolutely. Walton is one of the composers I've always felt closest to. There's that same slight cocking a snook – as in *Façade*. Walton also received influences from foreign music and popular music when he was very young.

PD Walton went on to write symphonies and concertos; Berners turned to ballet.

2 Elisabeth Lutyens (1903–83), pioneering English serial composer who also wrote film music.

RRB His music did become in a sense more respectable when he was writing for the ballet. That's not a judgement of quality, but pieces like *The Triumph of Neptune* are much more conventional than his early works, which are what I go back to. I've always been interested in music that was written in those chaotic years around World War I before anybody's style seemed to settle down. This includes Stravinsky, particularly Schoenberg, Bartók, Webern and Debussy, who, as far as I'm concerned, was in the most miraculous period of his life from a compositional point of view. Everything was such a melting pot at that time – in Europe and in music. This is why Berners is so extraordinary.

PD Do you regret that the panache of the *Funeral Marches* and the *Fragments psychologiques* wasn't followed up?

RRB I don't know how he could have carried on doing that without becoming a sort of naughty middle-aged composer – a bit tiresome. I don't see that those pieces could have expanded beyond the aphoristic frameworks he used. I can't conceive of him writing a large work in that style. In order to broaden his structures his music became slightly more conventional.

PD Isn't it extraordinary that a beginning composer should write highly dissonant music at the frontiers of technique and then go into something else?

RRB No. The same thing happened to Walton; Lambert to some extent; and perhaps Britten. It doesn't surprise me at all. When I was twenty I was writing demented music as a pupil of Boulez, and it was later that I found my own wings. But I'm interested in Berners because he seemed to have found his own eccentric wings early on.

PD How do you find Berners as a writer? Do the books stand the test of time?

RRB I hate to say this, but they aren't really for me. I was interested in them because he wrote them, but if I'd just found him as a writer I wouldn't have been that thrilled.

PD Have you any ideas about the paintings?

RRB What I've seen are magical, but I've seen very few.

PD What about a creative artist who spreads himself into three different media as well as an interesting life? Harold Acton thinks Berners would have been a better composer if he'd concentrated on his music.

RRB It's a depressing verdict. Berners' personality in the music, painting and the way he lived are so much part and parcel of the same thing that I can't dissociate him from the way he lived or the music from his style of living. He might have been a more solid composer if he had concentrated on music, but I think that would have lost a lot of his very special qualities.

PD Can one make a comparison between Berners and Satie?

RRB I think the same things apply. If Satie had suddenly turned respectable and started writing extended works of a conventional kind – I'm not talking about *Socrate* – he would probably have been a much duller composer. I like the fact that Berners was always skating round the edges of respectable music and never becoming a part of it. That's what gives him his special colour.

PD The fact that he hardly took anything seriously?

RRB Yes. There were bad writers in the 1920s such as Brian Howard, who was a silly butterfly socialite.[3] But Berners was a very good composer, and that fantastic aspect of his character doesn't in any way hurt the music.

PD What future do you see for Berners after the centenary?

RRB I don't think he will suddenly become a respectable famous composer. I think he was a quite individual minor talent of extraordinary charm and – I can't say importance – but somebody who'll always be a pleasure to go back to. Like a minor novelist who was nevertheless delicious to read and who you take off the shelf every now and again. I think Berners' most important music is the most eccentric, the small-scale pieces.

PD Isn't that unfair on the *Three Orchestral Pieces* and *Fantasie espagnole*?

RRB I've never heard them in the orchestral version. What I'm saying is not a criticism of Berners, but it's how I would place him. If I say 'a minor composer' I'm not putting him down. There are minor painters who are magical, but will always remain minor painters, not part of an important mainstream. I think this applies to Berners.

In their early atonal music the Viennese composers, particularly Webern and Schoenberg, seem to me to be proceeding entirely by instinct. They were fast getting away from the nineteenth century, and there was not yet a 'system' for writing atonal music. It was like choosing colours or words just for their meaning and not their coherence. They moved on to the twelve-tone system as a way of organising chaos. Berners went the other way – back to tonal music rather than continuing what he was doing in the early works.

PD Could we find a future for Berners as part of the new tonality – if people knew the music?

3 Brian Howard (1905–58), writer, Oxford contemporary of Acton and Waugh, who regarded him, in Byron's phrase, as 'mad, bad and dangerous to know'.

RRB I doubt if Berners had any influence after his death. I don't think he was a composer whom anybody has attempted to imitate nor are there conclusions to be drawn from his music. He has to be appreciated for exactly what he did – and no more.

PD Satie is fashionable now – why not Berners as part of the same thing?

RRB I think people read a great deal into Satie that wasn't necessarily there, drawing aesthetic conclusions that weren't actually in his music. I don't know if you could do the same thing to Berners: he doesn't point in any direction at all.

PD It's been said that Berners' apparently simple music is actually subversive.[4] It's not as simple as it seems – that's only the surface – but the particular dislocations from known models, as in the *Valses bourgeoises*, are slight but can seem threatening in some way.

RRB Heavens! I've never thought of it in that context. It seems to me to be a brilliantly twisted kind of parody – and a very musical parody as well. Threatening? I don't know.

PD You don't see anything sinister in *A Wedding Bouquet*?

RRB No. You can see a lot behind Satie's simplicity but Berners wasn't a simple composer or a *faux-naif*. The surface is what you get. It's a joy, but I wouldn't want to have a diet of Berners. I wouldn't want to have to play the *Valses bourgeoises* too often. I find his music hard to play chiefly because it's so wilful, particularly harmonically. It's hard to get your fingers round those chords, and this may account for the fact that his music hasn't been performed more. You have done absolutely invaluable service to his music, but you know that his piano music is hard to do.

PD The Valse in the film *The Halfway House* goes further back than the ballets – to Chopin.

RRB If I'd only known him from those late pieces I wouldn't have been interested in him. He was obviously a witty professional composer, but there are quite a lot of those. I'd like to know more about his film music. As a composer involved with film music myself, I'd like to know how he coped with the problems of the cinema.[5]

included in *The Collected Music for Solo Piano*, ed. Peter Dickinson (London: Chester Music, 1982; 2nd edn 2000). An orchestral suite, *The Halfway House*, has been edited by Philip Lane, and is recorded on Chandos CHAN10459 (2008).]

Champagne Charlie, opened at the Regal, Marble Arch, 25 August 1944. Producer: Michael Balcon; director: Alberto Cavalcanti; screenplay: Austin Melford, John Dighton and Angus McPhail; new music and lyrics: Una Bart, Frank Eyton, Lord Berners, Noel Gay, T. E. B. Clarke and Billy Mayerl. Ealing Studios. [Berners contributed the Polka as a piano piece, which was scored by the musical director Ernest Irving, and the song 'Come on Algernon' with lyric by T. E. B. Clarke (1907–89) sung in the film by Betty Warren (1907–1990) and recorded by Meriel Dickinson (Symposium 1278), Felicity Lott (Albany TROY290) and Ian Partridge (Marco Polo 8.225159). T. E. B. Clarke said: 'I had no experience of working with Lord Berners apart from *Champagne Charlie*, and so I knew him only slightly. He was a very kind and most amusing man.' Letter to Peter Dickinson, 29 March 1972. Clarke remembered that Berners wrote the music for their song before he added the words. They shared a sense of the ridiculous, since Clarke adapted illustrations cut from magazines of the 1890s and gave them comic captions. *Intimate Relations, or Sixty Years a Bastard* (London: Michael Joseph, 1971).]

The Life and Adventures of Nicholas Nickleby, released 7 April 1947. Director: Alberto Cavalcanti; screenplay: John Dighton based on Dickens; music: Lord Berners. Ealing Studios.

Ernest Irving (1878–1953) was appointed musical director at Ealing Studios in 1935. He was responsible for getting many of the most prominent British composers to write film scores. (Berners made a Suite from the film score, recorded by the Royal Liverpool Philharmonic Orchestra in 1986 under Barry Wordsworth – see Discography.)

---

4 See interview with Gavin Bryars, Chapter 15, p. 129.

5 Berners was involved in the following films:
The Halfway House, opened at the Regal, Marble Arch, 14 April 1944. Producer: Michael Balcon;

associate producer: Alberto Cavalcanti; director: Basil Dearden; screenplay: Angus MacPhail and Diana Morgan; music: Lord Berners. Ealing Studios. [The Valse used during the séance scene is a piano piece in the style of Chopin, and is

CHAPTER 17 Professor Fiamma Nicolodi

Interview with Peter Dickinson on 28 May 1983 at 19 Via Santo Spiritu, Florence

FIAMMA NICOLODI has been Professor of the History of Music at the University of Florence since 1987, and has taught musical dramaturgy there since 1995. She is a member of the Board of Directors of the Chigiana Academy, Siena, and of the Scientific Committee at the Observatoire musical français at the Sorbonne in Paris.

Her principal publications include *Luigi Dallapiccola: Saggi, testimonianze, carteggio, biografia e bibliografia* (1975); *Luigi Dallapiccola: Parole e musica* (1980); *Gusti e tendenze del Novecento musicale in Italia* (1982); *Musica e musicisti nel ventennio fascista* (1984) and studies of the language of musical literature *Le parole della musica* (1994, 2000).

Nicolodi is the granddaughter of Alfredo Casella (1883–1947), the friend and colleague of Berners in Rome. The basis for this interview took place in Florence on 28 May 1983 in a mixture of English and French. Professor Nicolodi saw a transcript and made a few corrections in 2007.

FN   Alfredo Casella came from Turin to Paris in 1896 and stayed there until 1914. In the first period he went to the Conservatory and became a pupil of Louis Diémer (piano), Xavier Leroux (harmony) and Gabriel Fauré (composition). This last class included at that time Roger-Ducasse, Charles Koechlin and Maurice Ravel, with whom Casella became a great friend. Casella wrote in his *Memoirs*:

> Ravel's culture was vast in literature as well as in music. I owe him my first knowledge of Russian music ... Once or twice a week we met at the home of Pierre Sechiari, the concertmaster of the Lamoureux orchestra, and read in four-hand arrangements all the operatic and symphonic repertoire of the Russian Five and of Glazunov, Liapunov, Liadov and others. Tchaikovsky was excluded from these sessions, because Ravel detested him. A great impression was made on us by the music of Borodin, Balakirev and Rimsky-Korsakov. There was developing, at least in the bold and unprejudiced circle headed by Debussy and Ravel, an anti-Wagnerian viewpoint which was also anti-Germanic ... I certainly do not regret my former enthusiasms. German music had been the essential basis of my artistic education until then.[1]

1 Originally *I segreti della giara* (Florence: Sansoni, 1941); trans. Spencer Norton as *Music in My Time*, (Norman: University of Oklahoma Press, 1955), 61.

After having conducted the first performance of the *Pavane pour une infante défunte* (1911: Concerts Hasselmans), Casella played the piano at the first performance of Ravel's *Trio* (1915: Salle Gaveau) and *Chansons madécasses* (1926: Salle Érard). In Vienna he and Ravel gave the première of *La Valse* for two pianos (1920: Kleiner Konzerthaussaal). They also wrote together in 1913 the second set of *À la manière de ...* – musical parodies of Borodin and Chabrier (written by Ravel), of d'Indy and of Ravel himself (by Casella).[2]

PD   Was Casella influenced by Stravinsky?

FN   Yes. He was affected first by Mahler, becoming a keen supporter of his music that he played often and imposed on the Parisians, who couldn't bear it. But after having heard the première of *Le Sacre du printemps* in 1913, he was greatly impressed by its violent energy: from that moment his style changed into something tougher and more dissonant. It was not as nuanced as before, but with Russian colours and much drier. That became his character – more geometric.

PD   So Casella brought to Rome a more advanced music back from Paris at the same time as he was meeting Berners. Who influenced whom?

FN   When Casella came back to Italy in 1915 at the time of World War I he became the centre of the Italian avant-garde and had a lot of charismatic power. He founded a society for modern music, which in 1923 became the Italian section of the International Society for Contemporary Music headed by Edward J. Dent, and organised many concerts where Italian listeners heard for the first time Ravel, Stravinsky, Falla, Debussy, Enescu, Fauré and Lord Berners. In his *Memoirs* Casella remembered the concert on 30 March 1917 when he played the *Trois petites marches funèbres* at the Accademia di S. Cecilia: '... it happened that a few weeks later an uncle died in London who left young Tyrwhitt his conspicuous fortune and the title of Lord Berners. Although the composer was not excessively superstitious, he always remembered that performance of mine in Rome. To which he attributed a mysterious relationship with the death of his rich uncle.'[3]

Casella and Tyrwhitt, who were the same age, were both certainly influenced by Stravinsky, but I couldn't say if they influenced each other. Berners, who was then an attaché of the British Embassy in Rome, became Casella's pupil. Casella was musical director of the Balli plastici, a marionette theatre founded by the futuristic painter Fortunato Depero (1892–1960) and based in Rome at the Teatro dei Piccoli, Palazzo Odescalchi. He asked Berners to transcribe for small orchestra some of his piano pieces for a ballet, *L'uomo dai baffi*, which he conducted on 15 April 1918 with other music

2   The first volume of *À la manière de ...* (Paris: Éditions SECA, 1911) was by Casella on his own, and contained realistic forgeries of Wagner, Fauré, Brahms, Strauss and Franck. The second, joint volume, contained Borodin, d'Indy, Chabrier and Ravel (Paris: Éditions SECA, 1914). Berners must have known these pieces, and they may well have prompted his own interest in parody.

3   *Music in my Time*, 143. The uncle died on 5 September 1918. See Chapter 1, p. 12.

(Malipiero's *Grottesco*, Casella's *Pupazzetti* and an arrangement of Bartók's *Ten Easy Pieces*).[4] Berners' autograph score, with some pencil corrections made by Casella, can be consulted at the Fondazione Cini in Venice, where Casella's archives have been placed by his family.

PD But where did the style based on minor seconds and major sevenths come from?

FN And also superimposed fourths.

PD Yes.

FN Stravinsky.

PD Only Stravinsky: not Schoenberg?

FN You are right. In 1913 Casella became enthusiastic about Schoenberg's music. In Paris he heard the *Kammersymphonie* op. 9 (with its superimposed fourths), String Quartet no. 2 and *Pierrot lunaire*. In the same year he wrote two articles on Schoenberg and his music in the journal *L'Homme libre* and bought the score of *Pierrot lunaire*.[5] Back in Italy, he invited Schoenberg for a tour in April–May 1924, where the Austrian composer conducted the first Italian performance of his melodrama. It was a tremendous scandal: the public didn't understand anything, and even composers like Goffredo Petrassi (1904–2003) admitted they were disconcerted by it. The only one who understood the originality of *Pierrot lunaire* was Luigi Dallapiccola (1904–75), who later became the first Italian dodecaphonic composer. But by 1924 Casella had changed his style, which became more fluent and *dépouillée*. Atonal influences can be found earlier in works such as *L'Adieu à la vie* (1915), *Sonatina for piano* (1916), *Elegia eroica* (1916) and *A notte alta* (1917).

PD The music of Berners and Casella at this period is not just an imitation of Stravinsky and Schoenberg: isn't it very original?

FN I feel an eclectic style in Casella's music written in the first period – Fauré, Ravel, Rimsky-Korsakov, Mahler – but the dissonance does come from Schoenberg, Stravinsky and Bartók.

PD Were there activities in the other arts that affected the climate in Rome, like the marionettes?

FN In Italy the main spectacle was the traditional opera of Verdi, Mascagni and Puccini. But other movements like Futurism wanted an alternative to the traditional theatre with variety, circus and music hall. So the marionette theatre of Fortunato Depero was really a new spectacle, and futurists wanted to shock the public with many colours, tactile

4 See interview with Sir Harold Acton, Chapter 3, p. 47.

5 A. Casella, 'Schönberg in Italy', *League of Composers Review* [*Modern Music*] 1/2 (June 1924), 7–10.

effects, and things like smoking on the stage. The futurists wanted movement rather than the static qualities of cubism.

PD Do you see the influence of Diaghilev?

FN Not in Depero's *Balli plastici*. But remember that the futurist painter Balla collaborated with Diaghilev on Stravinsky's *Feu d'artifice* (1908). The first Italian performance was in Rome on 12 April 1917 at the Theatre Costanzi.

PD Was it anything like the aesthetic of Satie's *Parade*?

FN I don't think so: the superimposition of music and noises is typical of Futurism. We find it earlier in *L'aviatore Dro* (1911–14) by the futurist Francesco Balilla Pratella and in many futurist performances produced with the collaboration of Luigi Russolo (1885–1947), the father of Rumorism (1913), who invented a mechanical device called the *intonarumori* (literally, noise-tuning) that made unconventional sounds impossible to produce with traditional instruments.

PD Casella and Berners were both the most avant-garde composers of their respective countries for a short period at the same time. Do you see any future for their work?

FN Yes, absolutely. Not only because we're looking for the historic avant-garde, and are very interested to discover the musical sources of the twentieth century, but because in their music we can find plenty of parody and irony. These are not Italian characteristics. Italian music in the years 1915–1920 was generally much more serious!

PD So those audiences in Rome during World War I would have found this kind of music strange?

FN Sure: very strange. I don't think the Italian public appreciated it very much because it rejected all the Germanic traditions and Italian opera.[6]

The two of them were very close in the years during World War I. After Berners left Rome, there seem to be no letters, but he sent Casella inscribed copies of two of his scores: *Le Carrosse du Saint-Sacrement* – 'a mon ami Alfredo Casella en tout sympathie', 1924; and *The Triumph of Neptune* – 'Alfredo Casella avec milles amitiés', 1927.

6 But Harold Acton was there – see his different account in Chapter 3, p. 47.

CHAPTER 18

Prose

[Narrative Paintings]

IF MY interest in music was aroused by its visual side, that is to say the actual appearance of the staves, clefs and notation, in the case of painting it was, perversely enough, the literary side of it that attracted me. I regret to have to confess that during my early stumblings in the art of connoisseurship, I used to like a picture that 'told a story', but it may perhaps be put forward as an extenuation that I preferred those that had something to do with Latin and Greek mythology.

The picture that made the most profound impression on me in my earliest youth was by Lord Leighton and it was called *Perseus and Andromeda*.[1] The effect of this painting was no doubt heightened by the fact that it was the 'picture of the year' in the first Royal Academy Exhibition to which my mother took me when I was very young; the experience stands out as one of the most exciting landmarks in my childhood. *Perseus and Andromeda* was on a vast scale and as it was customary in those days to judge works of art by their size, it was surrounded by a large crowd of people standing before it in an attitude of reverence, a circumstance which seemed to add to its awe-inspiring qualities. *Perseus and Andromeda* remains to this day as vividly impressed on my mind's eye as though I had the picture before me. A buxom Andromeda occupied the centre of the canvas. Over her sprawled the dragon huge and ominous with jaws aflame, while up above in the sky Perseus hovered on his winged steed. Andromeda was being very brave about the whole business, very British; indeed her phlegmatic attitude, given the alarming situation in which she found herself, almost made one suspect she knew all along that she was in the Royal Academy and that everything would come right in the end.

Another picture in the same exhibition that impressed me very much was one called *The Doctor* by Luke Fildes, and my taste in this instance was even more reprehensible from the absolute point of view, because it was based on pure sentimentality.[2] However it must be urged that the picture was a very moving one indeed and might well have softened the heart of the most out-and-out Art-for-Art's-Saker. In a humble cottage a doctor was sitting by the bedside of a sick child, peering into its face with a very earnest expression; there was a beautifully realistic blend of lamplight and faint daylight coming in through the window. The doctor was wearing a

1 Frederic, Lord Leighton (1830–96) was the most influential Victorian painter and sculptor, and the first to receive a peerage. *Perseus and Andromeda* (1891) is in the Walker Art Gallery, Liverpool. Their website explains: 'The painting shows Andromeda, daughter of the Queen of Ethiopia, tied to the rocks as a sacrifice to the sea monster sent by Neptune to ravage the country. She was rescued by Perseus, who eventually married her. Perseus is shown riding on his winged horse Pegasus, having already shot an arrow into the monster.'

2 Sir Samuel Luke Fildes RA (1844–1927) was widely known for his sympathetic portrayals of the trials of the poor depicted from life, a counterpart to the novels of Dickens, and for his pictures of Venice.

very elegant morning coat and he must have been a far more expensive doctor than such humble cottage folk as these could afford; but he looked a very nice man and no doubt he was giving his services at a reduced fee. One hoped passionately that the child, who appeared to be hovering between life and death, would survive, especially as neither the doctor nor the mother appeared to be sharing Andromeda's complacent belief in the security of the Royal Academy.

I thought the picture very beautiful and was much incensed by a caricature of it that appeared in *Punch* bearing the caption: 'Good gracious, I believe I've gone and given him the wrong stuff!'

But there was nothing really hostile in *Punch's* mockery, for those were the good old days when only the very advanced or the very cynical sneered at the sentiment displayed in Royal Academy pictures. Of course, people used to say occasionally that a picture was not quite as well painted as it might have been, or that the subject was a little too eccentric. Nevertheless the mentality that produced incidents in the lives of Oliver Cromwell, and Mary Queen of Scots, the Problem Picture, the loves of cavaliers and their ladies or little girls talking to Newfoundland dogs was thoroughly approved of and respected. Nowadays, alas, Royal Academicians have been frightened out of painting this kind of picture and except in the portrait department it is in vain that one searches the modern exhibitions for something really funny.

Richmond

A BOUT half an hour from London by car – a little longer by bus or tube – lies Richmond. Of that fact you are no doubt aware. You have heard of the Star and Garter, the Lass of Richmond Hill, of the associations of Richmond with the English kings. You have seen perhaps the views of Richmond that Turner painted – that lovely one of the bend of the river with groups of gaily dressed holiday-makers sitting about on the slopes. But have you done anything about acquiring a more intimate acquaintance of the place?

Possibly I am attributing to others my own lack of initiative, or that geographical snobbishness that leads people to make long journeys to visit some insignificant Italian hilltown or Bavarian hamlet while neglecting places of interest in their immediate neighbourhood. It was only through an enforced sojourn in a nursing home on Richmond Hill that I came to appreciate the attractions of the place.

No seeker after beauty could fail to be thrilled by the view from Richmond Terrace but, having caught sight of the new Star and Garter, the modern blocks of flats that disfigure the summit, depressed perhaps a little by the rather smug layout of the municipal gardens, he might murmur to himself: 'Too late. The place is spoilt' and go elsewhere in search of residential amenity. But he would be wrong, for there are many parts of Richmond Hill unravished by municipal taste and the speculator's hand, and in the general atmosphere of the place there remains much of that nostalgic old-world charm that he is seeking.

As an introduction I recommend a walk by the riverside from the Castle Hotel in the direction of Kew as far as the railway bridge (it will take you about five minutes) past the imposing façade of Trumpeter's House standing back in its gardens, and the lovely Italianate Asgill House looking out a little forlornly over the river. Here turn to the right through the Gate-House arch into Richmond Green, past the trim and stately houses of Maid of Honour Row, back into Richmond itself which at this point has the exhilarating air of a seaside town. Were Richmond in the Salzkammergut or in some foreign part of the world it would have been patronised by the wealthy and fashionable, for it holds all the delights of a foreign watering-place without the bother of the waters, and there are 'sights' enough within easy reach to satisfy the most voracious sight-seer; Walpole's fantastic neo-Gothic Strawberry Hill, Ham House, Hampton Court, Chiswick House with its cedar-flanked avenue of urns and sphinxes, Kew with its pagoda, its tropical water-lily houses, its distinctly Hanoverian flavour, where, if you like, you may evoke George III pursuing Fanny Burney among the rhododendron bushes.

If Richmond were a Continental resort it would certainly be more elegantly exploited. As it is, the places of entertainment, the tea-shops, the snack-bars and the cafés are not designed to attract a fastidious clientele. Richmond is democratic and seems to have no desire to do so. It has chosen the better part in the way of catering for the 'greatest happiness of the greatest number'. The holiday crowds at Richmond in the summer months are tremendous. I heard a woman say: 'We couldn't get anywhere near the river'. However, on less tumultuous days, for me at any rate, the holiday crowds are a delight. Walking by the river on a hot summer afternoon, one is transported back to the early nineteenth century atmosphere of Turner's pictures, the happy groups of holiday-makers disporting themselves on the banks, fishing, bathing, sailing, picnicking: a comfortable proportion of dear old ladies and dogs; all, one would like to think, a little chastened by the beauty of the scene, for there is no rowdiness only quiet, orderly enjoyment. It is a sight to make one almost in love with the human race which, I suppose, every good Christian ought and which, I fear, is becoming increasingly difficult.

The Time-Element in Music – A Plea For Brevity[3]

As music is a form of art that expresses itself in time, it is only natural that the time-element should play an important part in musical composition. By the time-element I mean the actual time that a piece of music takes in performance and the timing of effects, the length of developments, of modulations, the leading up to climaxes and so forth, all of which are just as important in music as proportion in architecture or emotional suspense in a play. Consideration of this aspect of musical composition does not as a rule figure in textbooks of musical instruction. No doubt because it is felt that such things cannot be taught.

There are no hard and fast rules to determine the exact length a piece of music should be; nor are there canons to determine the timing of entries, the length of development or the exact amount of suspense to be inflicted on the ear before it is relieved by resolution. These are matters which depend on the tact and sensibility of the composer. If he is lacking in this sensibility, the music which he produces is apt to be lacking in that, if he errs on the side of length, it will seem to drag; if on the side of brevity, it will appear spasmodic or trivial. My own point of view is that it is better to err in the latter respect, for music is not like a book in which we can skip passages when they begin to get boring. We cannot stop our ears for then we would miss the moment when the composer begins to get interesting again. We are obliged to listen all the time and being bored even for a few moments is liable to spoil what comes after.

Many composers seem to think that if the technical business of counterpoint, harmony and development is skilfully handled, it doesn't matter how long-winded they are. But it seems to me that there is no excuse for being long-winded. A work of art should never be boring, even for a moment – although a great many musicians and music critics do not seem to share this view.

In the works of the great composers prior to the nineteenth century you will always find perfect judgement with regard to the time proportion. How admirably in his fugues Bach brings in at exactly the right moment the reiteration of his subjects and counter-subjects and he always knows when to stop. In the symphonies of Haydn, Mozart and the earlier Beethoven you are never wearied by unnecessary expansion.

3 There are several drafts of this essay, one of which seems to have been timed for a talk, and I have amalgamated material using transcriptions from Bryars and Gifford. Notebook 42A.

Most of Beethoven's symphonies are perfect in their length though he is apt at times to linger a little too long over the threshold before bidding us farewell and I am always a little disconcerted by the almost abrupt ending of the scherzo of Sibelius' Fourth Symphony which gives the impression that he had got bored with it or had come to the end of his writing paper. Debussy's *Prélude à l'après-midi d'un faune* seems to me to be a perfect work of art, both in the timing of its climax and its length.

When the dramatic element enters into music as in opera, the time element assumes a different character and is dependent on dramatic structure and also on the fact that an opera is intended to be a whole evening's entertainment. It is also a question of the nationality of the composer. The operas of Bizet, Verdi, Puccini never seem too long. But here also the composer should beware of the prolixity that is apt to occur when literature gets the upper hand. He should have before his eyes, as a warning example, the tedious dissertations of Wotan and Fricker, Gurnemanz and King Mark. I must admit that Wagnerian opera seems less exhausting in Germany than elsewhere. In ballet music the time question is happily settled by the exigencies of choreography.

But in the nineteenth century there creeps into music a certain tendency to long-windedness which is no doubt due to the influence of the Romantic Movement, the substitution of the Gothic Cathedral for the classical temple and to the growth of subjectivity in art, involving lifeless and often rather formless outpourings of the soul. The symphonies of Schubert and Schumann, beautiful as they are, contain passages one feels might conveniently have been shorter, while in Bruckner and Mahler there are moments that even an audience of tortoises might find tedious.

Latin and Slavonic composers are on the whole less prone to prolixity than their Nordic colleagues. They say what they have to say concisely and effectively without unnecessary rhetorical trappings.

The moral of this little talk is that brevity is the soul of music as it is of wit. However serious, however weighty may be your message, deliver it as concisely as possible and avoid unnecessary rhetorical trappings. Padding in music is as insufferable as it is in literature, and it is a mistake to think that mere length is impressive and that a piece of music, like an English public character, can gain in importance through the length of its duration.

In the Manner of Gertude Stein[4]

1. Portrait of a Lady

Telegraph poles are taller but not so grand. So grand piano hearse-horses and state bed. A rummage sale is dustier and grimmer and grimmer but not so grand. Gaunt gaunt and Grimm's fairy tales with a little green stuff by Professor Freud. A little rabbit's fur dyed pink and some henna from the hen-house. Can hens lay ghosts? Ghosts covered with feathers and plumes of the past but feathers now and a little Renaissance Borgia dagger and poison but not really. She cherishes snakes in the grass. Snakes bite her and bite her and bite and bite her. She cherishes snakes. She cherishes snakes in the grass. Grass is green she is green. Purple does not go with green. She goes with purple and green and green and green and grin. Grimm's fairy tales and a little greenery-gallery from Professor Freud. She would like would like to have roses roses all the way green roses. All the way there and all the way back. Back water back biter of stack hair, back stair back ... back chat and back back back to the land. She sometimes hates her horse-faced husband.

2. Portrait of a Society Hostess

Give a canary champagne and it spins. Chandelier drops glitter and drop and are conversation. Bohemian glass is cracked in Mayfair. Mayfair-weather friends come and go come and go come and go. The house is always full full full full.

Are you there? Are you there? There! There! Are you not all there. Many are not quite all there but royalty are there and lots and lots and lots. Glitter is more than kind hearts and coronets are more than comfort. She praises and embarrasses she praises and embarrasses she confuses cabinet ministers. Some will not go.

What with one thing and another. What with another and one thing. What with what with what what wit and what not.

Squashed bosh is her favourite meringue.

3. Portrait of a Well-Known Conversationalist[5]

There was one who was wanting to be saying to be saying there was one who was wanting to be wanting to be saying there was one was wanting to be saying to be saying to be saying. There were many who were wanting who were wanting to be not listening. There was one there was one there was one who went on wanting to be saying who went on wanting who went on went on wanting to be saying to be saying to be

4 Berners Archive: from notebook 17B/Bryars.

5 Subtitled 'Portrait of Sir A. C.' – probably Sir Arthur Colefax (1866–1936), politician and lawyer, whose wife was the celebrated hostess.

saying. He went on saying. More and more and more were wanting to be not listening were wanting were wanting to be not listening. To be not listening to be not not not not listening. He is still saying. He is still saying saying saying saying. There are some who are not listening there are many who are not wanting to be not listening who are wanting wanting wanting to be not listening. He will not stop saying. He will not not not stop saying. He is saying this and this and this and this. He is saying this and that. He keeps on saying this and that. He is keeping on going on saying this and that. He means to be keeping on going on saying this and this and this. and that.

Many have left.

He is going on saying this and this and this and that. Nothing will stop him saying this and that. Nothing nothing nothing will stop him saying this and that. He means to be keeping on saying. He means to be keeping on going on saying. To be going on saying saying saying. He is determined to be meaning to be going on keeping on saying saying saying.

More have left.

Let us begin again. There was one who was wanting to be saying. There was one who was wanting to be wanting to be wanting to be saying. There was one. Stop. There was one. Stop. Stop. There was one who was wanting. Stop. Stop. Stop. He will not stop. He will not stop. He is determined not to stop. He is meaning to be wanting to be going on saying. He is going on saying. He is still going on saying saying.

All have left.

He is still going on saying, saying
saying
        saying
                saying
saying
        saying

CHAPTER 19   Poems

Red Roses and Red Noses[1]

(To a Young Lady who wished Red
Roses to be strewn on her tomb)

Some people praise red roses:
But I beg leave to say
That I prefer red noses –
I think they are so gay.

A Kempis[2] says we must not cling
To things that pass away:
Red Noses last a lifetime –
Red Roses but a day.

Red Roses blow but thrice a year –
In June, July or May:
But owners of Red Noses
Can blow them every day.

1 First published
in *Look! The Sun*,
ed. Edith Sitwell
(London: Gollancz,
1941), 32. Berners'
setting of this poem
is in *The Collected
Vocal Music*, ed.
Peter Dickinson
(London: Chester
Music, 1982; 2nd edn
2000).

2 Thomas à Kempis
(1380–1471), German
mystic, probable
author of *The
Imitation of Christ*.

From The Manual of Ornithology

1. The Motmots [3]

Oh what wot I of the Motmots,
The birds that are now all the rage?
It is better to eat them in hot-pots
Than to keep them as pets in a cage.
They strongly resemble the Jay
In its most disagreeable features,
And all ornithologists say
They are perfectly horrible creatures.

3 A family of
tropical birds
that also includes
kingfishers.

2. The Busy Boolah

The Boolah is a busy bird,
And all for our delight,
She sings and whistles all the day
And lays eggs all the night.

3. Robinson's Lesser Pitwit

Robinson's Lesser Pitwit
Is considered by some a nitwit.
The Cambridge dons however
Consider it awfully clever.

Surrealist Landscape [4]

On the pale yellow sands
Where the Unicorn stands
And the Eggs are preparing for Tea
Sing Thirty
Sing Forty
Sing Three.

On the pale yellow sands
There's a pair of Clasped Hands
And an eyeball entangled with string.
(Sing Forty
Sing Fifty
Sing Three.)
And a Bicycle Seat
And a Plate of Raw Meat
And a Thing that is hardly a Thing.

On the pale yellow sands
   There stands
   A Commode
That has nothing to do with the case.
Sing Eighty
Sing Ninety
Sing Three.
On the pale yellow sands
There's a Dorian Mode
And a Temple all covered with Lace
And a Gothic Erection of Urgent Demands
On the Patience of You and of Me.

[4] The full version of this poem was published in *Horizon* vol. 6, no. 31 (July 1942), 5–6. Six lines of it, in a slightly different form, are a footnote in Sacheverell Sitwell, *Spain* (London: Batsford, 1950), 154–5. It was included under the title of 'Queer' in *Spells*, collected by F. McEachran (Oxford: Basil Blackwell, 1955); reprinted as *Spells for Poets* (London: Garnstone Press, 1974). There is an earlier draft in the Berners Archives under the title 'More than Real'. The poem has been set to music by Peter Dickinson in *Surrealist Landscape* for medium voice, piano and tape playback (1973), recorded on Unicorn-Kanchana DKP(CD)9093 (1990). He has also set *Christmas Time* as the last of *Three Carols* (1998) for female voices. Philip Lane's *Lines from Mi'Lord's Perverse Verse* (c. 1985) for SATB unaccompanied or voice and piano, contains *Surrealist Landscape, Spring Thoughts, Epitaph, Warning to Children about Animals, The Were-Lamb, Christmas Time, From a Catalogue, Excursion to Innisfree*, 'Grandma made such a nice little nest' and 'No wonder Bertha's so morose'.

Spring Thoughts

In this merry month of May
Come let us read an Ibsen play
And may the sage of Scandinavia
Check all thoughts of bad behaviour.

When we look upon a flower
Let us think of Schopenhauer
And take a pessimistic view
Of all the things we'd like to do.

And when we walk by running brooks
With the girl of our affection
Let's find in them all Strindberg's books
And foster morbid introspection.

The Romantic Charter

I am not fighting for the Poles or Czechs,
And only indirectly for the Rex.
I do not greatly love the Slav or Greek,
I cannot bear the way colonials speak.
I loathe efficiency and Nissen huts,
And as for 'bonhomie' I hate its guts.
I am not fighting Germans just to get
My democratic share of 'blood and sweat'.
Dear Sir,
 I feel that you may get the gist
Of all MY War Aims from the following list …
Split pediments, breakfast at eleven,
Large white peonies in big glass bowls,
Asparagus au beurre, whitebait in shoals,
Close cropped grass, huge trees and cawing rooks,
A sunny breakfast room, a library with books,
Clean white housemaids in new print frocks,
Coachmen turned chauffeur, footmen on the box.
Dinner parties, all in evening dress,
Glamorous women drenched in Mary Chess.
Charades and paper games, hot-houses with the heat on,
Superficiality and Cecil Beaton.
Shrimps from Morecambe Bay, port that is tawny,
Claret and Beaujolais, soles that are Mornay,
Hot scones for tea, thick cream, the smell of logs,
Long country walks, thick shoes and spaniel dogs,
Ducks in the evening, swishing swans in flight,
Fires in the bedrooms flickering at night –
And of those 'autres fois', all those 'mœurs'
Which are epitomised in *Valse des fleurs* –
Fresh shiny chintzos, an herbaceous border –
Death and destruction to this damned new order.

To his Mistress

In Beauty, Virtue, unexcelled
Thank god with you I can't compete
Thank god you are unparalled
For Parallels can never meet.

Her Reply
I cannot say your views lack point
For therein lies their strength
For Euclid tells us that a point
Has neither breadth nor length.

Warning to Children about Animals

1. The Cat

Children, let me warn you
   Of the quaint capricious cat
Whose purring voice and graceful ways
Mislead you as to what she's at.
And when you see her face all smiles
And note her gentle homely habits
You must remember, on the tiles,
That cats are just as passionate as rabbits.

2. The Adder

The adder is a selfish snake
Who little does for others' sake.
You must not expect her to
Add up your accounts for you.

3. The Were-Lamb

Strange things happen in the night.
Worms may turn and lambs may bite.
And you may well be seized with fear
When shepherds say: 'The Lamb's gone were'.

Beware the Were-Lamb, oh my child,
Avoid the Were-Lamb's nightly prowling.
Wander not on moorland wild
If ere you hear the Were-Lamb howling.

Bolt the door, push down the latch
On every entrance keep a watch
And ask protection of the Lord
When'ere the Were-Lamb is abroad.

Excursion to Innisfree [5]

I will arise and go now, and go to Innisfree,
And tell them, at the little Inn,
That there'll be twenty-four for tea.
Twenty-four Ladies of the Band of Hope,
United in their hatred of the Pope,
Each one declaring loudly that she would rather
Serve the Devil than the Holy Father.
The bee-loud glade may hum with sounds, I fear,
Other than the murmur of the bee.
I do not fancy they'll be very welcome there –
At Innisfree.

5 Parody of W. B. Yeats, *The Lake Isle of Innisfree.*

Mrs Brown – A Love Poem

We are not glad for you
We are not sad for him
But we are glad
And we are sad
   Alas!
For Mrs Brown.

We do not fear the things that stand
Nor things that tumble down
But we are filled
With awful fear
   Alas!
For Mrs Brown

We do not bow to cleverness
Nor folly gets us down
But we perforce must bow
   And how!
   Alas!
To Mrs Brown

We are not moved by music
And painting makes us frown
But we would gladly practise both
   Alas!
For Mrs Brown

We do not want a cross
We do not want a crown
But crowns and crosses both combine
   Alas!
For Mrs Brown

We do not like a nobleman
We don't dislike a clown
But like, dislike
Are not the words
   Alas!
For Mrs Brown.

We do not like the country
We do not love the town
But we are not indifferent
   Alas!
To Mrs Brown.

Christmas Time

O Christmas Time
O hateful time
When posts are late
And there's a spate
Of Christmas cards from those we hate
   and almanacs and calendars
     and gifts from aunts of bad cigars.

O Christmas Time
O hateful time
When nights are long
And days are short
And we eat
   far more
Than we ought
and biliousness sets in
     And then
We're asked to feel
   Goodwill to Men.

O Christmas Time O hateful time
When all the rooms are decked with holly
Symbolic of a dreary folly
And mistletoe about the place
Invites to kiss some unloved face.

From 'Hints to Poets'

A plate of cold potato salad
Is not a subject for a ballad?
Although it may evoke delight
When seen through glass by clear moonlight.
A footstep echoing on the stair,
A locket with a lock of hair,
The midnight raven's warning croak,
A trumpet heard through fire and smoke
Of burning tombstones uninsured,
(What can't be cured must be endured)
Such things, and Love's entrancing passion,
Are now no longer in the fashion,
And while much wrath and no forgiving
May help, perhaps, to earn a living
For stern young men with scornful noses
Abominate the scent of roses,
My own subconscious mental state
Will never cease to iterate -
A plate of cold potato salad
Is not a subject for a ballad.

The Pig Faced Lady of Manchester Square

(The Pig Faced Lady is depicted, seated in a Regency chair,
her hand resting on a low table. Appended is an account of
her conversation, habits, her offers of marriage etc.)

The Pig Faced Lady of Manchester Square
Sat all day long in a Regency Chair
Resting her hand on a table low
The hand that was sought for by many a Beau
For you must not imagine the Lady so queer
For want of a Suitor did ever despair
An Italian Marquis, a Spanish Grandee
An American Merchant from over the Sea
Whose name was Emmanuel Emerson Potter
Were among those who sued for her elegant Trotter.

Epitaph (Translated from the Greek)

Here lies Emmanuel Bishop of Rhodes
He has an aversion for children and toads
He lived quite alone with his cook and his cat
And as for his morals – we'll leave it at that.

Epitaph

He did what he could
To be jolly[6] and good
But honest endeavour
Will never – no never!
Make some people clever.
But of such is the leaven
Of the Kingdom of Heaven.

6 This word is
difficult to decipher.

Epitaph [7]

Sacred to the memory
Of our dear little Emily,
At the same time the pride
    And the shame
Of her family.
Seduced by a Bishop when barely eleven
She's perfectly certain of going to Heaven.

7 Quoted in
Jonathan Guinness
with Catherine
Guinness, *The House
of Mitford*, 2nd edn
(London: Phoenix,
2004), 262.

Auto-Epitaph

Here lies Lord Berners
One of the learners
His great love of learning
May earn him a burning
But praise to the Lord
He seldom was bored.

Performing Mushroom

(To Professor Jebb, author of 'Inedible Fungi', 'The Toadstool
and all about it' etc.)

To walk the tightrope on a spider's web
Above the ditch where squats the humble toad
Who gasps and gapes and opens wide his eyes
And swells to many times his normal size
'neath wattled hedge beside the moonlit road,
    Just so, Professor Jebb.

To balance nimbly on the mouse's back
And canter round and round the mossy track
Waving the Tricolor and Union Jack;
To bow, all smiles, acknowledging the feb-
-rile shouts of pale enthusiastic tiers
Of water-newts, and other little dears
    And you, Professor Jebb.

To have one's portrait in the Picture News,
To be invited by a lovely deb-
-utante to autograph an album page.
That is pleasant also, and the rage
Of clumsy toadstools no one will engage,
Who vent their wrath in spiteful interviews
    With you, Professor Jebb.

To rest upon one's laurels late in life,
To settle down with children and a wife,
Enjoying wealth amassed by honest toil
And then, when life has ceased to ebb,
To die at home and fertilise the soil,
While other mushrooms fry in boiling oil
    For you, Professor Jebb.

Recipe

Take roots of immemorial oaks,
And tiles from tallest New York skyscrapers.
And well-minced brains of humble folks
Whose names have never been in newspapers.
    The combings of a mermaid's hair.
    A single line from Baudelaire
    And, if desired, the golden yolks
    Of Phoenix eggs reduced to ashes,
    And folded in with dots and dashes.
Season with the salt of tears
With pepper from an Anglo-Indian kernel
And flavour with the hopes and fears
That spring in every human breast eternal.
    Garnish with a lawyer's silk
    And kids seethed in their mother's milk.
    Decorate with donkey's years
    With flowers culled from mourners
    And bake for all eternity.

Sonnet [8]

To his Mistress

8 The first stanza was written on Berners' score of the piano duet version of Stravinsky's *The Rite of Spring*.

Shall I compare thee to a porcupine?
Or, with some quaint comparison, declare
The Armadillo's hide no match for thine
Nor Alligator's scales so gaunt and rare
As those that have not fallen from thine eyes
And hide from thee the things thou darest not see.

The unforgotten ghoul that strands and cries
Upon thy doorstep clamouring for thee.
The scales in which fatality is weighed
Have weighed thee and have found thee overweight.
And I who waited for the end have stayed
To see my hopes and fears fulfilled too late.

Oh would that these too solid bonds would break.
That bind the willing martyr to the stake.

Untitled Poems

1.

Aunt May was so funny
She left a sum of money
   In her will
To any girl who should succeed
   In producing
   A boy by the Pope
Or failing that
   In seducing
     John Stuart Mill.[9]

9 John Stuart Mill (1806–73), influential philosopher and social reformer.

2.

Grandma made such a nice little nest
Out of Grandpa's trousers, his
Drawers and his vest
and, right in the centre
    she placed –
    The Po!
Oh, Granny's the person
To make things go!

3.

No wonder Bertha's so morose
   Her view of life so bitter,
Her bottom is so adipose
   That no armchair will fit her.
And I imagine you'd look glum
If you'd been born with Bertha's bum!

4.

After reading Bentham[10] Charlotte
Determined to become a harlot
A course that did not fail to shock
The Reverend Spurgeon[11] and his flock
My! You should have heard them cackle
   When they met in the tabernacle.

10 Jeremy Bentham (1748–1832), lawyer and radical social reformer.

11 The Rev C. H. Spurgeon (1834–92), Reformed Baptist preacher renowned for the inspirational quality of his sermons.

5.

A thing that Uncle George detests
Is finding mouse-shit in his vests
But what he even more abhors
Is seeing Auntie in her drawers.

6.

There was a young lady of Samos
Who rode on a hippopotamus.
   This is the first time
   That our verse doesn't rhyme
And for this you will probably blame us.

7.

The intimate friends of the Dean
Will I'm sure understand what I mean
When I say that I think that the boys in the Choir
Should wholly be furnished with drawers of barbed wire!

8.

12 Nos. 7 and 8
were told to Peter
Dickinson by Sir
John Betjeman in
1972.

Uncle Fred and Aunty Mabel
Fainted at the breakfast table.
Isn't that an awful warning
Not to do it in the morning? [12]

9.

13 No. 9 was told to
Philip Lane around
1975 by a colleague of
Berners at the British
Embassy in Rome.

Imagine Aunty Jane's surprise
When Uncle won the fucking prize!
She never set much store by him –
Nor his brother Uncle Jim! [13]

APPENDIX 1

Foreword to
The Girls of Radcliff Hall

From the first, privately printed edition, and not included in the first trade edition.[1]

FOREWORD
By the Bishop of Brixton

WHEN first my friend and erstwhile parishioner Adela Quebec invited me to write an introduction to her little book, *The Girls of Radcliff Hall*, I must admit that I was filled with diffidence. I felt that, for a member of the Church of England, possessing no pretensions whatever to literary taste and above all handicapped by a complete ignorance of the subject of which the book treats, it would be a task that lay entirely outside my province.

But after I had finished reading her charming little work, all such diffidence fell from me. Here, I said to myself, is something that has an universal appeal. Nobody, in whatever walk of life, of whatever calling, could fail to be fascinated by the freshness, the delicious naiveté of this delightful chronicle of a Girls' School, with its charming descriptions of the romantic friendships of its inmates, descriptions that rival in their delicacy of touch, the illustrations of an early nineteenth century botany book.

Miss Quebec's little volume exhales so fragrant an atmosphere of charm and innocence that, after reading it, I felt as though I had been walking in a garden full of lilies and roses. In fact I was reminded of that exquisite picture by Sargent, 'Carnation lily, lily rose', except that here the theme is treated more naively and that in the place of Sargent's consummate mastery of technique one finds a fresher, less sophisticated treatment resembling that of Fra Angelico or some other primitive Italian artist.[2]

We follow the development of the various characters in the story with the same eager curiosity with which we watch the unfolding of the buds in our herbaceous borders, and upon laying down the book we are left with a longing to pursue still further the fortunes of the talented Cecily, the impulsive Lizzie, Daisy and Olive, with their vivid interest in the welfare of the school, Millie the Tomboy, and, above all, the benevolent Headmistress who watches over her little flock with such maternal solicitude.

It is sincerely to be hoped that Miss Adela Quebec will gratify us with a sequel.

1 *The Girls of Radcliff Hall* (under the *nom de plume* of Adela Quebec, *c.* 1935); ed. John Byrne (London: Montcalm, the Signet Press, 2000).

2 John Singer Sargent (1856–1925), American painter and outstanding portrait artist. 'Carnation, lily, lily, rose' is a phrase taken from a popular song by Joseph Mazzinghi (1765–1844) and given as the title to one of Sargent's most popular pictures dating from 1885–6 and now in the Tate Britain.

Unpublished foreword to *The Camel* (1936)

M Y OLD friend General Bouncer, to whom I showed the manuscript of this tale, was very scathing about the way I had written of camels. At one time in the course of his military career he had been in command of a camel corps and therefore considered that he knew everything that there was to be known about camels. He said that the animal depicted in my narrative was an impossible beast, that the picture I had drawn was highly unconvincing and that he was sure no camel would behave in the way my camel had done. He strongly advised me to destroy the manuscript and he said it would cover me with shame and derision and would certainly elicit protests from all people who knew anything about camels.

Similarly my friend the Reverend Ernest Thatcher, well known for his breezy sermons and his popularity among the lads of the East End, had several strictures to make on my accounts of parochial and clerical life.

He said they abounded in errors both of taste and observation.

Nevertheless I venture to assert that, apart from certain small technical mistakes relating to camels and clergymen, every word of this story is founded on truth. Slumbermere, though known by a different name, is a real village and all the protagonists of the story are real people.

Let not this admission, however, be an encouragement to anyone to bring an action for libel. I know that it is usual nowadays, when any writer produces a character who is in any degree disagreeable, for people to bob up on all sides crying 'That's me!' accompanying their assertion with a claim for substantial damages which, owing to the present state of libel law in England, they generally succeed in obtaining.

Such methods, in the present case, let me warn my readers, will meet with no success, because all the people taking part in this story (a record of events that took place in the eighteen-nineties) have long been dead.

Lady Bugle is dead. So is Admiral Clifton Porter, the latter leaving a clause in his will enjoining that he was to be buried at sea, thereby causing no little embarrassment to his heirs and executors, involving them in a good deal of trouble and expense.

The only possible exception to the general demise of my characters is the unfortunate Antonia. She vanished from the scene, but no positive evidence of her death is recorded. Maybe she still lives in some far off Arabian city, a second Lady Hester Stanhope.[1] Or perhaps, immured in some obscure convent, she meditates on the strange vicissitudes that so suddenly and unaccountably came to wreck the serenity of her peaceful parochial life.

But I should say that it was extremely unlikely.

---

1 Lady Hestor Stanhope (1776–1839), eldest child of 3rd Earl Stanhope, niece of Prime Minister William Pitt, for whom she acted as hostess until his death. She became intoxicated with the Middle East, where she travelled widely, which was then unusual for a woman on her own, and never returned. She dressed as a man, impressed the Arabs with her dynamic personality and large entourage including twenty-two camels, and was crowned Queen of the Desert at Palmyra. She settled in a disused monastery and declined into poverty in later life.

17 Denton Welch: portrait of Berners as a child (1941)

Lord Berners, making more sweetness than violence.

18 Max Beerbohm: caricature of Berners playing his Dolmetsch clavichord (1923)

19 Eleutario Riccardi: portrait of Berners,
published in *Ars Nova*, Rome, Anno III, N. 1
(November 1918), 7

20 Natalia Gontcharowa: cover for Berners'
Le Poisson d'or (1919)

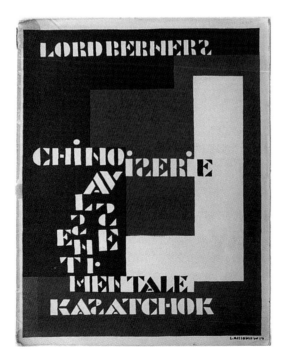

21 Michel Larionov: cover for Berners'
Three Pieces (1919)

22 Michel Larionov: cover for Berners'
Three Funeral Marches (1919) – not used

23 Berners: portrait of William Crack

24 Berners: 'Houses and Road' (1928)

25 Berners: 'Still Life' (1931)

26 Berners: 'Farm Buildings' (1931)

27 Berners: Hippodrome, Palatine Hill, rome (1930)

28 Berners: 'A Glade' (1931)

29 Berners: 'Faringdon House' (1933)

30 Jean-Baptiste-Camille Corot: 'Venise: Le Grand Canal vu du quai des Esclavons' (1828)

31 Berners: 'The Salute', Venice (1931)

32 Berners: 'The Piazetta', Venice (1933)

33 Berners: 'Piazetta and Columns', Venice (1933)

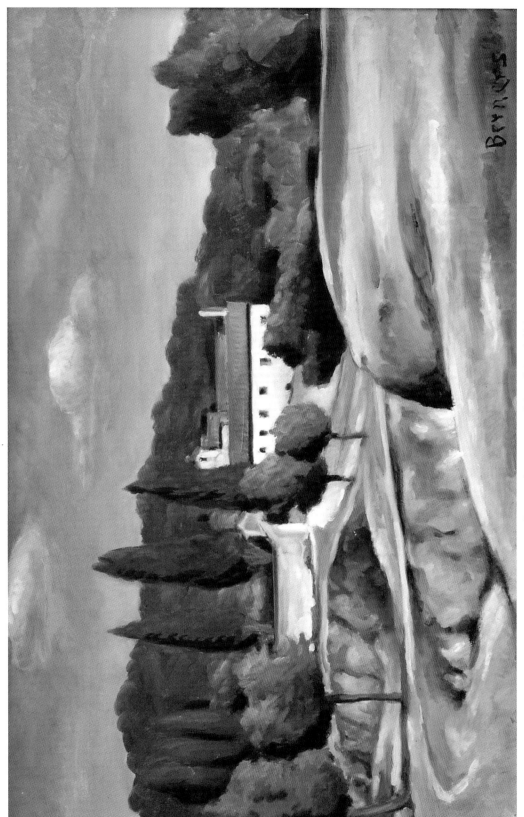

34 Berners: 'Monastery of Castel Gandolfo', Lazio

35 Berners: 'Castel Gandolfo' (1933)

36 Berners: 'The Forum, Rome' [1] (1933)

37 Berners: 'The Forum, Rome' [2] (1933)

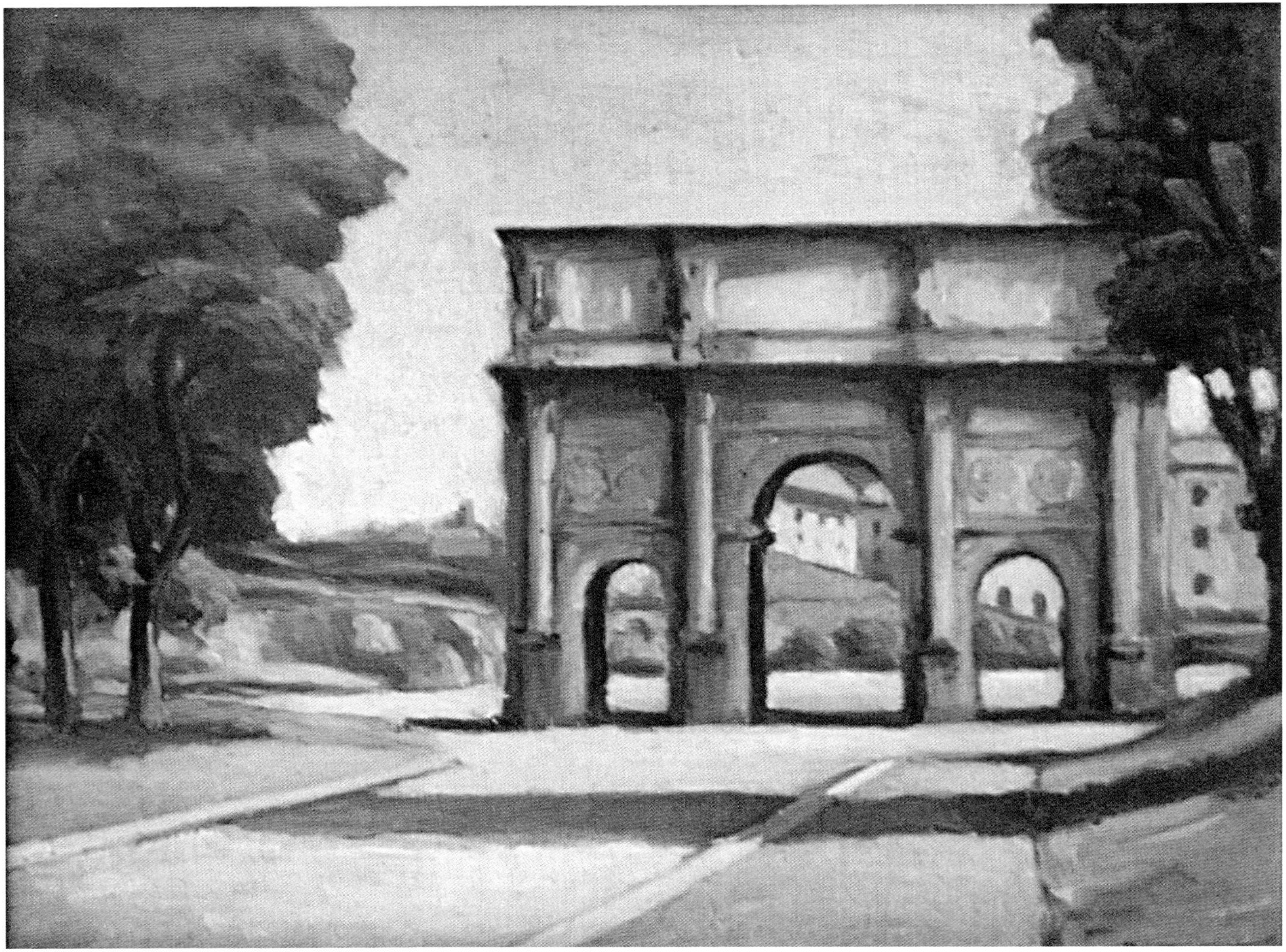

38 Berners: Arch of Constantine, Rome

39 Berners: View from the Acropolis, Athens (1933)

40 Berners: 'Olympia, Greece' (1933)

41 Berners: 'Tivoli', Villa Gregoriano

42 Berners: Peter Watson, Villa d'Este, Tivoli (1935)

43 Berners: 'View of Tivoli'

44 Berners: 'Chartres Cathedral'

45 Berners: 'The Podere, Florence'

46 Berners: 'Garden Gate, Mentone', French Riviera

47 Berners: 'House near Mentone'

48 Berners: 'Terraced Garden, Mentone' (Courtesy of the Tullie House Museum and Art Gallery, Carlisle)

50 Berners: Robert Heber-Percy [2]

49 Berners: Robert Heber-Percy [1]

51 Berners: 'Mottisfont' [Abbey], Hampshire

52 Berners: River scene

53 Berners: House

54 Folly Hill, Faringdon (engraving, 1792)

55 Berners: 'Faringdon Folly' (1936), used as a poster for Shell

56 Berners: Landscape (1938)

The Denton Welch portrait

Denton Welch was born in 1915 in Shanghai, where the family had business connections going back to his grandparents; he died in Kent in 1948. It was in 1935 that he suffered a nearly fatal accident when his bicycle was struck by a car. He remained an invalid.

His early childhood was spent largely with his mother, travelling about the world, but she died when he was eleven, and he was sent to a prep school in England. Then he went to Repton School, Derbyshire, as a boarder, but ran away: the story is told in Welch's autobiographical novel *Maiden Voyage* (1943). After a spell in China, also covered in the novel, he enrolled at the Goldsmiths School of Art. It was after his accident that he began to write whilst continuing to paint and draw as his health allowed. From about 1940 he began work on his travel books, stories and novels, and was encouraged by some of the leading literary figures of the day. These included Edith Sitwell and Cyril Connolly, who published him in *Horizon*, and Lord Berners.

John Lewis, a fellow student at Goldsmiths, remembered visiting Denton Welch at his house called the Hop Garden in Kent in 1940: 'In a clear area at one end of the room was an easel. On it was a painting of Lord Berners as a child that he was working on.' (See plate 17.) Lewis went on: 'It has been said that Denton Welch turned to writing as a result of his accident, but in the end he would probably have written anyway. His paintings were not of any great account, they were a reflection of his eclectic taste, but by painting he learnt to see. It is the power of acute observation and sensibility that gives his books such a special quality.'[1]

In 1941 the painting had a near escape. Welch was out to dinner and was called back because his house was on fire. When he reached the scene:

> I could not bear to look at my things. Curls of burning paper had fallen from the ceiling and stuck to the covers and carpets. I remembered my picture of Lord Berners, which had to go to the Leicester Galleries in a few weeks' time. I almost fought my way up the stairs. People stood on every step laughing and talking excitedly. Soldiers, villagers, firemen, A.R.P. Wardens, all had come as if to a victory celebration.
>
> At the top of the stairs was blinding, choking smoke collected in a heavy blanket ... I was nearly choking and felt my head reeling ... When I had recovered I ran back

1 John Lewis, *Such Things Happen: the Life of a Typographer* (Stowmarket: Unicorn Press, 1994), 65.

again, keeping my eyes shut. I twiddled the screws of the easel and pulled the picture away. It too was warm and the new paint had been made sticky. I was terrified to look at it for fear that my work of all summer had been spoilt.[2]

That was another tragedy in Welch's short life, but the picture lived on. Its full title is *Portrait of Lord Berners as a Child, dressed up as Robinson Crusoe*, and it was based on a black and white photograph in Berners' *First Childhood*, where it was captioned 'Myself aged eight'.[3] Welch corresponded with Berners about his choice of colours and he replied: 'I am very much flattered that you think my youthful portrait as Robinson Crusoe worthy of being made a conversation piece of. My hair in those days was brown and my eyes also.'[4] He went on to clarify the colours for the properties held by the child. One of Welch's stories is based on his attempt to interest Berners in buying the painting. They met at the Randolph Hotel in Oxford, where Berners

came in with a bounding step and sank down on the bed in front of the conversation piece I had made. I thought as he sat there that he bore a very faint resemblance to Humpty Dumpty. He immediately produced a little gold box and began furiously to take snuff. I was not offered any, and I cannot decide whether this was rudeness or true politeness.

"It's perfectly charming," he said in a sort of amused indulgent voice.

Berners made suggestions, but after forty-five minutes instead of offering to buy it, only said, "You'll let me have a photograph when you've finished won't you?"

"Oh, yes, of course," I said gaily, feeling rather miserable.'[5]

The picture was exhibited at the Leicester Galleries with a price-tag of £40, but failed to sell. Welch corresponded with Berners about the picture, but there were embarrassing confusions because a letter went astray in which Welch had offered to give Berners the picture.

Despite Berners' failure to rise to the occasion of helping a struggling young artist in wretched health, he nevertheless responded with consistent generosity when sent copies of Welch's books. On 20 February 1945 Berners wrote:

I must write to you a line to say how intensely I have enjoyed your book [*In Youth is Pleasure*, 1944]. It has caused a sensation in this house. In these days of so much turgid 'new writing' it is delightful to read anything so clear and limpid, so exquisitely written, so

2 *The Journals of Denton Welch*, ed. Michael De-la-Noy (London: Allison & Busby, 1984), 22.

3 *First Childhood* (1934), first edition only, opposite 114.

4 Mark Amory, *Lord Berners: the Last Eccentric* (London: Chatto & Windus, 1998), 202–3.

5 Denton Welch, 'A Morning with the Versatile Peer Lord Berners in the Ancient Seat of Learning', *Time and Tide*, 1946, quoted in Michael De-lay-Noy, *Denton Welch: the Making of a Writer* (Harmondsworth: Viking, 1984).

vividly exciting, so psychologically convincing. It will continue to haunt my memory and is one of the books I shall often reread.

That description fits Berners' own writing: no wonder he enjoyed it.

Finally Berners invited Welch to stay at Faringdon but he died shortly beforehand. Welch gave the painting to Helen Roeder, who had been a fellow student at Goldsmiths. She wrote to me on 10 December 1984:

He painted the picture from a photograph of Lord Berners as a child, which he came upon when he was reading Berners' autobiography sometime in the 1940s. I think he was fascinated by the little boy dressed as Robinson Crusoe standing on the terrace of a stately home. He wrote to Lord Berners about it and received a peppery reply.

It was exhibited at the Leicester Gallery *Artists of Fame and of Promise*.

It is an amusing and fantastic work – very Denton-esque – associated with two strange and talented people.

Welch was pleased that the painting was reproduced in *Vogue* in 1943. There was a rare opportunity to see an exhibition of Welch at Abbott & Holder in 1984. Mel Gooding thought:

Art seemed for him for the most part a form of dreaming. Given his temperament and the vitality of his imaginative life it is not surprising that the dreams are vivid and compelling. The principal interest of the drawings and watercolours ... with their whimsically attenuated trees, imaginary encounters and fairy-tale *dramatis personae* is as poignant visual documents of a tragically curtailed life.[6]

The *Portrait of Lord Berners* was reproduced then and again, more prominently, in conjunction with Alan Hollinghurst's review of books by and about Welch in the *Times Literary Supplement*.[7] For the Abbott & Holder exhibition Michael De-la-Noy wrote:

That Denton Welch was a writer of genius I have never doubted ... hitherto his best work as a painter has been considerably underestimated, and certainly it is only by regarding his contribution in both media that one can arrive at a rounded assessment of his role as a creative artist.

Something similar could be said about Berners in his various capacities.

6 Mel Gooding, 'Denton Welch', *Arts Review*, 23 November 1984, 586.

7 'Diminished Pictures', *Times Literary Supplement*, 21 December 1984, 1479.

Berners: Print orders of music

THE FOLLOWING details, provided by Chester Music in the early 1980s, show how many copies of Berners' works were printed up to the 1970s. The *Three Funeral Marches* began his association with J. & W. Chester Ltd, and by 1950 there had been as many as 3,100 copies printed. The first two works were contracted under the name of Gerald Tyrwhitt, but once he became Lord Berners he involved the Russian avant-garde artists and designers whom he must have encountered through Diaghilev's Ballets Russes – Natalia Goncharova (originally Gontcharowa) (1881–1962) and Michel (originally Mikhail) Larionov (1881–1964) – in making brilliantly attractive designs to go with some of his scores. The black and white designs made by Larionov for the *Trois petites marches funèbres* were not used, but his blue and chocolate designs for the piano duet version of *Trois morceaux* appeared, and so did Goncharov's dazzling sequence for *Le Poisson d'or*. (See plates 20, 21, 22.)

The terms of Berners' 1921 contract provided for him to pay all costs of production for the works cited. This is indicated on some of the print order sheets, but not all of them. However, charging Berners – at substantial rates – was probably the usual pattern.

The plates from which the music was engraved were stored at Novellos, who did most of the engraving and printing, and there are notes to say that they were destroyed in 1962. The print order sheets are sometimes revealing. Berners took his time with the full score of the *Fugue for Orchestra* and may have been uncertain about it, although the work had been well received. The first proofs were sent on 8 October 1926 but not received back until 7 May 1928; the second proofs were sent to him with admirable despatch on 25 May 1928 and came back on 14 August.

Titles of works are given as they appear on the sheets, not as shown in Catalogue 1: Musical Works (pp. 185–7 below). In his interview in this book Frederick Ashton recalled the subtitle of *Luna Park*. There is no print order sheet for the *Valses bourgeoises* or the late ballet *Les Sirènes*. If Berners paid all the costs below, he would have covered just over £1,543. In terms of the Composite Price Index, converting 1925 prices to those of 2003, that would be almost £60,000.[1]

1 Jim O'Donoghue and Louise Goulding, 'Consumer Price Inflation since 1750', *Economic Trends* 604 (March 2004), 38–46.

2 Berners, *The Collected Music for Solo Piano*, ed. Peter Dickinson (London: Chester Music, 1982; 2nd edn 2000).

Agreements

Trois Marches Funèbres [*sic*] – assignment of copyright in all territories for the sum of one shilling. Carbon copy of agreement with no heading, dated 30 June 1917. Signed Gerald Tyrwhitt, witnessed by Geoffrey Scott, British Embassy, Rome.

Three German Songs; Three English Songs; Three French Songs; The Rio Grande (Capstan Chanty); Theodore or The Pirate King; A Long Time Ago (Halliards Chanty); Dialogue between Tom Filuter and his Man by Ned the Dog Stealer; Fantaisie espagnole – formal Memorandum of Agreement, dated 16 December 1921, providing for Berners 20 per cent of the selling price of each score, fixed at half the marked price, after the first hundred copies used for promotion. He got 40 per cent of hire charges. In return Berners, as the vendor, agreed to 'defray all costs of engraving, printing and publishing of the works specified'. [These works marked with an asterisk.]

Print Order Sheets

Trois petites marches funèbres: piano solo by Gerald Tyrwhitt
August 1917: initial printing 600 copies; £17 18s 10d; reprints [as by Lord Berners] of 500 copies each time in April 1920, April 1924, March 1928, November 1938 and September 1950. [Total 3,100 copies costing £66 12s 8d.] Out of print in 1974, pending Peter Dickinson's new edition.[2]

Fragments pychologiques: piano solo by Gerald Tyrwhitt
January 1919: initial printing 300 copies £12 3s 4d; 1 January 1922: reprint of 500 copies £10 8s 9d

Le Poisson d'or: piano solo by Lord Berners with coloured designs by Natalia Gontcharowa [her signature spelling on the score]; June 1919: printing 1,000 copies; charged to Lord Berners £54 4s 9d

Three Pieces: piano duet
28 June 1919: printing 500 copies; charged to Lord Berners £55 9s 10d plus £28 6s 0d for coloured designs by Michel Larionov

*Lieder Album
20 April 1920: printing 500 copies; charged to Lord Berners £36 2s 6d

*Fantaisie espagnole: orchestral score
October 1920 (engraving order with Breitkopf & Hartel, Leipzig): 200 copies; charged to Lord Berners £57 3s 4d

*Three Songs in the English Manner
31 December 1920: printing 500 copies; charged to Lord Berners £23 0s 3d

*Three French Songs
January 1921: 500 copies; charged to Lord Berners £23 15s 9d

Three Pieces for Orchestra: orchestral score (engraving by Breitkopf)
31 January 1921: 200 copies; charged to Lord Berners £50 4s 0d

*Fantaisie espagnole: piano duet
30 June 1921: 500 copies; charged to Lord Berners £63 6s 0d

Miniature Essay
25 April 1922: 3000 copies; charged to Lord Berners £30 2s 0d

*Three Songs
April 1922: 1,000 copies £26 18s 7d; charged to Berners under contract

Le Carrosse du Saint-Sacrement: vocal score
14 June 1923: 300 copies £246 19s 6d; revised edition 30 June 1926, 300 copies £93 7s 6d

*Dialogue between Tom Filuter and his Man: song
30 April 1924: 500 copies £10 0s 3d; charged to Berners under contract

*Fantaisie espagnole: miniature score
30 December 1926: 500 copies £25 4s 10d; charged to Berners under contract

The Triumph of Neptune: piano score
31 October 1927: 500 copies £187 10s 5d.

Intermezzo from The Triumph of Neptune: piano solo
September 1928: 500 copies £6 8s 9d.

The Triumph of Neptune, Act I: orchestral parts
20 September 1928: £19 9s 9d; 6 October £3 11s 0d; 13 October (copying) £20 18s 6d.

Hornpipe from The Triumph of Neptune: piano solo
30 September 1928: 500 copies £10 3s 3d; reprint 30 September 1950, 500 copies, £6 17s 7d.

Fugue in C minor: full score (printed in France, plates stored at Bernard-Ernoult)
14 November 1928: 200 copies, £66 14s 0d.

Fugue in C minor: miniature score
21 October 1929: 500 copies, £38 1s 6d

The Triumph of Neptune, Act II: orchestral parts
6 January 1930, £17 10s 6d; 28 November (copying), £10 2s 6d

Luna Park (or The Revolt of the Freaks): piano score
5 April 1930: 500 copies, £67 7s 6d

Fantaisie espagnole: string parts
10 December 1930, £12 8s 0d

A Wedding Bouquet: vocal score
21 January 1938: 500 copies, £172 7s 6d

Luna Park: full score
19 March 1938: for library use, £4 3s 4d

Cupid and Psyche: orchestral score
30 June 1938: for private use only – charged to Lord Berners £13 13s 0d

APPENDIX 5   Stravinsky manuscripts and proofs

STRAVINSKY gave Berners a number of manuscripts and proofs of his compositions. The following were located at Faringdon in the 1970s.

Manuscripts

15 pages of *Les Noces* (1914–17) – vocal score in Russian only.

2 pages *Les Noces* – full score.

One cover page in Russian with three lines of text (translated as):

Small Wedding[1]
Songs and Dances (represented by) Characters
A Composition

Proofs

3 of 5 Easy Pieces for piano duet (1914–15): nos. 1, 3 & 5 – copyist's version with Stravinsky's notations in red ink.

Renard (1916): pages 4–47 vocal score proofs with corrections in red ink.

Berceuses du chat (1915): nos. 1 & 4 only. Ed. Adolf Henn, Genève 1917, signed.

Pribaoutki (1914): pages 10–21 only; nos. 3 & 4: 'Le Colonel'; 'Le Vieux'.

[Nos. 1 & 2 of *Pribaoutki* – apparently not in the collection above – signed and inscribed to Berners, were sold at Sotheby's on 21 May 1987 and bought by the British Library. Stravinsky's inscription runs: 'Prenez, mon cher Tyrwhitt cette première épreuve don't je n'ai plus besoin. A vous et à Dimanche I. Stravinsky'.]

---

1 In fact *Les Noces*, but with Russian diminutive ending.

Berners: Record collection

L ORD Berners' record collection was donated by Robert Heber-Percy to what was then the British Institute of Recorded Sound (now the National Sound Archive at the British Library). Patrick Saul, Director of the Institute, kindly provided this list with a letter to me on 15 June 1972. Apart from his own music, Berners' acetates contain three works by Stravinsky and Bartók's *Concerto for Orchestra*. His commercial recordings are overwhelmingly of Stravinsky (18), followed by Ravel (9), Debussy (7), Bach (4), Berlioz (3), Strauss (3), Prokofiev (2), Hindemith (2), Igor Markevitch (2), with other composers represented by single works or collections – and three recordings of the Gypsy Orchestra.

Acetates

3 discs: Columbia tests   Berners: Incidental Music from film *Nicholas Nickleby*

2 discs: electrical transcription   Berners: *Luna Park*; BBC Symphony Orchestra, 14 January 1938

6 discs: electrical transcription   Berners: Suite *The Triumph of Neptune*

5 discs: electrical transcription   Berners: *Valses bourgeoises* (piano duet)

3 discs: Columbia tests   Berners: *Les Sirènes*; Philharmonia Orchestra, 24 July 1947

5 discs: private recording   Bartók: *Concerto for Orchestra*; 6 March 1946

5 discs: private recording   Stravinsky: Symphony no. 3; BBC Symphony Orchestra/ Roger Désormière

5 discs: private recording   Stravinsky: *Dumbarton Oaks*; BBC broadcast, 4 November 1938

5 discs: Columbia tests   Stravinsky: *Concerto for Two Pianos*; Igor and Soulima Stravinsky

There are several further acetates with no indication of contents. However, two of them contained Berners' own performance of the Polka included on the CD of songs and piano music released on Symposium 1278 (2000).

Commercial discs

1	Columbia SDX 1/7	Delius: *Paris, Eventyr, Koanga* (closing scene), *Hassan* (excerpts); LPO/Beecham. 'To the Queen of my Heart', 'Love's Philosophy'; Heddle Nash (tenor), Gerald Moore (piano)
2	Columbia 12371D	Stravinsky: *Four Norwegian Moods*; NYPO/Stravinsky
3	Columbia L1422	Strauss: *Salomé* (Salomé's Dance); LSO/Strauss
4	Columbia G10210F	*Czárdás egyveleg*; Gypsy Orchestra
5	Columbia G10182F	*Ith az irás, Minden yo családban*; Béla Berker (tenor) and Gypsy Orchestra
6	Columbia G10198F	*Eger felöl jön, Nem jó nem jó*; Aladar Sió Gypsy Orchestra
7	Columbia LX311/3	Hindemith: String Trio no. 2; Szymon Goldberg, Paul Hindemith and Emmanuel Feuermann
8	Columbia 9656	Debussy: *Nocturnes* (Nuages); Paris Conservatoire Orchestra/Phillipe Gaubert
9	Columbia L2233/8	Debussy: *Pelléas et Mélisande* (excerpts); cond. George Truc
10	Columbia L1999/2001	Debussy: *Ibéria*; RPO/Paul Klenau
11	Columbia L2173/5	Stravinsky: *Petroushka* (suite); orchestra/Stravinsky
12	Columbia LX433/5	Prokofiev: Violin Concerto no. 1; Joseph Szigeti, LPO/Beecham
13	Columbia LX326/8	Stravinsky: *Les Noces*; ensemble/Stravinsky
14	Columbia DX949	Stravinsky: *Le Baiser de la fée* (Pas de Deux); LPO/Dorati
15	Columbia DX291	Berlioz: *Les Troyens* (Royal Hunt and Storm); Hallé/Harty
16	Columbia LF33/5	Poulenc, *Aubade*; Francis Poulenc (piano), Straram Concerto Orchestra/Straram
17	Columbia DB1790	Stravinsky: *Les Noces* (excerpt); cond. Stravinsky. Bartók: *Mikrokosmos* (staccato & ostinato); Bela Bartók (piano)
18	Columbia 5547	Byrd: *Justorum animae*, Mass for five voices (Agnus Dei); St George's Singers
19	Columbia DX1362	Berners: *Nicholas Nickleby*; Philharmonia/Ernest Irving
20	Columbia 1542	Berners: *Les Sirènes*; Philharmonia/Ernest Irving
21	Columbia LFX259/9	Ravel: Piano Concerto in G; Marguerite Long and orchestra/Ravel. *Pavane pour une infante défunte*; orchestra/Freitas Branco
22	Columbia LFX	Stravinsky: *Piano Rag Music*; Stravinsky (piano). *Ragtime for Eleven Instruments*; ensemble
23	Columbia L1041	Stravinsky: *Firebird* (excerpt); Beecham SO/Beecham
24	Columbia LFX82/4	Stravinsky: *Capriccio* for piano and orchestra; Stravinsky, Straram Concerto Orchestra/Ernest Ansermet

25	Columbia LX308/9	Stravinsky: Octet for wind instruments; ensemble/ Stravinsky
26	Columbia LX147/9	Stravinsky: *Symphony of Psalms*; A. Vlasoff Choir, Straram Orchestra/Stravinsky
27	Columbia D15126	Stravinsky: *Pulcinella* (excerpts); orchestra/Stravinsky
28	Columbia D15182	Stravinsky: *Three Pieces for String Quartet*; Krettly Quartet
29	Columbia L2373/4	Lambert: *The Rio Grande*; Hamilton Harty (piano), St Michael's Singers, Hallé Orchestra/Lambert
30	Columbia LFX92/3	Falla: Harpsichord Concerto; Falla and Instens
31	Decca X204/5	Ravel: Concerto for piano left hand; J. Blanchard, Paris Phil/ Charles Munch
32	Decca K815/6	Vaughan Williams: *Fantasia on a Theme of Thomas Tallis*; Boyd Neel String Orchestra/Boyd Neel
33	Decca AK1584/6	Ravel: *Daphnis et Chloé*, Suites 1 & 2; Paris Conservatoire Orchestra/Charles Munch
34	Decca LY6053/6	Moussorgsky, arr. Ravel: *Pictures from an Exhibition*; Berlin State Opera Orchestra/Alois Melichar
35	Decca X167/170	Stravinsky: *Apollon musagète*; Boyd Neel Orchestra/Boyd Neel
36	Gramo D1826/7	Ravel: *Daphnis et Chloé*, Suite no. 2; Boston SO/ Koussevitsky
37	Gramo DB2842/5	Bartók: String Quartet no. 2; Budapest Quartet
38	Gramo DB5067	Debussy: *Nocturnes* (Fêtes); Paris Conservatoire Orchestra/ Pierre Coppola
39	Gramo DB612/3	Debussy: *Images* (Gigues, Rondes de printemps); San Francisco Symphony Orchestra/Monteux
40	Gramo C3733/4	Stravinsky: Concerto in D major; Hallé/Barbirolli
41	Gramo W864/5	Bach: Concerto for three pianos in C; Pignari, Schavelson, Descarves, orchestra/Bret
42	Gramo W1066	Debussy: *En blanc et noire* (Scherzandi), Aubert: *Suite brève* (Air de Ballet); M. Ruff and D. Jeanès (pianos)
43	Gramo EH736	Weill: *Aufstieg und Fall der Stadt Mahagonny* (vocal selection); Lotte Lenya, vocal and instrumental ensemble/ Hans Sommer
44	Gramo W1029/30	Ravel: *Rapsodie espagnole*; orchestra/Piero Coppola
45	Gramo W1052/4	Debussy: *Ibéria*, *L'Isle joyeuse* (arr. Molinari); orchestra/ Piero Coppola
46	Gramo DB4935/6	Ravel: *Valses nobles et sentimentales*; Paris Conservatoire Orchestra/Piero Coppola
47	Gramo AG127	*Farruca* and *Cartaceneras*; La Niña de los Peines.
48	Gramo DB5069/71	Markevitch: *L'Envol d'Icare*; Belgian National Orchestra/ Markevitch

49	Gramo DB5072-4	Markevitch: *Le Nouvel Âge*; Belgian National Orchestra/ Markevitch
50	Gramo 4-2953	Raff: *Serenade*; John McCormack
51	Gramo DB3851/6	Berlioz: *Symphonie fantastique*; Paris Conservatoire Orchestra/Bruno Walter
52	Gramo DB2612-20s	Richard Strauss: *Also sprach Zarathustra*; Boston Symphony Orchestra/Koussevitsky
53	Gramo D1594	Ravel: *Alborado del grazioso*; orchestra/Coppola
54	Gramo D1564	Ravel: *Pavane pour une infante défunte, L'Enfant et les sortilèges* (Five o'clock), Orchestra/Coppola
55	Gramo DB3655/7s	Prokofiev: *Lt. Kijé* (suite); Boston Symphony Orchestra/ Koussevitsky
56	Gramo D1932	Stravinsky: *Chant du rossignol* (Marche Chinoise); LSO/ Coates
57	Gramo DB1952	Bach: Fugue in G minor, arr. Stokowski, *Christ lag in Todesbanden*, arr. Stokowski; Philadelphia Orchestra/ Stokowski
58	Parlophone R20109	Stravinsky: *Fireworks*, Suite no. 2 (Polka and Galop); Concerts Colonne Orchestra/Gabriel Pierné
59	Polydor 27163	Berlioz: Overture *Béatrice et Bénédict*; Berlin Philharmonic/ Julius Kopsch
60	Polydor 566019	Chabrier: Habanera. Falla: *El amor brujo* (Danza); Lamoureux Orchestra/Albert Wolff
61	Polydor G5295	Bach: *Komm, Gott, Schöpfer, heliger Geist; Schmücke dich, O liebe Seele*; Berlin Philharmonic/Joseph Horenstein
62	Telefunken SK2450/2	Stravinsky: *Jeu de cartes*; Berlin Philharmonic/Stravinsky
63	Telefunken E1647/9	Hindemith: Symphony *Mathis der Maler*; Berlin Philharmonic/Hindemith
64	Ultraphon E463/4	Bach, arr. Schoenberg: Prelude and Fugue in E flat major; Berlin Philharmonic/Erich Kleiber

Berners: Library of scores

THIS list is based on material seen by Peter Dickinson in the 1970s and by Mary Gifford more recently.[1] Most of it is in the Berners Archive, but it is unlikely to be complete. However, it shows the connections between Berners and other composers and, along with his record collection, confirms his interests.

1 Mary Gifford, *Lord Berners: Aspects of a Biography* (PhD thesis, University of London, 2007), table 10.

Audran, Edmond: *La Poupée* (1896) [operetta, signed, 1897]

Bach: 'O Praise the Lord' (motet); *48 Preludes and Fugues*, Book 1, BG edition

Bartók: *Mikrokosmos*, Vol. 1 (piano); *Bagatelles* (piano); Quartet no. 1

Berg: *Wozzeck* (vocal score)

Britten: *Variations on a Theme of Frank Bridge* (score)

Busoni: *Doktor Faust* (vocal score)

Chabrier: *Le Roi malgré lui* (vocal score)

Chopin: Concertos; Etudes, Vol. II; Ballades and Mazurkas [inscribed 'from his mother 1894']

Czerny: *Schule der Geläufigkeit*, op. 299 (piano)

Debussy: *Petite suite* (score); *Le Martyre de Saint-Sébastien* (vocal score)

Dvořak: *Poetické nálady* (piano)

Falla: *El amor brujo* [first edition with decorations by Gontcharova]

Fauré: Requiem (vocal score)

Granados: *Goyescas* (piano)

Hindemith: *Reihe kleiner Stücke* (piano); *Nobilissima visione* (vocal score); Piano Sonata III; *1922 Suite* (piano); *Mathis der Maler Symphonie* (score)

Holländer, Alexis: *Sumurum* (piano)

Honegger: *Amphion* (vocal score); *Les Aventures du Roi Pausole* (vocal score)

Lambert: *Music for Orchestra* ['to Lord Berners from Constant Lambert Hommage affectueux, September 1930']; *Horoscope* ['To Gerald from Constant with all good wishes Christmas 1938']; *Elegy* (piano, 1940) ['To Gerald with apologies for this prophetic piece. With love from Constant']

Lefébure-Wély: *Les Cloches du monastère: Nocturne* [piano, mentioned in *First Childhood*, 200 (1934); 184 (1999)]

Markevitch: *Psaume* (vocal score); *La Foire* (vocal score); *Le Paradis perdue* (vocal score)

Milhaud: *L'Album de Madame Bovary* (piano); *Trois valses* (piano); Violin and Piano Sonata no. 1; *Chanson bas* [inscribed 'à Lord Berners. Bien amicalement Milhaud']

Mozart: *Le nozze di Figaro* (vocal score); *Don Juan* (full score, signed); *Klavierstücke* (Peters Edition no. 6) [signed 'bought in Constantinople']

Moussorgsky: *La Foire* (vocal score)

Offenbach: *I ciarlieri* (vocal score)

Palestrina: *Ecce ego Joannes*; *Missa O sacrum convivium*

Porter, Cole: 'Wunderbar'; 'Night and Day'

Prokofiev: *L'Amour des trois oranges* (piano score)

Puccini: *Madama Butterfly* (vocal score)

Rawsthorne: *Bagatelles* (piano)

Salazar: *Trois chansons*

Satie: *Sports et divertissements* (piano); *Cinéma* (piano duet)

Sauguet: *La Chartreuse de Parme* [private printing, inscribed to Berners 1938]

Schoenberg: *Erwartung* [full score signed 'Berners']

Schumann: Piano Music Book 3 (Breitkopf)

Slaughter, W: *Dandy Dan, the Lifeguardsman* (1897) [musical comedy: inscribed by the
composer, signed 'G. Tyrwhitt']

Strauss: *Burlesque* (piano); Violin and Piano Sonata; *Feuersnot* (vocal score); *Intermezzo*
(vocal score); *Der Rosenkavalier Waltzes* (piano); *Ein Heldenleben* [signed 'Gerald
Tyrwhitt. November 1902]; 'The Stone-breaker' (song); *Kampf und Sieg* (score); *Die
schweigsame Frau* (vocal score)

Stravinsky: *Capriccio* [signed 'Berners, Nice 1929']; *Les Noces* (vocal score); *Duo
concertante*; *Quatre chants russes*; Sonata for Two Pianos; *Le Baiser de la fée* (piano
score); *Dumbarton Oaks* (two piano score); Violin Concerto in D (violin and piano
score) [signed 'Berners']; *Mavra* [signed 'Berners']; *L'Histoire du soldat*; *Apollon
musagète* (piano) [signed 'Berners']; *Jeu de cartes* (piano); *Le Sacre du printemps* [piano
duet: signed 'Gerald Tyrwhitt' with first verse of poem, Sonnet – see Poems, p. 162.]

Tchaikovsky: *1812 Overture* (score)

Wagner: *Tannhäuser*; *Album Leaf in C*

Walton: *Façade* (full score) ['for Gerald from William October 9 1936']; *Façade* (piano duet,
arr. Lambert)

An Egyptian Princess

Mary Gifford

1 Detail from family tree in the Berners Archive, also the obituary of Isabel Grace Denham (*c.* 1875–1933, née Vandeleur), *The Times*, 20 February 1933, 1a. Julia's eldest sister married Capt. Hector Stewart Vandeleur (1836–1909) in 1867.

2 Advice from an examination of the score by Chris Banks, Head of Music Collections, British Library, November 2003. The watermarks on the cover paper have not been identified, but the printed music paper is watermarked 'Strong and Hanbury London'. This has been traced to the early part of the twentieth century, probably the first decade. By 1915 the firm's designated watermark is listed as 'Strohan Ledger'. There are problems with dating music by watermark because the history of the paper before printing is not usually known. While the history of the company might provide a date before which the work could not have been printed, in the absence of any other information, this does not help with when the work was composed. The width of the printed page is 25cm (9⅞ ins) and the length 32cm (12⅝ ins), the paper is a dull grey, and the work has been glued and not bound.

3 Mark Amory, *Lord Berners: the Last Eccentric* (London: Chatto & Windus, 1998), 23.

4 Bryony Jones, *The Music of Lord Berners (1883–1950): 'the Versatile Peer'* (Aldershot: Ashgate, 2003), 127.

5 'Berners', *The New Grove Dictionary of Music and Musicians*, 2nd edn, ed. Stanley Sadie and John Tyrrell (London: Macmillan, 2001), vol. 3, 436–7.

ONE piece of evidence about Berners' earliest music survives – the vocal score of the privately printed operetta *An Egyptian Princess* by Gerald H. Tyrwhitt. In the Berners Archive there is one copy inscribed to a cousin: 'Grace Vandeleur with the "author's" compliments'.[1] The score has no identifying publisher's marks, and no date. The surviving three or four copies look as if they have not been used, and contain no markings. The music has been lithographically reproduced, and is probably free-hand apart from the titles of the separate numbers. The systems have been ruled up and bracketed individually, and the spacing between them is not even: no two bass clefs are identical.[2]

Mark Amory has suggested that *An Egyptian Princess* was probably the musical play that Berners wrote at Eton,[3] and Bryony Jones places the composition between 1897 and 1900.[4] There is no reference to the work in the British Library catalogue of published music. Peter Dickinson does not refer to it in the body of the text in his article for *New Grove 2001*,[5] but in his list of works it appears as: 'An Egyptian Princess (operetta), *c.* 1900'. If *An Egyptian Princess* had been written before 1900 it would indeed originate from his school days. The production of an operetta would have been a major event in Berners' life at Eton, and it would certainly have been mentioned either in his autobiography, in his letters home or in his mother's diaries, had it existed or been performed at that time. Details of printing the music and costs would also have been mentioned. Nor is there any reference in *A Distant Prospect* to any production while he was at Eton. The letter dated autumn 1898 provides the only possible information: 'I hope you will like my play. The music master played it through, and said it was good. Spring Rice even condescends to like it!! I have finished all the music, but have only written out the first act, so far.' I find this evidence insufficient to link the work with Eton.

Notebook 26 in the Berners Archive contains plans for a play or musical drama and some verses. There is no indication of music, apart from the use of the word 'chorus'. There is no plot outline, but the first few verses and choruses are nearly identical to those at the beginning of *An Egyptian Princess*. The notebook started life as an exercise book at Eton, and the cover is dark blue cloth, with 'Tyrwhitt', 'Div. 21' and 'SCIENCE' stamped in gold on the outside. Inside the book there is a date, Tuesday 25 January; the perpetual calendar shows that the year was 1898. The subject was 'Physiography',[6] and in the front of the book there are various science lessons or homework, written in a childish hand in ink. There are diagrams and amusing illustrations on the left side of the page, and information on the right in most places. The first page shows a very carefully drawn river, with cliffs and mountains, and later there is an amusing drawing of 'fish with phosphorous lungs'. The work has been marked, and on one occasion he was given 46 out of 50 and the comment 'good'. At the back of the notebook, upside down, there are apparently the answers to four tests on the subject, which have also been marked. 'Tyrwhitt' is written at the top of each of them, and the marks are circled. The last test has a '13' circled, and a note stating that the test was out of 14.

In the middle of the exercise book, in pencil and in a more mature hand, Berners has written pages of verse, starting with 'Opening chorus', and exactly the same words as in the printed libretto: 'Egyptians here you see, In marble hall reclining, Our raven locks are we, With lotus leaves entwining.' The second song in the exercise book, for Abanazar, 'The Necromancer', is also very similar to the second song in the printed version, but again only the first verse has been used, while the third song, to be sung by Iris, is headed 'The Greek Slave' in the exercise book, but is entitled by the first line in the printed copy: 'A dear little maid am I'. After this the words diverge. The exercise book has two pages torn out, with only the margins left. These show that the characters in the play were changed in the printed version, and as far as it is possible to tell, the plot as well. The notebook tails off, and some pages have a heading, for example '8: Duet. Abanazar and Sterope' followed by a blank page.

This use of a notebook from the middle is characteristic of Berners. He often appears to have used old notebooks, and the handwriting does not appear to be his schoolboy hand.[7] It looks as if he took the exercise book home and used the spare paper at a later date.

I estimate that around 1910, pre-Rome, is the most likely date for the complete composition and printing of *An Egyptian Princess*. This would explain the absence of any references to the performance or the printing in either letters or diaries when Berners was at school. The work would fit very appropriately into the amateur productions that were devised by diplomats as part of their social life abroad. There are references to such productions in Berners' letters – for example to the entertainment in Vienna.[8] Dorothy Wellesley, writer and wife of Berners' fellow diplomat and friend Gerald Wellesley, met Berners in Rome and knew him during the

6 *Concise Oxford Dictionary* (1990): 'Physiography: the description of nature, of natural phenomena, or of a class of objects, physical geography'.

7 See notes on notebooks: Mary Gifford, *Lord Berners: Aspects of a Biography* (PhD thesis, University of London, 2007), 'Sources', 21.

8 Gifford, *Lord Berners*, table 2, no. 68.

four years of the war. She said: 'He was a fine composer, writing comic operettas and a few books.'[9] This reference is particularly interesting because it mentions comic operettas. If this reference is to *An Egyptian Princess*, it gives weight to the dating of the work as later than Berners' schooldays and supports my assumption that it formed part of the entertainments devised for an embassy.

Berners' *An Egyptian Princess* is a light, inconsequential work that does little to suggest his later development and compositional style, all of which further supports a date before 1911. However, it does demonstrate his life-long sense of humour, and as Peter Dickinson pointed out in 1983: 'At all periods his music has the angled vision of parody. The early operetta, *An Egyptian Princess*, is a view of Gilbert and Sullivan much as the late song "Come on Algernon" looks at the music-hall genre.'[10] It might have been based on a fictional work by the famous Egyptologist, Georg Ebers, whose popular story went into four editions[11] and was used as the plot for a school 'Operetta for Ladies' by Charles Vincent, published in 1901.[12]

The work as it stands barely claims a plot, and there is no cast list or synopsis. There must have been dialogue, now missing, which supplied the narrative illustrated by the musical numbers. There are thirteen of these, spread over two acts that seem loosely connected to Egypt. The opening chorus of slaves, 'Egyptians are we', sets the life of comfort in 'this paradise of flowers'. The slaves are taking care of the beautiful Queen. In the second song Abanazar, the Necromancer introduces himself in a boastful patter-song, followed by a dance. No. 3, 'A dear little maid am I', introduces Iris, who has been captured and sold to Abanazar as a maid. This is close to Gilbert and Sullivan's 'Three little maids from school'.[13] No. 4 is a song by Hermoine: it describes a shepherd sleeping, while the chorus warns him to look after his sheep. No. 5 is a trio sung by Bombastes, Abanazar and Serapis, 'A nice little way'. This describes Bombastes' methods of rule that include beheading and torture for 'making one's subjects obey'. Abanazar then sings 'An ideal man', a cynical description of a man who was 'Beloved by ev'ry friend he had, Of enemies he'd none, Perhaps I'd better also add, Of friends he'd only one.' The last number of Act I is a song about the disappearance of two people, and how the woman must be rescued before nightfall.

Act II opens with a chorus and dance, 'Hail Osiris'. It is followed by a duet, 'Moderation', which employs the standard music hall type of repetition of the last phrase by another character. The first of two verses provides a description of a prophet who came to a miserable end, and the second the

9 Dorothy Wellesley, *Far Have I Travelled* (London: J. Barrie, 1952), 133.

10 Peter Dickinson, 'Lord Berners, 1883–1950: A British Avant-gardist at the Time of World War I', *Musical Times* 124, no. 1689 (November 1983), 669–72.

11 Georg Ebers (1837–98), *An Egyptian Princess* (London, 1870, 1882, 1887, 1907).

12 Charles Vincent, Operetta for Ladies: *The Egyptian Princess* (In Two Acts), The Vincent Music Company Ltd, 9 Berners Street, London, 1901. In the catalogue of the British Library, an 'Egyptian Princess' appears several times: there are three entries in the catalogue of printed music, two of which pre-date Berners' time in Constantinople, and the third is by Thomas Clapton, published in 1911 but dating from 1870. There are three entries in the general catalogue, also dating from the first decade of the twentieth century.

13 Sir Arthur Sullivan (1842–1900), *The Mikado* (1885). This connection has also been made by Philip Lane and Mark Amory, *Lord Berners*, 24.

story of a lad who goes fishing – with the customary luck of a beginner, he hooks a great monster, but the fish was so large that he has the lad for luncheon. No. 10 is a solo by Bombastes, 'I'm the ruler of the land', outlining his pleasure in himself. The next is a laughing song by Abanazar. The final song, sung by Iris, is 'The Conceited Owl', in which the chorus sings what may have been a pun on Berners' surname Tyrwhitt: 'To-whit, to-whit, to-whoo'. This entertainment in the tradition of the Gilbert and Sullivan operettas is quite different from the music of Berners' later modernistic style in Rome. And *An Egyptian Princess* is clearly marked 'Gerald Tyrwhitt' and not 'Lord Berners', which proves that it was composed before he inherited.

However, it hardly matters that the dating of *An Egyptian Princess* is uncertain. Whether it was written around 1900 or 1910 does not alter the judgement that it is a work of little significance. The interest lies in how it reflects Berners' musical education through Cheam and Eton, and his studies with Kretschmer and Tovey[14] – and, indeed, with his sense of humour. I am convinced that Berners did not write it for Eton, but that he must have used it in a diplomatic context such as Vienna or Constantinople and had it printed privately at that time.

14 Sir Donald Francis Tovey (1875–1940), pianist, composer, author of *Essays in Musical Analysis*. Berners had at least six lessons with him in 1908.

MARY GIFFORD returned to academic studies late in life to pursue her interest in music. Being neither a player nor a composer, she completed an MA in musicology at Southampton, where her research projects included 'Lord Berners and *The Triumph of Neptune*' and 'English Ballet music during the 1930s'. Her PhD thesis, 'Lord Berners: Aspects of a Biography', for King's College, London, was completed in 2008.

APPENDIX 9

Berners: Family tree

The Barony of Berners was created in 1455 for Sir John Bourchier (c. 1415–74). The 2nd Baron, his grandson, was also Sir John Bourchier (1467–1533), the translator of Froissart and an influential politician under Henry VIII. (See interview with Robert Heber-Percy, Chapter 9, p. 85.). Subsequently the barony fell into various abeyances, but it can descend through the female line, as with the two baronesses since the death of Berners, when the baronetcy became extinct.

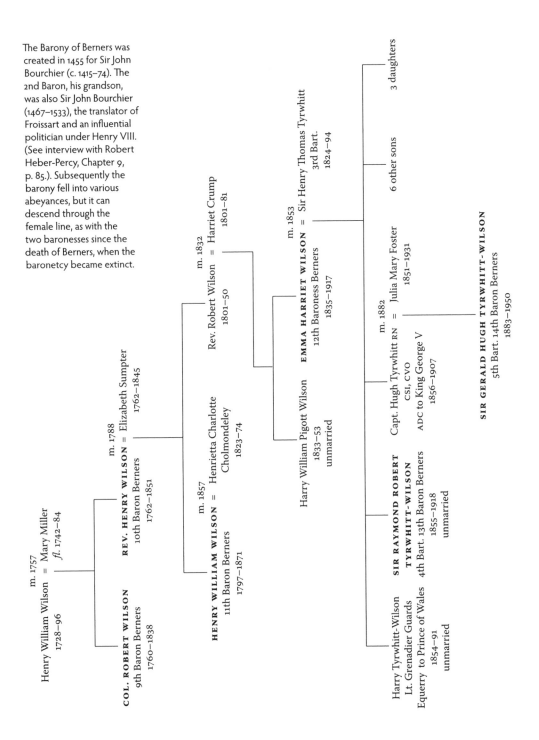

Henry William Wilson = Mary Miller
1728–96   fl. 1742–84
m. 1757

COL. ROBERT WILSON
9th Baron Berners
1760–1838

REV. HENRY WILSON = Elizabeth Sumpter
10th Baron Berners   1762–1845
1762–1851
m. 1788

HENRY WILLIAM WILSON = Henrietta Charlotte Cholmondeley
11th Baron Berners   1823–74
1797–1871
m. 1857

Rev. Robert Wilson = Harriet Crump
1801–50   1801–81
m. 1832

Harry William Pigott Wilson
1833–53
unmarried

EMMA HARRIET WILSON = Sir Henry Thomas Tyrwhitt
12th Baroness Berners   3rd Bart.
1835–1917   1824–94
m. 1853

Harry Tyrwhitt-Wilson
Lt. Grenadier Guards
Equerry to Prince of Wales
1854–91
unmarried

SIR RAYMOND ROBERT TYRWHITT-WILSON
4th Bart. 13th Baron Berners
1855–1918
unmarried

Capt. Hugh Tyrwhitt RN = Julia Mary Foster
CSI, CVO   1851–1931
ADC to King George V
1856–1907
m. 1882

6 other sons

3 daughters

SIR GERALD HUGH TYRWHITT-WILSON
5th Bart. 14th Baron Berners
1883–1950

Musical works

SOME dates in Berners are problematic. One would imagine that the dates he must have given to *Grove's Dictionary of Music and Musicians* and the *Musical Times* were accurate, but *Le Poisson d'or* is dated 1914 in such sources, and the manuscript has 1915. The *Three Funeral Marches* are dated 1914 in the early sources but the manuscript has 1916. The *Lieder* Album is a special case, since sketches for the last song suggest a very early date with additions made later. I discussed dates with Gavin Bryars in 1982 for the first edition of my two volumes *The Collected Vocal Music* and *The Collected Music for Solo Piano* (Chester Music, with second editions in 2000). This chronological list has been arrived at through further consultation with Mary Gifford and Philip Lane. Some dates are still conjectural, and some first performances are unknown. Berners' early works were originally published with French titles, probably because of his musical connections and performances in Paris; these titles have been retained. Publication arrangements between Lord Berners and J. & W. Chester for individual works can be found in Appendix 4. Additional information about the availability of all his music is in the Chester catalogue or online at www.chesternovello.com.

1 **Lieder Album: Three Songs in the German Manner** [Heine], 1913–18, voice and piano. 'Du bist wie eine blume' (The White Pig) – 'König Wiswamitra' (King Wiswamitra) – 'Weihnachtslied' (Christmas Carol). UK première: Olga Haley, Steinway Hall, London, 13 May 1920.

2 **Le Poisson d'or**, 1915, piano. Poème et musique, couverture, frontispiece, et vignette de Natalia Gontcharova. Dedicated to Stravinsky.

3 **Dispute entre le papillon et le crapaud**, *c.* 1915, piano. Première: Susan Bradshaw, Purcell Room, 8 December 1972.

4 **Trois petites marches funèbres**, 1916, piano. 'Pour un homme d'état' – 'Pour un canari' – 'Pour une tante à heritage'. Première: Alfredo Casella, Accademia di Santa Cecilia, Rome, 30 March 1917. 1st edition as by Gerald Tyrwhitt, dedicated to Madame Khvoschinsky; all three scored for chamber ensemble in *L'uomo dai baffi* (see item 7 below). No. 1, 'For a Statesman', scored for small orchestra.

5 **Fragments psychologiques**, *c.* 1916, piano. 'La Haine' – 'Le Rire' – 'Un soupir'. No. 2 scored for *L'uomo dai baffi*; nos. 1 & 3 scored by Philip Lane (see below).

6 **Portsmouth Point: Symphonic Sketch, after a drawing by Rowlandson**, arr. for piano solo, 1918; arr. chamber ensemble for *L'uomo dai baffi*; arr. two pianos by Richard Rodney Bennett (première: Richard Rodney Bennett and Susan Bradshaw: Wigmore Hall, 1 December 1983).

7 **L'uomo dai baffi** (The Man with the Moustache), 1918, puppet ballet for Fortunato Depero. Première: Teatro dei Piccoli, Rome, 15 April 1918; UK première: Aquarius/Nicholas Cleobury, Queen Elizabeth Hall, London, 18 October 1983. Five movements, arrangements of *Fragments psychologiques* no. 2; *Trois petites marches funèbres*; and *Portsmouth Point* for single woodwind, piano and string quintet. *Fragments psychologiques* nos. 1 & 3 scored as Interludes 1 & 2 by Philip Lane, 1995.

8 **Trois morceaux pour orchestre**, 1918. 'Chinoisérie', dedicated to Michel Larionow – 'Valse sentimentale', dedicated to Eugene Goossens – 'Kasatchok', dedicated to Natalia Gontcharova. Première: Hallé Orchestra/Eugene Goossens, Manchester, 8 March 1919.

9 **Trois morceaux pour piano à quatre mains**, 1918, arr. composer. Couverture, illustrations et ornement de Michel Larionow. Première: Mathilde and Helène Coffer, Société Musicale Indépendante, Salle Gaveau, Paris, 25 April 1919.

10 **Valses bourgoises**, *c.* 1918, piano duet. 'Valse brillante' – 'Valse caprice' – 'Strauss, Strauss et Straus'; orchestrated Philip Lane, 1995. Performed at the Festival of the International Society for Contemporary Music, Salzburg, 5 August 1923; Darius Milhaud and Jean Wiener, Aeolian Hall, London, 21 November 1923.

11 **Fantaisie espagnole pour orchestre**, 1919. 'Prelude' – 'Fandango' – 'Pasodoble'. Première: New Queen's Hall Orchestra/ Sir Henry Wood, Queen's Hall, London, 24 September 1919. Dedicated to G. Francesco Malipiero.

12 **Fantaisie espagnole pour piano à quatre mains**, *c.* 1920, arr. composer.

13 **Trois chansons** [Georges Jean-Aubry], 1920, voice and piano. 'Romance' –' L'Étoile filante' (The Shooting Star) – 'La Fiancée du timbalier' (The Drummer Boy's Sweetheart). Première: Olga Haley, Steinway Hall, London, 13 May 1920.

14 **Three English Songs**, 1920, voice and piano. 'Lullaby' [Thomas Dekker] – 'The Lady Visitor in the Pauper Ward' [Robert Graves] – 'The Green-Eyed Monster' [E. L. Duff].

15 **Three Songs**, 1920, voice and piano. 'The Rio Grande' [Traditional – capstan shanty] – 'Theodore or The Pirate King' [John Masefield] – 'A Long Time Ago' [Traditional – Halliards Shanty]. Première: Gladys Moger, Aeolian Hall, London, 26 January 1921.

16 **Dialogue between Tom Filuter and his Man by Ned the Dog Stealer**, 1921, voice and piano. Première: Gladys Moger, Aeolian Hall, London, 26 January 1921.

17 **Le Carrosse du Saint-Sacrement** [libretto by composer based on 'La Périchole' by Prosper Mérimée], opera comique en un acte; soloists – mezzo-soprano, 3 tenors, baritone, 2 basses, Théâtre des Champs-Élysées, Paris, 24 April 1924, rev. 1926; dedicated 'To my travelling companions in Italy. Perugia – Rome, summer 1920'.

18 **Suite: Caprice péruvien**, 1938, orchestra; arr. Constant Lambert from the opera.

19 **Fugue for orchestra**, 1924. Used as interlude in Diaghilev's Ballets Russes, His Majesty's Theatre, London, June/July, 1926; first concert performance, London Symphony Orchestra/ Sir Thomas Beecham, Royal Albert Hall, 7 November 1926. Dedicated to the Princesse Edmond de Polignac, Paris, May 1924.

20 **The Triumph of Neptune**, ballet, English pantomime in ten tableaux; book Sacheverell Sitwell; choreography George Balanchine; Diaghilev Ballet, Lyceum Theatre, London, December 1926; dedicated to Viscount Rothermere; complete ballet and suite; also reduced orchestration, arr. Roy Douglas; 'Adagio', 'Variations and Hornpipe', for strings; 'Harlequinade', 'Intermezzo' and 'Hornpipe' for piano solo; wind band, arr. Bram Wiggins; portions were also used for **Le Boxing**, Ballet Club, London, 16 February 1931 and **Waterloo and the Crimea**, Lyric Theatre, Hammersmith, London, 15 June 1931, both choreography Susan Salaman. The same music was used for **Mr Punch and the Street Party**, plus *The Expulsion from Paradise* and *Portsmouth Point*, orchestrated Philip Lane, choreography David Bintley, Sadlers Wells Royal Ballet, London, 1979.

21 **Luna Park, Fantastic Ballet in one Act**; book Boris Kochno; choreography George Balanchine; scenery and costumes Christopher Wood; in 'Cochran's 1930 Revue', Palace Theatre, Manchester, 5 March 1930; London Pavilion, 27 March 1930. Dedicated to Charles B. Cochran. Also regularly performed as **Foyer de Danse** (after Degas); choreography Frederick

Ashton, Opera House, Manchester, 20 February 1932; Mercury Theatre, London, 9 October 1932.

22 **Fanfare**, 1930, for 4 trumpets, 4 trombones and percussion. Première: BBC broadcast from the Annual Dinner of the Musicians' Benevolent Fund, Savoy Hotel, London, 8 May 1930; then Annual Musicians' Benevolent Fund Concert, Royal Albert Hall, 22 November 1931, both conducted by Captain H. E. Adkins.

23 **A Wedding Bouquet**, ballet, chorus and orchestra: text Gertrude Stein; choreography Frederick Ashton; costumes and décor Lord Berners under the supervision of William Chappell; Sadler's Wells, London, 27 April 1937; dedicated to Lilian Bayliss.

24 **Cupid and Psyche**, ballet; choreography Frederick Ashton; designs and sets Francis Rose (Ira Belline, Stravinsky's niece, realised Francis Rose's costumes); Sadler's Wells Theatre, London, 27 April 1939.

25 **'Red Roses and Red Noses'** [Lord Berners], *c.* 1941, voice and piano. 'To a young lady who expressed the wish that, when she died, red roses might be strewn on her tomb'. Concert première: Meriel Dickinson, Purcell Room, 8 December 1972.

26 **Polka**, 1941, piano; orchestrated Philip Lane, 1995. Première: Tom Bell and Lionel Gruenbaum, Tynchewyke Society Christmas Pantomime, Radcliffe Infirmary, Oxford, 29 December 1941. Used in film *Champagne Charlie*, released 25 August 1944.

27 **Valse**, 1943, piano. First 213 bars used in film *The Halfway House*, released 14 April 1944.

28 **Suite: The Halfway House**, orchestra, arr. from film score Philip Lane, 2007, includes his scoring of Valse.

29 **'Come on Algernon'** [T. E. B. Clark], voice and piano. Used in film *Champagne Charlie*, released 25 August 1944. Arr. voice and orchestra Philip Lane. Concert première: Meriel Dickinson, Purcell Room, 8 December 1972.

30 **The Expulsion from Paradise**, 1945, piano. For Penelope Betjeman's Nativity Play. Dedicated to Penelope Betjeman.

31 **March**, *c.* 1945, piano. Première: Susan Bradshaw, Purcell Room, 8 December 1972. Orchestrated Philip Lane, 1975.

32 **Les Sirènes**, ballet; choreography Frederick Ashton; designs and sets Cecil Beaton. Première: Royal Opera House, Covent Garden, London, 12 November 1946.

33 **Suite: Nicholas Nickleby**, orchestra; arr. Ernest Irving from film *The Life and Adventures of Nicholas Nickleby* released 7 August 1947; piano score of suite; dedicated to Ernest Irving.

Arrangements
In dulci jubilo – chorale prelude for organ by Bach, BWV729, arr. piano, in *A Bach Book for Harriet Cohen*, Oxford University Press, 1932. Première: Harriet Cohen, Queen's Hall, 17 October 1932.

Juvenilia
An Egyptian Princess, *c.* 1905–10, operetta. Privately printed vocal score, as by Gerald H. Tyrwhitt. [see Appendix 8: *An Egyptian Princess* by Mary Gifford]

Lost or Incomplete Works
St Valentine's Day Waltz, 1931, arr. Billy Ternent. Lost.

A Fascist March, piano, in the *Daily Express*, 19 April 1934. Incomplete.

Recordings Available in 2007

L'uomo dai baffi
    Harmonia Ensemble/Giuseppe Grazioli
    AS Disc AS5003 (1989)

Valse bourgeoise no. 3
    Isabel Beyer and Harvey Dagul, piano duet
    Four Hands Music FOUR FHMD8045 (1990)
    [originally 1984 LP FHM(C)842]

Trois morceaux
Fantaisie espagnole
Valses bourgeoises
    Peter Lawson and Alan MacLean, piano duet
    Albany TROY142 (1995)

A Wedding Bouquet
Luna Park
March (orch. Lane)
    RTE Chamber Choir; RTE Sinfonietta; Kenneth Alwyn, conductor
    Marco Polo 8.223716 (1996)

Les Sirènes
Caprice péruvien (arr. Lambert)
Suite: Cupid and Psyche
    RTE Sinfonietta/David Lloyd-Jones
    Marco Polo 8.223780 (1996)

Complete Vocal and Solo Piano Music
    Felicity Lott, soprano; Roderick Kennedy, bass; Peter Lawson, piano
    Albany TROY290 (1997)

The Triumph of Neptune (complete)
L'uomo dai baffi (with Intermezzo I and II orch. Lane)
Valses bourgeoises (orch. Lane)*
Polka from 'Champagne Charlie' (orch. Lane)*
    Royal Ballet Sinfonia*; English Northern Philharmonic/David Lloyd-Jones
    Marco Polo 8.223711 (1998)

The Triumph of Neptune (Suite)
Suite: Nicholas Nickleby (arr. Irving)
Trois morceaux
Fugue in C minor
Fantaisie espagnole
Three Orchestral Pieces
 Royal Liverpool Philharmonic Orchestra/Barry Wordsworth
 Campion Cameo 2054 (2006) [originally EMI Classics 7243 5 65098 2 5 (1986) and
 EMI CDC7 47668 2; then Olympia OCD662 (1999)]

Lord Berners, 1883–1950: Complete Vocal Music
Polka from 'Champagne Charlie'
Fragments psychologiques
Le Poisson d'or
Trois petites marches funèbres
Dispute entre le papillon et le crapaud
Valses bourgeoises
Fanfare*
Suite: Nicholas Nickleby (arr. Irving)†
Les Sirènes (Habanera, Farruca, Valse)†
Les Sirènes (Prelude, Mazurka)‡
Polka‡
 Meriel Dickinson, mezzo-soprano; Peter Dickinson, piano; Bernard Dickerson, tenor;
 Richard Rodney Bennett, piano; Susan Bradshaw, piano [from LP Unicorn RHS355
 (1978)]; Kneller Hall Musicians/Captain H. E. Adkins* [from HMV 32.2920, recorded
 1934]; Philharmonia Orchestra/Ernest Irving† [recorded 1937, 78 record C.DX1542];
 Lord Berners, piano‡ [private recording *c.* 1946]
 Symposium SYM1278 (2000)

Complete Piano Music [apart from Portsmouth Point]
Complete Vocal Music
 Ian Partridge, tenor; Len Vorster, piano
 Marco Polo 8.255159 (2000)

Fanfare and March (orch. Lane)*
Caprice péruvien (arr. Lambert)†
Le Carrosse du Saint-Sacrement (sung in English)
 Royal Ballet Sinfonia*/Gavin Sutherland; RTE Sinfonietta†/David Lloyd-Jones;
 BBC Scottish Symphony Orchestra/Nicholas Cleobury
 Marco Polo 8.225155 (2001)

Suite: Nicholas Nickleby
Suite: The Halfway House (ed. Lane)
'Come on Algernon' and Polka (orch. Lane)
 Mary Carewe, soprano; The Joyful Company of Singers; BBC Concert Orchestra/
 Rumon Gamba
 Chandos CHAN10459 (2008)

Some Historic Recordings

Fugue in C minor
BBC Symphony Orchestra/J. Ansell
Symposium SYMCD1203 [recorded 1929 on MB 354-1, MB 355-1]

'Come on Algernon'/Betty Warren
Columbia FB 3051 (1944)

The Triumph of Neptune: Suite
LPO/Beecham EMI CDM7 63405-2 (1992)
[recorded 1937]

The Triumph of Neptune: Suite
Philadelphia Orchestra/Thomas Beecham
Sony Beecham SMK93009 (1994) [recorded 1952; then CBS Classics LP 61431 (1974);
and Sony SMK46683]

Arrangements

Bach: In dulci jubilo, chorale prelude for organ, BWV729, arranged for piano
Gordon Fergus Thompson, ASV CDDCV759 (1991)
Peter Lawson, Albany TROY290 (1998)
Angela Hewitt, Hyperion CDA67309 (2000)

CATALOGUE 3   Published writings

1919

Correspondence between Berners and Ernest Newman. *Observer*, 13 July; 10, 17, 24, 31 August.

1925

'Happy Hampstead as a Ballet! Why not? – some suggestions for Diaghilev'. *Evening News*, January 1925.

Review: *The Psychology of a Musical Prodigy* by G. Révész. *Nation & Athenaeum*, 18 April 1925.

1926

Answer to questionnaire, *Our Symposium*. *The Gramophone*, December 1926, 263.

1929

'Fox-Hunting'. In *The New Forget-me-not: a Calendar*. London: Constable, 1929.

1930

Ronald Firbank: a Memoir by Ifan Kyrle Fletcher with personal reminiscences by Lord Berners, V. B. Holland, Augustus John and Osbert Sitwell. London: Duckworth, 1930.

1931

'The Swiss Governess' [later in *First Childhood*]. In *The New Keepsake: a Christmas, New Year and Birthday Present for Persons of both Sexes*. London: Cobden-Sanderson, 1931.

1932

'Neighbours' [later in *First Childhood*]. In *Little Innocents: Childhood Reminiscences*, by thirty authors including Lord Berners, preface by Alan Pryce-Jones. London: Cobden-Sanderson, 1932.

1933

'Chapters from an Autobiography' [later in *First Childhood*]. *Life and Letters*, September–November 1933, 311–24.

1934

'A Fascist March – original MS of opening bars of latest composition by Lord Berners'. *Daily Express*, 19 April 1934, 6. The column by 'William Hickey' (then written by Tom Driberg) contained a reproduction of eight bars of Lord Berners' manuscript.

First Childhood (to Robert Heber-Percy whose knowledge of orthography and literary style has proved invaluable). London: Constable, February 1934; reprinted April 1934; cheaper edition August 1942; American edition; Tauchnitz Edition: Collection of British and American Authors, Vol. 5168, Leipzig: Bernard Tauchnitz, 1934. In *First Childhood* and *Far from the Madding War*, with a preface by Harold Acton, Oxford: Oxford University Press, 1983; in *Collected Tales and Fantasies*, New York: Turtlepoint Press and Helen Marx Books, 1998; London: Weidenfeld & Nicolson, 1999; Phoenix paperback, 2000.

1935

Contribution to *Early One Morning in the Spring* by Walter de la Mare: London: Faber & Faber. 1935.

Shell Guide to Wiltshire, ed. Robert Byron. London: The Architectural Press, 1935. Outside cover designs, a photomontage, by Lord Berners. (See plate 16.) [New edition, ed. David Verey, Faber & Faber, 1956, using Berners' design for the back cover of the first edition on the dust-jacket without acknowledgement.]

The Girls of Radcliff Hall by Adela Quebec. Privately printed, *c.* 1935. As by Lord Berners, ed. John Byrne. London: Montcalm, the Signet Press, 2000. [Designed by Simon Rendall, 750 copies; 250 published in the USA, Asphodel Editions.]

1936

The Camel: a Tale (to John and Penelope Betjeman). London: Constable, 1936. In *Collected Tales and Fantasies*. New York: Turtle Point and Helen Marx Books, 1999. Trans. Swedish (1937); French (1951).

Shell Poster, painting of Faringdon Folly reproduced, 1936. In *The Shell Poster Book*, introduction by David Bernstein. London: Hamish Hamilton, 1992, no. 64. (See plate 55.)

1937

Kamelen: en berathelse av Lord Berners. Stockholm: Hugo Gebers Forlag, 1937.

1939

'Lord Berners, composer of the recently produced *Cupid and Psyche*, shows *Illustrated* cameramen round his country home and explains why there is a modern boom in ballet', *Illustrated*, 20 May 1939.

'Montages: Brighter Academy Pictures' in *Lilliput* 5/1 [issue no. 25] (July 1939), 26–34.

1941

Percy Wallingford (to Clarissa Churchill) and *Mr Pidger* (to Phyllis de Janzé). Oxford: Basil Blackwell, 1941. In *Collected Tales and Fantasies*. New York: Turtle Point Press and Helen Marx Books.

Far from the Madding War (to Rachel and David Cecil). London: Constable, 1941. In *First Childhood* and *Far from the Madding War*, with a preface by Harold Acton. Oxford: Oxford University Press, 1983. In *Collected Tales and Fantasies*. New York: Turtle Point Press and Helen Marx Books, 1999.

Count Omega (to Rosamund Lehman). London: Constable, 1941. In *Collected Tales and Fantasies*. New York: Turtle Point Press and Helen Marx Books, 1999. [Dramatised for BBC Radio 3 by Mike (now Maxwell) Steer, 10 March 1987.]

The Romance of a Nose. London: Constable, dated 1941, appeared 1942. In *Collected Tales and Fantasies*. New York: Turtle Point Press and Helen Marx Books, 1999. Trans. French (1945).

'Red Roses and Red Noses'. In *Look! The Sun*, ed. Edith Sitwell. London: Victor Gollancz, 1941.

1942

'The performing mushroom', in *Horizon* vol. 6, no. 31 (July 1942), 5.

'On the pale yellow sands', under the title of 'Surrealist Landscape' in *Horizon*, vol. 6, no. 31 (July 1942), 5–6; under the title of 'Queer' in *Spells*. Oxford: Basil Blackwell, 1955. Again in *Spells for Poets: an Anthology of Words and Comments*, collected by F. McEachran, London: Garnstone Press, 1974.

1945

A Distant Prospect (to Jennifer Heber-Percy). London: Constable, 1945; reprinted New York: Turtlepoint Press and Helen Marx Books, 1998; London: Weidenfeld & Nicolson, 1999; Phoenix paperback, 2000.

Le Nez de Cléopatra, trans. Marie Canavaggia. Fenêtres sur le monde 3. Paris: La Jeune Parque, 1945.

1946

Mr Pidger. In *Diversion*, edited by Hester W. Chapman and Princess Romanovsky-Pavlovsky. London: Collins, 1946.

1947

Books of 1947 – a Questionnaire: Twenty-One Answers. 'Lord Berners'. *Horizon*, vol. 16, no. 96 (December 1947)

1949

Answer to questionnaire in *Lilliput*, January 1949, 85.

1951

Le Chameau: roman. In *Les Œuvres libres: revue mensuelle ne publiant que de l'inédit* no. 60. Paris: Librairie Arthème Fayard, 1951.

2000

The Château de Résenlieu. New York: Turtle Point Press and Helen Marx Books, 2000.

2008

Dresden. New York: Turtle Point Press and Helen Marx Books, 2008.

[Not long after Berners death in 1950, Michael Sadleir of Constable & Co. wrote to Robert Heber-Percy about a third volume of memoirs. Ralph Arnold, representing the firm, took this up again in 1952/3. Gifford, table 4. Nothing came of this, although it is clear that Berners intended the third volume to consist of *The Château de Résenlieu* and *Dresden*, now published separately.]

Paintings

L ORD BERNERS was in the habit of drawing from an early age. Some of his watercolours dating from his time spent at Résenlieu are pretty but not remarkable, and he also made sketches of his friends when he was in Rome. There are watercolours of his costume designs for his ballets, some held at Covent Garden, which also has the backcloth he painted for *A Wedding Bouquet*.[1] Single examples of Berners' painting were exhibited at the Goupil Gallery and rated highly – *The Coliseum* in 1929, *Farm Buildings* (plate 26) and *Faringdon House from the Lake* (a later version appears as plate 29), both in 1931.[2] But the greatest impact undoubtedly came from the two exhibitions of his paintings at the Reid and Lefèvre Gallery, 1A King Street, London SW1, in 1931 and 1936.[3] Almost all the paintings reproduced in this book were shown there.

In the catalogue to the 1931 exhibition, the art critic Clive Bell thought the paintings were: 'the adventures of a man in love with all forms of subtle expression and equipped for excellence in all. For here is exquisite painting; here is the craftsman's understanding of the uses of paint.'[4] On 21 May 1931 Berners wrote to Bell: 'Thank you a thousand times for the admirable foreword for my picture show. It was just the sort of thing I wanted and I can't thank you enough.'[5] At the second exhibition *The Times* compared Berners with Corot (see plate 30), and concluded: 'nearly all his landscapes are sedate and satisfactory in their organisation and observed with quiet and unpretentious precision.'[6]

Soon after he had taken it up seriously, Berners went out painting with Christopher Wood (1901–30), and bought some of his pictures. Wood said of Berners: '... the only fault I find in his work is that it is just too perfect. He does everything as it should be done.'[7] In 1933 there was an exhibition at Sunderland House, Curzon Street, London W1, where Berners' portrait of Osbert Sitwell won second prize, and in 1935 his own collection of forty-eight French paintings, including fourteen Corots,[8] was shown at the French Gallery, Berkeley Square.[9]

Robert Heber-Percy confirmed that Berners signed a painting only when he was satisfied with it. It looks as if there were about a hundred paintings in this category; most of them were sold through the Reid and Lefèvre Gallery exhibitions. Unlike Berners' music and writings, there has been virtually no critical comment on his paintings since that time. With one exception, the pictures reproduced here are in private collections, so this selection makes it possible for Berners

1 See Gavin Bryars, 'Berners, Rousseau, Satie', *Studio International: Journal of Modern Art*, November/December 1976, 308–18. Bryars says that in 1938 Berners was president of the committee organising the *Salon d'automne* exhibition of *Peintres independants Brittaniques* at the Palais de Chaillot, Paris, where he exhibited 'at least three paintings'. See also Gavin Bryars, 'The Versatile Peer', *Guardian*, Arts, 20 February 2003.

2 Mentioned in *The Times* reviews 12 April 1929; 21 June and 16 October 1931.

3 Reviews in *The Times* 14 August 1931; 16 May 1936.

4 Clive Bell (1881–1962), art critic associated with the Bloomsbury Group, colleague of Roger Fry, with whom he supported Post-Impressionism.

5 King's College, Cambridge CHA/1/64.

6 16 May 1936.

7 Mark Amory, *Lord Berners: the Last Eccentric* (London: Chatto & Windus, 1998), 108.

8 Jean-Baptiste-Camille Corot (1796–1875) French landscape painter. Among the Corots owned by Berners was *Venise, Le Grand Canal vu du quai des Esclavons, 1828* (plate 30), which clearly affected Berners' own paintings of Venice (plates 31, 32, 33). This painting was sold at Christie's as 'from the collection of Robert Heber-Percy, Esq.' on 2 April 1990.

9 Reviewed in *The Times*, 30 May 1935.

to be assessed as a painter for the first time for over seventy years.

Unfortunately the pictures have not always been framed sensitively – often the date is obscured and sometimes even the signature. In some cases the title has disappeared from the back of the picture. All the pictures in the selection here are signed, except for those depicting significant people such as Robert Heber-Percy or William Crack, Berners' chauffeur. The list of illustrations below provides all the information available. Titles in quotes are those originally given to the paintings.

Paintings by Berners reproduced in this book

General bibliography

Aberconway, Christabel. *A Wiser Woman? a Book of Memories*. London: Hutchinson, 1966.

Acton, Sir Harold. *Memoirs of an Aesthete*. London: Methuen, 1948.

—— *More Memoirs of an Aesthete*. London: Methuen, 1970.

—— *Nancy Mitford: a Memoir*. London: Hamish Hamilton, 1975.

—— 'The Sweet Dove Dyed', *Harpers and Queen*, September 1983, 190–4. [Also as Preface to reissue of *First Childhood* and *Far from the Madding War*. Oxford: Oxford University Press, 1983.]

Adair, Gilbert. 'An English Eccentric', *Sunday Times: Books*, 8 March 1998.

Ades, Dawn. *Dalí*. London: Thames & Hudson, 1982; rev. 1995.

Allen, Brooke. 'Without Peer', *New York Times*, 6 December 1998.

Amory, Mark. *Lord Berners: the Last Eccentric*. London: Chatto & Windus, 1998; Pimlico, 1999.

—— 'Lady Dorothy Heber-Percy', Obituary, *Independent*, 20 November 2001.

Annan, Noel. *Our Age: Portrait of a Generation*. London: Weidenfeld & Nicolson, 1990.

—— 'The Camel at the Door', *New York Review of Books* 46/15, October 1999.

Anon. 'Nancy Mitford: an Outstanding Writer', Obituary, *The Times*, 2 July 1973.

—— 'Lord David Cecil: Eminent Man of Letters', Obituary, *The Times*, 3 January 1986.

—— 'The Hon Lady Betjeman', *The Times*, 16 April 1986.

—— 'Robert Heber-Percy', *Daily Telegraph*, 31 October 1987.

—— 'T. E. B. Clarke: Scriptwriter of Best Ealing Comedies', Obituary, *The Times*, 13 February 1989.

—— 'Betty Warren', Obituary, *The Times*, 27 December 1990.

—— 'Sir Harold Acton', Obituary, *The Times*, 28 February 1994.

—— 'Daphne Fielding', Obituary, *The Times* 16 December 1997.

—— 'Lady Dorothy Heber-Percy', Obituary, *Telegraph*, 17 November 2001.

—— 'The Hon Lady Mosley', Obituary, *The Times*, 13 August 2003.

—— 'Lady Harrod: Redoubtable Norfolkwoman who worked energetically to save her county's churches from dereliction', Obituary, *The Times*, 12 May 2005.

Armstrong, George. 'Sir Harold in Italy at 80', *Guardian*, 5 July 1984.

Avery, Kenneth. 'Lord Berners', *Grove's Dictionary of Music and Musicians*, 5th edn, ed. Eric Blom. London: Macmillan, 1954.

Bacharach, A. L., ed. *British Music of our Time*. Harmondsworth: Penguin, 1946.

Bailey, L. W. 'I Witnessed a Mosley Riot', *The Times*, 6 March 1998.

Banfield, Stephen. 'The Artist and Society'. In *The Athlone History of Music in Britain: the Romantic Age, 1800–1914*, ed. Nicholas Temperley. London: Athlone Press, 1981.

—— *Sensibility and English Song: Critical Studies of the Early Twentieth Century*. Cambridge: Cambridge University Press, 1985.

Bax, Arnold. *Farewell my Youth*. London: Longmans, 1943.

Beaton, Cecil. *The Wandering Years, Diaries, 1922–1939*. London: Weidenfeld & Nicolson, 1961.

—— *The Years Between: Diaries, 1939–44*. London: Weidenfeld & Nicolson, 1965.

—— *The Happy Years: Diaries, 1944–48*. London: Weidenfeld & Nicolson, 1972.

—— *The Strenuous Years: Diaries, 1948–55*. London: Weidenfeld & Nicolson, 1973.

—— 'Follies of the Famous', *Sunday Times Weekly Review*, 26 August 1973.

—— and Peter Quennell. *Time Exposure*. London: B. T. Batsford, 1941.

Beaumont, Cyril. *The Diaghilev Ballet in London*. London: Putnam, 1940.

Beecham, Sir Thomas. *Beecham Stories: Anecdotes, Sayings and Impressions of Sir Thomas Beecham*, compiled and ed. Harold Atkins and Archie Newman. London: Robson Books, 1978.

Beerbohm, Max. *Things New and Old*. London: William Heineman, 1923.

Berners, Lord. *Lord Berners: a Selection from his Works*, ed. with an introduction by Vivian de Sola Pinto. London: Sidgwick & Jackson, 1936.

Bernstein, David. Introduction to *The Shell Poster Book*. London: Hamish Hamilton, 1992.

Betjeman, John. 'Lord Berners: 1883–1950', *Listener*, 11 May 1950, 839.

—— *Letters*, vol. 1: *1926 to 1951*, ed. Candida Lycett Green. London: Methuen, 1994.

—— Foreword to *The Collected Vocal Music*, 2nd edn, ed. Peter Dickinson. London: Chester Music, 2000.

—— Foreword to *The Collected Music for Solo Piano*, 2nd edn, ed. Peter Dickinson. London: Chester Music, 2000.

Bland, Alexander. *The Royal Ballet: the First Fifty Years*. London: Threshold Books, 1981.

Bliss, Arthur. 'Reviews of New Music: Lord Berners', *Musical News and Herald*, 25 June 1921.

—— 'Berners and Bax', *League of Composers Review* [*Modern Music*] 1/1 (February 1924), 26–7 [Also in *Bliss on Music*, ed. Gregory Roscoe. Oxford: Oxford University Press, 1991.]

—— *As I Remember*. London: Faber & Faber, 1970.

Blom, Eric. 'Forecast and Review: Young Britons', *Modern Music*, March/April 1927, 34–7.

—— *Music in England*. Harmondsworth: Penguin, 1942; rev. edn 1947.

Boston, Richard. 'Lady Betjeman's last Trip: Richard Boston on an entertaining exchange', *Guardian*, 16 April 1986.

Bowen, Meirion. 'Berners', *Guardian*, 9 December 1972.

—— 'Berners' Centenary', *Guardian*, 26 September 1983.

Brain, Richard. 'Robert Heber-Percy', Obituary, *Independent*, 3 November 1987.

Brinnin, John Malcolm. *The Third Rose: Gertrude Stein and her World*. London: Weidenfeld & Nicolson, 1960.

Britten, Benjamin. *Letters from a Life: Selected Letters and Diaries of Benjamin Britten*, vol. 1: *1923–39*, ed. Donald Mitchell and Philip Reed. London: Faber, 1991.

Brooke, Jocelyn. *Ronald Firbank*. London: Arthur Barker, 1951.

Brophy, Brigid. *Prancing Novelist: in Praise of Ronald Firbank*. London: Macmillan, 1973.

Bryars, Gavin. 'Berners, Rousseau, Satie', *Studio International: Journal of Modern Art*, November/ December 1976, 308–18.

—— 'Satie and the British', *Contact* no. 25, Autumn 1982, 4–15.

—— 'The Versatile Peer', *Guardian*, Arts, 20 February 2003.

Buckle, Richard. *Diaghilev*, London, Weidenfeld & Nicolson, 1979.

Campbell, Margaret. *Dolmetsch: the Man and his Work*. London: Hamish Hamilton, 1975.

Carpenter, Humphrey. *The Brideshead Generation: Evelyn Waugh and his Friends*. London: Weidenfeld & Nicolson, 1989.

Cary, John. 'Discreet Charms of the Aristocracy', *Sunday Times*, 24 March 1985.

Casella, Alfredo. 'Schönberg in Italy', *League of Composers Review* [*Modern Music*] 1/2 (June 1924), 7–10.

——*L'evolution della musica: a traverso la storia della cadenza perfetta*. London: J. & W. Chester, 1924. 2nd edn, rev. Edmund Rubbra as *The Evolution of Music through the History of the Perfect Cadence*. London: J. & W. Chester, 1964.

——*I segreti della giara*. Florence: Sansoni, 1941. Trans. Spencer Norton as *Music in My Time*. Norman: University of Oklahoma Press, 1955.

Cecil, Lord David. *Two Quiet Lives: Dorothy Osborne and Thomas Gray*. London: Constable, 1948.

——*Max*. London: Constable, 1964.

——, ed. *The Bodley Head Max Beerbohm*. London: Bodley Head, 1970.

Chilvers, Ian, ed. *Concise Oxford Dictionary of Art and Artists*, 2nd edn. Oxford: Oxford University Press, 1996.

Clark, Kenneth. *Another Part of the Wood: a Self-Portrait*. London: John Murray, 1974.

Clarke, Mary. *The Sadler's Wells Ballet: a History and an Appreciation*. London: A. & C. Black, 1955.

Clarke, T. E. B. *Intimate Relations, or Sixty Years a Bastard*. London: Michael Joseph, 1971.

Cleave, Maureen. 'Acton in Aspic', *Observer Review*, 21 February 1982.

Connell, Brian. 'Sir Frederick Ashton: the Boy from Lima who Made Good', *The Times*, 20 March 1978.

Cooper, Diana. *The Rainbow Comes and Goes*. London: Rupert Hart-Davis, 1958.

——*The Light of Common Day*. London: Rupert Hart-Davis, 1959.

Courtauld, Simon. *As I was going to St Ives: a Life of Derek Jackson*. London: Michael Russell, 2007.

Cowley, Julian. 'The Neglected Satirical Fiction of Lord Berners', *Journal of Modern Literature* 19/2 (Fall 1995), 187–200.

Crichton, Ronald. 'Lord Berners', *Financial Times*, 11 December 1972.

——'Lord Berners'. *The New Grove Dictionary of Music and Musicians*, 1st edn, ed. Stanley Sadie. London: Macmillan, 1980.

——'Lord Berners Centenary/BBC Radio 3', *Financial Times*, 20 September 1983.

Cunliffe-Owen, Betty. *Thro' the Gates of Memory: from the Bosphorus to Baghdad*. London: Hutchinson & Co., [1924].

Dalí, Salvador. *Diary of a Genius*. London: Pan Books, 1966.

——*The Unspeakable Confessions of Salvador Dalí as told to André Parinaud*. London: W. H. Allen, 1976.

Dalley, Jan. 'Beauty and the Blackshirts', *Guardian Saturday Review*, 11 September 1999.

De Courcy, Anne. *Diana Mosley*, London: Vintage, 2004.

De-la-Noy, Michael. *Denton Welch: the Making of a Writer*. Harmondsworth: Viking, 1984.

Dickinson, Peter. 'The Music of Lord Berners', *BBC Music Weekly*, 6 May 1979.

——'Lord Berners: the Most Professional Amateur', *Radio 3 Magazine*, September 1983, 26–9.

——'Lord Berners, 1883–1950: A British Avant-gardist at the Time of World War I', *Musical Times* 124, no. 1689 (November 1983), 669–72.

——'Lord Berners (1883–1950): Composer, Author, Painter and Eccentric', *Royal Society of Arts Journal* 132, no. 5333 (April 1984), 313–24.

——'Stein Satie Cummings Thomson Berners Cage: Towards a Context for the Music of Virgil Thomson', *Musical Quarterly*, 72 (1986), 394–409.

——Lord Berners, CD booklet notes: EMI CDC 7 47668 2 (1986), EMI Classics 7243 5 65098 2 (1994), Olympia OCD 662 (1999), Campion Classics 2054 (2006).

——Reviews of Berners CDs in *The Gramophone*: 8/94; 4/96; 7/96; 7/98; 4/01.

—— 'The Trombone Effect'. Review of Lord Berners: *Count Omega* adapted by Mike Steer, BBC Radio 3, producer John Theocharis, 10 March 1987. *Times Literary Supplement*, 27 March 1987, 327.

—— *A Wedding Bouquet* and Profile, BBC Proms programme, 3 August 1990.

—— 'Lord Berners'. *Die Musik in Geschichte und Gegenwart*. Kassel: Bärenreiter, 1998.

—— *Marigold: the Music of Billy Mayerl*. Oxford: Oxford University Press, 1999.

—— 'Lord Berners'. *The New Grove Dictionary of Music and Musicians*, 2nd edn, ed. Stanley Sadie and John Tyrrell. London: Macmillan, 2001.

—— *The Music of Lennox Berkeley*, 2nd edn. Woodbridge: Boydell Press, 2003.

Dirda, Michael. 'Tales and Fantasies by Lord Berners', *Washington Post*, 20 June 1999.

Drabble, Margaret, ed. *The Oxford Companion to English Literature*, 5th edn. Oxford: Oxford University Press, 1985.

Dyer, Richard. 'Revisiting the Life of Lord Berners', *Boston Globe*, February 1999.

Eden, Clarissa. *A Memoir*, ed. Cate Haste. London: Weidenfeld & Nicolson, 2007.

Elborne, Geoffrey. *Edith Sitwell: a Biography*. Garden City, NY: Doubleday & Co., 1981.

Epstein, Joseph. 'Pink Pigeons and Blue Mayonnaise', *New Criterion*, 1 November 1998.

Evans, Edwin. 'Modern British Composers: VII – Lord Berners'. *Musical Times* 61, no. 923 (1 January 1920), 9–13.

—— 'Who is next?' *The League of Composers Review* [*Modern Music*] 1/3 (November 1924), 3–6.

—— 'Lord Berners', *Grove's Dictionary of Music and Musicians*, 3rd edn, ed. H. C. Colles, London: Macmillan, 1927.

Ezard, John. 'Harold Acton, Connoisseur and Philistine-Hunter, Dies Aged 89', *Guardian*, 28 February 1994.

Fielding, Daphne. *Mercury Presides*. London: Eyre & Spottiswoode, 1954.

—— *Emerald and Nancy: Lady Cunard and her Daughter*. London: Eyre & Spottiswoode, 1968.

—— *The Face on the Sphinx: a Portrait of Gladys Deacon, Duchess of Marlborough*. London: Hamish Hamilton, 1978.

Finkle, David. 'Twitting the Twits', *New York Times*, 24 October 1999.

Finlayson, Iain. 'Slow Berners', *Tatler* 278/8, September 1983, 93.

Firbank, Ronald. *Valmouth*. London: Grant Richards, 1919.

—— *The Complete Firbank: with an Introduction by Anthony Powell*. London: Duckworth, 1971.

Fletcher, Ifan Kyrle. *Ronald Firbank: a Memoir*. London: Duckworth, 1930.

Folway, Anne. 'The Making of Lord Merlin'. *Guardian*, 17 July 1999.

Forster, E. M. *A Room with a View*. Harmondsworth: Penguin, 1955.

Fryer, Jonathan. *Ronald Firbank: a Life*. London: Allison & Busby, 2007.

Gallup, Donald, ed. *The Flowers of Friendship: Letters Written to Gertrude Stein*. New York: Octagon, 1979.

Gifford, Mary. 'Ballet Music in England in the 1930s'. MA thesis: Southampton, 1998.

—— 'Lord Berners: Aspects of a Biography'. PhD thesis, University of London, 2007.

Girouard, Mark. 'Faringdon House, Berkshire', *Country Life*, 12 & 19 May 1966.

—— 'Lord Berners. Artist, Author, Musician and Wit', *The British Eccentric*, ed. Harriet Bridgeman and Elizabeth Drury. London: Michael Joseph, 1975.

Gooding, Mel. 'Denton Welch', *Arts Review*, 23 November 1984, 586.

Goossens, Eugene. 'Lord Berners', *Chesterian*, December 1919, 65–8.

—— *Overture and Beginners: a Musical Autobiography*. London: Methuen & Co., 1951.

Goreau, Angeline. 'Annoying the Victorians', *New York Times*, 26 December 1999.

Graves, Robert, and Alan Hodge. *The Long Weekend: a Social History of Great Britain 1918–1939*. London: Faber & Faber, 1940.

Gray, Cecil. *A Survey of Contemporary Music*. London: Oxford University Press, 1924.

Grierson, Mary. *Donald Francis Tovey: a Biography Based on Letters*. Oxford: Oxford University Press, 1952.

Grove, Valerie. 'Je ne regrette rien: Valerie Grove meets Diana Mosley', *The Times Weekend*, 27 April 2002.

Guinness, Desmond. 'At Home with a Musical Eccentric', *Irish Times*, 23 May 1975.

Guinness, Jonathan, with Catherine Guinness. *The House of Mitford*. London: Hutchison, 1984; 2nd edn Phoenix, 2004.

Hall, Radclyffe. *The Well of Loneliness*. London: Jonathan Cape, 1928 (banned); 1949. Cairo: Imprimerie El-Ettemad, n.d.

Harding, James. *Erik Satie*. London: Secker & Warburg, 1975.

Harrison, Max. 'Lord Berners: Purcell Room', *The Times*, 9 December 1972.

Haskell, Arnold, L. *Balletomania: the Story of an Obsession*. London: Victor Gollancz, 1934.

—— *Ballet: a Complete Guide to Appreciation*. Harmondsworth: Penguin, 1938.

Henderson, Sir Nevile. *Water under the Bridges*. London: Hodder & Stoughton, 1945.

Henderson, Robert. The Bubbling-over Berners', *Daily Telegraph* 10 September 1983.

—— 'An Evening with Lord Berners', *Daily Telegraph*, 26 September 1983.

Howes, Frank. *The English Musical Renaissance*. London: Secker & Warburg, 1966.

Hillier, Bevis. *John Betjeman: a Life in Pictures*. London: John Murray, 1984.

—— *John Betjeman: New Fame, New Love*. London: John Murray, 2002.

Holbrooke, Joseph. 'Lord Berners'. In *Contemporary British Composers*. London: Cecil Palmer, 1925.

Hollinghurst, Alan. 'Diminished Pictures', *Times Literary Supplement*, 21 December 1984.

—— 'An Unconveyable Aesthete'. *Times Literary Supplement*, 20 March 1998.

Howes, Frank. *The English Musical Renaissance*. London: Secker & Warburg, 1966.

Hoyle, Martin. 'Beautifully Drilled Puzzle Pieces', *The Times*, 27 August 1992.

Hughes, Spike. *Opening Bars: Beginning an Autobiography*. London: Pilot Press, 1946.

—— *Second Movement*. London: Museum Press, 1951.

Hurd, Michael. 'Civilising the Wealthy', *Times Literary Supplement*. 14 October 1983.

James, Edward. *The Gardener who Saw God*. London: Duckworth, 1937.

—— *Swans Reflecting Elephants: My Early Years*, ed. George Melly. London: Weidenfeld & Nicolson, 1982.

Jean-Aubry, Georges. 'Profile and interview: Lord Berners', *Christian Science Monitor*, 31 March 1923.

—— 'Le Carosse du Saint-Sacrement', *Chesterian*, June 1923, 244–51.

—— *French Music of Today*, trans. E. Evans. London: Kegan Paul, Trench, Turner, 1926.

Jones, Bryony. *The Music of Lord Berners (1883–1950): 'The Versatile Peer'*. Aldershot: Ashgate, 2003.

Kavanagh, Julie. *Secret Muses: the Life of Frederick Ashton*. London, Faber, 1996.

Kennedy, Michael. *Portrait of Walton*. Oxford: Oxford University Press, 1989.

Kenworthy-Brown, John, *et al. Burke's & Savill's Guide to Country Houses*, vol. 3: *East Anglia*. London: Burke's Peerage, 1981.

Lambert, Constant. *Music Ho!: a Study of Music in Decline*. London: Faber & Faber, 1934; Harmondsworth: Penguin, 1948.

—— 'The Uncommon Man: Lord Berners – The Musical Peer introduced by Constant Lambert, pictured by Osbert Lancaster', *Strand*, April 1947, 62–3.

—— 'Tribute to Lord Berners', BBC Third Programme, 16 February 1951.

Lambert, Herbert. *Modern British Composers: Seventeen Portraits with a Foreword by Eugene Goossens*. London: F. & B. Goodwin, 1923.

Lane, Philip. Unpublished biography (*c.* 1975). [Cited as Lane MS.]

—— CD booklet notes. Berners: Songs and piano music, Auracle AUC1001 (1981); *A Wedding Bouquet, Luna Park*, March, Marco Polo 8.223716 (1996); The Complete Vocal and Solo Piano Works, Albany TROY290 (1997); *The Triumph of Neptune, L'uomo dai baffi, Valses bourgeoises*, Polka, Marco Polo 8.223711 (1998); *Les Sirènes, Cupid and Psyche, Caprice péruvien*, Marco Polo 8.223780 (1995); Fanfare, *Caprice péruvien, Le Carosse du Saint-Sacrement*, Marco Polo 8.225155 (2001).

Larkin, Philip. *Required Writing: Miscellaneous Pieces, 1955–1982*. London: Faber & Faber, 1983.

Latham, Alison, ed. *The Oxford Companion to Music*. London: Oxford University Press, 2002.

Leach, Francis. *The County Seats of Shropshire*. Shrewsbury, 1891.

Lees-Milne, James. *Diaries: Ancestral Voices*. London: Faber & Faber, 1975.

—— *Prophesying Peace: Diaries, 1944–45*. London: Chatto & Windus, 1977.

—— *Harold Nicolson: a Biography*. 2 vols. London: Chatto & Windus, 1981.

Leslie, Cole. *The Life of Noël Coward*. London: Jonathan Cape, 1976; Penguin, 1978.

Lewis, John. *Such Things Happen: the Life of a Typographer*. Stowmarket: Unicorn Press, 1994.

Lovell, Mary S. *The Mitford Girls: the Biography of an Extraordinary Family*. London: Little Brown & Co., 2001.

Lyle, Watson, 'The Songs of Lord Berners', *Chesterian*, September 1934, 61–3.

MacCarthy, Desmond. *Desmond MacCarthy: the Man and his Writings*, ed. David Cecil. London: Constable, 1984.

Mackenzie, Compton. *My Record of Music*. London: Hutchinson, 1955.

Malcolm, Noel. 'The Lord of Many Talents'. *Sunday Telegraph*, 15 March 1998.

Manchester, P. W. *Vic-Wells: a Ballet Progress*, London: Victor Gollancz, 1946.

'Mandrake'. *Sunday Telegraph*, 23 September 1984.

Mannin, Ethel. *Young in the Twenties: a Chapter of Autobiography*, London: Hutchinson, 1971.

Marlborough, Laura, Duchess of. 'A Great Undertaking', *Harper's and Queen*, January 1980, 56–8, 98, 101.

Mason, Colin. 'Lord Berners: a Miniaturist in Music', *Listener*, 8 February 1951, 236.

Masters, Anthony. 'A Day in the Life of Lady Mosley', *Sunday Times Magazine*, 4 December 1983.

Masters, Brian. 'The Other Diana: Still Hated, after Fifty Years in Exile', *Night and Day, The Mail on Sunday Review*, 2 January 1994, 40–5.

Mellers, Wilfrid. 'Visionary Gleams'. *Musical Times*, October 1996, 17.

Melly, George. 'Strange Reflections', *Daily Telegraph*, Arts and Books, 11 April 1998.

Methuen-Campbell, James. *Denton Welch: Writer and Artist*. Leyburn: Tartarus Press, 2002.

Mitford, Nancy. *The Pursuit of Love*. London: Hamish Hamilton, 1945.

—— *Love in a Cold Climate*. London: Hamish Hamilton, 1949.

—— 'Faringdon House', *House and Garden*, August–September 1950.

——, ed. *Noblesse oblige: an Enquiry into the Identifiable Characteristics of the English Aristocracy*. London: Hamish Hamilton, 1956.

Mosley, Charlotte, ed. *The Mitfords: Letters between Six Sisters*. London: Fourth Estate, 2007.

Mosley, Diana. *A Life of Contrasts*. London: Hamish Hamilton, 1977.

—— *Loved Ones: Pen Portraits*. London: Sidgwick & Jackson, 1985.

Motion, Andrew. *The Lamberts: George, Constant and Kit*. London: Chatto & Windus, 1986.

Music Today: Journal of the International Society for Contemporary Music 1 (1949).

Nichols, Beverley. *The Sweet and Twenties*. London: Weidenfeld & Nicolson, 1958.

Nicolson, Harold. *Some People*. London: Constable & Co., 1927; Folio Society, 1951.

—— 'Marginal Comment', *Spectator*, 28 April 1950, 568.

Norman, Charles. *The Magic-Maker: E. E. Cummings*. New York: Macmillan Co., 1958.

Norris, Christopher. 'Radio and TV', *Music and Musicians*, February 1974, 31.

—— 'Lord Berners'. Review of LP of songs and piano music, Unicorn RHS355 (1978), *Records and Recording*, February 1979.

Nyman, Michael. 'Last Week's Broadcast Music', *Listener*, 27 December 1973.

O'Donoghue, Jim, and Louise Goulding. 'Consumer Price Inflation since 1750', *Economic Trends* 604 (March 2004), 38–46.

Orledge, Robert. *Satie the Composer*. Cambridge: Cambridge University Press, 1990.

—— *Satie Remembered*. London: Faber & Faber, 1995.

Osborne, Richard, and F. L. Griggs. *Till I end my Song. English Music and Musicians 1440–1940: A Perspective from Eton*. London: Cygnet Press, 2002.

Parton, Anthony. *Mikhail Larionov and the Russian Avant-Garde*. Princeton: Princeton University Press, 1993.

Payne, Anthony. 'Betjeman Gives Reading of Berners' Wit', *Telegraph*, 9 December 1972.

Percival, John. 'Travesty of Ashton's work', *The Times*, 10 November 1989.

Pirie, Peter J. *The English Musical Renaissance: Twentieth-Century British Composers and their Works*, New York: St Martin's Press, 1980.

Poulenc, Francis. *Correspondance, 1910–63*, ed. Myriam Chimènes. Paris: Fayard, 1994.

Pryce-Jones, Alan. Preface to *Little Innocents: Childhood Reminiscences* (thirty authors including Berners). London: Cobden-Sanderson, 1932.

—— 'Obituaries: Sir Harold Acton', *Independent*, 28 February 1994.

Pryce-Jones, David. *Unity Mitford: a Quest*. London: Weidenfeld & Nicolson, 1976.

Quennell, Peter. 'The Sage of Florence', *Guardian*, 28 February 1994.

Rainbow, Bernarr. *The Land without Music: Musical Education in England, 1800–1860, and its Continental Antecedents*. London: Novello & Co., 1967.

—— *Music in Educational Thought and Practice: a Survey from 800 BC*, 2nd edn. Woodbridge: Boydell Press, 2006.

Ratcliffe, Michael. 'Lord Berners, that Most Versatile Peer', *The Times*, 3 September 1983.

Reid, Charles. *Thomas Beecham: an Independent Biography*. London: Victor Gollancz, 1962.

Ritchie, Donald. 'The Return of the Eccentric Lord Berners', *San Francisco Examiner*, 15 July 1979.

Roberts, Andrew. 'Diana Mosley, Unrepentantly Nazi and Effortlessly Charming', *Daily Telegraph* 13 August 2003.

—— *A History of the English-speaking Peoples since 1900*. London: Weidenfeld & Nicolson, 2006.

Robinson, Derek. 'Hunting the Philistines – with Sir Harold Acton', *Listener*, 20 & 27 December 1979, 841–3.

Rose, Francis. *Saying Life*. London: Cassel & Co., 1961.

Rowse, A. L. *Friends and Contemporaries*. London: Methuen, 1989.

Salopian Journal, 16 August 1882.

Schmitz, Oscar A. H. *Das Land ohne Musik: Englische Gesellschaftsprobleme*. Munich, 1914. Trans. H. Herzl as *The Land without Music*. London: Jarrolds, 1925.

Sexton, David. 'Best of Amateurs', *Evening Standard*, 2 March 1998.

Shaw, John. 'Sixpenny Poster Become Classics'. *The Times*, 21 August 1992.

Shead, Richard. *Constant Lambert.* London: Simon Publications: 1973.

Shipman, David. 'T. E. B. Clarke'. Obituaries, *Independent*, 15 February 1989.

Shrewsbury Chronicle, 2 February 1894, 13 October 1899, 13 September 1918.

Sitwell, Edith. *The English Eccentrics.* London: Faber & Faber, 1933.

—— *Taken Care of: an Autobiography.* London: Hutchinson, 1965.

Sitwell, Osbert. *Laughter in the Next Room.* London: Macmillan, 1949.

—— 'The Love-Bird'. In *Collected Stories.* London: Duckworth & Co., 1953. [Originally in *The Argossy*, February 1934.]

Sitwell, Sacheverell. 'British Composers at the Proms (5): Lord Berners', *Radio Times*, 11 September, 1931, 556.

—— 'Been Everywhere, Seen Everything', *The Times Profile: Sir Sacheverell Sitwell, 85 Today*, 15 November 1982, 8.

Sorabji, Kaikhosru. *Around Music.* London: Unicorn Press, 1932.

—— *Mi contra fa: the Immoralisings of a Machiavellian Musician.* London: Porcupine Press, 1948.

Spender, Stephen. *The Thirties and After: Poetry, Politics, People (1933–75).* London: Macmillan, 1978.

Stanford, Peter. 'Great, Good and Ghastly', *Independent on Sunday*, 22 March 1998.

—— 'Wanted: Lords. Must be dotty', *Independent on Sunday*, 12 September 1999.

Stannard, Martin. *Evelyn Waugh: the Early Years, 1903–1939.* London: J. M. Dent, 1986.

Stein, Gertrude. *Everybody's Autobiography.* London: Heineman, 1938.

—— *Selected Operas and Plays of Gertrude Stein*, ed. with an introduction by John Malcolm Brinnin. Pittsburgh: University of Pittsburgh Press, 1970.

—— and Alice B. Toklas. *Dear Sammy: Letters from Gertude Stein and Alice B. Toklas*, edited with a memoir by Samuel M. Steward. Boston: Houghton Miflin Co., 1977.

Stein, Mark. 'Centenary of Lord Berners – a Brilliant Man', *Shropshire Magazine*, April 1983.

—— 'Lord Berners as a Painter', *Apollo*, August 1984, 128–31.

—— 'A Mellowed Mosley's Labour of Love', *The Times*, 22 March 1985

Stott, Catherine. 'The Mitford who Became a Mosley', *Sunday Telegraph*, 17 March 1985.

Stravinsky, Igor. *An Autobiography* (1936). New York: Norton Library, 1962.

—— *Selected Correspondence*, edited and with commentaries by Robert Craft, vols. 2 & 3, London: Faber & Faber, 1984, 1985.

—— and Robert Craft. *Memories and Commentaries*, London: Faber & Faber, 1960.

Swann, H. Kirk. *Dictionary of English and Folk Names of British Birds.* London: Witherby & Co., 1913.

Swynnoe, Jan G. *The Best Years of British Film Music, 1936–1958.* Woodbridge: Boydell Press, 2002.

Taper, Bernard. *Balanchine.* London: Collins, 1964.

Taylor, A. J. P. *A Personal History.* London: Hamish Hamilton, 1983.

Taylor, John Russell. 'An Evening of Lord Berners', *Music and Musicians*, December 1983, 24.

Templier, Pierre-Daniel. *Erik Satie.* Paris: Editions Rieder, 1932. English translation: Cambridge, MA: MIT Press, 1969.

Thomson, Andrew. 'Oh, Lordy!', *Musical Times* 139, no. 1863 (Summer 1998), 67.

—— Review: 'Music of Lord Berners (1883–1950): the Versatile Peer by Bryony James', *Musical Times* 144, no. 1884 (Autumn 2003), 68–9.

Tovey, Donald Francis. *Essays in Musical Analysis*, 6 vols. London: Oxford University Press, 1935–9.

—— *The Classics of Music: Talks, Essays and other Writings Previously Unpublished*, ed. Michael Tilmouth, completed by David Kimbell and Roger Savage. Oxford: Oxford University Press, 2001.

Vaughan, David. *Frederick Ashton and his Ballets.* London: Dance Books, 1977.

Vickers, Hugo. *Cecil Beaton: the Authorized Biography*, London: Weidenfeld & Nicolson, 1985.

—— 'Boys will be Girls', *Spectator*, 26 August 2000.

Walker, Ernest. *A History of Music in England*, 3rd edn, rev. J. A. Westrup. Oxford: Clarendon Press, 1951.

Walton, Susana. *William Walton: Behind the Façade*. Oxford: Oxford University Press, 1988.

Waterhouse, John C. G. 'A Futurist Mystery', *Music and Musicians*, April 1967, 26–9.

—— 'Continuita stilistica di Casella'. Florence: Leo S. Olschki Editore, 1981.

Waugh, Evelyn. *Put out more Flags*. Harmondsworth: Penguin, 1943.

—— *The Diaries of Evelyn Waugh*, ed. Michael Davie. London: Weidenfeld & Nicolson, 1976.

—— *The Letters of Evelyn Waugh*, ed. Mark Amory. London: Weidenfeld & Nicolson, 1980.

—— and Diana Cooper. *Mr Wu and Mrs Stitch: the Letters of Evelyn Waugh and Diana Cooper*, ed. Artemis Cooper. London: Hodder & Stoughton, 1991.

Welch, Denton. *The Journals of Denton Welch*, ed. Michael De-la-Noy. London: Allison & Busby, 1984.

Wellesley, Dorothy. *Far have I travelled*. London: J. Barrie, 1952.

Westrup, J. A. *British Music*. London: Longmans Green, 1943.

—— 'Lord Berners'. In *British Music of our Time*, ed. A. L. Bacharach. Harmondsworth: Penguin, 1946.

Whatley, Larry. 'Music Theory', in *The Athlone History of Music in Britain: The Romantic Age, 1800–1914*, ed. Nicholas Temperley. London: Athlone Press, 1981.

Wheeler, Sara. 'Don't Look Back' [interview with Sofka Zinovieff], *Telegraph Magazine*, 8 May 2004.

Widdecombe, Gillian. 'A Guru of the Ballet: Sir Frederick Ashton talking to Gillian Widdecombe, recalls memories of the late George Balanchine', *Observer* 14 August 1983.

—— 'Lord of music and mischief', *Observer*, 25 September 1983.

Williams, Gareth. 'Apley Hall: the County's Greatest Restoration Project: Past Deciphered, Future Assured', *Shropshire Magazine*, October 2005.

Wilson, A. N. 'The Diana I Knew', *Daily Telegraph*, 13 August 2003.

Wood, Henry J. *My Life of Music*. London: Victor Gollancz, 1938.

Wood, Hugh. 'Sheila MacCrindle: Business as usual', Obituary, *Guardian*, 24 July 1993.

Woolf, Virginia. *The Letters of Virginia Woolf*, vol. 3: *A Change of Perspective, 1923–1928*, ed. Nigel Nicolson and Joanne Trautmann. London: Hogarth Press, 1977.

—— *The Letters of Virginia Woolf*, vol. 4: *A Reflection of the Other Person, 1929–1931*, ed. Nigel Nicolson and Joanne Trautmann. London: Hogarth Press, 1978.

—— *The Diary of Virginia Woolf*, vol. 2: *1920–1924*, ed. Anne Oliver Bell and Andrew McNeillie. London: Hogarth Press, 1978.

—— *The Diary of Virginia Woolf*, vol. 3: *1925–1930*, ed. Anne Oliver Bell and Andrew McNeillie. London: Hogarth Press, 1980.

Wykes, Alan. 'Lord Berners', *Music and Musicians*, September 1983, 10–11.

Index of works by Lord Berners

General index